Creating the
Modern Man

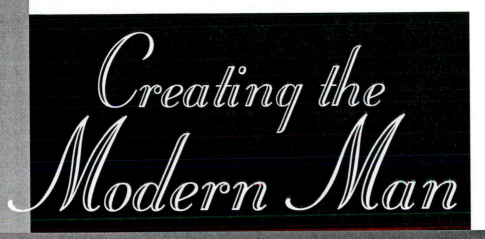

Creating the Modern Man

American Magazines and Consumer Culture

1900–1950

TOM PENDERGAST

University of Missouri Press

COLUMBIA AND LONDON

Columbia and London
Copyright © 2000 by
The Curators of the University of Missouri
University of Missouri Press, Columbia, Missouri 65201
Printed and bound in the United States of America
All rights reserved
5 4 3 2 1   04 03 02 01 00

Cataloging-in-Publication data available from the Library of Congress
ISBN 0-8262-1280-8

♾™ This paper meets the requirements of the
American National Standard for Permanence of Paper
for Printed Library Materials, Z39.48, 1984.

Text design: Elizabeth K. Young

Jacket design: Vickie Kersey DuBois

Typesetter: Bookcomp, Inc.

Printer and binder: Edwards Brothers, Inc.

Typefaces: New Caledonia, Stuyvesant, Helvetica Neue

Portions of Chapters 3 and 5 appeared previously in "Horatio Alger Doesn't

Work Here Any More': Masculinity and American Magazines," *American

Studies* 38, no. 1 (spring 1997): 55–80.

For Sara

Contents

Acknowledgments

This book could not have been written without the encouragement and assistance of a great many people. My academic debts are many, and they begin with Susan Curtis, whose example encouraged me to try to be a historian and whose advice, encouragement, and criticism sharpened my thinking at every step in the creation of this project. I could ask for no better booster than Bob Lamb, who expressed a belief in the quality of my work that I wish I could share and who never failed to make me laugh. Hal Woodman, Vernon Williams, Len Neufeldt, Nancy Gabin, and John Larson at Purdue University all contributed to this work in ways that they may not realize.

Librarians at Michigan State University, the Library of Congress, the Zimmerman Library at the University of New Mexico, and the University of Washington helped me to navigate my way through their collections, and the many members of the listservs H-AMSTDY, H-GRAD, and SHARP-L provided me with a virtual community of scholars when my wanderings took me far afield. For assisting me in acquiring photos I would like to thank Bonnie Coles at the Library of Congress and Betty Odabashian at the Schomburg Center. Clair Willcox and Jane Lago at the University of Missouri Press helped answer my many questions while preparing the manuscript, and Julie Schroeder did her best to right my wrongs. My sincere thanks go to the Purdue Research Foundation for supporting my research at several key stages in this project. Jacob Jones and Anne Boyd laughed and groaned with me through the travails of grad school and I thank them for their intelligence and humor.

One cannot finish such a project without the love and support of many people. My mom has offered unending support for my academic endeavors and has always been among my best friends. My grandfather and grandmother, Morton B. and Margaret Stratton, lifted me with their encouragement and assistance at key points in my academic career. Thanks also to my uncle and aunt, Joe and Peggy Bent, for being such gracious hosts during my extended research trips to the Library of Congress. My kids, Conrad and Louisa, have never known me not to be working on this project, and they often warmed my lap during early morning writing sessions. My wife, Sara, has been my first reader, my best critic, my unwavering companion, my business partner, and my very best friend. Without her, it wouldn't have happened.

*Creating the
Modern Man*

Introduction

During the time that I have worked on this project, a number of new forums for the discussion of masculine values have appeared on the pop culture scene: NBC introduced (and then killed) a television sitcom called *Men Behaving Badly* that follows the pratfalls of two guys in their late twenties who burp, drink cheap beer, and eat cold cereal out of boxes; magazines like *Men's Journal, Maxim, Details,* and many others promoted the rediscovery of men's recreation, leisure pursuits, and hobbies; and a variety of mediums commented on the reemergence of the male arts of cigar smoking and martini drinking. In 1996 and 1997, a group of Christian men organized themselves into the Promise Keepers, and they promoted a masculinity based on the patriarchal family. And just a few years earlier, Robert Bly had attracted a great deal of attention with his urgings that men reclaim long-lost elements of their identity through introspection and group interaction. Men who may have been seeking ways to make sense of their identities had a number of options to choose from, and I have hardly exhausted the list of possibilities.

The sheer variety of avenues for expressing male identity in American culture these days is astonishing. But it was not so long ago that the socially acceptable ways men could express their masculinity were rather more limited. For the better part of the nineteenth century, men had been channeled into embracing a sense of self that was closely tied to the ownership of property or other means of assuring economic success, and, secondarily, to a specified role in the family. By the latter half of the nineteenth century, men were encouraged to work hard, to practice self-control, to dedicate themselves to a career or trade (the remnants of the Puritan notion of a calling), and to strive to develop their character. Such a path to manhood was widely accepted by members of the white middle class and was deemed the only viable means to attain manly status in this white man's republic. This culture of manhood was very much a product of a social and economic system that coupled proprietary capitalism with Victorian culture. But the coming of corporate capitalism in the late nineteenth and early twentieth century brought sweeping changes to the culture of masculinity. By the end of World War II, most everyone still accepted that a man should hold a job and support his family, but men were encouraged to individuate themselves by pursuing a number of possible avenues toward self-expression. Pursuing a hobby, engaging in recreation, expressing an interest in sexuality or self-gratification, or developing a pleasing personality were all presented as viable ways for men to express their masculine identity. There were still confines on the way men were encouraged to behave—men were not yet encouraged to consider themselves as primary parents, nor were alternative forms of sexuality deemed remotely permissible—but men had been released from the narrow confines of defining their masculine identity solely through the ownership of property and the subscription to a narrow code of gendered morality. Cultural notions of masculinity had changed, and they now largely suited the corporate capitalist socioeconomic order.

Some of the best scholarship of the last decades has helped us understand the process of economic, social, and cultural transformation that occurred in the United States in the years surrounding the turn of the twentieth century. More recently, men's historians have added to this scholarship their understanding of the ways that the culture of masculinity has changed in relation to this transformation. Yet the former body of scholarship, which I will discuss at length, has shown a troubling tendency to cast the emergence of corporate consumer capitalism in largely negative terms, lamenting the undue influence of large corporate bureaucracies in determining the shape of modern culture and accentuating the tragic loss of a stable sense of selfhood that some scholars maintain existed in the pre-corporate consumer capitalist world. Such scholarship has tended to emphasize the extent to which consumer culture was foisted upon an American populace unable to resist its advance. The scholarship on masculinity has sometimes cast changes in masculinity in these negative terms, but it has more often uncritically embraced changes in male gender roles as positive evidence of male liberation from repressive and stultifying expectations. In this study, as I tell the story of the development of modern masculine images within the American magazine market, I hope to chart a middle course between tragedy and celebration. On the one hand, I intend to offer a more sanguine assessment of the impact of consumer culture on masculinity by suggesting, first, that the embrace of modern masculine imagery was largely a product of both purposeful and inadvertent choices made by numbers of participants in the American magazine market rather than the top-down imposition of values on a populace of unwitting dupes and, second, that the impact of cultural transformation was far more uneven and gradual than some would suggest, reaching black and working-class men much later than their white middle- and upper-class counterparts but, eventually, with largely positive results. On the other hand, I hope to suggest that while modern masculinity clearly expanded the roles that men could play, it was hardly the boon to men or to the larger culture that its celebrators have suggested. While the evolution of gender roles in the modern era opened up numerous areas of possibility and encouraged some socially progressive developments, the growth of modern masculinity created roles for men that suited them to a corporate consumer culture and left them with little input on how to deal with other areas of their life. I argue that the rise of corporate consumer culture largely shaped the masculine roles within which we operate even today, but that viewing these masculine roles as either a regrettable fall from an earlier Eden or an ascent into a virtuous present leaves us ill suited to grapple with the everyday effort of understanding and perhaps reconstructing our gendered lives today.

My study of the relationship between masculinity and the rise of a consumer culture is based in American magazines, which were themselves a product of the forces that drove economic transformation. American magazines underwent a significant transformation beginning in 1893, when *McClure's* lowered its price to ten cents a copy and subsidized the costs of production by carrying ever greater numbers of advertisements. The magazine revolution initiated by *McClure's* shifted the terms of success for American magazines and immersed them in a commercial marketplace in ways that they had never been before. In the years to come, magazines that wished for commercial success sought at once to attract readers and advertisers, for one led nearly inevitably to the other. Tracing the development of masculinity within the modern magazine is a way of assessing changes within a medium that was always inclined to promote consumerism, so it will come as no surprise to discover that those magazines that succeeded best at attracting advertising were those that promoted a consuming lifestyle, and thus a consuming masculinity. But what may come as a surprise is the persistence of Victorian masculine images within modern white magazines well into the 1920s, and the near invisibility of modern masculine images within black publications until 1940. Magazines provide a fertile and contained testing ground for assessing the impact of the forces of modernization and the rise of consumerism on images of masculinity, and it is within magazines that I have found the evidence for my arguments.

Before I venture into a sustained narrative of how magazines presented images of American masculinity, however, I want to make clear the historiographical contexts within which my argument has meaning. In the remainder of this chapter I will describe the arguments about the development of consumer culture and masculinity that I wish to call into question, make a case for magazines as a medium conducive to advancing my thesis, and explain the methodology I used to examine masculinity within American magazines.

Mine is in many ways an old story, for it revisits a historical era about which there has been an abundance of excellent scholarship and about which there is some consensus. Scholars now largely agree that the rise of what has been called corporate capitalism in the latter part of the nineteenth century was the driving force in the transformation of American social, economic, and cultural life. Whether they depict that transformation as the inevitable consequence of modernization or the full expression of capitalist organization, all agree with some basic facts: that by the turn of the century the U.S. economy had shifted from a system based on small capitalist shops to a system based on large-scale corporate enterprises, and the focus of these enterprises had shifted from increasing production (though this was still of vital importance) to encouraging consumption; that the movement of people to larger cities broke down small-town affiliations and encouraged identification with national rather than local culture; and that mass media such as magazines (and, later, radio and television) rose to prominence as a result of such changes. There were a host of other changes associated with these transformations—the development of national marketing and distribution systems, the decline of protest politics after 1900, the emergence of what has often been called a "professional managerial class"— but the decline of masculine ideals associated with proprietary capitalism, the emergence of networks to promote consumption, and the rise of mass culture are the most important for this study.

As the story has most often been told, in the late nineteenth century the forces of corporate capitalism progressively swept away the vestiges of proprietary capitalism and, in the process, undermined the cultural superstructure that grew out of proprietary capitalism and replaced it with modern consumer culture.[1] As this new culture emerged, there emerged with it new ways of conceiving of selfhood, ways that called into question the values that had

---

1. This particular narrative line is most pronounced in those works that I see my study responding to most directly. For example, in *Land of Desire: Merchants, Power, and the Rise of a New American Culture,* William Leach argues that "the culture of consumer capitalism may have been among the most nonconsensual public cultures ever created," for it was created by "commercial groups in cooperation with other elites comfortable with and committed to making profits and to accumulating capital on an ever-ascending scale" (xv). Richard Wightman Fox and T. J. Jackson Lears, in the introduction to their collection *The Culture of Consumption: Critical Essays in American History, 1880–1980,* claim that "The consumer culture is not only the value-system that underlies a society saturated by mass-produced and mass-marketed goods, but also a new set of sanctions for the elite control of that society. While nineteenth-century elites ruled through ethical precepts that they

adhered to the notions of self that dominated in the nineteenth century. The transformation of notions of selfhood has been described by scholars in a variety of ways. David Riesman, in his early and influential work *The Lonely Crowd,* described a transition from people who were "inner-directed" to those who were "other-directed"; Warren Susman, whose essays collected in *Culture as History* have now influenced two generations of scholars, depicted a movement from a "culture of character" to a "culture of personality"; Jackson Lears offered the movement from "salvation" to "self-realization" as characteristic of the changes associated with cultural transformation; and Christopher Lasch, in a number of his works, portrayed a progression from a time when people were concerned with family and community to a time when they were primarily narcissistic, concerned only with their minimal self.[2] Each of these highly influential treatments traces the movement of the notion of selfhood from a time when identity was securely anchored—in a stable self, a stable family, a stable (and often religious) community, a stable culture of meaning—to a time when the self was detached, free-floating, and oriented only toward selfish concerns. Each of these arguments posits a movement along a continuum, from the prior state (character, inner-direction, salvation) to the present state (personality, other-direction, self-realization). And each casts that movement as essentially tragic, full of profoundly negative connotations for both the self and the familial, social, and cultural relations in which the self operates.

Those who have decried the impact of the rise of consumer culture on the self have done so in various ways. In his acerbic style, Christopher Lasch has argued, "In earlier times, the self-made man took pride in his judgment of character and probity; today he anxiously scans the faces of his fellows not so as to evaluate their credit but in order to gauge their susceptibility to his own blandishments.

---

encouraged people to internalize, twentieth-century elites rule through subtler promises of personal fulfillment" (xii).

2. David Riesman et al., *The Lonely Crowd: A Study of the Changing American Character,* is a sociological evaluation of a long-term transition in the American character. Warren Susman's article " 'Personality' and the Making of Twentieth-Century Culture" points out that particular cultures call into being certain types of people. Jackson Lears has published a number of works relating to this theme, but he deals with it most directly in "From Salvation to Self-Realization: Advertising and the Therapeutic Roots of the Consumer Culture, 1900–1930" and in *No Place of Grace: Antimodernism and the Transformation of American Culture, 1880–1920.* Christopher Lasch's *Haven in a Heartless World: The Family Besieged; The Culture of Narcissism: American Life in an Age of Diminishing Expectations;* and *The Minimal Self* all sound his basic thesis that cultural modernization broke down social bonds that were rooted in property and replaced them with free-floating and narcissistic self-absorption.

He practices the classic arts of seduction and with the same indifference to moral niceties, hoping to win your heart while picking your pocket. The happy hooker stands in place of Horatio Alger as the prototype of personal success." Jackson Lears drew on the language of David Riesman to claim, "The older ethic had required adherence to an internalized morality of self-control; repressive as this 'inner-direction' had been, it helped to sustain a solid core of selfhood. The newer ethic of 'other-direction' undermined that solidity by presenting the self as an empty vessel to be filled and refilled according to the expectations of others and the needs of the moment." Under this new ethic, individuals felt "the need to renew a sense of selfhood that had grown fragmented, diffuse, and somehow 'unreal.'" William Leach, whose work has focused on the creators of consumer culture, suggests that "brokers"—those individuals or groups "committed to helping business in a mediating capacity"—developed a style that called for "repressing one's own convictions and withholding judgment in the interest of forging profitable relationships."[3] Each of these authors finds in this transformation of selfhood a real sense of decline.

Such depictions of the growth of consumer culture derive from a common interpretation, a common set of assumptions. In his article "The Politics of Pragmatism," James Livingston argues that since the 1960s, "historians and cultural critics have tended to present the rise of corporate capitalism (ca. 1890–1940) as a tragedy in two acts. In the first act, subaltern social movements finally succumb to the powers of a specifically corporate plutocracy—here we witness the eclipse of Populism, the 'fall of the house of labor,' and the 'decline of popular politics.' In the second act, accordingly, the proletarianization of freeholders, small producers, and skilled craftsmen is completed and, under the managerial auspices of the large industrial corporations, the 'reification' of all social relations is effected." Part of this second act, of course, is the creation of notions of selfhood that are dislodged from their traditional orientations and reconfigured in a relationship to the bureaucratic corporations and consumer goods and services that lay at the center of consumer culture. In the major narratives that describe changing notions of selfhood during this era, writes Livingston, "the self-mastering citizens characteristic of proprietary capitalism gave way to the rootless, hedonistic, apolitical, and artificial personalities—the 'other-directed' individuals—sanctioned by consumer culture."[4] Thus the rise of consumer culture led to the degraded individual and cultural life we are stuck with today.

---

3. Lasch, *Culture of Narcissism,* 53; Lears, "From Salvation to Self-Realization," 8, 4; Leach, *Land of Desire,* 10, 11.
4. James Livingston, "The Politics of Pragmatism," 149, 156.

Yet Livingston, in his *Pragmatism and the Political Economy of Cultural Revolution, 1850–1940,* offers an alternative framework for understanding the meaning of the rise of consumer culture between 1890 and 1940. In mounting a "more or less populist protest against the bureaucratization of bourgeois society by corporate-industrial business enterprise," the critics of consumer culture have assumed that there "is no alternative to modern subjectivity except the loss of selfhood as such." Positing that the nineteenth-century individual enjoyed natural relations with his or her property, community, and self, such critics contend that the disruption of those relations brought by the rise of consumer culture left the modern individual estranged from "real" selfhood. Livingston offers several grounds on which to critique this thesis: "[I]f the ethical principle that regulates the critique of consumer culture is the integrity of the 'natural individual,' the self-determining personality, and if the condition of that integrity is abstention from the historical process through which social relations, personal attributes, and political principles are commodified in theory and practice, then the critique becomes incoherent."[5] Furthermore, and more importantly for my own argument, such critiques of consumer culture ignore the fact that numerous writers and intellectuals were themselves offering alternatives for understanding the meaning of selfhood within a changing culture.

In Livingston's account, John Dewey, William James, Walter Lippmann, and others saw "the characteristic changes of their epoch—the reconstruction of business enterprise, the confusion of cultural spheres, and the remaking of class relations—not only as threats to modern subjectivity but also as sources of a new, *social* self." These young intellectuals "posited a reconstruction of subjectivity which they hoped would allow the articulation of the 'whole personality'—of the 'social self' whose ego-boundaries would be determined neither by ownership of private property nor by 'economic self-assertion' but by association with others in managing the 'collective property' of culture (e.g., parks, libraries, museums; religion, art, literature)."[6] By unearthing and reconsidering the thinking of such young intellectuals regarding the possibilities for selfhood in the modern era, Livingston offers a counter to the narrative of decline, one that makes it possible for us to view modern selfhood as more than the "tragic residue" of past actions.

The editors, writers, advertisers, publishers, and readers who contributed to the magazines that make up my study did not engage the philosophical issues raised by Livingston's intellectuals—such issues were hardly the stuff of the general magazine—but they did engage in an ongoing negotiation

---

5. James Livingston, *Pragmatism and the Political Economy of Cultural Revolution, 1850–1940,* 65, 81, 65.
6. Ibid., 66, 77.

over the meaning of masculine selfhood. The editors of and contributors to the magazines I have studied often discussed the changing economic and cultural scene, yet they rarely spoke of any anxiety with declining authenticity, with potential duplicity, or with the diffusion of selfhood. Such anxiety no doubt appeared in the sources consulted by Lasch, Lears, and Leach—in the writings of mugwumps, antimodernists, ministers, and intellectuals—but it rarely showed up in the general American magazine. The contributors to such magazines did not depict themselves as victims; indeed, they often wrote with a sense of excitement and anticipation that speaks more to their need to master a new situation than to any sense of fear or weightlessness in the face of changing cultural norms. Most editors and contributors to white magazines took an optimistic view of men's prospects, finding ample prospects for men to realize their goals, whether they were personal or work related. The editors and contributors to black magazines, while hardly filled with the optimism of their white counterparts, advanced views of black masculinity that took a narrative form all their own. Embracing first the standards of manhood associated with proprietary capitalism, then alternatives that recognized that without the vote and economic access there could be no viable American masculinity, black magazines finally adopted the modern standards of manhood associated with white mass-market magazines.

All in all, American magazines offer a compelling counternarrative to the narrative of declension offered most provocatively by Lasch, Lears, and Leach. In my narrative the direction of change is the same, but the meaning of that change is quite different. Masculine identity *did* become more closely associated with self-realization, other-direction, and personality as a result of the rise of corporate consumer capitalism, but it did so in ways that were more gradual, more freely chosen, and more dynamic than previous scholars have argued, and with results that need not be viewed as tragic. To approach the creation of masculine identity in this era as if it were an imaginative response to ongoing cultural change rather than a defensive reaction to the dominance of corporate bureaucratic interests is to suggest two things: that the rise of consumer culture was a more open cultural process than is often assumed and that the reconfiguration of gender roles that accompanied its rise is an ongoing process in which people today can still intervene.

My understanding of the larger contours of American masculinity derives from and reacts against several decades of men's history scholarship. I have benefited greatly from the efforts of men's historians to sketch out the framework for my understanding of major issues in the development of white, middle-class masculinity. Yet I have been troubled by the tendency of many such historians to follow women's historians in heralding the liberation involved in the slow loosening of gender role restrictions or to follow historians of consumer culture in embracing the tragic paradigm that equates modernity with a lack of authenticity. Both interpretive frameworks strip men of a determining role in the construction of their own identities, the former by largely ceding to women the impetus for initiating changes in destructive networks of gender relations, the latter by ceding to the impersonal forces of capitalism the power to shape men's conceptions of themselves. I hope to find room for an account that grants men more agency in crafting the images of masculinity that permeated the American magazine, even while recognizing the influence of other forces.

Beginning in the mid-1970s, a number of historians followed the lead of women's historians and began to trace the outlines of a history of masculinity. The first men's history, Peter Filene's *Him/Her/Self*, drew its depiction of men's roles in the nineteenth century from the "separate spheres" thesis of gender roles. According to Filene, Victorian manhood glorified men's aggressive tendencies in the marketplace but relied on the male's suppression of his own natural instincts in the home. While Filene's evocation of Victorian manhood was well-crafted, his presentation of the Victorian era as an age of repression from which men and women have been fleeing successfully for over a century indicated his presentist political desire to promote male liberation. Filene's *Him/Her/Self* is remarkable for providing such a useful account of masculinity without the benefit of a significant body of scholarship to draw upon. But his account of the repressiveness of the Victorian gender norms must be factored against his desire to read history in terms of the steady liberation from these repressive cultural tendencies. The publication of his book, Filene announced in the preface to the first edition, "is a part of my efforts to act on my conviction . . . that men as well as women would benefit by liberation from conventional sex roles." Joe L. Dubbert's less influential *A Man's Place* is also explicitly liberationist, arguing that "whatever chances male liberation may have will depend in large part on the ability of American males to understand more clearly where they are in relation to where they have been." [7] Later social histories, such as Stuart Blumin's *The Emergence of the Middle Class* and Mary Ryan's *Cradle of the Middle Class*, observed that male identity grew out of the separate roles that men were asked to play at home and in the workplace as a result of the development and expansion of a growing small-capitalist economy. However, these studies benefited by

7. Peter G. Filene, *Him/Her/Self: Sex Roles in Modern America*, xv–xvi; Joe L. Dubbert, *A Man's Place: Masculinity in Transition*, 5. See also Filene, "The Secrets of Men's History," 112–14.

not embracing the "liberationist" framework that guided Filene's work. The overall thesis offered by such scholarship held that nineteenth-century cultural norms for masculinity had largely taken shape within the context of a proprietary capitalist economy, democratic political institutions, and a Victorian family structure. Men were encouraged to form their identities around an ideology of hard work and dedication to one's chosen trade, around their status as citizens and property holders, and around a moralized vision of the man's relationship to his wife and family. Over time such cultural norms had hardened into a stable set of values that are often known as Victorian masculinity. The ideal Victorian man was a property-owning man of character who believed in honesty, integrity, self-restraint, and duty to God, country, and family; as such he upheld the social and economic order of which he was an integral part.[8]

Within the confines of this larger framework for understanding masculinity in the nineteenth century there are a number of variations. One important expression of masculinity in the nineteenth century to which I have devoted some attention is the self-made man. This image of the self-made man is crucial to my study, for most of those who wrote about masculine success in American magazines frequently paid homage to this enduring cultural ideal. Two early studies—Irvin G. Wyllie's *The Self-Made Man in America* and John Cawelti's *Apostles of the Self-Made Man*—helped flesh out this essential American figure. Wyllie examined the advice offered to men in advice books, commencement addresses, and success manuals to show how the cult of the self-made man grew up alongside American business and helped socialize men to the demands made by the business world. Cawelti looked to influential American leaders, both real and mythic, to understand how it was that the myth of the self-made man was able to reconcile the conflicting demands of a conservative middle-class Protestant tradition, an increasingly aggressive individualism, and a growing concern with individual self-fulfillment.[9] My own treatment of the self-made man figure corroborates much of their work while recognizing that this self-made man trope has been flexible enough to function—that is, to make sense of men's experiences—in both Victorian and modern times.

8. Nancy F. Cott's *The Bonds of Womanhood: "Woman's Sphere" in New England, 1780–1835* is the best expression of the separate spheres argument, but it concentrates on women's roles. Stuart Blumin's *The Emergence of the Middle Class: Social Experience in the American City, 1760–1900* and Mary Ryan's *Cradle of the Middle Class: The Family in Oneida County, New York, 1790–1865* both provide balanced accounts of the formation of male gender roles and their relation to work and family.

9. Irvin G. Wyllie, *The Self-Made Man in America: The Myth of Rags to Riches;* John Cawelti, *Apostles of the Self-Made Man.*

By the late 1980s, a number of historians frustrated by the top-down intellectual history approach to studying masculinity gathered to discuss new ways
of understanding the nature of masculinity in Victorian America. Complaining
that "until very recently, much of what has been written about the manhood and
masculinity of the Victorian era cannot serve as even a rudimentary foundation
for more elaborate analytical models such as those that have transformed
women's history," they gathered their work into a collection of essays called
Meanings for Manhood. With essays that explored masculinity from a variety
of perspectives, the collection indicated that cultures of gender were far more
various and multifaceted than had previously been recognized.[10] While this
collection certainly spurred a healthy interest in the varieties of masculinity, the
major works that grew out of the gathering continued to argue within existing
interpretive paradigms for understanding masculinity, for example, that men's
adjustment to corporate capitalism came at the cost of a stable identity or that
men's rejection of Victorian norms was the first step in a century of progressive
liberation.

Mark C. Carnes's *Secret Ritual and Manhood in Victorian America* and
E. Anthony Rotundo's *American Manhood* stand as cases in point. Carnes
studied fraternal orders such as the Masons, the Knights of Pythias, and others
in order to overturn the notion that these groups served the purpose of providing
business contacts and a web of community for an increasingly urbanized middle
class. In fact, he argued persuasively that fraternal rituals "facilitated the young
man's transition to, and acceptance of, a remote and problematic conception of
manhood in America," and "demonstrate man's ability to create cultural forms
to mediate the demands of society."[11] Thus Carnes views the fraternal order
as offering crucial outlets for the tensions in men's lives: the elaborate and demanding rituals satisfy those men unhappy with an increasingly liberalized and
deritualized Christianity, and the patriarchal organization of fraternal societies
subverts the forms and ideologies of capitalist social organization, thus easing
men's frustration with social change. Carnes's emphasis on the reactive nature
of these fraternal organizations smacks once again of the tragic paradigm, for
it puts men in the position of clinging to a past that they cannot hope to—nor
do they—retain. Nor does it offer a convincing explanation of why fraternal
organizations declined so rapidly in the twentieth century.

Rotundo's *American Manhood* is perhaps the single most important work of
men's history to date. Like nearly every other men's historian, Rotundo looks

---

10. Mark C. Carnes and Clyde Griffen, eds., *Meanings for Manhood: Constructions of
Masculinity in Victorian America*, 1–2.
    11. Mark C. Carnes, *Secret Ritual and Manhood in Victorian America*, ix, 146, 155–57.

at evidence generated by an economically privileged northern middle class, "a small proportion of the American population who used their vast economic and cultural power to imprint their values on the nation." Rotundo makes good use of existing scholarship to locate changes in American masculinity during the nineteenth century within the general context of individualism, self-control, and the doctrine of separate spheres, but he also taps into an extensive body of primary evidence to show how separate men's cultures fit into his general framework. Rotundo's book is important to men's history for at least three reasons: it explores boyhood, adolescence, and manhood as distinct sites for understanding masculine culture; it provides an important sense of what the doctrine of separate spheres meant for men; and it describes the close relationship between individualism and masculinity. Rotundo argues that the doctrine of separate spheres was created by men and women adjusting to a world in which individual self-assertion was becoming the basis for the social structure; it allowed men to pursue their political and economic self-interest while women were charged with guarding communal virtues. His work documenting men's active role in shaping their gender roles stands as a corrective to those who would see gender reacting passively to economic change. But Rotundo weakens his claims for male agency in his explanations of the decline of Victorian masculinity, discussing it in terms of men's reactions to the changing world of work, to women's efforts to undermine the doctrine of separate spheres, and to changing notions of individuality and self-expression.[12] Rotundo welcomes such changes, for they intimate the liberation that he contends has been the essential element in the development of modern masculinity.

While no full study of the transition from Victorian to modern masculinity yet exists, the existing scholarship provides the outlines for understanding the transformation. The cultural edifice that was Victorian masculinity had hardly set before changes in the American economy and the social structure started that edifice crumbling. By the 1890s, small-scale, competitive capitalism had given way to large-scale, corporate capitalism in a series of sickening economic jolts that made many Americans question the very stability of their way of life. The shifting economy was part of a larger transition in the social structure of the nation. These years also saw an influx of immigration, a concentration of population in cities, an increase in the availability of leisure, and, after the turn of the century, a boom in political reform followed by a decline in popular participation in politics. Finally, women's access to the vote and to jobs significantly changed relations between the sexes and within families.

12. E. Anthony Rotundo, *American Manhood: Transformations in Masculinity from the Revolution to the Modern Era,* 2, 294–97, 248–55, 279–83.

All of these changes, and many others, undermined the basis for Victorian masculinity: the republican notion of property ownership was obviated by the new corporate business structures, and many men began to question whether the virtues of self-restraint, dedication, honesty, and integrity really meant much anymore.

As men increasingly came to work in large, bureaucratic corporations rather than small shops; as they sought leisure in large, impersonal cities rather than in small towns; and as they viewed the world through mass-circulation magazines rather than local newspapers, they began to devise new ways to think about their identity as men. The masculinity that evolved alongside this modern culture came to emphasize personality, sexuality, self-realization, and a fascination with appearances, all traits that made men well suited to participate in the social and economic institutions of the period. Most works on masculinity intimate the direction of this change, but few have attempted to narrate the process through which Victorian masculinity evolved into modern masculinity. The general studies—Filene's *Him/Her/Self,* Peter Stearns's *Be a Man!* and Michael Kimmel's *Manhood in America*—tend to discuss modern masculinity in terms of the dizzying array of options made available to men by the collapse of Victorian masculinity and the vague challenges posed by the rise of corporate capitalism. The best monograph on modern masculinity, Kevin White's *The First Sexual Revolution* describes the masculine ideal that emerged out of urban youth culture and valued appearance, sexuality, and personality over hard work, solid morals, and good character. White's use of popular culture sources and the attention he pays to the impact of consumerism on masculine identity are welcome additions to the study of masculinity. But White's thesis harks back to the tragic paradigm, arguing that what drove the changes in masculinity "were the imperatives and urgencies of consumption," and thus were part of the process through which "ruling elites could maintain their power and hegemony." Thus gender roles are not crafted by people struggling to come to terms with their world but are instead created for people by an advertising machine intent on spurring consumption, and the "New American Man of the twentieth century . . . is the perfect dupe of the larger American hegemony."[13] As is probably obvious by now, I find much to reject in such a conclusion.

---

13. Peter N. Stearns, in *Be a Man! Males in Modern Society,* offers an interpretation of men's history that rejects the liberationist bias and grants men more agency than does Peter Filene. Moreover, Stearns locates the fundamental change in masculinity during the transition from a patriarchal agrarian economy to a market capitalist economy. Thus he finds more continuity in nineteenth- and twentieth-century manhood than any other scholar. Michael Kimmel's *Manhood in America: A Cultural History* is a useful survey of the variety of social influences that may have affected manhood, but it fails to offer a historical—that

Throughout this study I have used two terms to characterize the major constellations of masculine imagery that I see represented in this period: Victorian masculinity and modern masculinity. These terms are not meant to represent static or internally consistent cultural movements or moments; there is no one point at which American masculinity was strictly Victorian or modern. Indeed, elements of what I call modern masculinity emerged during the late Victorian era, while elements of Victorian masculinity lingered on well into the modern age. Rather, these terms are intended to designate loosely affiliated ideals and images that are associated with the major elements of manhood as discussed above. The terms are most useful when thought of as designating ends of a spectrum. It is not my intention to define the ends of that spectrum too precisely, but rather to use these terms to describe the movement of the majority of the representations of masculinity along this spectrum, from Victorian masculinity toward modern masculinity. My use of these terms is not intended to erase or deny the elements of American masculinity that I have not deemed relevant to this particular study.

While I am comfortable adopting the rough frameworks for understanding the dominant cultural markers for masculinity in America proposed by men's historians, I am eager to rework the interpretative paradigms that cast the rise of modern masculinity either as the story of tragic decline or happy liberation. The discourse on masculinity that pervaded American magazines between 1893 and 1950 cast men neither as "perfect dupes" nor as liberated good guys, but rather offered a variety of options within which men might understand their masculine identity. To the extent that men accepted the visions of manhood offered by advertisers concerned primarily with selling their goods, perhaps they were dupes. To the extent that they embraced notions of self-realization that were applicable across gender lines, perhaps they achieved a form of liberation. But what is certainly the case is that they were offered both options—and many more—within the pages of American magazines. In the end I argue that masculine images were actively created by publishers, editors, and writers who sought to make the best out of an emerging corporate capitalist culture in which they played a part.

A glaring gap in existing men's history that I hope to help to fill concerns the depiction of black masculinity. The existing scholarship on masculinity has concentrated nearly exclusively on white, middle-class masculinity, apologizing for this predictable focus while noting that black men (and working-class men) were largely absent from the sources that they used to understand masculinity

---

is, a causal—argument, and I have not found it very useful. Kevin White, *The First Sexual Revolution: Male Heterosexuality in Modern America*, 188–89.

and that it was white, middle-class men who were engaged in setting the terms for understanding masculinity.[14] For the better part of the nineteenth century, it is true that those African Americans whose voices were heard in public discourse had more pressing concerns than publishing advice books and success manuals. But beginning in the twentieth century African American magazines offered a medium for interrogating the way that black editors, publishers, and writers understood the meaning of masculinity. I have attempted to bring those magazines and those images into my study because I believe that we can obtain a far richer picture of what masculinity looked like at any given time when we consider it across boundaries of race and, for that matter, class. The presentation of masculinity within black magazines, for example, reveals that "Victorian" ideas of character, hard work, and integrity retained their validity within the black community well after historians of white masculinity depicted them as outdated. Moreover, tracing the impact of consumerism and the ethic of self-realization within black magazines reveals a great deal about the power and reach of these forces of transformation. Black magazines remained outside the commercial nexus for the better part of my study, indicating that the hegemony of consumer culture was hardly as pervasive as its advocates claim. Instead of discussing masculinity within the context of an expanding corporate economy and a world of goods, black editors and writers were predominantly concerned with access to jobs and with the rights of African Americans as citizens. Finally, black magazines actively sought to gain access to the commercial nexus that joined advertisers, readers, and magazines, and when one black magazine— *Ebony*—finally gained that access it rapidly reshaped the presentation of male images to conform to the logic of consumer culture. The readiness, indeed the zeal with which *Ebony* embraced modern masculinity makes it hard to view the forces that created modern masculinity as pernicious. The presentation of masculinity in black magazines thus provides a context for our understanding of both masculinity and consumerism that is crucial to our understanding of either.

By the turn of the century, it was clear that many men had become sufficiently aware of the dissonance between Victorian masculine roles and the emerging

14. Recent exceptions to this trend are Gail Bederman's *Manliness and Civilization: A Cultural History of Gender and Race in the United States, 1880–1917,* which examines the way a group of American thinkers used the "discourse of civilization" to rethink the relationship between race and manhood and is blessedly free of the interpretive dead ends that I have argued against (44), and Glenda Elizabeth Gilmore's *Gender and Jim Crow: Women and the Politics of White Supremacy in North Carolina, 1896–1920,* which devotes a chapter to understanding the self-presentation of (primarily young) black men as they sought a place in North Carolina's social structure.

modern culture that they began to reassess what masculinity might mean in this new age. One of the forums in which they began this reassessment was the magazine. The magazine market had been revolutionized by the very changing economy that had called Victorian masculinity into question. Where once magazines presented a refined cultural viewpoint to a select few, after the dime magazine revolution of 1893—during which key magazines dropped their price and subsidized their booming circulation by carrying an unprecedented number of advertisements—magazines became an immensely popular venue for the entertainment and education of great masses of Americans. The magazine revolution—which I cover in further detail in Chapter 1—not only brought magazines before a greater number of readers than ever before, but also changed the very nature of the magazine. After 1893 the general magazine typically offered both fiction and nonfiction, editorial comment, and a heavy dose of advertising. Each magazine crafted itself to appeal to a slightly different audience—some were for rural audiences, others for urban; some were primarily for men, others for women; some attempted to embrace all of the American experience, others focused on one aspect of it, like business or sports; most were for whites, a few for African Americans—but they all offered a combination of entertainment, information, and the inducement to buy. In discussing the various magazines I have covered, I have engaged a large and growing body of scholarship on the American magazine as a cultural phenomenon. Recent magazine scholarship has attempted to determine how it was that magazines participated in and helped shape cultural transformation, and it is this work to which I respond most directly.[15]

15. The standard history of the American magazine is Frank Luther Mott, *A History of American Magazines.* Theodore Peterson's *Magazines in the Twentieth Century,* John Tebbel's *The American Magazine: A Compact History,* John Tebbel and Mary Ellen Zuckerman's *The Magazine in America, 1741–1990,* and James Playsted Wood's *Magazines in the United States: Their Social and Economic Influence* all provide essentially celebratory overviews of magazine publishing.

More recent scholarship on magazines has attempted to understand the development of magazines within the context of arguments about the meaning of the cultural transformation associated with the rise of consumer capitalism. The most influential of this scholarship has been by Richard Ohmann, first in his essay "Where Did Mass Culture Come From? The Case of Magazines" and later in *Selling Culture: Magazines, Markets, and Class at the Turn of the Century.* In the latter work, Ohmann argues that magazines served as a crucial forum for articulating and advancing the cultural hegemony of the corporate capitalist class. Matthew Schneirov, in *The Dream of a New Social Order: Popular Magazines in America, 1893–1914,* insists that magazines were not merely vehicles of consumer culture but forums within which editors and contributors worked out their relationship to the emerging cultural order. Schneirov's argument has the advantage of granting agency to such editors and contributors, and of not assuming that they were merely swept along by the rising tide of consumerism.

Modern magazines were born out of the very transformative forces of corporate capitalism—they were children of mass production and distribution, large cities, and the existence of a "national" culture. Yet the editors and publishers, writers, advertisers, and readers who determined the shape of these magazines brought to the magazines an array of views about masculinity that were far more rich and complicated than might be expected by those who overestimate the transforming effects of corporate capitalism. Editors and publishers who embraced the culture of character clung to its ideals with some success into the 1920s, even as the medium in which they wrote was inundated with advertisements promoting the culture of personality. African American editors and contributors attempted to establish standards for masculinity in a context long untouched by commercial interests. And readers of the most modern of magazines contested the dominance of the culture of personality and the advertisements that celebrated it. Drawing on visions of masculinity offered in a wide range of magazines, I will show that the cultural reaction to the advance of corporate capitalism was various and multifaceted, producing numbers of ways of construing appropriate masculinity.

As magazines attempted to find and keep an audience, as they discussed the issues of the day, and as they peddled the goods offered by American manufacturers, they inevitably offered a kind of ongoing commentary on the nature of American masculinity. In commenting on the American scene, they commented on American masculinity. Thus I have used magazines as a window into the changing nature of masculinity during the first half of the twentieth century. I believe that magazines offer a particularly rich body of evidence to the scholar wishing to understand such a topic as masculinity. Because magazines strove to digest what was most important about contemporary goings-on in the culture, they provide a window into the concerns of the day. Yet because they are themselves commercial mediums, struggling to make it in a competitive market economy, they are attuned to providing images that are both appealing to readers and inoffensive to the corporations who wish to advertise themselves and their products. The history that one writes after studying magazines is not about social issues, but about social issues as they are filtered through the hands of editors; not about the economy, but about the economy as an indirect factor in shaping the content of magazines; not hagiography, but about stars as indicators of an emerging cult of personality.

The history that I have written is a cultural history, the history of developing and shifting notions of masculinity as they evolved within an increasingly commercialized medium. I argue not for one causal force that transformed American masculinity, but for a myriad of such forces, each of which was felt with differing intensity at different points in time. The persistent presence of American racism, the rise of sports heroes, the youth craze of the 1920s, the ubiquity of the salesman, and the tropes of popular fiction all play a role in reshaping masculinity within American magazines. I have, however, paid particular attention to two kinds of pressures that seemed especially important in understanding the evolution of modern masculinity: the pressure to succeed and the pressure to consume. American magazines were often obsessed with figuring out what it meant to succeed, and how success—economic success, of course, but success of other sorts as well—helped shape a man's sense of worth. The notion of masculine success crossed racial boundaries, and I have paid close attention to the ways that race shaped the presentations of success in African American magazines (keeping in mind that the dominant concerns of black editors and writers were jobs and citizenship rights). I have paid the most attention to the many ways that consumerism reshaped male identity. From the very beginning, the primary way that modern magazines survived was by attracting advertisers to their pages. These advertisers, over the course of time, developed sophisticated ways of recasting male images in terms that suggested to men that they needed to reshape themselves through the various means made available to them: bodybuilding exercises, personality-enhancing books, nice clothes, and an array of personal care products. It was not just advertisers who promoted the "improvement through consumption" agenda; many magazines crafted editorial content that suited the very same agenda. I have assessed the myriad effects that the consumerist agenda had on American magazines and American masculinity, again paying careful attention to the way race and class modified the impact of that agenda. In the end, modern men chose to be and were made to be consuming men within the pages of the American magazine.

Methodology and Organization

How does one begin to tell the story of a culture's changing notion of masculinity? What sources should one choose? How many sources are needed to tell the story? The very fact that such choices are wide open, and that any such sources are open to widely different interpretations, requires that I lay bare my own approaches to understanding this subject. Studying cultural notions of masculinity is not like studying a mine worker's strike or a presidential race; there are no notes of union meetings, no news stories devoted just to the subject. Historians once assumed that there was no need for the writing of men's history, or, rather, that all historical writing had been the writing of men's history. Feminists and women's historians, with their well-executed efforts to show the centrality of gender in constructing all facets of the human past, have proved and continue to prove that history is indelibly gendered.[16] We know now that notions of what constitutes appropriate behavior for men and women at different moments in time do not spring from stable truths or biological certainties. Gender is constructed in the maelstrom of social, economic, family, and individual life that we call culture.

To understand how gender is constructed, however, requires that we first recognize that until very recently the subject of the construction of gender has been largely invisible. Not long ago, it was unheard of for men to speculate in writing about their masculinity. There were no Robert Blys in the 1920s (although there was Ernest Hemingway). Gender and gender construction are modern concerns. The fact that the construction of gender was not the subject of past cultural conversations poses certain difficulties for the historian, difficulties that must be factored into the explanations that evolve out of the study of gender. There are, of course, the difficulties that face all historians, and these are certainly pressing. The lack of documentation on what seem to be key events, the scarcity of comment on certain issues, and so on, all constitute roadblocks for the historian wishing to offer the best possible account of past events. (For example, while I detected the shaping influence of advertisers all over the editorial content of the magazines I studied, I only once found direct evidence of an advertiser openly trying to influence editorial policy, and even that evidence appeared out of my time frame.) While I mean in no way to diminish the problems that a lack of evidence poses for any historian, it is not primarily a lack of evidence that bedevils the cultural historian. Indeed, it is the very abundance of evidence that I have found most bewildering. If, for example, too few people ever commented publicly about their perceptions of masculinity in the years between 1900 and 1950, it is also true that every utterance issued by men in this period could be interrogated for what it reveals about their underlying assumptions about masculinity.

The difficulty facing this historian, then, was in deciding which documents would be used to tell the story of a fundamental change in the way Americans thought about masculinity. When I began this study I hoped that I could study masculinity across several genres of mass culture—magazines, films, advertisements, music, and popular fiction. But the further I ventured into this study, designed to cover twenty years, the more I realized that portraying the changes in American notions of masculinity required a longer span of time. In order to narrate the changes in American masculinity over this time period,

16. The feminist and women's studies scholarship that has had the most impact on my approach to men's history includes Nancy Cott, "On Men's History and Women's History"; Cott, *The Bonds of Womanhood;* Joan Wallach Scott, *Gender and the Politics of History;* and Barbara Welter, "The Cult of True Womanhood."

I needed a medium that spanned the years from 1900 to 1950, and I wanted one that would allow me to chart the influence of commercialism and mark the differences between white and black representations of masculinity. Given these parameters, there was only one choice: magazines.

Choosing among the huge number of magazines that appeared before American readers was also a difficult decision. The decision was made easier in a very few cases by those magazines that explicitly identified themselves as "men's magazines": the *American Magazine, Esquire,* and *True.* The black magazines—the *Colored American, Alexander's,* the *Crisis, Opportunity,* the *Competitor,* and *Ebony*—also selected themselves, in this case because they were either the only magazines edited and published by African Americans or the only ones large enough to consider. (I should note that each of what I call black magazines had some white readership and, in some cases, substantial white editorial involvement. Nonetheless, they were primarily about African Americans.) From there, selection became more difficult. I always wanted those magazines that kept men's issues at the forefront of their agenda, but finding such magazines from the early years of the century was not easy.

George Lorimer's *Saturday Evening Post* had started out in 1899 as a magazine for men, but the difficulties of attracting both advertisers and readers to such a publication at the turn of the century had pushed the magazine to pursue a family readership while maintaining an emphasis on the concerns of men from about 1908. While the *Saturday Evening Post* plays a part in my study, it has been so well studied elsewhere that I have not made it a centerpiece of my own research. Several other magazines paid enough attention to men's work, to business, and to men's activities—fishing, camping, sports, and so on—to position themselves as clear competitors for a male readership. During the first period of my study—1893 to 1913—I chose to integrate the scholarship on the *Saturday Evening Post* with my readings in *McClure's* and *Munsey's,* two general-interest magazines with leading circulation figures. In the end, this period acts as a kind of precursor to my study of the commercial influence on American magazines, for while advertising was coming to dominate the finances of all American magazines of this time, advertising to men was still very limited and the representations of men were fairly consistent across publications.

In 1913 Condé Nast, publisher of the popular women's magazine *Vogue,* introduced *Vanity Fair,* a "smart" cosmopolitan magazine of culture with a distinctly masculine focus. Though its circulation during its early years was never large, the number of advertisements directed toward men and the tendency to construct men as consumers made this magazine a natural for my study. While *Vanity Fair* pitched itself to a male elite, the *American Magazine* was proving itself the magazine of the "self-made man, corporate style." With a circulation that rivaled that of the *Saturday Evening Post,* the *American Magazine* was the biggest magazine to appeal to the quintessential striving businessman of the 1920s. I looked intently at both of these magazines, reading the *American* virtually from cover to cover for the entire decade and reading all pertinent matter from *Vanity Fair* for its entire publishing run, from 1913 to 1936.[17] Another large-circulation magazine, *Collier's,* offered insights into a style of masculinity that was less urban, more traditional in its emphasis than the *American.* I also paid attention to a number of sports periodicals in this period, for they obviously were aimed at a male audience. *Sporting Life, Athletic World,* and *Athletic Journal* all spoke to different issues concerning men's interest in athletics. And I paid close attention to the *New Success* (later named simply *Success*), for this magazine struggled to reconcile Victorian notions of character with modern notions of personality.

In 1933, *Esquire* was launched as the magazine for American men, ushering in a new era in magazine publishing. I read *Esquire* very closely in its first seven years of publication, less intently in the following years (for reasons that will become clear in that chapter). During World War II, two magazines—*True* and *Argosy*—shifted their format to tap into the audience that *Esquire* had created. These magazines merited close attention, for they were so clearly trying to offer a consumerist masculinity to a working-class audience. In the end, I have devoted little space to the more derivative *Argosy,* however. And while I followed the careers of the *American* and *Collier's* into this last period of my study, they came to have less to say about American masculinity. But the first of the black magazines to reach a mass-circulation audience, *Ebony,* suddenly offered visions of black American men that were comparable to those of white American men. I read this magazine intently in its first decade.

I have selected for this study both magazines that were representative of the magazine market as a whole, and magazines that best reflected the concerns and interests of American men. I have selected magazines with huge circulation and magazines with relatively small circulation, but I have always tried to select commercial magazines, that is, magazines that subsidized their publishing efforts by attracting advertisements. Unlike the little magazines or those dependent strictly on subscriptions for their financial survival, commercial

---

17. Deciding what was "pertinent" was a judgment call I made every day I researched this study. In the end, I chose any article that seemed to reveal the author's understanding of what constituted acceptable or ideal notions of masculinity, whether that article be about boxer Jack Dempsey, succeeding in business, or attending college. I looked at—skimmed—every article in the first few issues of any magazine I consulted, and used that early information to guide my selections of what to read in future issues. Of course, *Vanity Fair* has since been revived as a popular magazine. I studied it only in its first incarnation.

magazines were immersed in the marketplace and thus ideally situated to offer insights into the influence of commercial pressures on masculinity. In the case of the African American magazines, however, I have had to bend this rule a bit. African American magazines tried very desperately to make it as commercial ventures, but it was not until the success of *Ebony* in 1945 that a black magazine succeeded in underwriting its publication with advertising dollars. Unable to attract enough advertisers, white or black, magazines like the *Crisis* and *Opportunity* were forced to rely on an institutional affiliation, and these affiliations made these magazines subject to a different dynamic. Rather than exclude black magazines for these reasons, I have used the lack of commercial support as a way of showing how black masculinity stayed centered around such issues as economic success, character, and citizenship long after those ideals became secondary in white magazines. Once black magazines entered the consumer market, black masculinity quickly shifted to embrace modern ideals.

Like many others who have studied American magazines, I have come to believe that magazines develop a kind of "personality." This personality is the sum of the components that make up a magazine—its editorials, its articles, its advertisements, and its illustrations. This personality is also something that develops over time, and changes and grows with passing issues. Studying a magazine as a personality, I have attended to the synergy between articles, ads, and editorials, and examined the relationship between what a magazine tried to do and how well it succeeded. Having said that magazines have personalities, I also believe that those are particularly interesting and engaging personalities, for in trying to create an identity that is distinctive they are also trying desperately to please subscribers who in their numbers will then lure advertisers, whose support will embolden and reinforce the identity created, and so on—and often in reverse.

The personality that a magazine develops is multifaceted. In some magazines the personality is most clearly defined by the editor's commentary and his selection of articles. Strong editors—like George Horace Lorimer of the *Saturday Evening Post,* W. E. B. Du Bois of the *Horizon* and the *Crisis,* John Siddall of the *American Magazine,* or Arnold Gingrich of *Esquire*—had a way of making their magazine an extension of themselves. But many editors took a lighter hand at shaping their magazine, and the personality indicated by the editorial matter was elusive. The advertising carried by a magazine deeply influenced a magazine's personality as well, and it certainly offered a narrative line that was just as important and just as persuasive as the narrative line constructed by editorial policy. Advertising tells a story that is far larger than the condensed words and images of an individual advertisement—it speaks to a whole culture of meaning and understanding, as its best interpreters have understood. Finally, reader comments have contributed to the magazine's personality as well. The "letters to the editor" section of many magazines revealed that readers had a depth of identification with the magazine that confirmed my assumption that magazines made a difference in the way people saw the world. Several magazines made such letters an important part of their editorial mix, allowing them to exert an influence on editorial policy. In the end, I have tried to read the narratives of advertising, reader comment, and editorial contents alongside each other, accepting each as a contributor to the magazine's overall personality. Placing the power to constitute images of masculinity in the hands of the hodgepodge of influences that create a magazine makes it difficult to ascertain exactly which forces are dictating the presentation of masculinity over time. This is as it should be, and I hope that is stands as a corrective to studies that place too much agency in the hands of editors or advertisers. In the end I have tried to balance what Richard Ohmann has called "the decisive power of economic forces and of those actors best located to harness them; and the equally crucial, if less decisive, agency of many others seeking their own ends with smaller means."[18]

Having said that I have paid attention to the input of readers, I should also acknowledge the real difficulties I faced in understanding exactly who was reading any magazine. Prior to the 1930s, there was simply very little information available concerning the readership of any magazine. Even the better studies of literacy and readership—such as Carl F. Kaestle's *Literacy in the United States: Readers and Reading since 1880*—offer only broad generalities about the social, race, and class makeup of magazine readers, and next to nothing regarding the readership of specific magazines during this period. By the 1940s survey researchers would begin to introduce the techniques that would allow magazine publishers to understand their readership and target their product more precisely, but for the better part of the first fifty years of the century one can best infer the audience—if one must infer it at all—from the way the magazine appeals to specific social and ethnic preferences. Even these inferences are fraught with peril. For example, one assumes that the *Crisis* was intended for African American readers, yet we know many of the NAACP members who received the magazine were white. In the end, my study is not about readership but rather about the images presented within magazines.

18. Ohmann, *Selling Culture,* 342; Matthew Schneirov's *Dream of a New Social Order,* for example, places too much emphasis on the ideology-creating role of magazine editors, while Stuart Ewen's *Captains of Consciousness: Advertising and the Social Roots of the Consumer Culture* places far too much power in the hands of advertisers.

I have paid a great deal of attention to words and images, for it is through words and images that magazines communicated to American men their expectations and idealizations of masculinity. The careful reader is going to get sick of some words—words like *self-made man, character, personality, integrity, perseverance,* and so on. Yet I have returned to these words again and again in order to explore how their meaning has changed over time, for they were the words that editors and contributors used to discuss the meaning of manhood. Magazines tap into a common language and they reinterpret that language constantly in order to suit their needs. Literary scholars may well wish that I had read more closely into some of the language I encounter, for much of what people had to say about masculinity is rich with meaning. I have tried to tease out what I needed to make my point and then moved on, believing that the abundance of many pieces of evidence is more persuasive than the eloquence of any one piece.

Having paid close attention to what was revealed by the words and images used by editors, advertisers, and contributors, I have also been deeply influenced by some things that were not said. As I combed through the memoirs, autobiographies, letters, and business correspondence of numerous of the editors I have mentioned, I looked closely for the "smoking gun": evidence that advertisers directly influenced editorial policy. Somewhere, I thought, there must be some reference to a clothing advertiser requesting that an editor make positive mention of his products, some quid pro quo arrangement that would suit both editor and advertiser. But, with one exception, such evidence was nowhere to be found. (The exception was in the papers of *Esquire* editor Arnold Gingrich, but well after the closing date of my study.) Nor was such evidence offered in other scholarly works on magazines, including those that argue that commercial interests helped determine the shape of editorial policy.[19] On the

19. The "smoking gun" that I found in the Arnold Gingrich Papers was a memo from an advertising salesman that suggested to Gingrich that some advertisers would be happy if the magazine would downplay its emphasis on sexuality; interoffice memo from Paul Olafsson of the New York office to Arnold Gingrich, April 22, 1953, Box 11, Folder: *Esquire Magazine* Office Files Advertising (3), Arnold Gingrich Papers, Michigan Historical Collections, Bentley Historical Library, University of Michigan, Ann Arbor (hereinafter referred to as Gingrich Papers).

In *The Adman in the Parlor: Magazines and the Gendering of Consumer Culture, 1880s to 1910s,* Ellen Gruber Garvey notes that while "magazines came to act in the interests of advertisers in the aggregate, and advertising came to shape magazines," there is virtually no evidence of direct influence (11–12). Participants on several academic listservs (SHARP-L and H-AMSTDY e-mail discussion lists) confirmed my sense that little such evidence exists. The piece of evidence that many people pointed out to me was an article in which *Ms.* magazine editor Gloria Steinem discussed the pressure the women's magazines faced to

one hand, perhaps such evidence is unavailable because it was in the best interests of both advertiser and editor not to let anyone know of any such quid pro quo arrangements. But the evidence that does exist offers the more persuasive explanation that advertisers did not need to pressure for such arrangements because editors were already convinced of the efficacy of providing a supportive editorial environment for advertising. Most of the editors I studied were first and foremost businessmen who saw no inherent contradiction in placing an editorial on the latest suits next to an advertisement for Arrow collars. As the American magazine market developed, such an arrangement became the norm in many commercial magazines.

The changing personalities of American magazines have had much to do with how I have read them. I have referred to two kinds of reading—intensive and selective—but I want to clarify these terms with respect to this notion of personality. At different times, different magazines seemed to be more or less concerned with questions of masculinity; this concern was an expression of that magazine's personality. Thus when a magazine's personality seemed oriented toward exploring concepts having to do with American masculinity, I read that magazine quite intently, and did so until it proved fruitless to do so any longer, until masculinity seemed no longer to be a primary concern. Those magazines that were never too explicitly concerned with masculinity, or were concerned with it in ways similar to publications I looked at intently, I read selectively.

When I claim to have read a magazine intently, I mean that I looked at every page of an issue, and often at every issue in the year. This was a habit I sometimes wished I could kick, for it drew me into spending far more time on some sources than may have been prudent. But understanding a magazine's representation of masculinity seems to me to rest on understanding the nuances of its many expressions, from asides dropped in editorials to fiction by writers that appeared only once, to the dizzying number of ads. And there is no way to gain an understanding of a magazine's nuances without reading it intently, month after month, and year after year. Those magazines I looked at selectively received a different kind of scrutiny. I decided to read a magazine selectively when, after reading intently from three to six months of successive issues, it seemed as if this magazine would not offer original insights that moved me beyond what I already knew. Once I decided to give a magazine a selective read, I read two issues a year every fourth year. In some cases, as with the *American Magazine* and *Argosy*, for example, a selective reading turned into an intensive reading (or vice versa) following a significant shift in editorial policy. I mention

---

"supply what the ad world euphemistically describes as 'supportive editorial atmosphere' or 'complementary copy'" ("Sex, Lies, and Advertising," 26).

my reading strategies for each magazine at the beginning of my discussion of it. Some readers may wish that my reading strategy were more consistent— that I had read four issues every other year, for example—but such a strategy would have allowed me too little time on some magazines and too much time on others. In the end I chose a strategy that would allow me to cover more total magazines and to spend more time on those magazines that dealt with masculinity most directly.

The bulk of my evidence comes from the pages of the magazines themselves—a necessity for an argument that is based on the presentation of masculine images within the peculiar cultural world that is bound within the pages of a magazine issue after issue. But I have also relied on other key kinds of documents—scholarship, memoirs, biographies and autobiographies, manuscript collections—when they were available. There have been several cases, however, in which I dearly wished that more information was available. The *American Magazine,* for example, provides my primary evidence for the transformation from Victorian to modern masculinity in the 1920s, yet the editor for most of those years, John Siddall, left astonishingly few traces of his existence, and the manuscript collections for the magazine consist nearly entirely of the manuscripts submitted to the magazine with brief reader comments attached.[20] Similar scarcities of secondary information pertained to numerous other magazines, including most of the black magazines and the less reputable white magazines, including *True, Argosy, Success,* and the sporting magazines. While I have not exhausted the research possibilities for every magazine, every editor, or every significant contributor to the magazines I have studied, I have tried to do so for those magazines that I deemed most important to my argument.

The notion of magazines having a kind of personality has helped to shape the narrative of my study as well. While my overall thesis is that over a fifty-year span America's notions of what constituted masculinity were reoriented through their relationship to the commercialization and "consumerization" of mass culture, that thesis does not lend itself to easy periodization. It is not that you cannot periodize changes in notions of gender, it is just that if you do so with any specificity you look like a fool. After all, people did not wake up to

---

20. My quest for more information on Siddall and the *American Magazine,* conducted with the assistance of librarians at the Library of Congress, Purdue University, and Michigan State University, turned up mere scraps of biographical details on Siddall. I had hoped that the voluminous Crowell-Collier Company Publishing Records, held at the New York Public Library, would be the gold mine for which I had longed, but the 808 boxes held there contained just a few boxes of information on the *American Magazine,* and these consisted almost entirely of articles and cartoons submitted by unknown people to which were paper-clipped brief notes of rejection.

modern masculinity the way they woke up to find that President McKinley had been shot. Indeed, my refusal to offer a strict periodization about the "birth" of modern masculinity is something of a thesis itself, for I refuse to do so in order to point out the fact that notions of gender give way slowly and nearly imperceptibly one to another, with new ideals appearing long before the death of the old; old ways maintaining viability long into a new age; and factors like race and class making normative masculinity quite elusive.

So, while I do not care to use changes in masculinity to periodize my study, changes in the magazines and in the way they represent masculinity stand as useful narrative signposts to point the way along this longer path of change. I have broken these periods into five chapters, with one chapter each describing the persistence of Victorian masculinity in white and black magazines, one chapter each describing the transformation from Victorian to modern masculinity within white and black magazines, and one chapter describing the triumph of modern masculinity in white middle-class and working-class magazines and in black magazines. Though I trust that the reader will come to see the logic of segregating white magazines from black magazines in the early chapters, let me say at this point that the separation reflects the absolutely different worlds within which black and white magazines—and indeed, black and white men—operated. The dynamic that motivated the white magazine market was consumer-oriented, while the one that motivated the black magazine was rights- and job-oriented until 1945, when John Johnson of *Ebony* took the "race journal" into the modern age.

In Chapter 1, "Old-Fashioned Manhood in a Newfangled Medium," I establish a baseline for understanding the changes that are to come in magazine's representation of masculinity and its relationship to the consumer marketplace. In this period, men were figured primarily as earners and producers, and much of the rhetoric that was used to describe them paid allegiance to the truisms of the Victorian age. In this chapter, I trace the careers of three magazines—*McClure's, Munsey's,* and the *Saturday Evening Post*—from their inception until World War I, an ending point that has nothing to do with the war and everything to do with the emergence of two new magazines that represent the interests of American men. I argue that the very nature of the commercial magazine mitigated against the expression of Victorian masculinity within its pages, but that the creators of the first magazines were themselves so indebted to the Victorian cult of character that they celebrated the old styles of masculinity regardless.

In Chapter 2, "African American Masculinity and the Great Debate: Rescuing Black Masculinity from the Success Ethic," I relate the difficulties faced by black magazines in establishing themselves as successful business ventures in a decade, 1900–1910, of intense discrimination. Believing that African Americans were ready to support a general-interest publication, several editors attempted to craft magazines that presented a respectable portrait of the race. But financial difficulties, lack of support from subscribers and advertisers, and—in one case—physical attack drove every magazine from the market. The difficulty of sustaining their publications informed the larger debate that pitted racial moderates against racial radicals in the first decade of the century and colored the way they presented black masculinity. By 1910, black masculinity was framed largely in terms of black men's access to the ground floor of white masculine status—citizenship.

In Chapter 3, "'Horatio Alger Doesn't Work Here Any More': The Emergence of Modern Masculinity, 1915–1935," I trace the emergence of modern masculinity in American magazines, paying special attention to the impact of consumerism on the images of masculinity offered by a large number of magazines. Beginning with a study of the elite masculine ideals offered by *Vanity Fair*, this chapter also explores the changing notions of masculine success that are articulated in the *New Success* and the *American Magazine*. I also pay close attention to the development of the sporting magazines *Athletic World*, *Athletic Journal*, and *Sporting Life*. I argue that the magazines published between 1913 and 1935 were enthralled with the image of the "up and coming" businessman, especially the salesmen, and increasingly inundated with advertisements that suggested the viability of self-creation through consumption. Such forces began to subtly transform American masculinity.

In Chapter 4, "From the Ground Up: Reclaiming the Basis for Masculinity in African American Magazines, 1910–1949," I discuss how the two dominant race journals, the *Crisis* and *Opportunity*, attempted to advance the place of African Americans through the articulation of a version of American masculinity that was out of step with trends in the white magazine marketplace. The expression of a rights-based masculinity stood in jarring contrast with the consumerist masculinity that was just beginning to penetrate black advertising.

In Chapter 5, "A Pleasing Personality Wins the Day: The Cultural Hegemony of Modern Masculinity," I argue that *Esquire* was able to pull together the disparate fragments of an emerging notion of masculine identity and package them into a coherent representation of a modern masculine ideal. Joining the male concern with self-creation and sexuality to a stridently consumerist agenda, *Esquire* became the publishing phenomenon of the 1930s. By the 1940s, magazines such as *True* and *Argosy* had borrowed the *Esquire* formula and repackaged it for a working-class audience, proving that the ideals of modern masculinity could be translated to a working-class idiom. And by 1945, *Ebony* magazine had learned to penetrate the commercial network and promote a view of black masculinity that was thoroughly in sympathy with the view offered by white magazines. The ability of *Ebony* to claim the language of modern masculinity—with its emphasis on personality, consumption, and self-creation—is a testament to the cultural hegemony of this particular set of ideals and images. By 1950, modern masculinity had attained a dominance akin to that which Victorian masculinity had held in the late nineteenth century. And it holds it to this day.

We are all still in the thrall of the masculine roles that were created out of the emergence of modern corporate consumer culture that began around the turn of the century. If anything, modern masculine roles have grown more pervasive with every passing year as ever more groups of men of every race and socioeconomic group were brought within the embrace of an ideology that celebrates self-creation through enlightened consumption. Yet even as modern masculinity has attained cultural hegemony in the realm of a highly commercialized popular culture that constantly reproduces itself, men have retained affiliations with older, perhaps more basic ways of understanding their male identity. Men still identify themselves with the jobs they hold—even if those jobs are inherently unstable. Men still claim their rights as fathers—even if legal challenges to those rights have not always appreciated the male role. And men still find a sense of belonging in their interactions with women and with other men. Even as cultural historians like myself work to describe the ways that masculinity is culturally constructed, scientists and biologists advance claims that much that defines gender is written in our genetic code, our DNA. For all that has changed about masculine norms during this century, there is much that endures.

I offer this study as one way of understanding the mélange of images and ideas that today make up our notions of masculine identity, fully cognizant that I have described just a small part of the formation of masculine norms in this century. This project has offered me a way of understanding how much of my own identity is constructed by the images and ideas that constantly bombard my consciousness, and how much of my identity is controlled by this vague sense of, for lack of a better word, "guyness," that seems to emerge unbidden from this biological package I call my body and soul. Yet I still wonder, how is it that people in the past and the present come to embrace certain ways of being, in this case, masculine? How much have I picked and chosen the behaviors and images that make up my own gendered self, and how much was simply passed on to me at my birth? Perhaps it is only human to think that we are creatures of our own making, yet I believe studies such as this can demonstrate the importance of culture in shaping human identities. If we wish to understand how we have come to be who we are, we can do far worse than to understand how those who have come before us determined who they were. I hope that my study contributes to our effort to understand ourselves, both past and present.

1
Old-Fashioned Manhood in a Newfangled Medium

The American magazine market underwent a profound revolution beginning around 1893, when within a short span of time *Munsey's, McClure's,* and *Cosmopolitan* slashed their cover price to ten cents and let advertisers bear the costs of reaching audiences that would soon number in the hundreds of thousands. Other magazines followed suit, and the magazine became the first true vehicle of mass culture in America, a medium that reached people of all classes all over the nation. Produced, even manufactured, by increasingly large corporations, edited by sharp businessmen attuned to the public interest, filled with reading matter intended for the broadest possible audience, and stocked with ads for nationally branded products, these magazines were the perfect expressions of the emerging modern corporate capitalist culture. Yet while these magazines participated wholeheartedly in the economic and structural transformations of the day, they were deeply conflicted regarding their presentations of American masculinity. In some instances, the magazines *McClure's, Munsey's,* and the *Saturday Evening Post* promoted visions of masculinity that were far better suited to an outdated web of social and economic relations. In other instances, they embraced the dynamism of modern masculinity. These conflicting representations indicated a very real uncertainty about the meaning of manhood at the dawn of the modern age. In this chapter I explain this conflict in terms of the dissonance between these modern magazines and their old-fashioned creators, and set the stage for the emergence of magazines that resolved this paradox by sharing the consumerist ethos of the magazine's main source of support—advertisers.

The magazine revolution occurred because a good idea—lowering the price of magazines—was set to work within an ideal set of circumstances. Conditions were ripe for distributing magazines to a large audience spread across the entire nation: distribution networks established to move matériel during the Civil War were now capable of moving masses of goods across the country; population movement toward more urban environments concentrated potential audiences; and low postage rates granted to magazines by Congress in 1879 made the costs of sending magazines much more reasonable. Such conditions made nearly the entire American population potential magazine subscribers or buyers, but prior to 1893 no magazine managed to take advantage of these conditions to reach a mass audience.[1]

The failure of existing American magazine producers to take advantage of these conditions to boost circulation and revenues owes much to their conception of the role of the magazine. The leading magazines of the post–Civil War years, *Harper's* and the *Atlantic,* were products of publishers and editors who thought it their duty to put the best reading matter before the best people, not the most people. These magazines ran long, serious articles that were often about European subjects, and they published serious fiction in serial form. Their editors consciously set standards for literary and social taste, acting as a kind of gatekeeper to refined culture. As such, they reached a limited audience of educated people, primarily on the eastern seaboard (or at least educated there), who could afford to pay twenty-five to thirty-five cents an issue. Advertising was simply not part of the mix. In the end, it seems that these magazines would not have wished to reach a mass audience even if they had thought it possible.[2]

But there were publishers who did care to reach a larger audience if only they could figure out how. These publishers were a new breed, concerned more with making money than with making their magazines cultivators of good taste. The entrance of this kind of publisher into the magazine marketplace was itself a precondition for the magazine revolution and a sign of the changing economic times. While improved distribution channels and postal rates made mass-market magazines possible, it was the entrance into the publishing world of men with the attitudes and expectations of manufacturers and industrialists—in short, the entrance of capitalist entrepreneurs—that precipitated the magazine revolution. The new magazine publishers took their cues from other American businesses that were learning to concentrate and streamline production in

1. Frank Luther Mott's *A History of American Magazines, 1885–1905,* vol. 4, and his "The Magazine Revolution and Popular Ideas in the Nineties," were among the first attempts to explain this period as a revolution. See also Ohmann, *Selling Culture,* 24–38.

2. Algernon Tassin's *The Magazine in America* was one of the first efforts to look back at nineteenth-century magazine publishing. The standard magazine histories all devote attention to what John Tebbel calls the "Golden Age" of American magazines. See Tebbel, *American Magazine,* 47–90, 121–30; Wood, *Magazines in the United States,* 41–59; and Tebbel and Zuckerman, *Magazine in America.*

order to cut the cost of goods, thus making more goods available to ever more consumers. Publishers also adopted and perfected the use of advertising. Magazines made themselves known to their readers through advertising in traditional channels—regional publications, local newspapers, and so on—but they soon attracted advertisers to their own pages in such droves that this advertising became the magazine's dominant source of profit. In mass-market magazines, advertising developed into a medium for schooling Americans in the benefits of nationally recognized brands, and magazines soon learned to work with advertisers to their mutual benefit.[3]

Realizing that there was a market for a midlevel magazine at a low price, S. S. McClure introduced his magazine, *McClure's*, on May 28, 1893, at the low price of fifteen cents. A little over a month later John Brisben Walker of *Cosmopolitan* cut his magazine's price to twelve and a half cents. But Frank A. Munsey trumped them both when he offered his magazine, *Munsey's*, for ten cents an issue beginning in September of 1893. His competitors soon lowered their prices as well, but not quickly enough to catch *Munsey's* in what amounted to a race to expand circulation. The furious round of price cutting was, in its way, a bidding war, and Munsey won. He won, curiously enough, not because his magazine carried better articles or illustrations—nearly everyone agrees that the other magazines were "better"—but because he was the first to lower the price enough to haul in the thousands of Americans who had declined to pay more for a magazine. In gathering this new group of American magazine readers, Munsey also snared his real prey: American advertisers. Within a short span, advertisers eager to get their message before the largest number of readers paid Munsey for space in his magazine. The other magazines joined *Munsey's* in increasing their circulation and their advertising, creating, seemingly out of the blue, a new medium, the low-price, mass-circulation magazine whose costs of production were paid by advertisers.

"Publishers mass-produced a physical product, which they sold at a loss," writes Richard Ohmann, "and used it to mass-produce an immaterial product, the attention of readers, which they sold at a profit." The content of the magazines mattered little. Munsey was rather indifferent to the content of his magazine; or rather, he was more concerned with not paying too much than with such issues as maintaining a consistent editorial stance or attracting the very best writers. *Munsey's* was better known for its illustra-

3. On this generally accepted depiction of the relationship between advertising and the magazine revolution, see Wood, *Magazines in the United States*, 304–5, 310–30; Peterson, *Magazines in the Twentieth Century*, 18–39; Tebbel, *American Magazine*, 195–202; and Daniel Pope, *The Making of Modern Advertising*, 136–37. On the marketing of national brands, see Susan Strasser, *Satisfaction Guaranteed: The Making of the Mass Market*.

tions and for the number of its pages than for any of its articles or fiction. *McClure's* was more noted for its content, and it was, all in all, a more serious publication. When it was at its best, during the muckraking days, *McClure's* was probably the best-known magazine in America. But for most of its life it was not all that different from its higher-selling competitor.[4] Like *Munsey's*, *McClure's* was buoyed by its advertising, which it carried in abundance.

Those who loved the older style of magazines sniffed that these new rags did not compare to the likes of magazines edited by such luminaries as William Dean Howells, Horace Elisha Scudder, Henry Mills Alden, or Bliss Perry. But such a comparison, based on the literary quality of the contents, was beside the point. *Munsey's* and *McClure's* and the other magazines that followed in their footsteps represented a new direction in magazine publishing, and they had to be judged on a different standard. "The effect of this purely merchandising idea," wrote Munsey biographer George Britt, "was not only to enrich a new generation of publishers and elevate advertising to the peerage of big business, but to make the editing of a magazine an exciting and vital undertaking as never before. The popular magazines were yeast at work within the population. Into a field long resigned to the remote dignity of graybeards, they brought a journalism highly personal, intimate, vital and new."[5] In the old-style magazines, editors sought to bring together the best that was thought and written; their emphasis was on the dignity and sophistication of the act of reading. In these new magazines, the goal was to catch readers' attention with the most arresting pictures, the most entertaining stories. The emphasis was on satiating the reader's desire for information that was new and exciting.

For all that was revolutionary about these magazines, there was yet one area in which they chose to remain defenders of the gender status quo. Despite profiting from their ability to take advantage of the new means of economic organization that were transforming the American economic and social landscape; despite their real innovations in marketing, distribution, and image creation; despite being lifted by the very tide of economic change, these publishers continued to offer visions of masculinity that were rooted in Victorian culture and increasingly outdated economic ideas. *Munsey's* and *McClure's* were joined in the early years of the twentieth century by the *Saturday Evening Post*

4. This assertion no doubt runs contrary to most people's understanding of the magazine, but the muckraking phase of the magazine's career lasted for only five years, beginning ten years after the magazine's first issue.

5. George Britt, *Forty Years, Forty Millions: The Career of Frank A. Munsey,* 91. On the earlier magazines, see also Christopher P. Wilson, "The Rhetoric of Consumption: Mass-Market Magazines and the Demise of the Gentle Reader, 1880–1920."

in offering to Americans images of male success thoroughly rooted in the proprietary stage of capitalist development, images that encouraged men to adhere to ideals of character, honor, honesty, industry, and self-reliance in the hopes that through adherence to these ideals they could create for themselves an economic island of their own. Thus magazines that were deeply enmeshed in new webs of economic relations—indeed, were partially responsible for creating those new webs of economic relations—continued to promote visions of manhood that were appropriate to antiquated modes of economic relations. "Rational" processes like corporate organization and mass-marketing quickly penetrated and revolutionized American magazine production, yet *Munsey's* and *McClure's* echoed with the archaic expressions of Victorian masculinity.

Munsey's and *McClure's*: The Dime Magazines

Frank A. Munsey had been publishing a magazine for boys titled the *Golden Argosy* since 1882, but that venture had earned him little money and even less distinction. Another publishing effort, *Munsey's Weekly*, had succeeded for a brief period as a campaign organ for James G. Blaine, but by the early 1890s it too was struggling to survive. Unabashed by his lack of success and schooled in a decade of publishing, Munsey believed there existed a mass of readers who were still looking for an appropriate magazine. "I began to analyse [*sic*] the magazines," Munsey later recalled. "They seemed made for anaemics and their editors editing for themselves and not for their subscribers. Living in an artificial literary world, they got out publications which wofully [*sic*] lacked human interest. . . . If a magazine should be published at ten cents, and made light, bright, and timely, it might be a different story."[6]

Putting a price tag on a magazine was one thing, but getting it on the market was another. In order to get his magazine out, Munsey needed the cooperation and assistance of the American News Company, which held a virtual lock on magazine distribution and newsstand sales. When the American News Company refused to give him the six and a half cents a copy he asked for his magazine, Munsey took his case to the public, running huge advertisements in newspapers and initiating the formation of his own distribution company. To shorten a long story told in many other places (most notably by George Britt in *Forty Years, Forty Millions: The Career of Frank A. Munsey*), Munsey won his battle with the distributor and gained his new magazine valuable publicity to boot. Within a short period of time, *Munsey's* was a circulation leader: The magazine sold 200,000 issues by February 1894, 275,000 by October 1894, and

6. Frank A. Munsey, quoted in Tassin, *Magazine in America*, 342.

500,000 by April 1895; by 1898 its publisher claimed for it the largest circulation of any magazine in the world.[7]

Of course circulation did not matter in itself, for at ten cents an issue no amount of circulation could ever pay for the magazine. Circulation was only a means to an end, to realizing a profit from the advertisers who wanted their ads to appear before the greatest number of people. Munsey recognized early on that what he was after was advertisers: "I knew too that the great big circulation toward which we were pushing with such tremendous strides meant that the advertisers of the country could not afford to remain out of *Munsey's Magazine,* and that from the advertising pages a big revenue must inevitably come." And come it did. The number of advertising pages rose from sixteen pages in September 1894 to eighty pages in May 1895. In March 1896 Munsey reported that his magazine had netted $30,323.92 in advertising revenue. Some fifteen years after becoming a publisher, Frank A. Munsey had revolutionized the magazine market and become a very rich man.[8]

In its heyday—roughly 1893 to 1898—the magazine's most notable feature, according to preeminent magazine historian Frank Luther Mott, was a department entitled "Artists and Their Work," "copiously illustrated by good halftone reproductions of paintings and portraits of artists."[9] This section sometimes included seminude women, but over time the number of "illicit" pictures declined dramatically. *Munsey's* reputation was made, however, and some public libraries actually refused to carry the magazine. Other sections were also liberally illustrated with pictures of art, people, and places, making *Munsey's* a kind of window on the world for its subscribers.

Munsey's was always one of the thickest magazines on the market, with the number of its pages growing from 112 to 160 to 192 and finally, in its later pulp days, to 260. Of these pages, one third to one half were devoted to advertising; such ads brought in some $25,000 to $35,000 a month for the magazine and were, in many ways, its *raison d'être.*[10] And then there was the rest of the magazine: light fiction by writers of no renown; departments featuring information about the stage, literature, and current events; occasional poetry and editorials; and a department called "In the Public Eye," which lauded the successful. *Munsey's* was always fascinated with royalty and whenever it could it ran articles on kings and queens, princes and princesses. Nor did such royalty need to be alive: In April 1898 the magazine ran an article titled "The Six Queens of Henry VIII," which combined the thrill of royalty with the titillation

7. Mott, "Munsey's Magazine," in *History of American Magazines,* 4:611.
8. Britt, *Forty Years,* 86–87.
9. Mott, "Munsey's," 611.
10. *Munsey's,* March 1896, 760, cited in Mott, "Munsey's," 611.

of multiple wives. *Munsey's* was also noted for its features on foreign lands, often written by ambassadors who could publicize their own activities with such copy.

S. S. McClure was already a wealthy man when he began his magazine in 1893, but for the first few years his new venture added nothing to his fortune. McClure had made his money building the first newspaper syndication business in the United States. His syndicate bought novels and sold them to newspapers for publication across the country. Through this business, McClure became convinced that there was a market in the American Middle West for a magazine offering good fiction—he had, after all, sold the Midwest on fictions by Rudyard Kipling, William Dean Howells, William Hardy, and others—and articles about affairs of the world. The first few issues of *McClure's*, priced at fifteen cents, consisted of syndicated fiction, editorial comment, and nonfiction articles. It was a magazine of the quality of *Munsey's,* though without special distinction—and it lost money.

"At first," writes magazine historian James Playsted Wood, "*McClure's* was a financial flop."[11] The magazine lost one thousand dollars a month for its first months, and more as circulation increased. McClure had cut the magazine's price to ten cents an issue shortly after Munsey's innovation, but the price cut seemed only to exacerbate his problems, for the circulation gains won by the price cut were not matched by an inflow of advertising dollars. As circulation boomed—from 40,000 in 1894 to 120,000 in August of 1895 to 250,000 in December of 1895—McClure struggled to keep up with the costs of producing the magazine.[12] By 1896 McClure had raised his advertising rates in line with his circulation and finally lifted the venture out of the red. Success had nearly wiped him out, but it proved Munsey's lesson: lower the price, and the masses will come. And when the masses come, advertising will follow.

A typical issue of McClure's from 1898 included a "A Story of Wall Street" by Hamlin Garland, a pirate tale, an article on Scottish soldiers, several articles on railroading, "Reminiscences of Men and Events of the Civil War" by Charles A. Dana, and a serial story by Anthony Hope. By 1902 and 1903, however, the content of the magazine had grown far more serious; a typical issue contained an installment from Ida Tarbell's history of Standard Oil, an article on municipal corruption by Lincoln Steffens, perhaps something on the "Negro problem" by Thomas Nelson Page, and some lighter filler. Where in the earlier years editor and publisher McClure had used a few pages to trumpet his magazine's success,

11. Wood, *Magazines in the United States,* 10.
12. Mott, "*McClure's,*" in *History of American Magazines,* 4:591, 596.

in the muckraking days he used his column to trumpet the merits of his articles for helping to reform the country.

By the turn of the century, both *Munsey's* and *McClure's* had found a secure place in the American magazine marketplace. Both magazines had strong circulations and carried abundant advertising, advertising that made the magazines the profitable enterprises their publishers had always hoped they could be. But what messages did these magazines send to their readers about the place of the American man in the world that they were helping to change? How did these magazines frame American masculinity? The following stories, culled from over a decade of these magazines, offer conflicting ideals: On one hand, they suggest that both *Munsey's* and *McClure's* believed that the way for American men to cope with the modern world was to rely on the values that had sustained a generation of men raised years earlier, men much like Frank Munsey and S. S. McClure; on the other hand, they offer a tentative embrace for the new styles of masculinity that were equated with new economic ways.

The Anxiety of Manhood

Five American men gathered to smoke on the deck of a ship four days out in the Atlantic. As a thick fog gathered about them, one man—Lynder—wondered whether "a group of average intelligent Americans" could navigate the ship to safety if there were an accident. "Every educated man has a tremendous accretion of haphazard knowledge," he reasoned, "combined with a faculty for sustained and clear reasoning, which is, or should be, his chief differentiation from the ignorant man. Ordinarily you wouldn't think that haphazard knowledge worth while; in fact, you wouldn't *dare* use it. In an emergency, however, you would be constrained to sift out every remote particle bearing, however amateurishly and indirectly, on the problem at hand. I believe you have more knowledge, practical available knowledge, than you think possible."

Lynder and his companions soon got the chance to test their theory, for the *Almeria* struck something in the open sea and listed seriously to the side. The passengers and crew abandoned ship, but the men aboard Lynder's boat returned to the ship when it remained afloat the next day. Bardon, the oldest man in the group, assessed the situation: "We're evidently in a serious predicament, . . . although it isn't yet by any means a desperate one. Our ship has been in collision [*sic*], and has been deserted. All the other passengers seem to have gone. We are back again. The ship has not sunk yet; but we do not know but that it may at any time. We should plan a course of action at once." One by one they solve the problems of reviving the ship and rescuing themselves: they calculate their location, fire the ship's engine, fix the steering mechanism, operate the bilge pumps, and make contact with the outside world through the

"HE BEHELD THE MIRACLE OF LIFE PULSE SLOWLY INTO EVERY FIBER OF THE GREAT
TRIPLE-EXPANSION ENGINE"

A staple of *McClure's* and the other early magazines was the tale of manly competence, in which men confronted a complex, daunting problem and conquered it through their skill and knowledge. In Fremont Rider's "Bringing in the *Almeria*" a group of men start this massive engine and guide an abandoned ship to safety. Such tales helped men envision the ways that their skills would remain viable in the rapidly changing American economy (*McClure's*, May 1913, 101).

"wireless." And finally, they make their way to land, where they are paid $29,000 each for salvaging the ship. One of the heroes of the voyage says to his wife that they can stay on the island a few days longer now, and she responds "I'm ready to tackle *any*thing with you."

"Bringing in the *Almeria*," written by Fremont Rider and appearing in *McClure's* magazine in May of 1913, neatly dramatizes one of the central dilemmas facing men in this era.[13] Faced with a world grown suddenly complex, filled with giant machines and complicated technology, could American men maintain their mastery? Rider's answer is an emphatic yes, an affirmation that good men are still in control, for they can tap into their innate knowledge of how things work, drawing upon resources that they hardly knew they had. The very storytelling makes the triumph of these American men even more dramatic. Of the wireless system, the narrator laments, "It is difficult to conceive of anything that to a layman would seem more hopeless to attempt." But Norris, with his Yankee ingenuity, solves the puzzle. The lone illustration accompanying the story, drawn by André Castaigne, depicts a colossal engine dominating the belly of the ship; the caption reads "He beheld the miracle of life pulse slowly into every fiber of the great triple-expansion engine." The problems that the men must solve involve both complexity and scale; nevertheless, they triumph. This tale is a version of an American classic, a tale of manly competence, nearly a genre in itself. But it is not the only kind of tale about men that appeared in the pages of American magazines during this period.

"The Mower from Wall Street," by Lynn Roby Meekins, is one of many stories that used Wall Street as a kind of synecdoche for the world of high finance and corporate triumph. In this story, a young farmer's son named Hamilton is hired to do office work for Mr. Dodson, a farmer who also runs a store. Hamilton is a natural businessman, and Dodson predicts a bright future for him even while lamenting the fact that it is getting harder and harder to find good farm laborers. Hamilton wagers that he can mow Dodson's hay field in a day, and the men agree. A prize will be named later. Dodson's daughter comes out to watch Hamilton swing the scythe under the hot sun and comments:

> "You've no idea," she remarked, "how much better you look here than on an office stool. It's just fine to see a strong man work hard—so much finer than to see him standing behind a fretwork of iron or sitting in a revolving chair, like a Sampson chained to routine."
> His scythe kept up its steady, conquering strokes.

13. Fremont Rider, "Bringing in the *Almeria*," *McClure's*, May 1913, 99–109.

> "I read a story the other day," she continued quizzically. "It was about a people among whom wife beating was an amusement. With them beauty and savagery went together; but the men became more tender and less heroic, till the wives complained that their husbands no longer loved them because they left them without bruises."

Hamilton exclaims that he does not believe in that kind of love, for he loves her in a far purer way, and he proves it by finishing the job by the deadline. Not surprisingly, Hamilton names as his prize the hand of Dodson's daughter in marriage, and all ends happily.[14]

On the one hand this is a tale like the shipwreck story, for Hamilton shows his competence in both the world of business and the world of agriculture, and for that competence he is rewarded with the affections of the girl. But the girl's bizarre comment midway through the story skews the way we understand these issues. While Hamilton maintains his "steady, conquering strokes," the girl seems to lament the passing of a civilization where men were hard, even savage, and women beautiful, if bruised. It is a society in which men and women occupy distinct and very different social roles, much like the separate spheres occupied by men and women in Victorian society. Dodson's daughter is pleased to see Hamilton take up the hard work of a farmer, for it seems that he is thus capable of maintaining the gender status quo, leaving his woman bruised but sure that she is loved. Hamilton rejects the gendered logic of her formulations, for he is capable of success in both arenas, yet he returns to his modern job and proves himself a successful husband. The institution of marriage thus remains secure even with a modern man at the helm.

The story that was most closely associated with *McClure's* was, of course, the muckraking exposé. In "The Fight of the Copper Kings," the first of a series of articles about "mining wars" in the American West, C. P. Connolly offers the larger-than-life figure of F. Augustus Heinze, who is characterized in this brief sketch:

> Tall, well-proportioned, physically powerful, a combination of the Bohemian and the calculating man of affairs, he displays at all times a grace of pose which one is puzzled whether to characterize as a bit of splendid by-play or a natural quality from birth. With this personality at his command, he has played the boldest game of bluff that the West, accustomed to the methods of desperate challengers, has even seen. His feats of legerdemain in business affairs have dazed his enemies; his boldness, no less than his eloquence, has governed mobs; his lightning changes of front have hypnotized courts.[15]

14. Lynn Roby Meekins, "The Mower from Wall Street," *Munsey's*, April 1903, 115–17.
15. C. P. Connolly, "The Fight of the Copper Kings," *McClure's*, May 1907, 1ff.

Here was another kind of man altogether, a man so bold that he seemed to play outside the rules and conventions that govern other men. He was a kind of man that *McClure's* helped to both make and unmake, for if the magazine's muckraking series started out as an attempt to portray the good side of America's biggest business men, it soon ended up exposing many who were unscrupulous and immoral. Such powerful and potentially unscrupulous men obey neither Victorian or modern masculine dictates: They are too brazen and primitive, too free of concern for their communities to be proper Victorian men; yet they are too self-made, too unconcerned with pleasing others, to be stereotypical modern men. By exposing the more unscrupulous and immoral of the corporate giants, such exposés drew attention to proper behavior and validated the moral elements of Victorian masculinity.

In the May 1902 edition of *McClure's*, J. George Frederick told the story of "Breezy, Grocer's Clerk," who "was at the bottom of the commercial hill, and was preparing to run up to the top." The grocers who hire Breezy—his real name is Hezekiah Smith—place him in charge of the fruit counter, which he turns into a shrine to cleanliness. But Breezy is not satisfied with the fruit counter, so in his spare time he prints up five hundred business cards advertising fruit delivery. Gaining the approval of the boss, the energetic youth is soon making phone sales, offering daily specials, and bringing the miracles of modern salesmanship to this small-town concern. But his ambition soon gets ahead of his boss's tolerance, and when Breezy tries to corner the market on butter before the prices rise, his boss gets so angry he fires him. Then, just as Breezy predicted, they sell all the butter. As the story closes, Breezy is offered the position of superintendent and advertising manager of the store, at thrice his former salary. Leaving the store, Breezy "rode madly up the full length of the steepest hill in the city on his way home, to rid himself of surplus nervous energy."[16]

Breezy's story also belongs to a genre, the story of a man's rise to business success. But Breezy's story is not typical of the genre, for he has not risen to his success through the usual Victorian routes—hard work, integrity, thrift—but rather by displaying more modern traits—aggressiveness, salesmanship, pluck. One can read this story as an example of how a new, more modern style of masculinity gets incorporated into a magazine, and to some extent I think it is right to read it in this way. But Breezy is no hero; his method of succeeding is not held up for emulation. Instead, Breezy is a source of humor, as the illustrations accompanying the article make clear. Rather than a lesson in how to be a self-made man, Breezy's story tells the comic tale of how even a nervous, high-strung

16. J. George Frederick, "Breezy, Grocer's Clerk," *McClure's,* May 1902, 41–48.

fellow can make his way in the world—and perhaps illustrates the nervousness with which many men confronted the likes of Breezy.

As this small sampling of articles and stories attests, these magazines entertained many visions of American manhood in the years between 1900 and 1913. Men might be presented as naturally capable, able to handle any emergency; as possessed of an abundant natural energy that must find an outlet; or as dominating and forceful. The very variety of these images—and there were many more—lends credence to the notion that American manhood was undergoing a kind of transformation, if not a "crisis," in this era. In *Manliness and Civilization*, Gail Bederman takes pains to put to rest the notion that manhood was going through a crisis in this period, suggesting rather that "men were actively, even enthusiastically, engaging in the process of remaking manhood"[17] Such is the framework within which I understand these images of masculinity— these stories indicate the openness of gender roles in a time of flux. Each of the stories I have selected is a story of male achievement, but of achievement pursued along such different paths as to speak to the myriad ways that men might orient themselves in a rapidly changing social and economic environment.

A crucial function of these stories is to narrate a way out of the anxiety that men felt at being confronted with sweeping social and economic changes.[18] In the first story, moneyed elites and intellectuals confront their fear that they have become distanced from the workings of "real" life by taking charge of the physical manifestations of industrial production. The lesson they draw from their adventure is that even though they are distant from the forces of production and distribution, they can still master those forces. The Wall Street trader turned farm laborer learns a similar lesson when he proves himself as capable in the field as he is in the trading room. And his "victory" has the added reward of "winning the girl."

These first two stories are told from the point of view of the man in control, the man achieving. But what of the other stories, the stories of the nervous sales clerk and the overaggressive business tycoon? These stories are not about the protagonists but about those who must deal with the protagonist, and

17. Bederman, *Manliness and Civilization*, 10–15.

18. On the anxiety felt by men during this time of transformation, see Joe L. Dubbert, "Progressivism and the Masculinity Crisis," in *The American Man,* ed. Elizabeth H. Pleck and Joseph H. Pleck, 303–20; Filene, *Him/Her/Self,* 69–93; John Higham, "The Reorientation of American Culture in the 1890s," 73–102; Michael S. Kimmel, "The Contemporary 'Crisis' of Masculinity in Historical Perspective," in *The Making of Masculinities,* ed. Harry Brod; Kimmel, *Manhood in America,* 81–116; and James R. McGovern, "David Graham Phillips and the Virility Impulse of the Progressives."

the lessons they offer benefit from this perspective. Readers are not asked to identify with Breezy, the sales clerk, but to find him amusing. Amusing as he is, Breezy is nevertheless a transformative presence, possessing a kind of energy and drive that seems new to the stolid grocers who employ him (and who no doubt buy the magazine). These grocers learn how to contain and profit from Breezy's flair for advertising and promotion, and Breezy is naturalized into the business landscape. Men like F. Augustus Heinze—robber barons, tycoons, bold speculators, and so on—must also be absorbed into the social fabric, and the muckraking stories served some of this function. Men like Heinze were presented as oversized, possessed of too expansive and explosive an energy. They were, in important ways, hypermasculine. By framing the exploits of such men within a narrative climate of censure, the muckraking stories placed limits.

These stories contain the traces of changing cultural notions of masculinity and the anxiety men felt about their changing role in culture, yet they also serve to reinforce and conserve late-nineteenth-century notions of manhood, notions that are stereotyped as "Victorian." In each of the stories, there is an implicit privileging of the values of discipline, hard work, self-control, and integrity. The hay mower succeeds because he works hard and uses his self-control to resist the odd temptations of the girl's allusions to aberrant sexual practices. The men aboard the *Almeria* live because they strive to master that which they thought beyond them. Breezy will be a good worker—a good man—when he learns to tame his natural energy, to contain his tempestuous nature within a single-minded pursuit of profit. And Heinze, who had all the makings of a good man, is a fearsome failure when he acts without concern for morality or integrity. This pattern—this narrative trope—propelled both fiction and nonfiction month after month.

Most of the stories told in *Munsey's* and *McClure's* reflected a general lack of consensus about the meaning of manhood in this transitional period, though there remained a preference for—perhaps a greater level of comfort with—Victorian masculine standards. But the stories and the self-presentation of the magazines' editor/owners betrayed no such ambivalence or uncertainty. The men behind these magazines—their own stories of manhood and of how they reacted to change—need to be considered if we are to understand the manner in which Victorian ideals persisted within the modern magazine.

Self-Made Men: Frank Munsey and S. S. McClure

When it comes to self-made men, Frank Munsey and S. S. McClure were the real thing. Both Munsey and McClure had lifted themselves up by their bootstraps, created successful businesses out of years of hard work. In the chapter of his biography called "Alger Story," George Britt describes Munsey arriving in New York in 1882: "Tall, gawky, dour, hollow-cheeked, wide-eyed, . . . his mother's wedding ring on his finger, in flight from country and poverty but hardened against city distractions. . . . Lowliness was his ladder. He might be a Yankee grimly on the make, not out for a good time or for charity, but to improve his condition in life, nevertheless the folk quality and the youth of the man assert claims upon our sympathy such as he was to reveal seldom again." This hardscrabble Munsey put together a magazine, the *Golden Argosy*, which he nursed along for years, scrimping on his personal needs, cudgeling people to lend him just a few more dollars, and all the while waiting for the day when his magazine would catch the public fancy. Munsey even wrote some of the stories for this magazine for youth, and the stories were modeled after the Horatio Alger stories. It was these stories that seemed to make the magazine, for once they appeared circulation increased dramatically. Munsey published his story "The Boy Broker," and his circulation rose 20,000, taking the magazine's circulation to 150,000 copies by May 1887. "Less than five years, and he had put over his dream by sheer determination and the resources of his own life. It was spun no less than a spider's web out of the inner content and stuff of his person. The *Argosy* was himself," wrote Britt.[19]

Munsey's first success was not to last, for the *Argosy* quickly declined. But Munsey kept working and finally, when he saw his chance, with *Munsey's*, it was a chance he felt he had earned, for he had dedicated his life to work for an entire decade. Munsey was never known as a playful man, and the years of hard work in pursuit of a goal did not give him a sense of humor. He took himself and his work seriously and never found time for a wife or a close companion. When asked what were his pastimes, Munsey always replied, "Hard work." Something of this attitude comes across in one of the rare instances in which Munsey addressed his readers, a 1902 call for investors titled "To the Readers of Munsey's Magazine." Issued on the occasion of his incorporating his company, the article recounts the story of Munsey's rise to success—a story he was said to have told dozens of times without ever cracking a smile—and calls for subscribers to his stock, sold at a hundred dollars per share. The appeal to investors is both diffident and personal: He does not want anyone to buy who is not willing to take a risk or who does not believe that this company will succeed. He would just as soon keep all the stock to himself, he says, but should incorporate for posterity's sake. "I perhaps lean backward a bit in my seeming independence in this matter, but my reason for doing so is my desire to make it clear that this is no scheme to unload a worthless stock on you or the public generally. I believe thoroughly in the property; I know what it has done, and

19. Britt, *Forty Years,* 58, 63, 77.

believe I know what it is capable of doing along the broad lines laid out for its future development."[20]

For Munsey, his success and the success of American businesses in general was nothing to joke about. He and his fellow businessmen had earned what they had through hard work and perseverance, and Munsey was offended by the whole muckraking movement, seeing it as "an attack upon men of his own kind, whose philosophy he shared," writes Britt. When the muckraking movement died, Munsey crowed that "The people of this country have come to realize that prosperity rests on upbuilding, not in destruction."[21] Munsey took special pleasure in profiling people who had built themselves into successes; his favorite subject was J. P. Morgan and United States Steel. In short, as a self-made man who most admired other self-made men, Munsey was adept at selecting reading material that trumpeted the cultural values of his own kind, but he was far less adept at seeing how those values might integrate into the emerging and soon-to-be dominant cultural economic matrix.

McClure suffered from many of the same biases as Munsey, though they manifested themselves in very different ways. Like Munsey, McClure was a self-made man in the peculiar nineteenth-century American meaning of that term. An Irish immigrant who was raised in poverty, McClure was educated at Knox College, where, McClure recalled in his autobiography, he "lived on bread and grapes varying this with soda crackers and grapes." It was a place where "A boy's standing among the other boys depended entirely upon his scholarship, and every one did his best."[22] After college McClure struggled to develop a business syndicating fiction to newspapers and magazines around the country. Slowly and with great effort, McClure convinced known authors that they could make more from their works in syndication than in one-time publication and built a profitable business. When he thought he could make no more profits of his syndication business, McClure decided to launch a magazine of his own,

20. Frank A. Munsey, "To the Readers of *Munsey's Magazine,*" *Munsey's,* April 1902, 104.

21. Britt, *Forty Years,* 93.

22. S. S. McClure, *My Autobiography,* 65, 69. Though the autobiography (ghostwritten by Willa Cather) is the most revealing source on McClure, a number of McClure's friends and colleagues left revealing portraits of him in their autobiographical works. See Ida M. Tarbell, *All in the Day's Work,* chs. 8–13; Ray Stannard Baker, *American Chronicle,* chs. 9–24; Lincoln Steffens, *The Autobiography of Lincoln Steffens,* part 3, chs. 1–26; Charles Hanson Towne, *Adventures in Editing,* 165–81. Peter Lyon's biography of McClure, *Success Story: The Life and Times of S. S. McClure,* was described by Harold Wilson as "a readable apology for the muckraker's career written by his grandson" (McClure's Magazine *and the Muckrakers,* 327). Wilson's *McClure's Magazine* is the most reliable modern history of McClure and his magazine.

using material he already had purchased to get the new publication off the ground. To help him run the new magazine he contacted an old Knox friend, John Sanborn Phillips. With $7,300 in capital, the men launched *McClure's Magazine* in May of 1893, at a price of fifteen cents an issue.[23]

The men could not have picked a worse time to launch a magazine, for a nationwide financial collapse kept banks from providing any support for the fledgling enterprise. With personal loans and hard work, however, McClure rode out the storm and soon found his circulation rising dramatically. Like Munsey, his circulation so outpaced his ability to raise advertising rates (which were pegged to circulation counts) that his very success nearly did him in. But as stories like Ida Tarbell's "Early Life of Lincoln" (complete with dozens of never-before-published pictures of the adored President) attracted thousands of new readers, the magazine drew advertisers and gained in prestige. Soon McClure and Phillips found themselves able to achieve their fondest dreams: to publish a magazine that featured fine fiction and progressive nonfiction articles. McClure and Phillips sought and published nonfiction that reinforced their notion that there was a moral order that ought to lie behind progress; such nonfiction praised those who innovated for the public good, and soon came to criticize those who triumphed without respect for the public good.

Like Munsey, McClure was fond of telling his success story. According to Robert Stinson, McClure told Ida Tarbell of his struggle to succeed the very first time they met, and regularly related his Horatio Alger–like tale on the lecture circuit. "The Springfield (Mass.) *Republican* gave three long columns to a 1910 speech which was typical. 'MCCLURE TELLS HIS STORY,' the headline read. 'TALE OF HARD WORK AND PLUCK,' and, in small type, 'The autobiography of a Hustler.' "[24] That story, retold in print form in McClure's *My Autobiography,* was consistent with the conventions of the self-made man story and with the thrust of much of the fiction in McClure's magazine. The more laudatory of McClure's biographers and historians have embraced this narrative as well. One such historian wrote that "McClure in real life was the American dream come true, an actual Horatio Alger."[25] Clearly McClure succeeded in creating an indelible association between himself and the ideology of the self-made man.

Of course McClure expressed his disposition to favor the values of a receding economic system quite differently than Munsey. While Munsey smiled

23. Robert Stinson recounts the variety of influences that encouraged McClure to found his magazine in "McClure's Road to *McClure's:* How Revolutionary Were 1890s Magazines?"

24. Stinson, "S. S. McClure's *My Autobiography:* The Progressive as Self-Made Man," 206.

25. James Woodress, "The Pre-eminent Magazine Genius: S. S. McClure," 173.

on all that was capitalist, believing that the very big capitalists were simply small proprietors who made it big—like himself—McClure and his stable of muckrakers were deeply suspicious of the methods of those tycoons and magnates who had come to dominate the American corporate landscape. When they attacked some of America's biggest companies and bureaucracies, it was with the sense that their very bigness was rotten somehow, proof that they had not acted in accordance with the moral dictates of the old order. Where George Horace Lorimer and the *Saturday Evening Post* hoped to make modern corporate capitalism safe for the man of character, McClure and the muckrakers questioned whether corporate behemoths could achieve what they did without relinquishing cherished moral values.

McClure spelled out to his readers what the muckraking effort meant in an editorial promoting the ongoing publication of Tarbell's "History of Standard Oil":

> There is no right thinking person who is not willing and glad to have the best man win if he plays fair. There is no right thinking person who does not feel that the most important thing in the world is that men play fair whatever the game. . . . It is of vast importance to the future manhood of this country that scorn of unfairness should be universal. Above all, let it be applied strenuously to unfairness in business. We are a commercial people. Our boys must go into commerce. Our professions are so mingled with commerce that it is often hard to distinguish if they be professions. If we are to wink at unscrupulousness in commerce, then we are doomed to become a race of tricksters and manhood is dead within us.[26]

Munsey and McClure were both self-made men in the old sense of the word—they had started with little and through hard work and dedication had built successful businesses without sacrificing their principles. They expressed their dedication to the gendered moral framework by which they rose in different ways, Munsey by acclaiming all capitalist achievement, McClure by declaiming that achievement which was earned without adherence to principle. For all the modernity of their methods, they remained committed to Victorian manhood. Yet there were elements of their Victorian masculine ideology that would begin to temper their achievements, even lead to their decline. Both men believed that part of what brought them to their elevated position was a strict adherence to what one believed was true, a single-mindedness of purpose, a steadfast vision. What they did not know was that the magazine market they had helped to create would grow increasingly capricious. The public taste for magazines, editors and publishers soon came to understand, could shift as

26. S. S. McClure, "Editorial Announcement of Miss Tarbell's History of the Standard Oil Company—Part Second," *McClure's,* November 1903, 112.

audiences tired of one format and looked to another. This too was a condition of modernity, and one Munsey and McClure were ill-suited to embrace.

By the middle of the first decade of the twentieth century, a shift in the balance of power had begun in the American magazine marketplace. That shift was both quantitative and qualitative; it could be measured in issues sold as well as in the personality of the magazines, reflected by their collective contents. *Munsey's* had reached its peak around the turn of the century, claiming a circulation of seven hundred thousand and stunning the publishing world with its number of pages, the volume of its advertising, and, as critics often noted, the mediocrity of its contents. But circulation had slowly declined until, in 1905, Munsey ordered a freshening of the magazine's departments and its layout. Following a brief surge in circulation, the magazine's numbers slowly dwindled until the circulation manager claimed only four hundred thousand readers in 1912. *Munsey's* hung on for years after that, adding features, raising and then lowering its price, and changing to an all-fiction pulp format in the early 1920s, before it finally disappeared into *Argosy All-Story* in 1929. "*Munsey's* was never a first-class magazine," wrote Frank L. Mott. "Sometimes there was quality as well as quantity in the magazine, but there was a shocking amount of mediocrity."[27] In the end, *Munsey's* will be remembered for pioneering a genre—the cheap general illustrated magazine—though for little else.

Munsey's declined so quickly for several reasons. First and foremost among the reasons for its decline was the magazine's lack of a coherent editorial "personality." *Munsey's* was born as a marketing idea, an idea so successful that competitor S. S. McClure once called Munsey "the greatest business man that ever entered the magazine field." But its contents were cobbled together on the cheap by a man with no real sense of what values or ideas he wanted his magazine to embody. (This is not to say that Munsey was without values or ideals, for he certainly valued a particular set of standards, but that he had not made those ideals the basis for his magazine.) The magazine was a reflection of one man, and that man was a tinkerer. He once said in a speech, "I keep on experimenting, creating and killing, till I happen to hit the public's taste."[28] Those experiments involved not only *Munsey's* magazine but also the variety of other magazines Munsey bought, created, combined, or killed in his career as a publisher. Many of Munsey's magazines hit it big for a time, but none lasted and none were ever beloved by their readers.

If Munsey was an inconsistent editor, it was also true that the magazine-buying public represented an inconsistent market. While the magazine-buying

27. Mott, "*Munsey's*," 619.
28. Britt, *Forty Years*, 92, 100.

public that Munsey helped to create would maintain a consistent appetite for magazines, they would, over the course of the next fifty years, rarely buy the same magazine over too long a span of years. With few exceptions—the *Saturday Evening Post* being the most notable—American magazines would enjoy a surge of popularity that might last from one to ten years, making one magazine or another the "hot read" of the era before changing tastes or editorial innovations killed its popularity. Most magazines struggled to develop an editorial package that would attract a large audience, and when they had won that large audience they struggled to keep it. *Munsey's*, with its lackluster and ever-shifting editorial package, did not remain in the public favor for very long.

McClure's is an excellent example of a magazine that struck on a particular editorial package that appealed to the public and rode that appeal to mass circulation. McClure had purchased Ida Tarbell's "Life of Lincoln" and achieved such circulation gains that he was convinced to bring Tarbell on his staff and encourage her to write a history of the Standard Oil Company. In January 1903 an installment of Tarbell's piece appeared alongside Lincoln Steffens's "The Shame of Minneapolis" and Ray Stannard Baker's "The Right to Work" and, according to magazine historian Theodore Peterson, "the era of the muckrakers officially opened." For several years after that issue, *McClure's* led the journalistic critique of corruption and dirty dealing that seemed to come along with the growth of massive corruption and large cities. McClure himself claimed that his magazine's forte "came from no formulated plan to attack existing institutions, but was the result of merely taking up in the magazine some of the problems that were beginning to interest people a little before newspapers and other magazines took them up."[29] Planned or not, muckraking lifted *McClure's* to the top of the American magazine market, prompting one contemporary observer to note that "the special character of the American cheap magazine as we now know it is mainly due to one man—Mr. S. S. McClure."[30]

The success of *McClure's* was not to last, however. For all the vigor with which they offered their case, and for all the indignation they stirred up in a nation of people themselves suspicious of the values and motivations of these new captains of industry, the muckrakers were fighting a battle of retreat. The muckraking movement proved short-lived, and when the public taste for scandal

29. Peterson, *Magazines in the Twentieth Century*, 16; McClure, *My Autobiography*, 246.

30. William Archer, "The American Cheap Magazine," 922.

receded, so did the fortunes of the magazine.[31] It did not have to be that way, for McClure had published a successful magazine prior to the muckraking years, tapping a public thirst for quality fiction and nonfiction at a reasonable price. Yet in muckraking S. S. McClure found his life's purpose, and his enthusiasm for reform soon exceeded that of his notable staff and his audience. But McClure, like the self-made men he admired and thought himself to be, was nothing if not single-minded. By 1905 he had become so devoted to criticizing the established corporate order that he began to concoct plans to establish his own business schemes to operate free of the snares that corrupted other businesses. These schemes called for a major restructuring of the entire McClure organization.

McClure's staff was gradually worn down by their boss's singular dedication to reform and they grew wary of having their significant investment in the magazine tied up in what they thought were ill-begotten schemes. In 1906, John Sanborn Phillips, Lincoln Steffens, Ray Stannard Baker, Ida Tarbell, and a lesser-known assistant named John Siddall left *McClure's* and shortly thereafter purchased a new magazine that they renamed the *American Magazine.* McClure continued to wield the muckrake, but his magazine was in decline and never realized a profit after 1905. By 1911, beset with financial difficulties, McClure sold the magazine to a group led by his son-in-law. The new owners continued the magazine in a similar fashion, but muckraking had gone out of style, and they sold it in 1919. After 1919, writes Mott, "it was kicked about, knocked out, revived, and knocked out again—a sad spectacle as far as Samuel McClure's part in it was concerned, and a ridiculous one in other aspects."[32]

Frank Munsey and S. S. McClure were, at the turn of the century, representative figures of a cultural ideal—the ideal of the self-made man—that was already falling apart. Throwing themselves into work, holding themselves to a high moral standard, they lifted themselves from lowly origins and built something prominent and, in some sense, important. There was something incongruent about their privileging of Victorian masculinity within magazines that were representative of forces that were rapidly draining Victorian masculine ideals of their meaning. When the monuments that Munsey and McClure had built collapsed—for reasons that had nothing to do with their visions of manhood—they created a kind of space in which another way of representing masculinity could thrive. Modern masculinity did not rush in to fill this void. But

31. On the rise and fall of muckraking, see C. C. Regier, *The Era of the Muckrakers;* Wilson, *McClure's Magazine;* and Wilson, "Circulation and Survival: *McClure's Magazine* and the Strange Death of Muckraking Journalism."

32. Mott, "*McClure's*," 607; on the travails of *McClure's,* see Diana A. Chlebek, "*McClure's,*" in *American Mass-Market Magazines,* ed. Nourie and Nourie, 247–52; Wilson, *McClure's Magazine,* 168–89; Woodress, "Pre-eminent Magazine Genius," 189–92.

the masculinity that was offered by the *Saturday Evening Post*, while partaking of many of the images that constituted Victorian masculinity, was a step in the direction of modern masculine norms.

The First Magazine for Men: The *Saturday Evening Post*

While the changing turn-of-the-century magazine market hastened the demise of *Munsey's* and *McClure's*, it provided the perfect circumstances for the emergence of a new magazine, a magazine that was to bring the persistence of Victorian manhood in modern society into much clearer focus. The *Saturday Evening Post*, founded by successful publisher Cyrus Curtis and edited by George Horace Lorimer, was the first American magazine to appeal directly to a male audience, and for the first four decades of the twentieth century was the champion of Victorian masculine ideals. Where publishers Munsey and McClure naturalized their conceptions of manhood into the background of stories and articles, Lorimer brought questions of manhood to the fore. His goal was no less than to find a place within modern corporate capitalism for the nineteenth-century self-made man of character. What is most remarkable is that he clung to that goal for more than thirty years.

In August of 1897, Cyrus H. K. Curtis, publisher of the successful *Ladies' Home Journal*, bought a failing periodical called the *Saturday Evening Post*. The magazine had little to recommend it other than a pedigree that traced its roots to Benjamin Franklin and his *Pennsylvania Gazette*.[33] (This pedigree was uncertain at best, since the most that can be known with certainty is that the magazine's predecessor was published from the same shop where Franklin's *Pennsylvania Gazette* had been published six years earlier.) Though it had a pitiful circulation and no identity, the *Post* could call itself the oldest magazine in America. Curtis set out to reinvent the magazine, to make it as popular with another audience as his *Ladies' Home Journal* was with middle-class American women. If Curtis had learned one lesson from the *Journal* it was the lesson of advertising. Though he had difficulty attracting advertisers to his men's magazine at first, Curtis spent heavily on placing ads for the new *Post* in newspapers and magazines across the country. Circulation grew, but costs grew more quickly, until Curtis had spent nearly $750,000 on promotions in the first two years of the magazine's publication. What the magazine clearly needed was an identity, and Curtis soon found an editor to give it one.[34]

33. Mott, *"Saturday Evening Post,"* in *History of American Magazines*, 4:683.

34. While there are any number of books and sketches about the *Saturday Evening Post*, the one to which I am most deeply indebted is Jan Cohn's *Creating America: George Horace Lorimer and the* Saturday Evening Post. Thanks to Cohn's book I was able to strike the *Post* from the list of magazines I felt that I needed to read closely, for her interpretation of the

Curtis hired George Horace Lorimer to edit the *Post* beginning in June of 1899. "Although in 1899 the *Saturday Evening Post* had no identity, no voice, and no focus," writes Jan Cohn, "Lorimer remedied this with astonishing sureness and speed. . . . He intended to create a national magazine by appealing to the average American; he would, in fact, *invent* the average American—some compound of nineteenth-century values and twentieth-century opportunities."[35] Lorimer would invent that American based on what he had already learned from the magazines that preceded his and from the sense of his own masculinity, developed in his own rise to success. Like *Munsey's* and *McClure's,* the *Post* would carry a mix of fiction and nonfiction, pictures and advertisements. But under Lorimer's charge, the *Post* would establish a reputation for quality and consistency that its competitors might sometimes match but could never sustain.

There were several secrets to Lorimer's success at the *Post*. Every editor asked for quality fiction, but from day one Lorimer was willing to pay for it. The *Post* was known to read stories quickly and pay for them upon acceptance rather than upon publication; writers learned of this policy and learned to submit their best work to the *Post* first. For nonfiction, Lorimer turned to experts when he could and to big names whenever possible: within the first year of his editorship he had featured articles by former President Grover Cleveland and up-and-coming Senator Albert J. Beveridge. But Lorimer could never be comfortable with taking the contributions of "outsiders," who where unlikely to bend their stories to his will, and he soon trained a cadre of nonfiction writers to take the *Post* line on topics that were hand chosen. Perhaps the real secret to the consistency of the *Post,* however, was the fact that "The Boss," as Lorimer was known to others in the office, personally approved every word that appeared in his magazine.

With a more secure identity came the success that Curtis and Lorimer craved for their magazine. Circulation rose from 108,000 a week in December 1899 to 153,000 in May 1900, and from there continually upward until it reached

---

Post's approach to questions of masculinity is quite in line with my own. Having said that my interpretation of the *Post* is deeply indebted to Cohn's work, I should also note that Cohn claims a great deal from her sources. That is, she uses the magazine itself and the documents associated with its creators to make claims for the magazine's influence and significance. Scholars of magazines will certainly recognize how easy it is to overstate the conclusions one can draw from a magazine's contents.

On the *Post,* see also Mott, *"Saturday Evening Post,"* 671–716; Otto Friedrich, *Decline and Fall;* John Tebbel, *George Horace Lorimer and the* Saturday Evening Post; Frederick S. Bigelow, *A Short History of the* Saturday Evening Post: *"An American Institution" in Three Centuries.*

35. Cohn, *Creating America,* 28.

over half a million Americans in 1903.[36] This success came as Lorimer very carefully crafted a magazine designed to appeal to the American businessman based on a message of optimism and progressivism. This is not to say that the *Post* was a business magazine—it focused no special attention on markets or on business topics. Rather, it was a magazine that offered general reading material to an audience that was expected to consist of white, middle-class, male readers who anticipated further success. "The representative American, in Lorimer's view, was a compendium of nineteenth-century values; he worked hard, saved money, and assumed the duties of citizenship responsibly," writes Cohn. "The American was pragmatic and self-reliant, dedicated to his own social and economic betterment, but always within the constraints of law and decency." Lorimer made the ideology of the businessman of character the ideology of his magazine. And as the *Post's* readership grew to be the largest in America, argues Cohn, the *Post* "creat[ed] and continually refram[ed] a set of attitudes and beliefs that, at least until the time of the New Deal, constituted an American ideology."[37]

While the editor/publishers of *Munsey's* and *McClure's* had no clear program for their depiction of masculine images within a changing culture, and presented masculine ideals within an ambiguous and shifting context, Lorimer had a clear notion of how men were to behave and how they should be portrayed. Perhaps the clearest statement of Lorimer's own position can be found in his serial *Letters from a Self-Made Merchant to His Son,* which appeared anonymously in the *Post* beginning in 1901. Written as a series of letters from a successful meat-packer to his son, who is attending Harvard, the story offers a handy lesson in the moral verities of the older generation. The meat-packer, John Graham, tries to guide his son into an embrace of honesty, industry, common sense, and character, and the son tries to use those values to help him find his way through college and his first years in business. It was the perfect telling of Lorimer's essential tale: that the values of the last century are still of use in the modern world.

Other elements of the *Post* told a similar story. In a series of pieces called "Why Young Men Fail," successful businessmen indicated that those who did not practice diligence, thrift, and honesty were unlikely to make it in today's competitive corporate world. "The lack of an undeviating application to one pursuit is a cardinal weakness in the younger generation of toilers," claimed Thomas B. Bryan, who was described as a "lawyer, capitalist, scholar, and man of affairs and of society"; William A. Pinkerton, the founder of a detective agency,

36. Ibid., 44, 46.
37. Ibid., 10, 5.

blamed young men for "vanity . . . [and] the desire to get money without earning it"; while Postal Telegraph Company executive Edward J. Nally cited a "lack of concentration of purpose and energy." Such advice was echoed in such articles as Robert C. Ogden's "Getting and Keeping a Business Position" and Albert Beveridge's "The Young Man and the World."[38] Lorimer was pleased to publish confirmation of his essential views whenever he could.

In many ways, Lorimer was the perfect man to offer an education in the relevance of the values of the self-made man in the corporate world. Born in Louisville, Kentucky, in 1867, Lorimer attended Yale University for just one year before going to work for one of his father's acquaintances, Philip D. Armour of meatpacking fame. Within a few years Lorimer headed a department and earned $5,000 a year, but he soon quit to build a business of his own. When that business failed, Lorimer returned to college to study journalism and later took a position as a writer for the *Boston Post* and *Herald* newspapers. Lorimer soon used his father's connections to get another job, this time meeting with Cyrus Curtis, who was looking for a literary editor to work on his fledgling *Saturday Evening Post*. Lorimer's work pleased Curtis, and he soon moved up to acting editor while Curtis searched for a permanent editor. When Lorimer produced issues that were all that Curtis desired, he landed the job permanently. And the rest, as they say, is history.

Lorimer's rise to success bore just enough resemblance to what was expected of the self-made man that he was able to adopt the ideals and values associated with that masculine norm. While he had not built a business up from scratch by hard work and unstinting sacrifice—in fact, his one attempt at building his own business failed—he had risen up through the hierarchy of other organizations through those very methods, methods that men had long been taught to value. As the son of a famous Baptist minister, born into some privilege, he had not had to travel the path of Horatio Alger, lifting himself up from his bootstraps. But his late move into a journalism career did educate him in what it was to start anew. Furthermore, Lorimer's father introduced him to many men who were themselves "self-made," people like Armour and Curtis himself, and Lorimer grew to admire their accomplishments and to wish to emulate them. If he was not truly a self-made man, Lorimer had gotten to his current elevated position by at least trying to be one.

Or, if we wish to be skeptical about how self-made Lorimer really was, we might say that Lorimer got to his position by reflecting back to nineteenth-

38. "Why Young Men Fail: A Clear Explanation by Shrewd Business Men," *Saturday Evening Post,* October 28, 1899, 327; Robert C. Ogden, "Getting and Keeping a Business Position," *Saturday Evening Post,* November 4, 1899, 345–46; Albert J. Beveridge, "The Young Man and the World," *Saturday Evening Post,* July 7, 1900, 3–5.

century men the values those men admired. It is clear that Lorimer got to his position through the patronage of powerful men, men who themselves adhered to the cult of the self-made man. Perhaps Lorimer's real skill lay in offering to his patrons the reassuring image that the next generation would make it in the same way their generation did, though all while he made it on the manipulation of large egos, the careful balancing of many talents in the production of a magazine, and the power of a winning personality. Whether Lorimer's stance as self-made man of the modern world was real or a mask, it is true that getting ahead in a new world by respecting the values of the old was a lesson Lorimer was well prepared to teach. He had developed some of the habits of modern masculinity and used them to preach the values of Victorian masculinity.

While the passage of time saw *Munsey's* and *McClure's* fall by the wayside, the *Post* thrived. Backed by a wealthy and experienced publisher, edited by a man with a clear sense of how to shape a magazine to appeal to a distinct and sizable audience, and with a personality that would offend no friend of capital, the *Saturday Evening Post* grew into what its editor was proud to call "the greatest weekly magazine in the world."[39] On December 12, 1908, the *Post* was able to boast on its cover that it had reached a circulation of more than a million a week. The *Post* would remain among the circulation leaders well into the 1920s, and it maintained—Lorimer maintained—this leadership by doing what few editors in the history of American magazines have ever figured out how to do: to change just enough to attract new readers while changing so little as not to alienate old readers. It was a balancing act that worked because, well into the 1930s, many Americans held dear the ideals around which Lorimer built his magazine. And it worked because it reflected so well the developing personality of its creator.

The trick for Lorimer was to bring ever more Americans within the embrace of an ideology that kept the hardworking, thrifty, honest businessman of character at its moral center. When Lorimer and others referred to the archetypal figure of the self-made man in America, they referred not to a static figure but to an entire narrative of becoming. The self-made man was someone who started with little and, through the diligent application of habits and values, became something and someone much richer. The narrative of the self-made man was thus a narrative of ascent; it took a man higher. When he began editing the *Post*, Lorimer aimed his editorial matter at readers who saw themselves at a particular stage in that narrative of ascent, a stage several removes from the bottom but not so high that they did not need to continue to strive to succeed.

39. Letter from George Horace Lorimer to Albert J. Beveridge, May 4, 1903, Beveridge Papers, Library of Congress, quoted in Cohn, *Creating America*, 59.

Lorimer pitched the *Post* at the young man entering the world of business, a young man in, say, his early thirties, who had had a few jobs but was ready to settle down and dedicate himself to a life's work. In short, Lorimer edited the *Post* for himself and for men in his position.[40]

Lorimer continued to edit the *Post* for men in his position even as his position advanced. Cohn illustrates a number of ways that the *Post* changed to reflect the views of businessmen who were becoming more successful, who had reached positions of security and even influence. Where in its first years the *Post* had run an article on how to land a job, by 1910 it was running articles on financing a business or hiring and managing employees. Where the focus of short articles in the early years was on thrift and overcoming financial obstacles, the *Post* now began running articles that "were clearly addressed to an audience for whom the exercise of thrift had already paid off in accumulation of some capital."[41] It was not that the *Post* abandoned the interests of those Americans who were just beginning to climb the ladder of success; far from it. A number of departments continued to carry Horatio Alger-like stories and advice to young businessmen. But Lorimer's magazine was definitely broadening its appeal to include the stable and successful middle and upper-middle class.

As Lorimer broadened his magazine to embrace those at different stages on the path to business success, he subtly reshaped the rhetoric of the magazine to be more broadly consensual. The trope around which this change centered was that of common sense and easy rationality. The kinds of decisions that a businessman made—based on careful investment of resources and designed for long-term profit—were the kinds of decisions that all people made, or so articles that rationalized all areas of life seemed to imply. In pieces like "Making a Living by Literature," "The Business End of Baseball," and "The Business Side of the Church," the *Post* made it clear that the logic of the businessman of character was the logic of all America.[42] Common sense was, as the *Post* practiced it, as American as apple pie. But it was not necessarily the logic of modernity, or at least of modern publishing.

"Advertising," wrote Lorimer in a 1910 editorial, "is true pioneering. It is the great creator of new business, the great expander of old." Nowhere was this more true than in magazine publishing, for advertising had allowed for the flourishing of mass circulation magazines that made the *Post* phenomenon

40. Cohn, *Creating America*, 27–33.

41. Ibid., 88–89.

42. Anonymous, "Making a Living by Literature," *Saturday Evening Post*, November 11, 1911; B. B. Johnson, "The Business End of Baseball," *Saturday Evening Post*, July 19, 1913; James H. Collins, "The Business Side of the Church," *Saturday Evening Post*, February 1, 1913; all quoted from Cohn, *Creating America*, 86 n. 32.

possible. Yet by 1908 the *Post* was experiencing some unanticipated troubles with advertising. It was not that advertisers no longer placed ads in the *Post*. Indeed, the *Post* regularly carried advertising on over 40 percent of its available pages. But as the *Post* grew more manly, so did its ads, with the majority of advertising offering goods and services of interest to men, things like investment opportunities, business supplies, clothing and shoes, correspondence courses on business, and a variety of other items. But such ads were rarely large, and they were never placed by the manufacturers who were learning to use advertising so effectively to sell masses of goods. In magazines that appealed to the whole family, manufacturers of foods, household supplies, furniture and appliances, children's goods, and all goods related to women advertised regularly and lavishly. These ads appeared in the *Post* with much less frequency. It was not that the ads for men were less effective or desirable, but rather that ads for men represented a small share of the total advertising market.[43]

"The advertising pages of the periodicals," wrote Lorimer, "are the great world-market in which every one may display his wares on equal terms and secure customers in fair competition, according to the merits of his goods and the brains in his arguments."[44] But by the end of the first decade of the 1900s, increasingly professional advertisers must have recognized that the *Post* offered a market that excluded the very people they assumed were the primary consumer of goods, women. And so Curtis, whose primary motivation in running a magazine (if not his editor's) was to offer American manufacturers an attractive venue for selling their products, took steps to make sure that the *Post* was reaching the right audience. The *Post* began appealing to the consumers of the world more directly beginning in 1908, when it declared that henceforth, the *Post* was "Not for Men Only." From that point on, the *Post* regularly ran articles of interest to women, departments that addressed stereotypically "feminine" concerns, and, perhaps most important, an abundance of ads aimed at women. By the end of 1909, the proportion of the magazine devoted to ads jumped to 60 percent and, according to Cohn, "advertisements for domestic products made the difference."[45]

43. Both Marchand and Lears cite the "conventional wisdom" that 85 percent of all consumer spending was done by women. See Roland Marchand, *Advertising the American Dream: Making Way for Modernity, 1920–1940*, 66, and T. J. Jackson Lears, *Fables of Abundance: A Cultural History of Advertising in America*, 209. Quote by Lorimer is from "Twentieth-Century Pioneers," *Saturday Evening Post*, February 5, 1910, 22.

44. Lorimer, "The Popular Magazines and Their Advertising," *Saturday Evening Post*, December 17, 1910, 23.

45. Cohn, *Creating America*, 71.

In making the *Post* a hospitable place for female readers, Lorimer was careful not to make it a woman's magazine. Indeed, with someone so self-consciously manly as Lorimer it would have been amazing if he had. (A widely quoted anecdote depicts a conversation in which the powerful publisher Curtis tells his young editor that Mrs. Curtis had not liked a story he was about to run. Lorimer replied, "I'm not editing the *Saturday Evening Post* for your wife.")[46] What he did was somehow bring the woman reader into his ideology of commonsense Americanism without feminizing that ideology. After all, Lorimer firmly believed that what united Americans was their shared experience, their shared embrace of common sense and rationality. Lorimer once wrote that magazines like the *Post* "are simply giving more or less coherent expression to facts that business men are finding in their ledgers, mechanics in their pay envelopes and housewives in their bills, and crystallizing already existing public opinion."[47] That he attempted to conflate the world of the businessman, the mechanic, and the housewife into one ideology, transcending issues of class and gender, was truly remarkable.

As it began its second decade, the *Post* was the representative American magazine. Edited for a family audience, chock full of ads, and reaching millions of American households, the *Post* had achieved the kind of influence that made many Americans consider it essential reading. The *Post* maintained this position of preeminence for years to come, rightfully claiming itself to be America's magazine into the 1930s (when Lorimer's hatred for Roosevelt's New Deal and his isolationism finally put him out of touch with the mainstream). Lorimer's *Post* articulated a vision of manhood that echoed with the truths of the Victorian era into an era when those truths seemed outdated, and it did so in the face of an onslaught of advertising that offered images quite contrary to Victorian masculinity. The masculinity articulated in the *Post* would remain, from 1910 onward, basically the same. While other magazines would take up the task of interpreting the changing meaning of masculinity to men trying to make sense of the world, Lorimer would stick to his guns. Those who would overestimate the transforming power of consumer culture would do well to look to the example of the *Saturday Evening Post*, which carried the banner of Victorian masculinity well into the modern era.

The Transformative Rhetoric of Modern Advertising

Lorimer's ability to champion images of Victorian masculinity is all the more surprising in the face of the changes he made in the magazine after 1908, changes

46. Tebbel, *George Horace Lorimer*, 25.
47. Lorimer, "The Popular Magazines," *Saturday Evening Post,* December 10, 1910, 18.

aimed at drawing a more general audience and enticing more advertisers to advertise in the *Post*. When Lorimer invited women readers into his magazine, he initiated a process that had the potential to contradict the very notions of manhood he held most dear. It was not that Lorimer's vision of manhood could not stand the company of women. Neither Lorimer nor his ideology were antiwomen, but they did hold that women were to occupy a separate space in culture from men. This was a view that Lorimer shared with many in his day. Rather, bringing in women readers also brought in advertisers who crafted their appeals to women. By their very nature, these appeals were different from those made to men.[48] Such advertisers soon began to suggest to men that they too might consume for the same reasons women did: because goods made them more successful at what they did, because goods made them look better and feel better. This suggestion had a power that I believe Lorimer did not realize, for it was the power to reorient notions of manhood away from self-control, rational autonomy, and character and toward self-expression, desire, and personality. This latter view of manhood had more in common with the spirit of corporate consumer capitalism than did Lorimer's self-made man, though it would be a few years before this view found expression in a popular magazine.

In the first decade of the century, the advertising that was directed toward men offered visions of masculinity that were largely consistent with the visions of manhood being offered by all of the magazines I have examined, though perhaps most closely aligned with the *Saturday Evening Post*. (This is true primarily because the *Post* actually had a vision of masculinity, while both *Munsey's* and *McClure's* offered representations of masculinity haphazardly.) That is, in both articles and in advertisements, American magazines tended to offer images of men that stressed their self-control, their rationality, their autonomy. Both ads and articles venerated the self-made man and imagined that they could "sell" to that man by appealing to his common sense, his practicality.

According to David Maxcy, author of a quantitative study of the advertising that appeared in both the *Ladies' Home Journal* and the *Saturday Evening Post* over a twenty-five-year span, the advertising in the *Post* was consistently "directed to the Victorian image of the self-directed, autonomous, rational individual, in control of the natural and social relationships which surround him." While from early in the century advertisers had learned to couch appeals to women in terms of the concrete domestic space that women were believed to occupy, and to offer goods as a way to improve that domestic space, they had a

---

48. On the nature of advertising's appeal to women, see Marchand, *Advertising the American Dream*, 66–69, 167–88; Garvey, *Adman in the Parlor*, 171–83; and Lears, *Fables of Abundance*, 118–20, 209.

difficult time determining a space in which men might be thought to consume. "Man inhabits the world beyond the home," writes Maxcy. "He is identified with the broad forces of the marketplace, business, industry, technology."[49] While advertisers were able to develop an array of emotional appeals to the woman's desire to beautify her domestic space, prior to the 1920s they largely contained their appeals to men within the rational paradigm that characterized the *Post's* representation of manhood. Thus while women might be convinced to purchase a new dress because it flattered her figure or a new kind of cereal because it offered to boost the energy and vitality of her entire family, men were asked to purchase typewriters for their office because of their efficiency and speed, to buy carriage tires because of their price and durability. In short, while women were being taught the logic of desire, a logic that was based on what the product could do for them, men were schooled in the more familiar logic of reason, a logic based on the intrinsic quality of the merchandise. For women, goods could transform; for men, goods would perform.[50]

Maxcy quantifies this "gender system" in terms of the rhetorical appeals that advertisers made to different genders, and his model characterizes those appeals on a spectrum ranging from an appeal to pure utility to desire/image/utility/text to desire/utility. In a typical issue of the *Ladies' Home Journal* for 1906, 59 percent of the appeals were to pure utility, 12 percent of the appeals were to desire/image/utility/text, and 6 percent of the appeals were to desire/utility. By comparison, a typical issue of the *Saturday Evening Post* for 1904 contained 88 percent appeals to pure utility, 3 percent to desire/image/utility/text, and 4 percent to desire/utility.[51] At mid-decade, then, advertisers considered men more susceptible to appeals to pure utility, while they were beginning to offer a mix of appeals to women. While this gender dynamic held true during the first decade of the century, it began to change in the 1910s as advertisers crafted more and more of their appeals to women based on desire and image. This was precisely the period during which the *Post* opened its doors to women and women's advertising. While the pure utility appeal was quite consonant with Lorimer's vision of manhood, the appeals to desire and image were not. And these were the kinds of appeals that would slowly increase over the years to come, both to women and to men.[52] The introduction of women's advertising

49. David Joseph Maxcy, "Advertising, the Gender System: Changing Configurations of Femininity and Masculinity in Early Advertising in the United States," 307, 335.

50. See note 40, above, and Marchand, *Advertising the American Dream*, 188–91.

51. Maxcy, "Advertising, the Gender System," 309–10.

52. The proportion of ads in the *Ladies' Home Journal* that were based on pure utility dropped steadily through the 1910s and 1920s, reaching 27 percent in January of 1926. While the ads in the *Post* followed this trend, the drop in the percentage of appeals to pure utility

into the *Saturday Evening Post* could only hasten the increase of appeals to desire and image that readers encountered in the magazine. It was the beginning of a process through which men would slowly be oriented into the world of consumption based on desire and image.

Maxcy concludes that "advertisers took the communicative techniques honed in women's advertising and applied them to advertising to men, bringing the figure of man for the first time into clear focus within the feminine field of consumption."[53] But it is one thing for advertisers to offer images of men as nonrational, self-improving consumers, quite another for the editorial policy of a magazine to accommodate itself to those images. In the case of Lorimer and the *Post,* the editorial policy of the magazine remained committed to essentially Victorian notions of manhood long after the advertising within the magazine—and the images of manhood contained within those ads— had become thoroughly modern. Lorimer was reputed to be obstinate about refusing to allow advertisers to influence the content of the magazine. As Otto Friedrich reports, " . . . once an advertising man wandered into the art department and admired a cover painting of a golfer. 'Gee, that's fine,' he said, 'that'll help us sell some pages of advertising.' 'I'm sorry you said that,' Lorimer answered. 'Now we can't use that cover.'"[54] Lorimer could resist the inducements of helping his advertisers to sell their product because he knew that he was providing them with access to the largest purchasing audience in the world through the family of Curtis magazines. But other editors with other magazines would prove unable to resist the temptations to assist advertisers by creating a magazine context in which consumption was inherently validated. In its steadfast refusal to come to such terms with advertisers, the *Post* would be the exception to the rule among mass-market magazines in the years to come.

In this chapter I have tried to outline the conditions out of which there developed the phenomenon we now know as the mass-market magazine, and to show how the representations of masculinity found in those magazines grew out of the conceptions of manhood held by publishers and editors who were themselves schooled in the imagery and ideology of Victorian masculinity. Toward the end of the nineteenth century the right conditions met with the right idea to bring forth magazines that were edited for a general audience

---

was far less marked, declining to 52 percent in September of 1924. See Maxcy, "Advertising, the Gender System," 309–10.

53. Ibid., 351.

54. Friedrich, *Decline and Fall,* 9. Friedrich was a *Post* editor and executive who viewed the magazine's collapse in the late 1960s; he reports many such anecdotes about Lorimer that seem to have been company lore.

and priced to sell. The conditions that allowed for the mass-market magazine were very much a part of the developing economy of national brands, corporate structure, and mass production that was transforming the American economic and social landscape, and yet the content of the magazines sometimes resisted the implications of the very culture that had created those magazines. As such, the major American magazines *Munsey's, McClure's,* and the *Saturday Evening Post* offered to the reading public views of American manhood that contested or belied the very economic transformation that had brought the magazines forth.

This paradox is largely explained by the personality (or perhaps I should say the character) of the editors of these magazines. Either self-made men themselves, like Munsey and McClure, or dedicated adherents to the self-made man ideal, like Lorimer, these editors sustained a connection to the masculine ideals of the old economic order—the one they grew up in—even while they participated in shaping the new economic order. In the case of both Munsey and McClure, the paradox was ultimately unsustainable. Munsey had made it as a tinkerer, but his tinkerings with the editorial content of his magazine ultimately drove it out of favor with his audience. McClure rode his progressive vision to a brief preeminence in the American magazine market, but when the appeal of muckraking faded so too did his magazine. Neither Munsey nor McClure succeeded at turning their disposition to favor self-made men into the kind of editorial policy that would sustain a readership over the long haul; indeed, their expressions of approval for self-made manhood came out not as policy but as a kind of byproduct of other intentions. Lorimer, on the other hand, consciously created his editorial policy to suit the needs of men who embraced the old ideals for masculinity yet acknowledged the changed and changing economic order. Lorimer embraced the paradox of which I speak and attempted to resolve it. That he did so for over thirty years speaks to the enduring appeal of the self-made man ideal and the resources it offered to men.

By 1910, the nature of the mass-market magazine had changed in important ways. The leading magazines were no longer products of a single man's vision in the way that *McClure's* and *Munsey's* so obviously were. The model for future magazines would be set by the *Saturday Evening Post,* which rose to prominence with the backing of the strong corporate structure provided by Curtis Publications. It was Curtis's backing that allowed Lorimer the freedom to establish a coherent editorial policy while his magazine struggled to make its way into the black. The magazines that would hit it big in the coming decades—*Collier's, American Magazine, Time, Life*—would do so with the backing of a strong national corporation. Just as Curtis wished his magazine to be a profit generator, so too would future publishers demand that their magazines produce an income. This profit motive had profound implications for the editorial policies of American magazines, as we shall see.

Corporate backing did not mean that editors could no longer exert a distinct influence over the content of their magazines, for every magazine that "made it" in the coming years did so by introducing an editorial formula that attracted readers, which in turn attracted advertisers. But the editors of magazines would grow increasingly concerned with the bottom line of their enterprises, losing the kind of independence that Lorimer somehow maintained. In several cases, editors of magazines were more attuned to the selling of goods than they were to the formation of a coherent editorial agenda. With the rise of professional advertising firms in the 1920s and their efforts to find the best medium to sell their goods, editors would come under increasing pressure to ensure that their magazines provided a forum conducive to the flow of goods. Frederick Lewis Allen, a veteran magazine editor, explained the modern editor's attitude in a speech to future journalists in 1945: "The editor will say to himself, 'You want the magazine to make money, don't you? You want all the advertising you can get, don't you? Well, don't go round insulting the people whose favor you need. Flatter them. Eliminate anything disrespectful to them. Play ball with them.' That's how the pressure works."[55] Such pressure from a hypothetical "them" was further compounded when, as members were already part of the corporate structure, editors and publisher were a member of "them."

A latter-era *Post* editor named Clay Blair once said of George Horace Lorimer: "I think Lorimer was the guy who sold out to big business. When McClure was doing all those exposés—Lincoln Steffens and Ida Tarbell and those people—really telling the truth about the outrageous things that were happening, graft and swindles and price-fixing and everything, Lorimer was saying that everything was just great. And big business rewarded him for it. That's how Lorimer became such a big success. He sold out."[56] If this was true, then most of the editors of mass-market magazines sold out. But we ought not to rush to the conclusion that "selling out" necessarily meant relinquishing one's true values to the dictates of advertisers. "Selling out" takes on a pejorative sense only if one suspects corporations and advertisers of attempting to subvert the real interests of magazines and their editors. In the case of Lorimer and in the case of other editors I will cover, there is no evidence to suggest that they were coerced into advancing the interests of advertisers and their corporate clients. In fact, the interests of the corporate class may well have been their interests. If selling out meant embracing the culture of consumption, then the

55. Frederick Lewis Allen, "The Function of a Magazine in America," 6. Allen spoke based on his experience as the editor of *Harper's*, a magazine far more inclined to keep American business at arm's length than those magazines I have studied.

56. Friedrich, *Decline and Fall*, 11.

big magazines incorporated selling out into the very fiber of their being. Selling things was why they existed.

The commercial nature of the American magazine marketplace affected every magazine that attempted to find a reader. In the chapters to come, I will survey many magazines that attempted to find and appeal to a male audience, and every single one of them was deeply influenced by their attempt to stay afloat by simultaneously attaining advertising dollars and attracting readers. At the same time, commercial influences were not the only factors involved in the reshaping of masculinity within the magazine market. The editors of the magazines that sprang up after 1910 tended to be younger, more dependent on the publishing corporations for whom they worked, and more inclined to accept the logic of self-realization, to value the influence of personality. They were different men working in different contexts, and they began to reshape the way masculinity was presented to American readers.

$\mathscr{A}$frican $\mathscr{A}$merican $\mathscr{M}$asculinity and the $\mathscr{G}$reat $\mathscr{D}$ebate

Rescuing Black Masculinity from the Success Ethic

There was another revolution in the American magazine market, occurring just seven years after *Munsey's* changed the face of the mass-market magazine. Like the earlier revolution, this one took advantage of the decreased costs of publishing photographs through the halftone reproduction process and the increased literacy of potential audiences. Like the earlier revolution, this one offered a new kind of editorial product to potential readers, one aimed to encompass a variety of interests in its readers' lives. And as in the earlier revolution, the participants in this one hoped that advertisers would subsidize the costs of producing the magazine. Yet for all the similarities in conditions and intent between the two revolutions, this latter magazine revolution was indelibly altered by one factor: race.[1]

As with everything else in American culture, race changed everything. Where white magazines had available to them distribution channels that gave hundreds of thousands, even millions, of readers access to their magazine at newsstands, African Americans had no such network. Where white publishers had access to large amounts of capital, black publishers could count on meager sums from white philanthropists or black businessmen, who saw little chance of making a profit. Where white magazines were inundated with ads from

1. For background on black magazines of this era, see William Braithwaite, "Negro America's First Magazine"; Penelope L. Bullock, *The Afro-American Periodical Press, 1838–1909;* Frederick Detweiler, "The Negro Press Today"; W. E. B. Du Bois, "The Colored Magazine in America," *Crisis,* November 1912; Charles S. Johnson, "The Rise of the Negro Magazine"; and Abby Arthur Johnson and Ronald M. Johnson, *Propaganda and Aesthetics: The Literary Politics of Afro-American Magazines in the Twentieth Century.*

national manufacturers, black magazines went begging for ads, even from local merchants. Finally, where white magazines could count on a readership both literate enough and wealthy enough to purchase their product, black magazines could expect neither. Despite what seemed at times to be insurmountable odds, black editors and publishers worked intently to promote their magazines.

Though black magazine editors and publishers no doubt derived some motivation from the explosive growth of white magazines, and hoped that they might achieve the kind of success that these magazines achieved, there were precious few lessons to be learned from those magazines. For one thing, while white magazines offered themselves to a "general" audience, black magazines were always conscious of the "race" audience. White magazines clearly presented a race-centered view of the world, but they did so without the acute race consciousness that would characterize black magazines well into the century. For example, white magazines could write of success without recourse to racial explanations; the story was first and foremost about success, and the whiteness of its exemplar was assumed to be natural. But when black magazines wrote of success, they wrote of success that was notable for what it had triumphed over, success that was notable because it was achieved by a black man despite the forces arrayed against him by the bulwark of American racism. In the black magazines, everything was seen through the filter of race.

Without access to the major distribution channels used so well by white magazines, black magazines reached their audience either through local networks of black newsstands or through subscriptions. The effect of these limited means of distribution was to concentrate readership in the city of publication and in the small portion of the black population willing and able to spend their money on a year's subscription. This locally concentrated readership placed limits on the kinds of advertisers the magazine could hope to lure into its pages, and advertising in black magazines was restricted to local businesses for a number of years. But a more daunting limit on the number of advertisements a magazine could carry was, again, race. Major advertisers, white advertisers, the ones who placed so many ads in white newspapers and magazines, did not care to place ads in a black publication. In part this reluctance can be attributed to simple business sense—why waste advertising dollars reaching an audience that numbers in the hundreds and has little money to spend? But in large part this reluctance must also be attributed to the racism that suffused white America during this era.

Deprived of advertising support and acutely conscious of race, black magazine editors and publishers nevertheless tried to offer magazines that were of interest to large numbers of African Americans. The stories of these magazines' attempts to reach a large audience offer in themselves interesting parallels to those of their white counterparts, but more interesting yet are the ways that black magazines framed and debated the issues facing black men in this period. For black magazines in the first decade of the century were participants in a pitched debate over the future of black advancement, and that debate had far-reaching ramifications for the way black men would conceive of their identity. Like their white counterparts, black editors drew on the masculine ideals that had animated nineteenth-century social and economic development. Again, always, race informed the way they drew on those ideals: on the one hand, the small capitalist path to success might still be possible within a segregated black economy still in the early stages of its development; on the other hand, Victorian notions of manhood were based in the very ideas of freedom and citizenship that were systematically denied to black Americans in this period. Like their white counterparts, black editors strove to make masculinity meaningful within this rapidly shifting cultural milieu.

Booker T. Washington entered the twentieth century as the acknowledged leader—at least by white folks—of the black race, and he counseled blacks to lift themselves up to citizenship by concentrating on earning a place in the economic life of the United States. "Industrial Education" was the slogan for Washington's program of instructing blacks to take jobs in agriculture and the trades, to build up businesses within their own communities; it was a program taught at his well-funded Tuskegee Institute. We often know Washington's agenda today by the term "accommodationism," a term used by critics to fault the Washingtonians for adjusting black aspirations to the limits imposed upon the race by white—especially southern white—racism. Take away the pejorative sense and accommodationism remains a useful term, for Washington was clearly trying to stake out some territory within which blacks could begin to pursue successful lives.

Though critics had long faulted Washington for accepting the limits placed upon race advancement, a coherent alternative program for race advancement was slow in coming. W. E. B. Du Bois eventually emerged as an articulate opponent of Washington's race program, however, joining with like-minded people of both races to express what was then called the "radical" agenda. The radical agenda, formed slowly throughout the early 1900s and institutionalized with the formation of the Niagara Movement (later the NAACP), insisted that blacks not accept the limits imposed by a racist social structure. Radicals would have blacks advocate for their full rights as citizens, seeking the protection offered (though not always granted) by the Constitution of the United States. Though they too sought the success of the race, radicals rejected the "go slow" attitude of the accommodationists and demanded justice now. Much of their agitation was aimed at drawing attention to the injustices dealt out to blacks, notably lynching, and to the achievements of blacks that equaled or superseded those of their white peers.

This great debate among African Americans over such issues as citizenship, equality, and economic progress had real implications for the representation of black masculinity. On the one hand, African American publishers, editors, and writers adopted some of the language of white Victorian masculinity. Both radicals and accommodationists, for example, stressed the importance of character, honesty, hard work, and duty, though the two groups departed in stressing what it meant for a *black* man to act with character, what duty meant to a *black* man. Accommodationist editors and writers, for example, insisted that acting with character meant ignoring the snubs and hostility of white racism and persevering in one's chosen profession. They argued that black men could rise to success by following such prescriptions, and that while the success they might achieve would be within the segregated black world, that it would stand as an example of black potential and would ultimately lead to the decline of widespread racism. Radical editors and writers suggested that acting with character meant standing up to insults and demanding the equality that was every man's due. They believed that there could be no end to racism without the widespread acceptance that black men had full access to the rights of white men, beginning with the vote and proceeding to economic opportunity. At the base of these disagreements was a shared acknowledgment that black men were systematically denied the very fundamental elements of white Victorian masculinity: citizenship and the ownership of property. Indeed, American black men were all too aware that they and their ancestors were once the property of others. Thus as radicals and accommodationists debated their differing racial programs, they began to articulate notions of black masculinity that were as different from each other as they were from those images of masculinity offered in white magazines. They adopted some of the language of Victorian masculinity, but they brought to their use of that language an entirely different set of expectations and experiences, and they developed unique representations of masculinity as a result.

According to Abby Arthur Johnson and Ronald M. Johnson, authors of *Propaganda and Aesthetics: The Literary Politics of Afro-American Magazines in the Twentieth Century*, "Nowhere did the controversy [between Washington and Du Bois] appear more clearly and dramatically than in contemporary Afro-American journals."[2] In this chapter I will use several key African American

2. Johnson and Johnson, *Propaganda and Aesthetics;* the quote comes from an earlier version of one chapter, "Away from Accommodation: Radical Editors and Protest Journalism,

magazines—*Colored American, Alexander's Magazine, Horizon,* and *The Voice of the Negro*—to reveal how images of black masculinity developed out of the great debate and out of the efforts of these magazines' editors to develop successful publishing enterprises. Each of these magazines strove to achieve financial success, and much of the drama of these magazines lies in the editors' struggle to keep the ship afloat. Moreover, each editor felt it necessary to position himself in relation to the great debate between radicals and accommodationists (if he was not a prime proponent for one or the other approach). In advancing both the financial and ideological agendas of their magazines, these editors staked out a view of black masculinity, even if offering a view of masculinity was not their primary aim. The result of this pivotal decade in black publishing was the relative triumph of the radical school of thought and the radical program for black masculinity, and a real retrenchment in the expectations and aspirations of black magazine publishers and editors. These developments—the argument over black masculinity and a new approach to publishing the black magazine—evolved largely independently of the forces of consumer capitalism that reshaped the white magazine market.

The *Colored American Magazine*

The first Negro magazine of the new century had an auspicious start. Its founders—Walter W. Wallace, managing editor, and his associates H. A. Fortune, Jessie Watkins, and Peter B. Gibson, who joined together as the Colored Co-operative Publishing Company in Boston, Massachusetts—claimed that their purpose was "the introduction of a monthly magazine of merit into every Negro family, which shall be a credit to the present and future generations."[3] Such a magazine, they hoped, would "develop and intensify the bonds of that racial brotherhood, which alone can enable a people, to assert their racial rights as men, and demand their privileges as citizens"; such a magazine was much needed at a time when the "South is attempting to crush the manhood and self-respect out of the negro; the South is determined to smile upon the servile, fawning, cowardly and sicko fantine negro and to frown upon the grave,

---

1900–1910," 325. There is an abundance of scholarship discussing the "great debate" between Du Bois and Washington, most of it accounted for in Jan Miller, "Annotated Bibliography of the Washington–Du Bois Controversy."

3. *Colored American Magazine,* May 1900, 2. Note that although I have used the terms *African American* and *black* in my framing paragraphs, when I write about the magazines of the period I will use the racial terminology used by that magazine at that time. This too will lead to multiple usages, for the *Colored American,* for example, referred to African Americans as Negroes and as colored people.

manly, and aggressive negro. . . . What we desire . . . is justice; merely this and nothing more."[4]

Though their editorial policy announced a strident stand on race matters, the actual contents of the magazine proved to be a mix of defenses of Negro rights, light fiction, promotion of Negro success, and humor, and the magazine was sprinkled with photographs of reasonably high quality. Pauline E. Hopkins, who would later become literary editor of the magazine, contributed a short and sensational ghost story, and Maitland Leroy Osborne penned a romance set in the hills; such fiction was remarkably similar to that found in *Munsey's* and *McClure's*, the largest of the white magazines. I. D. Barnett, president of the National Colored League, reported on the shooting of a black postmaster and his child in Lake City, South Carolina, and on the efforts of the league to prosecute the killers and care for the family. Again, this type of story—of a sensational event and the effort to absorb it by a solid American community—differs little from that found in white publications. In its very early editions, then, the *Colored American* was indeed a typical general magazine albeit with a singular focus on race.

In its first year the *Colored American* presented a view of black masculinity that also differed little from the portraits of masculinity offered in white magazines. White magazines of the day heralded the virtues of the self-made man, the man who through hard work and self-control had risen to some success. In June of 1900 James Warren Payton contributed a giddy sketch of his experiences as a student at Yale, noting of the black student that "if he only has ambition and self determination, nothing can keep him from making a successful college issue." Such a view was seconded by none other than its most famous proponent, Booker T. Washington, in a later issue. In "The Storm before the Calm," Washington asks Negroes to bear through this difficult time in race relations and advises whites that "What the Negro does ask is, *equality of opportunity,* that the door which rewards and encourages virtue, intelligence, thrift, economy, usefulness, the possession of property, to be kept wide open to the humble black man from one shore of the continent to the other."[5] Such articles urged Negro men to subscribe to the Victorian notion that faithful

---

4. "Editorial and Pubishers' [*sic*] Announcements," *Colored American,* May 1900, 60–61. Johnson and Johnson read this comment as an avowal of distance from Booker T. Washington, who stands in as the "servile, fawning, cowardly and sicko fantine negro," but the evidence presented by succeeding issues indicates that the magazine offered no principled opposition to Washington's program. Abby Arthur Johnson and Roland M. Johnson, "Away from Accommodation: Radical Editors and Protest Journalism, 1900–1910," 328.

5. James Warren Payton, "Some Experiences and Customs at Yale," *Colored American,* June 1900, 87; Booker T. Washington, "The Storm before the Calm," *Colored American,* September 1900, 210 (italics from source).

adherence to certain cardinal virtues created men of character who were bound, as if by the laws of nature, to succeed.

But the world did not quite work that way for African Americans, as any reader realized. The deeply ingrained racism of white America placed strict limits on black success of any kind. Before I examine the ways that success rhetoric came to reconcile itself with those limits, most notably in the philosophy of Booker T. Washington, I want to make clear how black magazines like the *Colored American* defined the difficulties facing Negroes, for the ways those difficulties were defined had much to do with the advice offered to men about how to overcome them and thus with the very vision of masculinity constructed within the magazine. Most pressing was the South's attempt to crush the Negro referred to in the opening editorial and described at greater length in Robert W. Carter's "The Tyranny of the South," appearing in October 1900; such articles posited a uniform effort by southern whites to reduce Negroes to as near a condition of slavery as they could. One element of that oppression was the attempt to deny the vote, a device for denying full citizenship that the *Colored American* fought in editorials and by aligning itself with the activities of the Constitutional Rights Association of the United States, for which it declared itself the "official organ."[6] The other element of oppression, noteworthy for its absence in the *Colored American*, was the lynching of Negroes, usually men, and often for alleged rapes of white women. The sum of white oppression was often best encapsulated as an utter denial of justice, a recognition that without justice Negroes had no standing in America.

These two chords—one suggesting that the path to masculine success lay in adherence to Victorian values, one denying that any success was available to black men in an environment characterized by oppression—were played lightly in the early years of the *Colored American*, but they were to become the crucial issues in defining black masculinity and black magazines in the years ahead, both in the *Colored American* and in such black magazines as *Alexander's Magazine, Horizon, The Voice of the People* (later simply *The Voice*) and later the *Crisis* and *Opportunity*. Up until the time of Booker T. Washington's death and the subsequent decline of his influence on magazine publishing, these ideas also defined the editorial agenda of every black magazine.

The *Colored American* began its career as an "independent" magazine, awaiting "its success or failure, on the proposition that there is a demand for

6. The members of this organization were largely the editorial staff of the magazine, which makes the "official organ" moniker not too surprising. The magazine published the addresses and declaration of purposes in October 1900 and appealed for contributions to be sent to the magazine.

such a magazine."[7] And for a time the magazine seemed to succeed, prompting publisher Wallace to crow that they would no longer hand-set the type but move to a linotype machine and inducing R. S. Elliott to announce that the magazine has gone "from a handful of readers in May, 1900, to one hundred thousand readers at the present time" without the assistance of philanthropists.[8] The magazine's success was no doubt helped along by a growing number of ads, including full-page spots from Oatnuts breakfast cereal and the Rubber Soled Leather Shoe Co., that totaled as much as six pages by late in 1901, nearly 10 percent of the magazine's pages.[9]

For its first few years of publication, the *Colored American* offered an eclectic vision of black masculinity. On the one hand it seemed to embrace character-based Victorian masculine ideals, as in the story "The Test of Manhood: A Christmas Story," by Sarah A. Allen. The story tells of a light-skinned Negro, Mark Meyers, who forsakes his mother and his race and moves north to compete as a white man in the world of business. In the North he is given every opportunity to succeed, rises quickly in a law firm, and stands poised to marry the lawyer's daughter when his mother appears upon the scene, a poor wretch taken in for a Christmas dinner by the lawyer's family. In the climactic scene, Meyers is faced with a momentous choice of embracing his mother and his past and potentially falling from the position he has attained, or denying his mother and continuing to enjoy his false ascension as a white man. The story concludes: "All that was noble in his nature spoke at last. Another instant his arms were about his fond old mother, while she sobbed her heart out on his breast." With this ending Allen embraces the cult of character, as the protagonist adopts the "correct" position of loyalty to mother over all else. Yet the author's and Meyers's embrace of the "correct" position is problematic for a black man trying to rise in the world, for to act with character in this instance is potentially to damn himself to a return to the netherworld of the Negro experience he was so glad to escape. And there is yet another point to this Christmas story with a happy ending, one aimed at white men who regularly deny their blood ties to mulatto children. Meyers acts with character when he embraces his mother at the end of the story, yet his action begs the question of whether a white father of a black child would act the same way in those circumstances. Thus Allen, while seeming to herald an act of character, also calls into question

7. *Colored American,* June 1910, 61. By "independent" they meant that they professed allegiance to no "philanthrophical, political, sectarian, or denominational clique."

8. R. S. Elliott, "The Story of Our Magazine," *Colored American,* May 1901, 43.

9. Successful white magazines, by comparison, carried between 40 and 60 percent of their pages in ads.

the very meaning of that word in a moral world muddied by racism and miscegenation.[10]

Mariner J. Kent's short story "Three Times Met" conveys a different set of expectations about what constitutes appropriate masculine behavior.[11] This historical adventure story recounts the circumstances of three meetings between an escaped former slave, Hinton, and a white slave hunter, Faversham. In the first meeting, Faversham sicced attack dogs on Hinton, nearly killing him; in the second meeting, Hinton secretly observes Faversham using his racial position as leverage to try to bed the woman Hinton loves, but cannot reveal himself for he is in the midst of leading a band of slaves to freedom in Bloody Kansas; in the final scene, Hinton and Faversham meet in the Battle of Gettysburg, soldiers on opposing sides, and Hinton kills Faversham by driving a bayonet through his heart. A lurid story that enacts Hinton's desire to avenge the wrongs done to him, to the women of his race, and to his nation, it places the black man in the position of powerful hero at the center of an important historical struggle. Such an image of black masculinity paralleled the position of white heroes, but was to prove a very rare kind of image indeed.

Such complex and potentially disruptive images of black masculinity as these stories were not the norm in the *Colored American,* however. More common were stories that heralded the hard work and slow rise to status of "ordinary" people. Hopkins herself wrote a regular feature on "Heroes and Heroines in Black" that recounted success stories of Negroes known and unknown; such stories were unremarkable except for the fact that they countered the fictions of Negro savagery and barbarism that appeared in the white media. Hopkins's biographical pieces, and many like them, simply established that Negro people built their lives through hard work and dedication—just like any other people. Also typical were stories such as J. Shirley Shadrach's piece called "William Pickens, Yale University," which combined biography with analysis of the current racial climate. The piece opens:

> This country owes us compound interest on the toil of our ancestors invested as capital stock in the upbuilding of this opulent and powerful Republic. We intend to have our interest in spite of the insane ravings of our malicious enemies.

10. Sarah A. Allen, "The Test of Manhood: A Christmas Story," *Colored American,* December 1902, 113–19; Brian Joseph Benson notes in his essay on the *Colored American* in Walter C. Daniel's *Black Journals of the United States* that Sarah A. Allen is a nom de plume of Pauline Hopkins, but the best biographical piece on Hopkins, Ann Allen Shockley's "Pauline Elizabeth Hopkins: A Biographical Excursion into Obscurity," fails to confirm this assertion.

11. Mariner J. Kent, "Three Times Met," *Colored American,* August 1903, 568–71.

> "The pound of flesh, which we demand . . .
> Is dearly bought; 'tis ours, and we will have it."[12]

The actual biography is blander fare, describing Pickens's success at winning the Ten Eyck Prize for an essay as a result of "hard work" and "determined effort," but the essay concludes with another stirring call to arms: "Under a republican form of government, without the franchise men might as well be monkeys; the ballot makes the man."[13] While such an odd assemblage of paeans to hard work and radical calls for full suffrage might indicate a failure in editing, it ought also to alert us to the real turmoil facing black men trying to understand how to get ahead in life. Did one buckle down, never complain, work hard, and wait for the promised rewards? Or did one agitate, demand full justice now, insist upon one's equality before the law? This question, which lay at the core of the battle between radicals and accommodationists, was one which black magazines would eventually all choose sides on, for it defined the very nature of black masculinity.

That such questions remained open and contested in the *Colored American* in the years between 1900 and 1904 is a greater testament to the impartiality of the magazine than any editorial pronouncement. Readers of the magazine were presented with a number of alternative ways of conceiving of the place of Negro men, of the ways Negro men should act in order to survive and thrive. But the *Colored American* was not to remain independent for long. Financial instability would soon push the magazine into the hands of a publisher who was intent on having the magazine represent just one of the possibilities for black advancement and black manhood.

Despite the early and notable successes that made the Colored Co-operative the largest Negro-owned publishing house in the nation and the *Colored American* the most successful magazine, internal bickering among the company's principals and Wallace's alleged difficulties with getting the magazine out on schedule led to Wallace's ouster. In his place came William H. Dupree, a wealthy black Bostonian who placed Hopkins in charge of editorial matters. But Dupree's assistance failed to rescue the magazine from its financial difficulties,

12. J. Shirley Shadrach, "William Pickens, Yale University," *Colored American,* July 1903, 517. Pickens's speech later became something of a *cause célèbre* when William Monroe Trotter cited it as an example of how Washington's accommodationist philosophy was twisting the minds of Negro youth, for Trotter saw the speech as "slavish servile and sycophantic." Pickens would later repudiate the speech and Washington's approach to race relations and eventually become the field secretary of the NAACP. This incident is covered in Sheldon Avery's highly readable biography of Pickens, *Up from Washington: William Pickens and the Negro Struggle for Equality, 1900–1954,* 16–18.
    13. Shadrach, "William Pickens," 521.

and after another year of struggle the magazine was purchased by Fred R. Moore of New York. A friend and follower of Booker T. Washington, Moore soon made the magazine into a promoter of Washington's distinct views about the path to success for Negroes.[14]

Washington's participation in the shaping of the *Colored American* was always indirect, as both Washington and the press outlets he used to promote his views sought to assert their independence.[15] But Washington's ideology was written all over the magazine, from as early as Edward Elmore Brock's barely fictionalized 1903 account of the life of Booker T. Washington titled "For the Sake of Elijah."[16] In this biography turned hagiography, Brock tells of a young black man named Elijah Washington, born to a lazy though good-hearted father and a saintly mother, who commits his life to doing good and rises to a position few blacks have reached, all on the strength of his hard work and integrity. A brilliant scholar, a soldier so celebrated that the son of a Confederate general stands up at a public celebration and proclaims the dawn of universal brotherhood in tribute to Elijah, finally a college graduate who founds his own college and wishes to lead his race to the promised land of opportunity, he stands before his people at the conclusion of the story and gives Booker T. Washington's Atlanta Compromise address of 1895!

But what did it mean for a magazine to align itself with a particular way of representing the black experience such as that offered by Washington? On the one hand such a decision was no doubt a product of the editor's and publisher's own ideological view of the progress of race advancement.

14. The story of the magazine's two-year odyssey from Wallace's hands to Moore's is complicated and obscure. Though various editorial comments promised to explain the management changes, no such explanation was ever offered. Later comments by participants and historians have also failed to explain the reasons for some of the changes; see Benson, *"Colored American,"* 123–30; Braithwaite, "Negro America's First Magazine," 21–25; Johnson, "Rise of the Negro Magazine," 7–21; and August Meier, "Booker T. Washington and the Negro Press: With Special Reference to the *Colored American Magazine.*"

15. On Washington and the Negro Press, see Horace M. Bond, "Negro Leadership since Washington," *South Atlantic Quarterly* (April 1925), 115–30; Bullock, *Afro-American Periodical Press;* Louis R. Harlan, "The Secret Life of Booker T. Washington"; Harlan, "Booker T. Washington and the *Voice of the Negro,* 1904–1907"; Johnson and Johnson, "Away from Accommodation"; Johnson and Johnson, *Propaganda and Aesthetics;* Meier, "Washington and the Negro Press"; and Emma Lou Thornbrough, "More Light on Booker T. Washington and the *New York Age.*"

16. Edward Elmore Brock, "For the Sake of Elijah," *Colored American,* July 1903, 539–45. This piece was written when the magazine was in transition from the "independence" of Wallace's editorship to the partisanship of Moore's. Once Moore gained control of the magazine such blatant adoration of Washington declined in favor of more subtle forms of worship.

Washington's emphasis on industrial education and on Negroes slowly building up an economic base beginning in those areas like agriculture and the trades where they had experience, coupled with his desire not to arouse white anger over charges that Negroes were trying to get too much too fast, appealed to many people in this period. Moreover, adopting such a stance seemed in many ways to make good business sense, as G. Grant Williams makes clear in his portrait of "Conductor Henry Vanness" in the October 1903 issue of the magazine. Williams praises the *Colored American* for bringing before the American people a portrait of Negro America that has been obscured by the "Southern white Democratic press": "The inception of 'The Colored American Magazine' was as balm in Gilead for our wounded feelings. . . . [It] has shown [the Anglo-Saxon press] that Negroes support such enterprises—there's money in the Negro reader, and therefore white editors are ready to cater to a black clientele. This is what Negro enterprise in business will do for us in every part of the world. There is no corner of this vast globe that will not bend to the power of the mighty dollar."[17]

In this paragraph we find condensed all the hopes for this publication: that it can present to the world a more industrious and attractive vision of the Negro population, that this new view of the Negro race will lead to the end of racism and bigotry, and that the race will then enter into the commercial nexus that was raising the quality of life for so many white Americans (not to mention enriching magazines). And this is all merely in the way of introduction to the profile of one conductor, Henry Vanness, a train conductor on a line that runs through New England. What is most important about Vanness, says the author, is his ability to get along with all the people on board his train, to do a good job, to laugh off any jokes, "for he is not at all sensitive because of his dark skin, and knows a joke when he hears one."[18] Thus an embrace of the Washingtonian program implies that Negroes will slowly increase their incomes through success in entry-level jobs, eventually earning the respect and acceptance of fair-minded white Americans, and emerging as full participants in an expanding economy.[19]

17. G. Grant Williams, "Conductor Henry Vanness," *Colored American,* October 1903, 703–4. Williams had some attachment to the magazine as one of the stockholders in the Colored Co-operative Publishing Company.

18. Ibid., 706.

19. I have chosen representative examples of the magazine's dedication to the Washington/accommodationist line, but interested readers might also see Cyril H. McAdam, "Booker T. Washington's Recent Trip through the Southwest," *Colored American,* January 1906, 773–75; "Publishers' Announcements," *Colored American,* June 1906, 434–35; editorial, *Colored American,* August 1906, 78; editorial, *Colored American,* October 1906, 217; J. M. Henderson, "How the Negro Can Secure His Full Rights," *Colored American,* June 1908, 331; and "Industrial Education," *Colored American,* September 1908, 455.

Colored American Magazine publisher Fred Moore denied charges that his publication was subsidized by Booker T. Washington, but he offered full support for Washington's accommodationist agenda, urging black men to reject radical agitation and settle down and work hard to build businesses and run farms (*Colored American,* October 1904, 619).

But it is difficult to say which came first, the adoption of a Washingtonian approach by an independent editor making a business decision over how best to represent Negro America in order to attract readers and advertisers, or the decision by Washington secretly to fund the purchase of an organ edited by someone sympathetic to his views. Those critical of Washington, notably W. E. B. Du Bois and J. Max Barber, editor of *The Voice of the Negro,* asserted that Washington underwrote the *Colored American* and other Negro publications to provide good coverage for his vision of Negro America.[20] The fact that the magazines promoting what I will call a Washingtonian masculinity might not have survived as long as they did without Washington's subsidy calls into question the viability of the masculine images presented. But it is equally difficult to say whether the readers were aware that they were being offered images of masculinity carefully tailored to Washington's ideology. To the reader unaware of the political battle being waged between Washingtonians and radicals, such images of masculinity might well have appeared as legitimate options for emulation.

That the *Colored American* was firmly in Washington's camp became clear soon after Moore announced his acquisition of the magazine in June of 1904, though a variety of format changes and an ongoing series of articles on the question "Industrial Education—Will It Solve the Negro Problem?" indicate that he had begun to exercise control over the publication even earlier. Moore soon moved the magazine's offices to New York, where he could control the publication along with his other venture, the newspaper the *New York Age.* Moore announced that the magazine would "record the doings of the race along material lines," and thus would publish the news of the National Negro Business League and start a Masonic Department.[21] As president of the National Negro Business League, Moore was a frequent booster of what he called "race patronage"—urging blacks to support the businesses of other blacks (not least his magazine)—and his magazine certainly was a supportive medium for black enterprise. Long "reading ads" in September featured the Afro-American Investment and Building Company (which was headed by Moore himself) and the Afro-American Realty Company, and a complete lack of fiction and stories provided further evidence of the magazine's changing editorial direction. At times, as in March of 1908 when the magazine devoted nearly every article to Negro banking, the magazine's absorption in business seemed to threaten

20. Moore sought to deflect this charge in several instances, though he did comment in July of 1904 that he roundly supported Booker T. Washington against those "would-be leaders" who voice only "words and criticism" (Fred T. Moore, "In the Editor's Sanctum," *Colored American,* July 1904, 522).

21. "Editorial and Publisher's Announcements," *Colored American,* August 1904, 566.

its very viability as a "general" magazine. Moore seemed to sense when the magazine was becoming too focused on business, however, and he remembered to run a short story, a light article, or some poetry.

T. Thomas Fortune, editor of the *New York Age*, soon began writing intro-ductory editorials that confirmed the Washingtonian bias: "Work is the basis for living, and there can be no intelligent living without intelligent work. That is the main reason why some nations are prosperous and others poor, why some people are wealthy and others impecunious." Thus begins an argument that blacks need access to the bread-and-butter jobs in order to lift themselves up. Professor Alexander Hawkins penned "Success in Life" to advance the same cause, noting, "No man gains a fortune by wishing for it. It is only by hard toil and the sweat of a man's brow that he can make a success of his future in life." And Moore furthered the point in an editorial, adding that "it will readily be conceded that the Afro-American people . . . need most in the basis of education, whether of State or Church, self-reliance, self-dependence, a character rounded out to make the most of favorable opportunities and to regard obstacles only as incentives to greater effort." But Moore probably expressed the magazine's vision of Negro masculinity best and briefest when he appended this aphorism to his "Publishers' Announcements" page: "BEGIN to be producers."[22] Such an admonition cut to the core of the magazine's and Washington's notion of the path to success, for they both believed that the key to gaining the respect of others that was so crucial to success in America lay not in advocating for rights or protesting ill treatment but in slowly building up a business.

While Moore and his contributors certainly did their best to promote the more optimistic face of the Washingtonian ideology, when faced with conflict they also revealed the approach to race relations that earned Washington the term "accommodationist." When Reverend Reverdy Ransom, a prominent speaker, was evicted from a train for speaking to a white woman, Moore seemed on the same side as the white racists who had evicted him. Reporting on the National Negro Business League meeting that was held in Atlanta in late August of 1906—a time when other magazines were reporting that the entire state was at a fever pitch of racism thanks to a political campaign led by white supremacists—Moore chose to emphasize the cordiality of relations between the races. Although the "abolitionists" of the race served a purpose, he commented, "It is . . . a fortunate thing that the great mass of the Negro

22. T. Thomas Fortune, "Way of the World," *Colored American,* September 1904, 572; Alexander Hawkins, "Success in Life," *Colored American,* September 1904, 593; Moore, "In the Editor's Sanctum," *Colored American,* September 1904, 601; "Publishers' Announcements," *Colored American,* February 1905, 113.

people are willing to toil on and up, by the slow processes of industry, thrift, sobriety, inspired by a desire for peace [and] the common welfare of the whole people, black and white." Even after the riots that got *Voice of the Negro* editor J. Max Barber run out of Atlanta, Moore's only comment was, "All we ask is even handed justice." Nor was outright accommodationism merely Moore's agenda; contributor J. M. Henderson, M.D., in an article titled "How the Negro Can Secure His Full Rights," argued that "the way of politics has been tried" and that Negroes ought to realize that "The ballot is not all, it is only one of the rights and voting is only one of the duties of the good citizen."[23]

The combination of business boosterism and hat-in-hand racial thinking also had implications for the way the magazine framed black masculinity. Though Moore tried to stay above mudslinging, he often compared those who "do" (the Washingtonians) to those who only talk (the radicals), implying that the former were more manly. "There is growing up among the Negroes of this land a class of persons who spend their time and strength in talking and writing about their 'manhood.' This talk has the tendency to give one the same feeling one has in the presence of the woman who is always talking about how sacred she holds her virtue. Superiority, manhood, and virtue never speak of themselves." Not long after, Moore made a set of New Year's resolutions, concluding with "We believe in the virtue of manly protest, but, much protest and little 'do' is as bad as the reputed African regiment with two-thirds officers and one-third enlisted men—too many commanders and too few fighters." And when Du Bois, writing in the *Horizon*, accused Moore's editorials of lacking vigor, Moore shot back: "Just what is meant by *vigor* we can judge from what this magazine seems to endorse and stand for, to wit: continuous and loud-mouthed 'cussing' from a long distance off at white folks." But we need less vigorous talk and more work, said Moore. "We insist that the emphasis at this time should be placed on doing and being rather than talking and writing so-called *vigorous* editorials."[24]

This emerging formulation of ideas about black masculinity was given a more coherent focus by W. R. Lawton, who wrote:

> Our peculiar situation in this country calls for a wise, manly, conservative leadership. This statement may seem paradoxical to those who regard the terms manly and conservatism as incompatible. But conservatism is not cowardice, but

23. Moore, *Colored American*, August 1906, 78; *Colored American*, October 1906, 216–17; *Colored American*, November 1906, 334; J. M. Henderson, "How the Negro Can Secure His Full Rights," 331.

24. Moore, "Black and White," *Colored American*, June 1906, 373; Moore, "In the Editor's Sanctum," *Colored American*, March 1907, 232; Moore, "Editorial Vigor," *Colored American*, December 1907, 409.

manhood in wisdom. While there should be no retreat or surrender . . . there are times when a truce or a compromise is the best means to an end and seize the best method by which a desired result can be obtained. . . .

The impulsive and the radical men of the race serve a purpose. They deal some telling blows during the fighting, but their place to-day is in the ranks, not to plan and lead the battle nor direct the fight. . . . The gravity of the situation calls not for political hirelings and agents, neither for the impulsive nor radical, but for a conservative and disinterested leadership.[25]

Thus what critics labeled as truckling under to white supremacy was converted not only to wisdom but to a valid way of behaving manfully. Linking their ideological position to character traits like stoicism, wisdom, patience, and pragmatism, legitimate markers of Victorian masculinity, both Moore and Lawton sought to defend themselves from the attacks of the radicals and stake out some means of being both manly and accommodating. Their position, however, would come to seem out of touch with the spirit of the modern Negro, as well as with the spirit of the modern man.

The new emphasis the magazine took under Moore seemed to work as a business venture, no doubt confirming his belief that hard work, application, and a careful management of resources represented the path to success for Negro Americans. In January of 1905 Moore announced that circulation had reached 12,500, and that they wished to reach 15,000 by the end of the year. A year later, Moore was pleased to announce that "We have the largest bona fide circulation of any periodical published in behalf of the race."[26] To what can we attribute this boom in circulation? Not least among the factors to be considered is the magazine's affiliation with the Negro Business League, of which Moore was the founder. As the official organ of the League, the *Colored American* had a built-in subscriber base that no other magazine of the time had. Moreover, the magazine's close affiliation with Washington made the magazine a natural purchase for those associated with his program, both at Tuskegee and throughout the nation. But we should not overlook Moore's own efforts to increase circulation, for Moore aggressively solicited subscribers, offering premiums to those who could bring in subscriptions and reminding readers that though "We appreciate very much the many letters of congratulation[,] . . . we would be better pleased and it would be more encouraging to have a subscription accompany such letters hereafter. To publish a magazine requires money, and bills cannot be satisfied with congratulatory letters. Send us a subscription."[27]

25. W. R. Lawton, "Our Present Situation," *Colored American,* April 1908, 230–31.
26. *Colored American,* January 1906.
27. *Colored American,* November 1904, 700.

The magazine succeeded in other ways as well, most notably in bringing back some of the advertisers who had fled when the magazine had gone through its hard times back in 1903. Moore pumped his magazine as a good medium for ads hard and often, claiming that "as an advertising medium the columns of this Magazine are not surpassed. We circulate throughout the East, West and South, the Philippines, South Africa and the West India Islands. We place our space at your disposal and feel that as a business man you will be helped through advertising with us."[28] A number of advertisers agreed, and ads for the Loftis System for selling diamonds on credit, Dr. Scott's Electric Hair Brush, Free Hair Grower, and a variety of local (New York) merchants began to appear, occupying as many as fifteen pages each month.

The actual content of these ads is less important than their existence in a black publication. For the better part of the first forty years of the twentieth century, black magazines had a notoriously difficult time attracting advertisers, either black or white. (The notable exception was ads for hair straighteners, skin bleaches, and insurance, the first two of which posed real problems for both readers and editors, with their implication that the natural condition of the Negro was somehow repugnant and must be changed.)[29] When magazines did prove successful at attracting ads, it was largely because they provided a hospitable atmosphere for advertising. Like plants that fail to thrive in an environment that is too cold or dry, advertisements fall flat in an editorial environment that rails at the racial status quo, that supports sweeping economic change, or that is radical or confrontational.[30] The *Colored American* attracted more ads than other black magazines because it subscribed to the core economic values of white middle-class American culture, and was willing to subordinate calls for racial progress to its advocacy of hard-work, self-help, and slow economic progress. Thus the magazine's advocacy of a masculinity based on production, with all the various values that went along with the long tradition of masculine production in nineteenth-century America, helped to make it a viable venue for the limited stream of ads that would potentially flow to black magazines.

28. *Colored American,* October 1904.

29. *Ebony* was the first black magazine to openly address the problem of such ads. It announced in 1948 that it would no longer accept ads for "sex books, skin lighteners, hair straighteners" and other such products that were in bad taste. But it soon began running just such ads, prompting a number of letters to the editor complaining about them. See "Backstage," *Ebony,* November 1948, 12, and "Letters to the Editor," *Ebony,* November 1950, 8.

30. This is a lesson that W. E. B. Du Bois would learn all too well as the editor of *Horizon.* See Du Bois, *Horizon,* November 1909, 1, and "The New Horizon," *Horizon,* January 1910, 1.

Some of the few advertisements that early black magazines were able to land were for products such as skin lighteners and hair straighteners, advertised here in the *Colored American* in 1908. Though many black magazines carried such ads at one time or another, editors were all too aware that such ads only reinforced the notion that black Americans were somehow faulty or inferior (*Colored American,* September 1908, 508).

But the magazine did not remain viable for long, though it is difficult to ascertain why. Moore often used his "In the Editor's Sanctum" and "Publishers' Announcements" columns to ask for more advertising support and more subscribers to his magazine, but he never warned that the magazine was in dire straits (and dunning for subscribers seemed to be the black editor's primary occupation, anyway). Indeed, when he announced in November of 1907 his plans to incorporate and capitalize at $25,000 and served notice that he had acquired a controlling interest in the popular race newspaper the *New York Age,* all seemed to be going well. In March of 1909, however, Booker T. Washington wrote to Moore that he would no longer be able to provide financial assistance to the magazine. This announcement brought a series of changes, as Moore handed over the editorial reins to George W. Harris without fanfare or announcement in May of 1909.[31]

The quality and character of the magazine changed quickly under Harris, who seemed to have no vision of how to maintain a coherent editorial policy and no support from Moore or Washington. Articles from Washington antagonists Du Bois and Kelly Miller soon appeared in the magazine, incongruent beside the usual business boosterism that occupied the other pages. The magazine finally confronted lynching in October 1909, a topic it had long avoided. Advertising dropped off and deteriorated in quality as well, with no ad more bizarre than the one placed by Fred Moore, publisher, himself. "Education and Personal Appearance," it announces, "Are Sometimes Better Than Money! *They Are Necessary Requisites to Get Money!* We Offer You Both For The Price Of One. Read Our Offer Below." The education he offers can be gained by subscribing to the *Colored American Magazine,* but of personal appearance he asks: "What will create a more favorable impression than a head of beautiful hair? What can add more to one's personal appearance than a healthy scalp, entirely freed from the dreaded scalp disease of Dandruff, Eczema, Itchings, Tetter and Scurf. . . . Remember that Personal Appearance and Education in this day of activities count for much and the fortunate possessor of those most important requirements is the success."[32]

In August 1909 the *Colored American* published a poem called "The Man Who Wins," by Charles R. Barrett. The first and last stanzas read:

> The man who wins is an average man,
> Not built on any particular plan,
> Not blessed with any particular luck;
> Just steady and earnest and full of pluck.
>
> For the man who wins is the man who works,
> Who neither labor nor trouble shirks,
> Who uses his hands, his head, his eyes;
> The man who wins is the man who tries.[33]

31. Booker T. Washington to Fred R. Moore, March 9, 1909, Booker T. Washington Papers, Library of Congress, quoted in Meier, "Washington and the Negro Press," 72 n. 23.

32. *Colored American,* September 1909.

33. Charles R. Barrett, "The Man Who Wins," *Colored American,* September 1909.

Perfectly consistent with the magazine's earlier philosophy of manhood, the poem nevertheless represents a kind of death knell. Just three months later the *Colored American* appeared for the last time. Du Bois's postmortem declared that the magazine became "so conciliatory, innocuous and uninteresting that it died a peaceful death almost unnoticed by the public."[34]

Alexander's Magazine

Alexander's Magazine began publication on May 15, 1905, in Boston, offering to take up "important events and questions of vital and present-day interest and [give] its readers the outcome of calm, deliberate, and critical thought. The weekly paper has its place, but the race now needs strong monthly journals." Notable in its absence is any mention of the *Colored American Magazine*, which had departed Boston not long before Charles Alexander started his self-named magazine. Charles Alexander was no stranger to Negro periodicals: he had worked as a journalist for the *Reflector* newspaper in the early 1890s, founded and edited the *Monthly Review* magazine in 1894 and 1895, cowritten a history of a black cavalry regiment, and contributed a number of articles to the *Colored American* magazine, as well as a number of other black periodicals. From 1899 to 1901, when he taught printing at the Tuskegee Institute, Alexander came under the influence of Booker T. Washington. Though Alexander left Tuskegee to teach printing at Wilberforce College in Ohio, Washington soon called on Alexander to help his cause by editing the *Colored Citizen* newspaper in Boston, where William Monroe Trotter's *Boston Guardian* was proving one of Washington's harshest critics. Alexander took on the assignment, but it was not an easy one, for the paper was mired in debt and its new editor was forced to accept a subsidy from Washington to keep it afloat. When the *Colored Citizen* failed, Alexander founded *Alexander's Magazine* with the financial help of Washington.[35]

34. Du Bois, "The Colored Magazine in America," *Crisis*, November 1912, 34. Johnson and Johnson have speculated that the magazine began a long decline after losing the confidence of Washington, who felt that Barber's *Voice of the Negro* was a better publication. The final cause of the magazine's death, they contend, was the withdrawal of Washington's financial support (Johnson and Johnson, "Away from Accommodation," 329).

35. *Alexander's Magazine*, May 1905, 41; Cathy Packer, "Charles Alexander," in *Dictionary of Literary Biography*, vol. 91, *American Magazine Journalists, 1900–1960; First Series*, Sam G. Riley, ed. (Detroit: Gale Research, 1990), 11–16. Packer's contention that Alexander received subsidies from Washington is not supported by the work of Louis Harlan, August Meier, and others who document the impact that Washington had on the Negro press; see note 15 above. On Trotter, see Stephen R. Fox, *The Guardian of Boston: William Monroe Trotter*.

Charles Alexander, founder and editor of *Alexander's Magazine,* struggled to keep his magazine afloat during the first decade of the century, but discovered that neither subscribers nor advertisers were as yet willing to support a black magazine (*Alexander's Magazine,* November 1905, 14).

Alexander's Magazine was, from its very first issue, a very well put together magazine. Combining nonfiction articles on such subjects as "Missionary Work and African Education" and "Socialism and the Negro," with light fictional romance and adventure, biographical sketches, an abundance of photographs, and reprints and snippets penned by various public figures, including Andrew Carnegie, Booker T. Washington, and Charles Chesnutt, *Alexander's* tried with much success to emulate the white "general" magazines of the period. It imitated those magazines as well in achieving an editorial stance that was designed to offend no one and to appeal to, even to court, those commercial interests that could make or break a magazine. Though Alexander may have received assistance from Booker T. Washington, he was no Washington lackey, offering a reasonably balanced presentation of racial issues.

While other Negro magazines tied themselves to one or the other schools of thought concerning racial progress, Charles Alexander guided his magazine to a truly moderate position that combined a recognition of the conditions limiting Negro advancement with a genuine optimism for the outlook of Negroes who dedicated themselves to success in business.[36] In part this position seemed to reflect his own sunny outlook, but it became clear from a number of his comments that he also thought it the most likely strategy to attract advertisers and sponsors for his business enterprise. That such an outlook failed proved to be a bitter disappointment to Alexander, who complained about the lack of support his enterprise received as it failed a mere four years after its founding. Still, *Alexander's* provides us a with a portrait of black masculinity that differs in important ways from the consolation prizes offered by accommodationists and the dangers and risks associated with racial radicalism. *Alexander's* vision of masculinity is as close to white middle-class manhood as any Negro magazine before *Ebony*.

What is most striking is how faithful the tales of masculine success in *Alexander's* are to the principles of white Victorian masculinity. Self-control, self-reliance, character, honesty, integrity, hard work, and investment are repeatedly hailed as the keys to success, from the first issue, which praises Patrick Healy, whose "honesty, integrity, faithfulness . . . stamped him as a man of fine quality and a model for young men," to a later issue, which tells the "Story of a Self-Made Man," whose "efficiency and reliability" are held up as qualities that no individual or race can succeed without.[37] The import of such stories was reinforced by Alexander's editorials, one of which claims that "In life or in any of the pursuits of life very much depends on the foundation and by this we really mean character, for character is the foundation of life." Though I will not beat the reader over the head with the repeated references to such "keys to success," Alexander did, running frequent stories that explicitly announced themselves as advice and reinforcing the lessons of these stories in his upbeat

36. Advertisements for the magazine in other publications labeled *Alexander's* "the most conservative monthly publication issued at the present time in the interest of the race"; see *Horizon* for most of 1907.

37. *Alexander's Magazine*, May 1905, 40, and June 1906, 35. Such stories appeared in nearly every issue of the magazine in its first two years, though they declined as Alexander increasingly padded the magazine's content with reprints from other sources.

editorials.[38] Alexander, like John Siddall of the *American Magazine* some years later, was trying to drive home a point.

What makes Alexander's invocation of such masculine traits so interesting is his resistance to mentioning the constraints that limited black advancement and his persistent optimism. Stories of success in other Negro magazines often relied on a formula that registered black success "in spite of" the persistent racism facing African Americans. In fact, later magazines such as the *Crisis* and *Opportunity* incorporated the "in spite of" formula into their series of stories on black success, ending such accounts with the explanation that "he did it all despite persistent efforts to keep him down." But Alexander seemed to wish to record the stories of black success without the racial qualifier, as if to argue that Negroes ought to be pleased with the successes they have had and need not mention those factors that kept those successes from being even greater. This was a very "manly" and stoic pose itself, for it indicated that real men did not appeal to the limits they faced when explaining what they had achieved.[39]

Alexander recognized the limits facing African Americans in this period, but he chose not to complain about them. For complaining was not a good way to invest one's energy, and Alexander thought black men needed most to learn the proper way to invest their energies. Alongside the urgings to work hard and be self-reliant, Alexander urged men to shepherd their resources, to invest their time and efforts (not to mention their money) wisely. In an editorial called "As to the Big Negro," Alexander complains of the attention given to the big Negroes who "make their money on uncertain investments of wit and 'hot air,'" rather than on hard work and perseverance like the good businessmen who make up the National Business League. If they invest their efforts well, Negroes will in turn *be* a good investment, Alexander explains: "The Negro race is making a tremendous progress in the South. Thirty-one banks have been established by representative men and women of the race and great headway has been made

38. Charles Alexander, *Alexander's Magazine,* June 1905, 44. See also "He Knew How to Say No," *Alexander's,* June 1905, 33–34; J. C. Napier, "Opportunity and Possibility: A Message to Young Men," *Alexander's,* July 1905, 28–33; profile of Joseph Seamon Cotter, *Alexander's,* August 1905, 25; E. C. Brown, "A Bit of Personal Experience," *Alexander's,* September 1905, 36; untitled poem, *Alexander's,* January 1906, 57; editorial, *Alexander's,* May 1907, 9–10; "The Need for Enterprise," *Alexander's,* July 1908, 127–29; and "The Man Who Wins" and "A Man with an Aim," *Alexander's,* November 1908, 25–26.

39. The magazine's stoicism was not monolithic, of course, and some stories did use the "in spite of" trope (see profile of Dr. James Robert Norrel, *Alexander's,* June 1905, 15–16), but it was all in all a consistent approach to male success. Even John Daniel's glowing review of Du Bois's *Souls of Black Folk* faults the author for presenting the sorry state of affairs for Negroes instead of singing a "song of triumph" ("Booknotes and Comments," *Alexander's,* September 1905, 10).

along purely commercial lines. Let us not grow disheartened and discouraged. *A sick race, says Dr. Washington, is a poor investment.* This is true. Let us not get the reputation of being sick."[40]

Critics seeking easy labels might have used such evidence to call Alexander an accommodationist, but Alexander was no mere subscriber to the views of Booker T. Washington.[41] Instead Alexander offered a vision of progress through constructive endeavor that did not limit Negroes to agriculture or the trades but encouraged them to seek business success wherever they might find it. By couching his advice in that regard in the most optimistic possible light he sought to create a black middle class around the very values that had made the white middle class so prosperous in the nineteenth century. And optimism was certainly Alexander's guiding star in editing the magazine, as he made clear in any number of editorials. In November of 1905, six months into his publishing career, Alexander wrote, "My magazine teaches optimism. It selects the best examples of race development as a means of inspiration to others." Later in the same issue, an editorial titled "Happiness Often Depends on the View Point" promoted optimism as a way of life, arguing that "winning or losing in the game of life is a question of attitude," and concluding by asking, "Are you a pessimist or an optimist?"[42]

This persistent optimism was itself part of Alexander's overall philosophy concerning the prospects for his race; it was both a creed for the individual and for the race. In the magazine's first two years, such optimism, while rare in Negro magazines, was in keeping with the other content of the magazine, which told tales of black success. And it seemed in keeping with the general fortunes of the magazine, which increased in length and succeeded in attracting an increasing number of advertisers. Indeed some of the ads themselves wore editorial clothing, as with the November 1905 "article" on the Spencer Red Brick Company of Spencer, New York, which sought investors for a business built on "hard work and limited capital." By May of 1906 there were ten pages of advertising in the magazine, including spots for the Metropolitan Mercantile & Realty Co. of New York; Johnson's Hair Food; a book called *The Aftermath of Slavery*, offered by Alexander; a variety of services (mostly in Boston); hair products; Tuskegee Institute; printing by Charles Alexander; and a hair

40. Alexander, "As to the Big Negro," *Alexander's Magazine,* September 1905, 44; Alexander, "The Optimist," *Alexander's,* April 1907, 271.

41. Du Bois himself refused to place Alexander in the enemy camp, noting in *Horizon* that *Alexander's* was well worth reading. Du Bois, "The Race Magazines," *Horizon,* February 1907, 20–21.

42. Alexander, "Happiness Often Depends on the View Point," *Alexander's,* November 1905, 39.

straightener. A number of stock companies, presuming that *Alexander's* readers had money to invest, hawked their products; the popular *Youth's Companion* magazine (a white publication) even placed an ad in October of 1907. It is estimated that circulation reached as high as five thousand.[43]

For two years, then, all appeared to be going well with *Alexander's Magazine* as it carved out a unique editorial position, presented a cleanly set and nicely laid out magazine, and attracted advertisers and subscribers. In May 1907 the magazine absorbed the Indianapolis-based *National Domestic*, adding "thousands of new readers." The acquisition set Alexander off on new rhapsodies: "Nothing in the world compensates for self-confidence—a man must believe in himself if he is to make any real progress among his fellows . . . ," he editorialized. "We cannot help being largely what we think we are, because mind controls matter."[44] But such optimism began to seem oddly out of place in a magazine that was obviously struggling for survival. No clear records of *Alexander's* demise remain; there is no way of knowing if Alexander lost what fortune he had in some misadventure, if he simply mismanaged the magazine, if he was unable to continue to fund the magazine from his own money, or if he simply grew tired of the fight. I must infer the cause of the magazine's demise from the cryptic traces of its decline left in the magazine, and from what else I know of the market for Negro magazines in this era. But one thing is certain: from as early as 1906 Alexander began scrambling to keep the magazine together. It was a scramble that ultimately failed.

The difficulties of what he was attempting dawned slowly on Alexander. In March of 1906, in an editorial on Negro journalism, Alexander lamented the difficulties of his job, which required so much work and yet paid so little. Such a complaint is understandable, since Alexander not only had to publish his magazine but also manage the business of his book printing company, which printed a number of race titles and which was always the major advertiser in the magazine. By April of 1907, Alexander hoped for one kind of deliverance from what must have been increasing financial problems: "So strong is our confidence in the good we are doing that we believe firmly that sooner or later some noble soul of means will relieve us by substantially endowing our magazine with sufficient funds to render it possible for us to do our very best work and to extend our influence for good a thousand fold." And in May of 1907, following his acquisition of the *National Domestic*, he hoped that "advertisers everywhere will now be more generous in their patronage of our enterprise." Alexander got

43. Daniel, *"Alexander's Magazine,"* in *Black Journals*, 27. No source for the circulation figure is given.
44. *Alexander's*, May 1907, 11; *Alexander's*, May 1907, 9.

even more creative with his pleas for advertisers when he published a poem titled "The Editor and the Advertiser," which tells of a businessman whose ad has brought in so much business that he pleads for a rest.[45] But neither form of deliverance came—no wealthy donor stepped forward (though one must wonder if Washington offered his assistance) and advertisers seemed not to renew their ads after they had run for a span of three to six months.

Like many editors seeking to revive a magazine's fortunes, Alexander tinkered with the magazine's format and content. He began running more and more material reprinted from other magazines and often "dedicated" an issue to one group or another, seemingly wishing to attract the subscribers of that group. Catholics and Masons were courted in succession; followers of Booker T. Washington were treated to an issue heaping praise on the race leader; women were offered stories on cooking and housekeeping. In September 1907, Archibald H. Grimke stepped in as guest editor and penned a number of pointed political articles roundly condemning all political candidates but singling out presidential candidate William Howard Taft for the bitterest remarks. But after Grimke advised Negroes to abandon the Republican Party, Alexander stepped back in and urged Negroes not to "lend encouragement and strength to the Demcratic [sic] party"[46] and gave a whole issue over to the interests of the Republican party. F. H. M. Murray, coeditor of the black magazine *Horizon*, accused Alexander of selling his editorial soul to the Republican party, noting that "the entire 'editorial' out put, which is nearly all there is in the last issue, gives off a strong odor of a campaign headquarters' typewriter. . . . But whose fault is it? . . . If our race wants 'clean,' presentable, healthy periodicals we must ourselves see to it that the laundry bills are paid, and with untainted money, too."[47]

In December of 1908, Alexander published a bitter poem called "The Editor's Dream." In the poem, an angel takes an editor to the pits of hell and shows him all his delinquent subscribers burning in eternal damnation. Offered an opportunity to then go to heaven, the editor mutters: "This is heaven enough for me."[48] But Alexander lived through his hell a few months longer, offering as his final effort a combined March/April issue with Lincoln on the cover and an abundance of reprinted material inside, some of it from earlier issues of his

45. Alexander, *Alexander's Magazine,* March 1906, 19; *Alexander's,* April 1907, 269; *Alexander's,* May 1907, 11; "The Editor and the Advertiser," *Alexander's,* September 1907, 253.
46. Catholics were courted in June of 1907, and Masons in July of 1907; *Alexander's,* May 1908, 29.
47. F. H. M. Murray, "The In-Look," *Horizon,* August 1908, 19.
48. *Alexander's,* December 1908, 83.

own magazine. On the last page of the last issue was this plea: "Try to Secure Ten Subscribers for *Alexander's Magazine*. This note is to our Subscribers who know the mission of this publication. Ask your friends to send us One Dollar at once to help develop a good, strong medium of optimistic news of value to the Colored people. Charles Alexander, Editor and Publisher." And so ended the career of another black magazine.

Horizon

In the first years of the new century, Professor W. E. B. Du Bois dreamed of founding a magazine that would offer opposition to the accommodationist policies of Booker T. Washington. As he set about investigating the possibilities for making a success of such a magazine, Du Bois estimated that there were one million Negro families who were literate, and a hundred thousand Negroes who were well educated enough to appreciate a Negro magazine.[49] Du Bois's first effort to reach this audience was the *Moon Illustrated Weekly*, published out of Memphis, Tennessee, beginning in December 1905. Though the *Moon* attracted a surprising number of advertisements, including some from prominent white businesses in Memphis, the magazine was poorly put together and achieved a circulation of between 250 and 500 subscribers. The magazine ceased publication a mere eight months later, to the delight of the several magazines and newspapers who advocated the Washingtonian cause.[50]

Du Bois renewed his efforts at editing a magazine in January of 1907 when he, along with coeditors Freeman Murray and Lafayette M. Hershaw, began publishing *Horizon: A Journal of the Color Line*. The magazine was, as it intended to be, "a radical paper," offering an interpretation of the black experience in America that differed greatly from that offered by the *Colored American* or *Alexander's,* its two primary competitors. Murray expressed the magazine's approach well in July of 1907 with this borrowed quote: "Don't flinch, don't foul, and hit the [color] line hard.—T. Roosevelt and We."[51] In its three and a half years of publication, the *Horizon* attacked accommodationists and Jim Crow with equal vigor, and it did so while advancing a construction of black masculinity more stridently rights-based than that proposed by the

---

49. W. E. B. Du Bois to Jacob Schiff, April 4, 1905, Broderick Notes, Schomburg Center, quoted in Paul G. Partington, "The *Moon Illustrated Weekly*—The Precursor of the *Crisis,*" 209.

50. Partington's claim that *"The Moon Illustrated Weekly* remains an enigma" is belied only by Partington's own work to recover the history of a magazine of which only three copies have survived. See Partington, *The* Moon Illustrated Weekly: *Black America's First Weekly Magazine.*

51. *Horizon,* July 1907, 19. Brackets are from source.

other magazines. The *Horizon's* vision of masculinity was muscular, demanding that black advancement begin with a full recognition of the rights of Negroes as men.

The *Horizon* was a unique editorial product, consisting of three separate sections containing the writings of the three editors. Du Bois wrote "The Over-Look," taking as his terrain any element of the black experience he felt needed comment. In this section of the magazine, Du Bois began to hone what would become one of the most distinctive editorial voices of the era; his *Horizon* editorials are among the most acerbic and pointed of his vast body of writings. Du Bois clearly imagined himself writing to a literate and intelligent audience, for he nearly always offered a list of books worth reading and he extolled the virtues of literacy, urging "Do not merely read [books] but buy them, own them, make them yours. Do not simply use libraries, but use books."[52]

"The In-Look," edited by F. H. M. Murray (as he signed the column), surveyed the Negro experience from the vantage point of the Negro himself, and especially the vantage point of the Negro press. Murray's opinions were every bit as pointed as Du Bois's, though expressed with somewhat less erudition, and he took particular delight in skewering what he clearly saw as the "opposition" press. Murray was fond of beginning his section with a quote from some noted American that commented ironically on the present situation, as was the case with this quote from Benjamin Franklin in the May 1907 issue, clearly aimed at Booker T. Washington: "Those who would give up essential liberty to purchase a little temporary safety, deserve neither liberty nor safety."[53] Hershaw edited "The Out-Look," which generally discussed the Negro experience as it was perceived by the white world. Hershaw's was the least coherent and least memorable of the three sections. In each of the three sections, the editors combined their comments with excerpts and clippings from other sources, producing a unique mix of news and comment.

Uniting the three sections were open attacks on the subsidized Negro press in general and on Booker T. Washington, as subsidizer and as false leader of the Negro people, in particular. Du Bois had launched general attacks on Washington for subsidizing the Negro press while writing for the *Voice of the Negro*, but such attacks became even more pointed in the *Horizon*. Murray claimed that "Not the least particular thing (in race journalism) about this periodical is —the editors own the magazine and not the magazine the editors. Another peculiarity is—while we endeavor to 'digest' every thing we read and hear about the race we do not 'swallow' everything." Murray concluded this

52. Du Bois, "The Over-Look," *Horizon,* April 1907, 5.
53. Murray, *Horizon,* May 1907, 19.

early jibe by asking, "Who hath woe? Who hath sorrow? Who hath trepidation? He that tarries long at the subsidy trough." Such comments were directed primarily at T. Thomas Fortune, editor of the newspaper the *New York Age*, and Fred Moore of the *Colored American*, as well as a number of editors of other black newspapers. "Subsidy is degrading and dangerous because it implies the secret buying of a paper's policy by persons unknown and often unsuspected by the readers. When Negroes know that today editorials are being written at the dictation of that same despicable Hitchcock who made 'lily-whiteism' triumph at Chicago, they lose faith in their 'Negro' paper."[54] Similar comments lamenting the lack of freedom of the Negro press were tossed off as asides in nearly every issue of the magazine.

T. Thomas Fortune came in for the most pointed criticism for accepting subsidies, not least because he had once seemed sympathetic to the radical cause. In May of 1907 Du Bois penned this portrait of Fortune:

> I remember my first knowing of the man. It was about 1883, while I was a lad in the High School. I became agent for his paper and wrote crude little news notes from our town. He wrote me an encouraging letter—a good long sympathetic letter. That letter I shall not forget. No matter how far the writer has fallen and groveled in the dust, I shall ever remember that hand of help. He worked on. His fierce brave voice made men of the nation hearken, even while it scared them. "A dangerous Negro," they said "muzzle him." Thus his voice became bitter, wild and strained and his own people joined the critics and deserted him. Temptations gathered; drink, women, debt; he staggered downward. The Arch-Tempter came, smooth-tongued and cynical, with gold: "I have a commission from the Gods-that-be to buy your soul." And the man, bitter at those who had criticized and deserted and refused to support him, mortgaged his Soul and Home to Hell. His slavery began—a bitter, cringing, maddening serfdom. His soul—that fierce old untamed soul—lashed him. Ever and again he breaks forth in fury; flashes in fierce denunciation, cynical fury or eloquent silence—then the smooth cold gold drops on his brow and he slinks cowed and trembling into his hired kennel. O, it is pitiable; thrice pitiable in a day when as never before his voice and pen are needed in the madness of the battle. And yet I cannot attack him. I receive his curious mad jibes silently. Why? because the fault is ours as well as his. Who refused to hold up his hands? Who refused his wiser youthful leadership? Who withheld the money and bread and clothes due him and his suffering family? We did. Shall we crucify him today for his venality, his weakness, his unbridled passions, his tottering over-aged manhood? No, rather let us bow our heads, for his shame and failure are ours. The lash that goads him, goads us, O Unfortunate!

Du Bois's ire strikes out in any number of directions—at Fortune for failing to resist the entreaties of the devil (Washington); at the Negro people for failing to

---

54. Murray, "Nodules," *Horizon*, January 1907, 19, 20; Du Bois, *Horizon*, July 1908, 2–3.

support an honest and eloquent man (as Du Bois no doubt pictured himself); at Washington for using his gold to buy men's souls.[55] Several months later, Murray echoed Du Bois's critique; in an editorial titled "Tom Fortune—Our Shame" he wrote that "the Frank-stein [sic] he has helped create now devours him. Not suddenly, at a gulp, but insidiously, relentlessly."[56] When Fortune left the *Age* and tried to set up an independent magazine of his own, Du Bois and Murray were the first to cheer him on, but the magazine never materialized.

The problem with magazines that were subsidized by Washington and the powerful Tuskegee machine was that they promoted a view of racial progress that was fundamentally weak, asserted the editors of the *Horizon*. In April of 1907, Hershaw writes that radicals are to accommodationists as freemen are to serfs, and that Washingtonians are simply afraid to demand equality before the law: "Civil and political equality have no place in the lexicon of [Washington's] uttered conviction." Murray hit Washington even harder, writing "Peculiar, that white men who despise 'molly-coddles' and nincompoops in their own race should apparently lend a willing ear only to 'mushmouths' and flunkies of our race." A month later, Murray attacked Washington for recommending that Negroes not let their children read race papers because they carry too much news of black oppression, asking "Will you be satisfied to continue licking the 'united' hand that smites or must you now, to prove your docile 'loyalty,' fawningly, meanly, suck the very skin off its 'separate' fattened fingers?"[57]

The editors were outraged not only that Washington capitulated to white southerners, but that Washington proposed to teach the rest of Negro America to do the same. Murray attacked Tuskegee for teachings that encouraged Negroes to blame themselves for their sorry position in American society instead

55. Du Bois, "The Lash," *Horizon,* May 1907, 5–6. Du Bois's comments are both self-congratulatory—for he had resisted Washington's advances (or so Partington maintains, based on a letter from Du Bois; see "The *Moon:* Precursor," 207 n. 7)—and a little fearful—for he too was a Negro editor dependent for his success on a people who had not offered much support for Negro magazines. Du Bois was to return to the difficulties faced by Negro editors in later issues, posing the choice between subsidy and commercial failure even more clearly than he does here. Fortune is a more sympathetic character than Du Bois would admit, as Emma Lou Thornbrough indicates in her nicely written biography, *T. Thomas Fortune: Militant Journalist.*

56. Murray, "Tom Fortune—Our Shame," *Horizon,* October 1907, 23–24. Du Bois and Murray track Fortune's fortunes in a series of asides, indicating that he traveled to Chicago, almost started a magazine with former *Voice* editor J. Max Barber, then floated several abortive issues himself. The point, I believe, is that whatever personal enmity they bore Fortune paled in comparison to the hatred they had for subsidization. See also Thornbrough, *T. Thomas Fortune.*

57. Hershaw, *Horizon,* April 1907, 14, 26; Murray, *Horizon,* May 1907, 25.

of the oppressive white society, offering as proof this poem published by an Instructor Hill:

> "We call upon thee now no more in chains
> Such as our fathers wore—from these we're freed—
> But clanging still the fetters of the soul.
> The liberation of ourselves remains.
>
> "The gleam we follow weakly, *for we need*
> The Freedom of a sturdy *self-control.*"

"Now candidly," Murray asked his readers, "would you desire your child schooled in an atmosphere reeking with such low-flung race accusation? 'Self-control,' indeed—but we'll stop, as the strain on the girth of ours has almost reached its modulus of rupture."[58] Murray was not launching a modernist critique of the abstract notion of self-control or the idea that principles should guide actions, key elements in Victorian masculine norms, for he was quite comfortable with the idea that principles should guide a man's life. Rather, he was attacking the Washingtonians for teaching the wrong principles, for teaching Negroes to internalize the blame for their position and use the white man's principles for achieving success. Murray and Du Bois had other ideas.

For the editors of the *Horizon,* to be radical was to claim forthrightly, as the Negro man's due, the rights guaranteed to him by the Constitution and by his status as a man. They bitterly resented the image of Washington going hat in hand to plead with white southerners for their recognition of anything less than full equality. Each of the editors heaped scorn on those following Washington's example and praised those who stood defiantly for the Negro man's rights. In an article titled "An Eagle in a Pewee's Cage," Murray quotes with approval the following lines from the *Atlanta Independent* newspaper: "The race is far more in need of real manhood than it is of money and material wealth. . . . Racial integrity and unflinching manhood must be our fort, and from behind this breast-work we can best our most determined enemies. . . . When the political emissary comes to the South and offers you the custom house, tell him you do not want the custom house, but your rights as an American citizen, and if the custom house comes incidentally thereto you will consider it, but you are not going to sell your 'seed corn' for a mess of pottage."[59] Such

---

58. Murray, *Horizon,* June 1907, 25–26.

59. Murray, "An Eagle in a Pewee's Cage," *Horizon,* May 1907, 19–20. Murray followed these lines with the comment: "It is not likely that any of the white Negro-baiters nor the colored referees and middle-men who anoint black copper-heads with commendation and continually squeeze sustenance into their pudgy paws, will quote with approval, any of that" (20); he never could resist a jab at subsidized editors.

expressions of Negro manhood countered much of Washington's program, for they placed material gain secondary to the recognition of Negro rights, refused to accept the social inferiority demanded by southern whites, and disdained the crumbs—the Custom House and Post Office jobs—offered by Republican politicians. Moreover, such expressions announced their goals explicitly in terms of an active, aggressive manhood, a manhood based foremost on equality and citizenship. To sell one's seed corn for a mess of pottage, as the Washingtonians had done, was to be neutered, unmanned.

The publication of the notes from the Niagara Movement's fourth annual meeting in September of 1908, run as part of Du Bois's column, reinforced this message. "First, we say to our own: Obey the law, defend no crime, conceal no criminal, seek no quarrel; but arm yourselves, and when the mob invades your home, shoot, and shoot to kill. Secondly: We say to voters: Register and vote whenever and wherever you have the right. Vote, not in the past, but in the present."[60] Readers were thus encouraged to associate the magazine's policy with the policy of the Niagara Movement, with all the meanings that association entailed.

The manhood that the *Horizon* advocated was not for the old or the weak; it required strength and courage. The editors damned weakness of expression, and hailed conviction, as Murray indicates in this comment about the *Voice:* "Editorially—where weakness, puerility and truckling generally occupy—there is conviction, ability, insight, and above all and dominating all, high ideals and unlimited aspiration. If you are a *man* or would attain a man's status, read 'The Voice.'"[61] The manhood that the *Horizon* advocated was also often associated with youth. Suggesting that those who followed Washington did so out of a fear that came with age, Du Bois answered a letter from a white reader who complained about the "bumptious" and aggressive behavior of northern Negroes by writing: "What is this you describe so well and complain of so bitterly? Is it aught but that consciousness of power, that ill-balanced but just ambition, that sense of boundless but unrealized possibilities which characterizes all Youth—the youth of the individual as well as the youth of a race or of a nation?"[62] Du Bois and Murray both suggested that it was time for the old men to step aside and let the spirited and manly youth take over the

60. *Horizon,* September 1908, 2–3.

61. Murray, "The In-Look," *Horizon,* June 1907, 20. It is unclear in this instance whether the man's status refers to the right to vote, which *Voice* editor Barber always advocated, or to Barber's recent critical stance toward white Atlantans following the race riots, a stance that got him run out of town and forced him to move his magazine to Chicago, where it soon failed.

62. Du Bois, *Horizon,* May 1908, 2.

mantle of race leadership. In many ways this rhetoric matched that of those who supported the policies of the youthful President Teddy Roosevelt.

Not surprisingly, the boldest and most forthright expression of Negro masculinity came from Du Bois's pen, in the form of a poem called "The Song of the Smoke." This poem was the strongest statement of race pride seen in any Negro publication of this era:

> I am the Smoke King
> I am black!
> I am darkening with song,
> I am hearkening to wrong!
> I will be black as blackness can—
> The blacker the mantle, the mightier the man!
> For blackness was ancient ere whiteness began.
> I am daubing God in night,
> I am swabbing Hell in white:
> I am the Smoke King
> I am black.
> . . . .
> Souls unto me are as stars in a night,
> I whiten my black men—I blacken my white!
> What's the hue of a hide to a man in his might?
> Hail! great, gritty, grimy hands—
> Sweet Christ, pity toiling lands!
> I am the Smoke King
> I am black.[63]

Such images of masculinity—powerful, judgmental, wrathful, strong—stood in stark contrast to the hardworking, obedient Negro who asks only for the right to prove himself capable of earning a living.

Advocating an aggressive and powerful black masculinity was one thing, building a successful magazine another, but the two were not unrelated. The editors announced from the beginning that they would try to finance the magazine on advertisements and subscriptions rather than subsidies, and they called for advertisers from the first issue: "Persons minded to advertise within this periodical should consider the selected character of our clientele and also note the necessary conspicuity of the display; the size of the pages preventing any particular adv. from being buried."[64] They offered a "first advertisers discount" and promised that all ads will be marked plainly as such, a reference to

63. Du Bois, "The Song of the Smoke," *Horizon,* February 1907, 5–6.
64. *Horizon,* January 1907, 25. The size issue referred to the *Horizon's* "magazinelet" format, which appears on the microfilm to be about 6 × 9"; the magazine usually had only two ads per page.

the "reading ads" that appeared to be portraits of a company's growth but were in fact calls for investors—like those that appeared in the *Colored American* and *Alexander's*. The magazine soon carried ads for sympathetic (or at least not hostile) newspapers and magazines, including the *Guardian,* the *Voice,* and *Alexander's,* as well as for the Murray Bros. printing firm, and some local (Washington, D.C.) services and stores. But the advertising was never abundant, and it dropped off considerably after the first year.

It is difficult to know how many subscribers the magazine had, though magazine historian Walter Daniel estimates that circulation reached as high as three thousand. The magazine was linked to the Niagara Movement, and Du Bois regularly commented on the activities of the movement's annual meetings, but the link between the magazine and the movement was never such that the magazine was guaranteed a certain number of Niagara Movement subscribers. But Du Bois knew from the first that building a successful magazine would be difficult, noting that "Newspapers and magazines for the general public have achieved national circulation by two methods: a high subscription price or multitudinous advertisements. Both of these methods are at present impossible for the Negro; we are a poor people. The only methods are these: to seek secret subsidy or openly to make up the annual deficit."[65] A year and a half into their venture, the editors of the *Horizon* sought openly to make up the annual deficit. "Of course it might struggle on by appeals, campaign funds and graft—but as a straight-out, independent, business proposition a national Negro magazine will not pay yet. . . . This means that somebody must foot the bill." Thus began a regular series of calls for "guarantors" to offer twenty-five dollars to help the editors pay the annual deficit they incurred in putting forth a magazine so obviously helpful to the race.

Such a call for help was usually a death knell for Negro publications—as for white publications—but in the case of the *Horizon* it portended instead a kind of rebirth. Rather than deteriorating in quality and shrinking in size, the *Horizon* took a ten-month break from publishing, improved its typesetting, revitalized its design, and increased its size to the more standard 8 1/2 × 11" format. When it returned to the newsstands in November of 1909, Du Bois, now listed as the main editor with unnamed assistant editors, announced:

> This is a radical paper. It stands for progress and advance. It advocates Negro equality and human equality; it stands for Universal suffrage, including votes for Women; it believes in the abolition of War, the taxation of monopoly values, the gradual socialization of capital and the overthrow of persecution and dogmatism in the name of religion. . . . No periodical that advocates unpopular

65. Du Bois, "The Horizon," *Horizon,* July 1908, 2.

or partially popular causes, can be a self-supporting business proposition. A modern magazine gets its support from advertisements. Paying revenue of that sort cannot be expected for such a monthly as this. We must depend upon subscription and donations.

Du Bois further amplified on these comments several months later when he explained that "Certain vehicles of thought, defense and exposition are often needed even when they are not commercially profitable—that is even when many of those for whom they work are not convinced of their need."[66]

These statements indicate a monumental and crucial step in the development of the Negro magazine, for they announce that the issues Du Bois found most crucial to Negro progress could not be contained within a commercial medium, both because advertisers did not wish to be associated with such radicalism and because an insufficient number of Negroes had or were willing to spend the money to support such an endeavor. What was needed for such a magazine to survive was affiliation with an organization, and Du Bois now placed the *Horizon* "under the patronage of the Niagara Movement," an organization that enjoyed enough philanthropic backing and had enough paying members to float a small magazine. The July 1910 issue of the *Horizon* was its last, but an announcement inside boded well for the future of Du Bois as editor, for the Niagara Movement had transformed itself into the National Association for the Advancement of Colored People and would soon begin publishing a new magazine, the *Crisis*, with Du Bois at the helm. With the NAACP's backing of the *Crisis*, Du Bois would prove that an editor need not truckle to white opinion or court commercial interests to succeed. With the *Crisis*, Du Bois would advocate Negro strength and equality and soon gain a hundred thousand subscribers.

Du Bois's recognition that radical black magazines were unlikely to attract advertisers also had implications for the impact of consumer culture on images of black masculinity. In white magazines, images of modern masculinity were first introduced and promoted by advertisers eager to cast men as consumers of their products. In black magazines, such images simply did not appear and thus black men were not exposed to images that explicitly constructed them in terms of consumption, self-realization, and personality. Obviously, black men came across images of masculine consumption in white magazines, but those images were neither about black men nor aimed toward them. (And the very fact that black men had to struggle to achieve the rudiments of white manhood meant that such images must have been viewed with a sense of bitterness.) The absence of images of consuming masculinity from black magazines, and

66. Du Bois, *Horizon*, November 1909, 1; "The New Horizon," *Horizon*, January 1910, 1.

of the pressures that those images entailed, meant that the editorial agenda drove presentations of masculinity in black magazines far more than in white publications.

The *Voice of the Negro*

No early black magazine made as strong a start as the Atlanta-based *Voice of the Negro*. When it first appeared in January of 1904, the magazine boasted that it was "the first magazine ever edited in the south by Colored Men." This is not to say that the magazine was funded by colored men; in fact, the venture was underwritten by the Atlanta branch of the Illinois-based Hertel, Jenkins, and Company Publishing House. According to Daniel, the company's managers thought that a magazine could be a profitable accompaniment to the company's extensive southern publishing ventures.[67] Backed by an established publishing firm, the magazine had from the first issue a more polished look than its competitors: the type was distinct, the pictures of high quality, the page layout clean. Perhaps attracted by the attractive layout and the strong financial backing of the magazine, a number of advertisers signed on from the first issue.

The editorial board was equally well chosen. Consisting of John Wesley Edward Bowen, president of Gammon Theological Seminary in Atlanta; Emmett J. Scott, Booker T. Washington's personal secretary; and the lesser-known Jesse Max Barber, a recent graduate of Virginia Union University, the editorial board seemed chosen to pursue a moderate path in promoting racial causes, a path well-suited to Atlanta's self-styled role as the leading city of the New South. There can be little doubt that Washington used his substantial leverage as the best-known American Negro to place Emmett Scott on the board, but Washington's distance from the editorial offices and Scott's differences of opinion with Barber kept them from unduly influencing the character of the magazine. As the least known and the least busy of the editorial board members, Barber became the editorial voice and the workhorse of the magazine.

Despite his youth and his relative inexperience in running a magazine— he had merely managed his university's promotional publications—Barber proved an able and farsighted editor. From the first issue he attempted to set a clear course for the magazine's development, a course that would steer directly between the Scylla and Charybdis of racial politics, radicalism and accommodationism. "*The Voice of the Negro* enters the field of magazine literature modestly but with a high purpose. In these strenuous days of literary and commercial competition, none but the best is able to stand and receive the

---

67. *Voice of the Negro,* January 1904; Daniel, *"Voice of the Negro,"* in Daniel, *Black Journals,* 369.

patronage of the reading public," Barber wrote in his first editorial. The *Voice of the Negro* "is not a political magazine . . . ; [i]t is our purpose to steer clear of the prophets, seers and visionaries who dream dreams and prophesy out of their lurid imaginations or unreasoning hopes. . . . [T]he magazine will be all that the best cultured taste will demand and superb skill can command."[68] And indeed it was, for, from the first issue and for the first several years, the magazine featured some of the best race writers of the day, from both camps of race policy. In the first issue alone, Booker T. Washington, who used his familiar parable of the sweet potato farmer to preach uplift through labor, was paired off with Kelly Miller, who argued for the "Negro as a political factor." Succeeding issues included essays by W. E. B. Du Bois, Archibald Grimke, Reverdy Ransom, and other notables.

Though the *Voice of the Negro* maintained its quality of production and continued to gain advertisers in its first six months, the peaceful middle way of the editorial board was soon shattered by disagreements between Scott and Barber. Barber's editorials, while tamer than the fiery briefs that Du Bois would pen for the *Moon* and the *Horizon*, indicated his growing sense of alignment with the radical cause. "We shall cry aloud against anything short of manhood recognition for our people. . . . We ask no excuse of our friends anywhere for our lack of refined cowardice," Barber explained in response to letters asking him to tone down his pleas for racial justice. In September he declared that "A Voteless citizen is not a citizen; he is a subject and subjects belong to monarchies while citizens rule republics." Such comments carried an implied critique of Washington's policies to which Scott could not help but object. According to Scott, what he objected to even more was Barber's "malevolent spirit," his "nagging propensities," and his "overweening egotism and acceptance of everything as an insult."[69] Scott resigned his position as associate editor, leaving the editorial policy entirely in the hands of Barber and Bowen, the latter of whom seemed to exercise little influence at all.

However such editorial disputes might have ruffled the participants, they had little apparent effect on the success of the magazine. On the first anniversary of the magazine's publication Barber boasted that "the literary outlay of THE VOICE OF THE NEGRO from North to South has been the best that the Negro race has ever produced, the equal to the best in other magazines of its grade and work, and has been unsurpassed by the best in any of the

68. J. Max Barber, "First Words," *Voice of the Negro,* January 1904, 33.
69. Barber, "With Malice toward None," *Voice,* April 1904, 208; Barber, "Our Political Number," *Voice,* September 1904; Emmett Jay Scott to Hertel, Jenkins, and Company, August 4, 1904, in *Booker T. Washington Papers,* ed. Louis R. Harlan and Raymond W. Smith, vol. 8, *1904–1906,* 38–39.

best." It was no idle boast, for the *Voice* outclassed all of its competitors in layout and execution. Moreover, Barber crowed, "We have a larger bona fide, paid up subscription list than any other Negro periodical in the land, newspaper or magazine, and that list is greater than many published by the more favored race. We believe that in another year we will begin to take our place along side some of the great magazines in point of subscription list." Barber had reason to be proud, for his publication had indeed reached the highest circulation of any Negro periodical of the time: twenty thousand subscribers at a time when five thousand was considered successful for a Negro magazine.[70]

The magazine attracted more than the usual number of advertisers as well. During 1905, the *Voice* typically carried five pages of advertising in the front and nine pages in the back. The dominant advertisers were railway companies—often offering fares for those leaving the South for parts west and north—hair treatments, herbal medicines, and, in the July and August issues, black colleges; the Metropolitan Mercantile and Realty Company and Coca-Cola regularly ran full-page ads. Though the magazine was clearly more successful than its competitors in gaining advertisements, it lobbied for more in one of the first attempts by a black magazine to convince advertisers of the value of the Negro market. "Why would it pay you to advertise among colored people?" asks a full-page ad in July of 1907. The ad suggests four reasons: because "this is a class of people that have to buy as well as any other"; "they have the money to buy good stuff"; "the day has come when the idea that having a colored trade is injurious to the business, has been dispersed"; "the colored people have not been flooded with advertisements, and the quicker you begin the better." "To reach these people you must place your advertisements in the largest circulated colored periodicals. The 'Voice' guarantees a larger circulation than any other colored magazine in THE WORLD."[71]

Though Barber grew to defend the principal tenets of radical journalism—which in his case meant primarily advocacy for voting rights, insistence on equal justice before the law, and reasoned ridicule of Washington's programs—his depiction of black masculinity remained distinctly moderate. Where Du Bois and his fellow editors at *Horizon* would declare that the soul of manhood required fierce advocacy for equal rights, indeed that to be a man was to be willing to die for those rights, Barber blandly declared that "the writer believes that the race should contend manfully for the right of suffrage. . . . We have

70. Barber, "In the Sanctum," *Voice,* January 1905, 694, 695. The circulation of twenty thousand was claimed by Barber, while Daniel cites the magazine's highest circulation as fifteen thousand.

71. *Voice,* July 1907, 436.

no sympathy with the gratuitous counsel given the race at times that it should keep out of politics. On the other hand, we advise the race not to give up any right."[72] To the extent that Barber prescribed for men the qualities that they would need to bear their burden, he counseled black men to cultivate character, an ill-defined quality that seemed to rest on a disdain for money for money's sake and a belief in the uplifting potential of a liberal education.

Nor did Barber encourage his regular contributors to debate the qualities of manhood suitable to racial advancement. While the *Voice* never included the biographical features that other magazines used to champion certain styles of achieving success in the world, John Henry Adams occasionally contributed "Rough Sketches" of notable Negroes. A better cartoonist than writer, Adams began each sketch with a tribute to the power of biography "to lead, to teach, to inspire man" and proceeded to lay out the lives of his subjects with such a lack of detail and an abundance of abstract descriptors that a reader could easily lose the man amid the flurry of words like "strength," "honesty," "vigor," "honor," and "fame."[73]

Adams's point was far clearer, however, when he gave up the attempt to talk about any one individual and mused instead upon the distinguishing characteristics of what he called "The New Negro Man." Tracing the life of this representative man from the cradle through boyhood and college days and on into a productive life, Adams points to the pitfalls that await the black youth—the passions of the body, the urging of others to accept a life of menial labor, the pull of the seamier side of Negro life—but asserts that the new man "clings to his aspiration to be a man," aided by his "mother's ringing words of love-truth," and "his pastor's soul inspiring sermons." A college graduate—in fact, a valedictorian—he moves out into the community and in a half-dozen years that "black man . . . has gone where there seemed to be no water and brought forth the sparkling flow to which his people may go and quench their longing thirst."[74]

"The new Negro man . . . sees nothing but vital principles to sustain him in his struggle for place and power," writes Adams in his concluding passages. "He will do this not for his own sake entirely, but for the sake of humanity. . . . The present fight is a fight for manhood—not man. Man dies. Manhood lives

---

72. Barber, "Hands Off," *Voice,* March 1906, 216. The "gratuitous counsel" came from Washington, who Barber skewers in several other editorials as well; see *Voice,* January 1905, 670; *Voice,* February 1905, 126; *Voice,* November 1905, 3; *Voice,* May 1906, 317.

73. While the "man" in Adams's "to inspire man" is ungendered, the fact that all the examples he uses are of men indicates that the real lessons of these sketches are meant for men.

74. John Henry Adams, "The New Negro Man," *Voice,* October 1904, 449, 450.

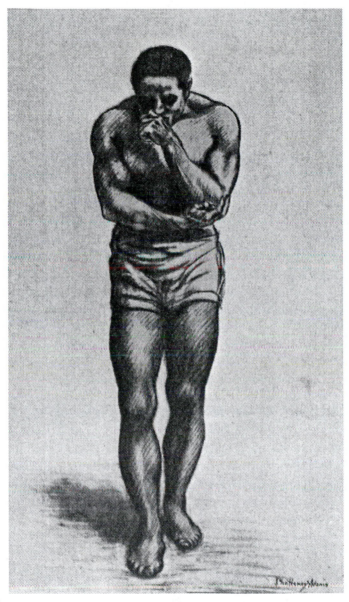

"Why Stand Ye There Face Down, Strong Man," asked the caption to this illustration from the *Voice of the Negro*. The *Voice* urged black men to reject Booker T. Washington's accommodationist policies and advocate for full citizenship. Editor Jesse Max Barber was run out of Atlanta after he published unflattering accounts of the 1906 race riots that shook the city, and the magazine soon died (*Voice of the Negro*, April 1906, 282).

forever."[75] Such a paean to the principles of Victorian manhood makes perfect sense within the context of white publications of this era and earlier; exclude the references to race and it would fit nicely in *Munsey's* or in a Teddy Roosevelt speech. While such constructions of manhood may not have been as bold or forthright as those offered by Du Bois in the *Horizon,* they probably reflected an accurate assessment of how strong a presentation of black manhood could be offered within the southern city of Atlanta at a time of white backlash. Though there is no direct evidence to prove that Barber restrained expressions about masculinity, it is easy to imagine that he was aware of the very real dangers involved in expressing ideas about black strength and equality in a city where newspapers like the *Atlanta News* regularly incited hatred and even violence against "uppity" blacks. In any case, the *Voice of the Negro* hewed to a safe way of heralding the qualities of Negro men in this polarized time. Perhaps it required bravery enough merely to advance the radical cause from a southern base.

That there were limits to what a black magazine editor could express in the South was soon confirmed to Barber and his readers by a series of events that led to Barber's fleeing the city and to the eventual demise of a very healthy magazine. The October 1906 issue of the *Voice* was late in coming, and Barber began his editorial remarks with this "Notice": "We wish to apologize to our subscribers for the lateness in the appearance of the October number of the magazine. On account of recent disturbances in the city of Atlanta, it has been deemed advisable to move the office of publication from Atlanta, Ga., to Chicago, Ill."[76] This rather bland announcement masked what was in fact an incredibly tumultuous few weeks for Barber and the *Voice.* On September 22, the city of Atlanta had erupted in rioting, as reports of black men attacking white women brought out white mobs who attacked and killed numbers of black men and terrorized the black community. *Atlanta Constitution* editor John Temple Graves wired the *New York World* with news that a "carnival of rapes" had invited recriminations against Atlanta's black community. Incensed, Barber wrote a letter of his own to the paper, laying the blame for the riots on a "carnival of newspaper lies" and a political campaign by Hoke Smith that was aimed at inciting race hatred. Moreover, Barber claimed that the riots were instigated by white men disguised as Negroes who feigned attacks on white women to alarm the white population. Though he signed the letter "A Colored Citizen," white community leaders quickly traced the letter to Barber and called on him to, in Barber's words, "leave the city or suffer any penalty the community might see fit to inflict. He [Barber] left not because he feared

75. Ibid., 450.
76. Barber, "Notice," *Voice,* October 1906, 437.

a mob but a legal lynching." Barber was one of the many African Americans to leave Atlanta, according to historian Charles Crowe, who claimed that the riot "burst into reality with the full impact of a long expected nightmare . . . [as] white Atlanta seemed to be surrendering to its own sense of inevitability."[77]

Barber's eviction from the South—"the land of our birth and rearing, and the place where all we have is dear to us"—inspired some of his most passionate and exciting writing. In articles titled "Why Mr. Barber Left Atlanta" and "The Atlanta Tragedy," Barber recounts in dramatic detail the events that led up to the riots and to his being run out of town. "I have had the audacity to beard a coterie of politicians in their den and to expose their cowardice to the people. They are out for my scalp. Let them get it." From his safe address in Chicago, he was able to blast at southern whites with a venom he had heretofore had to restrain.[78]

While the personal attack and relocation inspired more powerful and indignant rhetoric from Barber, it also placed the magazine in grave financial danger. In the very first announcement of the magazine's move, Barber announced that the Voice Publishing Company, incorporated only six months earlier, had lost much of its property. The extent of the magazine's losses would not become clear for some months, but Barber took several immediate steps to right the financial boat. He implored subscribers to pay their late subscriptions now, and to get friends to subscribe as well. He offered Voice Publishing Company stock at four dollars a share, a substantial discount from the ten dollars at which the stock had been selling before the relocation. And he began to tinker with the format of the magazine, changing the name to simply the *Voice* and recrafting the titles, though not the content, of the editorial sections. The name change, he explained, was meant to situate the magazine better in its northern context, for "we expect to do a large amount of business with the white people. . . . In the long run we have got to live from the advertisements we carry. We expect a majority of those from white firms because such an overwhelming preponderance of business is in their hands." Such an admission seems to reveal that the Voice Publishing Company was without money and no longer receiving any help from the magazine's white founders. Little did Barber know how difficult getting white advertising dollars into black magazines would be.[79]

For several months the *Voice* continued on as a healthy and seemingly intact magazine, but the stresses of the relocation began to show as advertising slowly

77. Barber, "Shall the Press Be Free?" *Voice*, October 1906, 392; Charles Crowe, "Racial Massacre in Atlanta, September 22, 1906," *Journal of Negro History* 54 (1969): 151–52.

78. Barber, "Why Mr. Barber Left Atlanta," and "The Atlanta Tragedy," *Voice*, November 1906, 470–73, 473–79.

79. Barber, "Our Name Changed," *Voice*, November 1906, 464.

disappeared and as fewer and fewer articles were published. Finally, in May of 1907, Barber admitted that "It cost us tremendously to start over in business here in Chicago," and that they had had to pay for publication of the magazine on a month-by-month basis. "In trying to wipe out our indebtedness we appealed first to certain wealthy Negroes who claimed to admire our magazine. We did not care for the general public to know of our condition for the reason that we feared that public confidence would be crippled and in the end we would suffer. Not one of them responded favorably to our call and some never even acknowledged our letter." Next, Barber said, he had appealed to white friends, who helped out enough to finance one more issue. "Now," he continued, "we take the public into our confidence. We need $3,000 in the next sixty days. . . . Can we have that money? Is it worth $3,000 to the race to save THE VOICE? We firmly believe our 15,000 subscribers will answer, 'Yes.' " This plea bought the magazine five more months, but by October 1907 Barber was again calling for help: "Finally, friends, while we are saved for a year and will be able to give you the magazine regularly and promptly, the future is in your hands. You must rally around us if you would always have us grow and continue. A dollar is not much to risk on us. We are risking our reputation and the best years of our life on you. And we do it gladly."[80] But in the end, they sacrificed to no avail, for this issue of the *Voice* was to be the last, and the magazine disappeared.

The *Voice of the Negro* is clearly one of the most important of the early black periodicals, its importance diminished only by its short life span. Just after incorporating in May of 1906, Barber mused that "it is not too much to believe the THE VOICE OF THE NEGRO will enjoy a bona fide circulation of 100,000 within three or four years."[81] While such hopes were probably too optimistic, the *Voice* had become the best-selling magazine of its type and had managed to promote a cautiously radical agenda from a southern base. One has to wonder what the magazine might have achieved had Barber not run afoul of the Atlanta power structure and been forced to make a go of it on his own, severely limited resources. As it is, the *Voice* provides a way of seeing radical ideas tempered by the conservative social climate of the South.

If black magazine publishing in the first decade of the century was a battle, it can truly be said that there were no winners. But then, there were not even

80. Barber, "Announcement Extraordinary," *Voice,* May 1907, 162–63; Barber, "Title," *Voice,* October 1907.

81. Barber, *Voice,* May 1906, 308. Barber based this optimistic estimate on a population of ten million Negroes in the United States, of which "nearly 50 per cent are intelligent enough to appreciate a good, bright, well edited and well illustrated magazine." Of course no black magazine would reach a circulation of a hundred thousand until the *Crisis* reached that figure in April of 1918. On the final days of the *Voice,* see also Johnson and Johnson, "Away from Accommodation," 332.

survivors. Each of the magazines I have examined experienced extreme financial difficulty, either because they could not attract advertisers and subscribers or because they attracted the ire of the southern white power structure. In the end, all of the African American magazines begun in the 1900s failed. Depending on the ideological disposition of the magazine editor, that failure was interpreted in different ways. Washingtonians were clearly the more dispirited by their lack of success, for their very message was that blacks could succeed in enterprises aimed at addressing the needs of the black community. In their case, the failure of the publication must have also represented in some way the failure of their mission. Du Bois took the financial difficulties of running his magazines much to heart as well, though he derived different lessons from their failure. The failure of his magazines to make a commercial success—to draw advertising dollars—only confirmed Du Bois's belief that the commercial power structure would not underwrite black dissent, and that the key to success lay in attaining philanthropic and institutional support for his radical platform. For the next three decades the only magazines that succeeded—that survived— were those that sought their support from an institutional affiliation and from philanthropists. The lesson learned by black editors was that the magazine that addressed race issues had as yet no place in the marketplace.

The failure of these magazines as business ventures had lessons for editors' and writers' understanding of black masculinity as well. Both Washingtonian and Du Boisian versions of masculinity relied on an adherence to principle, though the principles adhered to are quite different. In adhering to principle, both partook of the larger commitments and visions of Victorian masculinity, which held that masculinity emanated from a deeply held commitment to a set of shared values; that is, both forms of black masculinity reflected an interpretation of the cult of character. The failure of Washingtonian publishing ventures, and eventually the wide abandonment of the Washingtonian program for racial advancement, especially after Washington's death in 1915, left proponents of Washingtonian masculinity little reason to trumpet the virtues of the self-made man. It seemed that black masculinity must rest on something other than economic success, for that success was to remain circumscribed for some time to come.

While Du Boisians and other radicals would continue to lay claim to a vision of black masculinity that paid homage to traits like character and duty and honor, they would do so in magazines that were, to a large extent, divorced from the commercial markets that helped to shape white masculinity. When white editors paid tribute to Victorian masculine values, they were doing it in large part to continue to channel men's behavior into socially and economically acceptable paths, the paths of business success that they believed still applied to masculine endeavor. With their own publishing ventures as object lessons, black editors had little reason to believe that adhering to Victorian masculine values would lead to economic success, and with that goal removed, their treatment of black masculinity would begin to take on very different tones. Unchained from any imperative to link their notions of masculinity to a socioeconomic structure from which they had reaped few rewards, they could couple their notions of character and manliness to a strong advocacy for citizenship and basic manhood rights. And untouched by the pressures of advertising and consumption, their notions of masculinity would remain distant from those of their white counterparts.

Moreover, the radicals' association of their stance on masculinity with youthfulness—recall Du Bois's conflation of ambitiousness and consciousness of power with youth—was a decisive step away from Victorian notions that manhood was something earned over time through the long-term application of effort and toward the visions of modern manhood that would soon penetrate white magazines. The quintessential Victorian man was the patriarch, the man who had earned his place at the top of the heap after a long struggle. The quintessential radical man was an aggressive youth determined to claim now that which was due him. In important ways, the radical formulation of masculinity recalled the days when white American men claimed their rights as men based on lofty principle and youthful assertiveness. It was a rich heritage of associations from which radicals could draw, and they did so successfully in the years to come.

3

"Horatio Alger Doesn't Work Here Any More"

The Emergence of Modern Masculinity, 1915–1935

The mainstream American magazines published between 1915 and 1925 largely followed the *Saturday Evening Post* in their depictions of American masculinity. Though the *American Magazine* and *Collier's Weekly* aimed at slightly different audiences, their presentations of masculinity echoed the *Post's* contention that the path to manhood still lay in following the dictates of the Victorian cult of character in order to achieve success. Yet even as these magazines continued to reach millions of Americans, forces within and outside the magazine market began to chisel away at the base of Victorian masculinity, offering in its place a set of prescriptions for masculine behavior that were radically different. New magazines like the *New Success* and *Vanity Fair* created visions of masculinity based on personality and self-creation, wealth and appearances; older magazines like *Sporting Life* reoriented the idea of the sportsman to suit the needs of sporting goods salesmen. In creating images of men that were based around consumerism, the cult of personality, and the urge toward self-improvement, such magazines expressed the ethic of corporate marketers and advertisers who were coming to understand the cultural import of mass production and corporatism. Yet these magazines—their editors sometimes and their advertisements especially—were also tuned in to the dynamic of cultural modernism, a dynamic that in the 1920s came to emphasize (among other things) glamour, youth, optimism, and a sense of boundlessness tempered by anxiety. Taken together, and filtered through the hands of editors and contributors who presented these changes with a sense of delight and exhilaration rather than anxiety, these changes announced the emergence of modern masculinity. By the mid-1920s the force of such trends had reached the *American Magazine* and *Collier's* and had begun to transform them: the cultural imperatives of youth, consumerism, personality, and self-improvement echoed through the old magazines in odd ways, challenging editors to modify their editorial policies and adjust their presentations of masculinity. And then the Great Depression came along to challenge the remnant representations of Victorian masculinity, clearing the way for modern masculinity to dominate the magazine market and, by extension, mass culture.

The story that I tell in this chapter is one of transition, from a time when the major American magazines continued to champion the tenets of Victorian masculinity to a time when they embraced modern masculine images and ideals. The chapter spans roughly twenty years, from the emergence of the *American Magazine* as a vehicle for promoting old-fashioned masculine values in 1915 to the same magazine's abandonment of masculine issues in the early 1930s. By 1933—the year that *Esquire* magazine offered itself as "the magazine for men"—American masculinity had undergone a profound transformation. That cultural norms for masculinity should have undergone significant changes in these years should come as no surprise, for little in American culture was left untouched by the cycles of economic boom and bust, by the sweeping political realignments, and by the social fads—the youth craze, changing sexual norms, and so on—that matured into general cultural dispositions in these years. Yet existing explanations of this transition do not go far enough in explaining how it was that economically driven change got translated into new cultural notions of gender identity. What I offer in this chapter is an explanation of how what James Livingston calls the consolidation of consumer capitalism helped reorient the advice and images about masculinity offered within American magazines.[1]

Several forces combined to effect the transformation of American images of masculinity in magazines between 1915 and 1935. The force that scholars understand best is the underlying economic transformation that resulted in the consolidation of consumer capitalism. Editors and advertisers interpreted this transformation primarily in terms of how masculinity might need to be reconfigured in order to best suit men to participate in a bureaucratic corporate workplace in which coworkers and clients were, in effect, strangers. The *American Magazine* especially spent a great deal of its time explaining such issues to American men. If all that the rise of a corporate consumer culture entailed was adjusting men to a changed workplace, however, modern masculinity might not have emerged so rapidly or represented such a decisive break with the past.

Corporatization brought along with it an array of other changes—including urbanization, economic prosperity, mass production, the growth of mass enter-

---

1. Livingston, *Pragmatism and the Political Economy*, 85.

tainment, and the proliferation of consumer goods and their advertisements—
that taken together reshaped and modernized American culture. The American
magazine market reacted to such changes in a number of ways: they took
on an ever greater number of advertisements, and in so doing became ever
more indebted to advertising dollars for their support; they diversified, offering
magazines for more specialized interests and demographic groups; and they
hired editors who saw no contradiction between their editorial and financial
interests. This last point is important, for how we interpret this lack of contradiction is key to whether we view modern masculinity as the calculated creation
of corporate interests or the honest expression of new ways of expressing
masculinity. I argue that modern masculinity was both an honest expression of
freely chosen opportunities and a product of corporate interests eager to create
a populace of eager consumers. In this chapter I trace how modern masculinity
emerged out of the meeting of all these forces, as editors, contributors, and
advertisers asserted their notions of appropriate masculinity within increasingly
commercialized magazines.

Following the *Post:* Victorian Masculinity Lingers On

In 1911, Crowell Publishing Company president Joseph Palmer Knapp added
the *American Magazine* to a roster of periodicals that included *Woman's Home
Companion* and *Farm and Fireside* (later *Country Home*). The *American* had
been run by a group of famous muckrakers, including Ray Stannard Baker,
Lincoln Steffens, and Ida Tarbell, who had become dissatisfied with *McClure's,*
and included William Allen White and Finley Peter Dunne on its editorial
board. Originally a stridently progressive, muckraking organ, the magazine
soon "tempered the severity of its muckraking with material dealing with the
homely affairs of average people."[2] Knapp, recognizing that muckraking had
run its course, offered the editorship of the magazine to the staff member who
could come up with the best idea for saving the magazine. The winner of the
"contest" was John M. Siddall. His idea, a friend later recounted, "was that
people are more interested in themselves than in anything else in the world.
That personal problems mean more to the average man and woman than social
or community problems. That the question, 'How to make a living,' is more
vital than the question, 'How to regulate the railroads.' "[3] Under Siddall, the
American Magazine began to specialize in inspirational biographies of well-

2. Wood, *Magazines in the United States,* 141.
3. John E. Drewry, *Some Magazines and Magazine Makers,* 151. On the magazine's
beginnings, see also Drewry, "The *American Magazine* Adopts a New Success Slant," in
his *Contemporary American Magazines: A Selected Bibliography and Reprints of Articles
Dealing with Various Periodicals,* 1–3.

known men, many of whom ran America's largest corporations. Such stories would inspire men to improve their lives, believed Siddall, by showing them that anything could be accomplished with hard work.

Beginning in 1915, editor Siddall made the *American* into the magazine for the self-made man, corporate style. Few editors ever made their presence better known in a magazine than Siddall, who shaped the work of his stable of writers to make the magazine an unashamedly optimistic booster of American businessmen. Like George Horace Lorimer of the *Post*, Siddall wanted to show that "daily business life was adventure just as surely as life in the remote and romantic regions far from the drab city and the workaday farm." While Lorimer of the *Post* tried to keep himself hidden from public view, never signing his editorials, for example, Siddall seemed to hover over the shoulder of the reader, pointing out the important lessons to be learned in each article in a box that accompanied most articles and some fiction. He wanted to be sure readers got the point; "Give this article a good read," he advised, "for you will benefit from it." Siddall also spoke directly to readers in his monthly editorial, "Sid Says—," sharing his views on the issues of the day. It was in this column in 1921 that "Sid" explained the purpose of the magazine: "Victory. Victory for the individual. Victory over the difficulties and obstacles that beset you."[4]

At the heart of "Sid's" magazine were profiles of men who achieved success through hard work, integrity, dedication, and self-control. It was in the profile that the masculine ideals of Victorian man reigned supreme. A composite portrait of the corporate leader depicted in the early 1920s would show a man in his fifties or sixties who had worked his way to the top of a large company, usually one he had started himself. The man wore a beard and looked directly into the camera. The caption below his picture was a variation on this theme: "Captain Dollar is one of the biggest business men in the United States. He is the creator and owner of the Dollar Steamship Line. He was once a penniless lumberjack. Captain Dollar is a man whose reputation for integrity and ability is such that he was recently commissioned by the United States Government to arrange a thirty-million-dollar shipbuilding contract with the Chinese Government, and was made the depository for receiving these millions without even being asked by either nation to put up a bond!"[5] Such profiles, written under Siddall's

4. Drewry, *Some Magazines,* 152; one boxed comment told readers that in this article they would find "ideas about the *spirit that wins:* whether the game is football, or business, or the greatest game of all—Life itself" (Allan Harding, "How to 'Play Your Game'—Whatever It Is," *American Magazine,* November 1922, 25); John M. Siddall, "Victory—Victory for the Individual," *American Magazine,* July 1921, 14.

5. B. C. Forbes, "A Wonderful Scotchman's Story and Advice," *American Magazine,* January 1919, 17.

In its early years, the *American Magazine* celebrated the self-made business man, usually an older man known for his stalwart character, like businessman Captain Robert Dollar (*American Magazine,* January 1919, 7).

editorship by B. C. Forbes, Bruce Barton, Mary B. Mullett, Merle Crowell, and several others, were mini-bildungsromans, showing how a man committed to hard work and integrity from his early days steadily rose to the top. They were portraits of a unitary male self, a self launched on an upward trajectory toward success in a world of other men.

It was not only businessmen who taught readers the values associated with *American*-style manhood. Football coaches, professors, athletes, and preachers were also called upon to do their duty. Fielding H. Yost, the illustrious coach of the University of Michigan football squad, advised readers, "Never lose your self-control. . . . Never stop fighting. . . . Be aggressive," and concluded that character is the number one thing that wins ball games. James H. Foster, president of the Hydraulic Pressed Steel Company of Cleveland, Ohio, wrote his own copy for an article titled "Men are *Square*." His own way of dealing with disputes between labor and capital was simple: he reminded himself that workers were men just like himself. Putting himself in the worker's shoes, he wrote: "You wanted your boss to recognize that you were men—with all the pride, the self-respect and the right to happiness of every other human being." Dr. Frank Crane listed the "Ten Good Points" that defined the religion of everyday man: Truth, Law, Justice, Work, Democracy, Mercy, Monogamy, Optimism, Science, and God.[6] Again and again, articles in the *American* in the early twenties drove home the essential tenets of success unsullied by qualification or doubt. All a man had to do was model his character after these essential attributes and he would succeed.

The fiction published in the *American* served the same ends. Harold Titus's "The Stuff of Heroes" is a telling example of an *American* staple, the workplace story. The story opens, "Until his brother-in-law died and left Emmy with two children . . . and without a roof or a dollar, the details of living had been of little consequence to Henry Boggs." Shouldering these obligations, Boggs becomes a dynamo in his workplace, unselfishly and almost single-handedly resuscitating the flagging department in which he works as a clerk. The story concludes with Boggs winning a big promotion and the heart of the girl he has admired. The lesson: honor family responsibilities and work hard, and the rewards you desire will follow. A nearly identical conclusion is drawn in "Where Their Roads

6. Allan Harding, "How to 'Play Your Game'—Whatever It Is," 25, 84; James H. Foster, "Men Are *Square*," *American Magazine,* February 1920, 16; Dr. Frank Crane, "Ten Good Points about the 'Everyday Man,'" *American Magazine,* January 1919, 44–45. See also Allison Gray, "'Chick' Evans on Golf as a Test of Character," *American Magazine,* July 1919, 34, 150–54; James Harvey Robinson, "The Seven Greatest Americans," *American Magazine,* June 1923, 13–15, 136–42; and Grantland Rice, "Do Your Stuff," *American Magazine,* July 1924, 45, 169–71.

Parted," by Mella Russell McCallum. In this story, two college chums who once longed for literary success meet after several years apart. Bachelor Bob Daynes finds his old friend Dick married and haggard, tied to the obligations of a wife and family, and he thinks, "Something young was slipping from Dick." Yet for all his vaunted freedom, Bob cannot find the motivation to complete the book he hoped to write. And despite his responsibilities, Dick does write a fine and popular book. In the end, the "victorious" Dick says to Bob, "When are you going to get yourself a wife and family, old bystander?" Again, the lesson is that obligation and duty and sacrifice are the qualities that make the man, not youth and energy and vitality.[7]

While the *American Magazine* reinterpreted the basic ideals of Victorian manhood to an urban male audience, *Collier's: The National Weekly* attempted to do the same for a rural audience. *Collier's* was a magazine with a long and fairly distinguished history. Founded in 1888 by Irish immigrant Peter Fenlon Collier, the magazine joined with other participants in the magazine revolution of the 1890s in offering decent fiction, plentiful photos, and a variety of articles at a cheap price. *Collier's* published better material than many magazines, featuring such writers as Henry James, Frank Norris, James Whitcomb Riley, Rudyard Kipling, Robert Chambers, and others. In the first decades of the twentieth century *Collier's* was a leader in color magazine illustration and featured southwestern scenes by Frederic Remington, Maxfield Parrish's "Arabian Nights" scenes, and Charles Dana Gibson's famous Gibson girls. Under Norman Hapgood's editorship, from 1902 to 1912, *Collier's* was known as "one of the most influential magazines in the country."[8] But the magazine declined following Hapgood's departure, churning through a succession of editors from 1912 through the early 1920s.

Despite frequent changes of editor, *Collier's* maintained an editorial policy that appealed predominantly to a small-town business class, a class neither too close to the farm to be rubes nor too distant from it to be unmoved by pastoral, republican visions. The magazine's editorials were often delivered by a fictional character named Uncle Henry, who ruminated upon the concerns of the day in a down-home, "aw shucks" kind of way. A regular column called "What the Folks

7. Harold Titus, "The Stuff of Heroes," *American Magazine,* August 1924, 23–25, 72–74; Mella Russell McCallum, "Where Their Roads Parted," *American Magazine,* June 1923, 31–33, 102–8. In "Outwitting the Flapper," *American Magazine* (March 1923, 30–31, 104–15), Dorothy Sanburn Phillips delivered a similar rebuke to single youth when she tells of a Victorian mother teaching her college-age son how to avoid the snares of loose modern girls. Suspicion toward youth remained constant in the *American Magazine* in the 1920s.
8. Norman Vogt, *"Collier's,"* in Nourie and Nourie, *Mass Market Magazines,* 54.

Are Thinking About . . ." featured the opinion of a reader from a small town in the heartland, an opinion that the magazine implicitly supported. In 1924, editor Loren Palmer responded to a long-standing request to announce the magazine's editorial policy with a credo he titled "It Is Our Firm Conviction." Palmer claimed that *Collier's* was for prosperity and opportunity for all, but believed that to "get there we don't need to try new and unusual ways of doing things" but rather must stick with methods "which have already been tried and proved."[9] The magazine's biggest concerns, he continued, were with raising standards of education and health, with arguing the cause of the farmer, with ending waste in government and in the productive economy, with awakening an interest in public affairs, and with assuring peace. In all, it was a pleasant, liberal expression of the views of small-town America.

The magazine's depiction of the roles of men was equally benign, echoing with the variations on Victorian manhood initiated by the *Saturday Evening Post* and updated by the *American Magazine*. Walter Camp, whose writings on football were ubiquitous in the 1920s, took the recently concluded war as the cue for his ruminations on the man-making qualities of the gridiron game: "As long as we are breeding youths with virile mind and body, youths to be the backbone of this nation, football will be played and played in deadly earnest. Every boy who is to become a real man in the light in which we now have learned to view the real man has bred in the very marrow of his bones the desire for personally physical combat with boys his own age on the athletic field, and no game so simulates the features of such personal combat as does the sport of football. . . . [B]est of all, that grand do-or-die spirit that holds the attack on the one-yard line was what made Chateau-Thierry."[10] Camp and other writers took the war as evidence that America's youth were up to the standards of old, believing in the same standards of honor and fair play that had sustained earlier generations.

"Fear," a story penned by Lucian Cary for *Collier's* in 1919, relates a similar vision of traditional masculinity. Mechanic Jim Fallon was, like his father, a "man who knew steel as few workmen ever know it. Fine workmanship was his religion. He dealt in ten-thousandths of an inch as other men deal in halves and quarters." Yearning to be a pilot, Fallon goes on a pilgrimage to Detroit, gets a job in an aircraft engine shop, and soon conquers his fear of heights in order first to fly and finally to become a pilot. As the story progresses, Fallon achieves mastery as a pilot and eventually ventures to become the first pilot to fly across

9. Loren Palmer, "It Is Our Firm Conviction," *Collier's*, April 5, 1924, 5.
10. Walter Camp, "The All-America Team: Annual Review of the Football Season," *Collier's*, January 4, 1919, 13.

the Atlantic. Disdaining the applause of the crowds, Fallon is most proud of his mastery over his machine and over his own fears. Like the tales told in the *Post* and the *American Magazine*, Fallon's is a tale of self-control, of perseverance, and of the attainment of a long-held ambition.[11]

"A Man's Job," by Walter A. Dyer, tells the story of a Coast Guard rescue during a yacht race, closing with this paean to manhood:

> There at Race Point we came in contact with about the finest thing in the world, it seems to me—not culture, not wealth, not social distinction, not fame, not genius, not princely power, but simplicity, unquestioning courage, obedience to the rules of the game, devotion to the job, strength, competence, the dignity of a noble calling, duty, manhood, honor. . . . There are dastards enough in the world . . . but there are men, too, and they go on, in the hidden places, quietly doing their appointed work, saving lives, saving honor, keeping the faith, giving much and asking little. That, and not Wall Street or Washington, is America![12]

Such views of masculinity were characteristic of *Collier's* despite the instability of the editorial staff. The continuity in representations of manhood should not be too surprising, for the magazine merely represented those views that were most prevalent in American magazines and indeed in American culture. Through the early 1920s, the language of Victorian masculinity—the web of references to character, self-control, and so on—was the common language of any magazine that did not purposefully set out to reinterpret the meaning of gender roles.

Though he managed a much smaller empire in print, John L. Griffith, editor of an amateur sports monthly called the *Athletic Journal* and the Commissioner of Athletics of the Big Ten Conference, was also interested in preserving the Victorian masculine ethic. Griffith launched his magazine in March of 1921, hoping to draw upon the heightened public interest in athleticism that had been promoted by the recent war. "The world war demonstrated the value of athletics in the life of the nation," noted Griffith in the first of his regular editorials, and he hoped his magazine would promote the athletic training of men in the college and high schools of the nation.[13] Griffith's magazine carried little advertising, especially in the first few years, and then only for athletic equipment and sports-related education and camps; many of the articles were written by Griffith himself, many others by college coaches and athletic directors; though no definite circulation figures are available, the audience Griffith addressed

---

11. Lucian Cary, "Fear," *Collier's*, June 7, 1919, 7–8, 30–36.
12. Walter A. Dyer, "A Man's Job," *Collier's*, June 2, 1923, 28.
13. John L. Griffith, *Athletic Journal*, March 1921, 8–9.

included those interested in promoting athletics and could not have been large.[14] Yet Griffith elaborated upon the prevailing versions of masculinity, constructing in his pages an ideal of manhood more vigilant in its self-control and stern in its asceticism than anything imagined by more mainstream editors.

Though Griffith began his magazine with the simple idea of promoting athletics, that agenda quickly expanded to saving the souls of American male youths, indeed the soul of America. "The Journal . . . believes that if our sports are properly coached, are extended to include large numbers of competitors and are in the hands of men who are concerned with improving the quality of manhood in America, that then our athletics are second in importance to no other constructive agency." Athletics taught men how to win at life, argued Griffith, and "when a true sportsman loses or fails to succeed, he doesn't blame society or the government and turn bolshevist, but he takes off his coat and fights a little bit harder to win."[15] Griffith's justification for beginning the magazine soon turned into a crusade to maintain the standards of "Spartan" amateur athleticism in the face of a wide array of challenges posed by an American culture that often appeared hostile to those standards.

Griffith feared that the values of strenuous athletic competition were coming under attack in the 1920s and, especially, in the 1930s. Professional athletics posed one sort of challenge to his virtuous athletic code, for they promoted winning over competition and encouraged men to use any means to attain their end. More dangerous yet were those who wanted to curb competition to allow "weaker" sorts to participate and enjoy sports. In 1925, Griffith complained that "ladies of both sexes are preaching a doctrine of athletics which . . . would develop men of weak and insipid character. What we need is more of the strenuous life, more of the rugged sports, more of the idea that a man should do his best in athletics and in everything else." Griffith carried this idea to its logical conclusion by 1932, when he argued that "Today, whether we like it or not, we are working out the principle of the survival of the fittest. The weak will perish and the strong will survive. . . . [T]he men with fighting hearts and with minds that think straight, will be in the forefront."[16]

In the end, the American Magazine, Collier's, and the Athletic Journal all worked the soil that was sown for them by the Saturday Evening Post. The

<hr/>

14. Griffith cites a circulation of fourteen thousand in 1939 ("An American Type," Athletic Journal, June 1939, 20), but that is the only circulation figure I saw quoted in the years under study.

15. Griffith, "The Journal Next Year," Athletic Journal, May 1922, 16; Griffith, "A Challenge," Athletic Journal, October 1922, 14.

16. Griffith, "Competition," Athletic Journal, May 1925, 14–15; Griffith, "Athletics in a Time of Depression," Athletic Journal, December 1932, 7.

larger magazines were all roughly alike: they carried the same ads, published short fiction from many of the same writers, and hewed to a liberal Republican party line. If anything, *Collier's* was more like the *Post* in not commenting self-consciously on the nature of masculinity. All of these magazines subscribed to the notion that manhood was central to the vitality of the American republic, and that all would be right with the nation as long as men continued to practice the virtues that had built the country in the nineteenth century. Yet for all the certainty with which these magazines promoted their visions of masculinity, their magazines and American masculinity were soon to be changed by trends in American culture and in the American magazine market.

Modernizing Influences: Consumerism and Personality

While magazines like the *American Magazine, Collier's,* the *Athletic Journal,* and the *Saturday Evening Post* continued to pay homage to Victorian masculinity, a new breed of magazine began to offer new ways to conceive of masculine gender roles and new ways to conceive of the relationship between advertising and editorial content. In some cases—*Sporting Life* and *Athletic World*—these were old kinds of magazines changing direction to try to find an audience in the competitive magazine marketplace, while in other cases—the *New Success* and *Vanity Fair*—they were entrepreneurial ventures hoping to offer an entirely new kind of journalistic product. Modifying or rejecting altogether the traits associated with Victorian masculinity, aligning their interests with those of the advertisers who underwrote their publications, these magazines articulated over the course of a dozen years some of the fundamental elements of a new, more modern style of masculinity. The new ideal that they came to embrace, the ideal of modern masculinity, proved far more amenable to the fast-paced culture of commercial society and to the agenda of corporations and marketers. In short, these magazines began to represent and articulate visions of American masculinity that better suited men to function in a corporatized consumer culture.

No single magazine better narrates the emergence of modern masculine norms from the ashes of Victorian clichés than Orison Swett Marden's the *New Success,* which began publication in January of 1918. The *New Success* was not Marden's first publishing venture, for he had begun publishing a magazine called *Success* in 1897. The first *Success* cataloged the qualities that would lead to success—"purity, perseverance, patience, prudence, . . . concentration, courage, character"—but it failed to attract a large readership and it foundered when its editors tried to ride the coattails of the fading muckraking movement. By 1911 the magazine was sold and quickly disappeared. Taking his own advice, Marden persevered and found a new financial backer, Chicago manufacturer

Frederick C. Lowrey, who bankrolled the founding of the magazine aptly named
the *New Success.*[17]

"The purpose of *The New Success,*" wrote Marden in his opening editorial,
"is to clear the vision, stir the ambition, to strengthen the will of every one of
its readers." Marden still promoted a set of traits and habits that were needed
to make a success, but those traits and habits were now shaded with a new
emphasis, what would later be called the power of positive thinking. Marden's
opening words are worth quoting at length.

> *The New Success* is a magazine with a personal message. It is a forerunner
> of the new order of things, the new ideals and the new times, the new day
> which is dawning, the new conditions which are being evolved. . . . *The New
> Success* will give inspiring examples of success. These stirring life stories of
> great lives will show our readers how to develop their own resourcefulness,
> their own inventiveness, ingenuity, and originality. They will show them how to
> become independent, self-reliant, courageous, masterful, and will spur them
> to attempt the greater things which they are able to do and ought to do. . . .
> *The New Success* will show its readers that we tend to get what we expect, and
> that ill-health, poverty, unhappiness, are largely the result of our own negative
> thought. Only thru right thinking can we bring ourselves into conscious union
> with the great Source of infinite life, the Source of health, harmony, abundance,
> success. . . . *The New Success* will show you how, coupled with your highest
> endeavor, you can think yourself out of discord into harmony, out of disease into
> health, out of poverty into plenty, out of darkness into light, out of hatred into
> love, out of poverty into success and prosperity. . . . *The New Success* will put
> great emphasis upon the truth that to build a superb personality, a magnificent
> character, to acquire personal power for use in the service of mankind is the
> highest success.[18]

Many of the words and images Marden uses to characterize his vision of success
were no doubt familiar to readers of American magazines, words like *character,
self-reliance, perseverance,* and so on. They were the common stock-in-trade
of any wordsmith discussing success and the American man. Yet Marden also
drew on a new set of ideals when he used terms like *personality, inventiveness,
originality,* and *personal power* to suggest to men that there were other ways to
pursue success. That set of ideals came out of the New Thought movement that
had started in the 1880s and gained a number of adherents in the ensuing years.
At the core of the New Thought ideology was the notion that one could think
his way to success, that concentrating on what one wanted—success, money,

17. On Marden and his magazines, see Margaret Connolly, *The Life Story of Orison
Swett Marden,* Mott, "Success," in *History of American Magazines,* 5:286–94; and Richard
M. Huber, *The American Idea of Success,* 145–64.

18. Orison Swett Marden, "Not Just 'Another' Magazine," *New Success,* January 1918,
3; Marden, "A Foreword by Orison Swett Marden," *New Success,* January 1918, 12–13.

power—would eventually lead to its acquisition.[19] Marden's combination of New Thought ideas with the character ethic led him to frame masculinity in ways that opened new possibilities for the meaning of manhood.

Though Marden's opening editorial paid homage to Victorian masculine values, the magazine soon became a dedicated proponent of personality, appearance, and self-realization, and it attracted readers and advertisers along the way. An early article urging readers to make a New Year compact to improve their life was a testament to the belief that people can recreate themselves. The lesson that Marden draws from Lincoln's life is that people should smile, have courtesy, and be enthusiastic. A profile praising Governor Alfred E. Smith claimed that "his popularity was due to personality—the personality that is a power in life." Most striking was the magazine's emphasis on appearance. In an article titled "Look Successful If You Would Be Successful," Marden counsels: "If there is no sign of a winner in your appearance, if you look as tho you have lost your nerve, nobody is going to give you a responsible position." Several issues later he expands on this point:

> Your personal appearance, your dress, your manner, everything about you, the way in which you keep yourself groomed, how you carry yourself, what you say, . . . all these things are to you what the show windows of a merchant's store are to his business, the way he advertises and displays his goods. Your appearance will be taken as an advertisement of what you are. It is constantly telling people whether you are a success or a failure; and where people place you in their estimation will have a powerful influence upon your career.

Lost in all this encouragement were any reminders to work hard, to pursue a cause without swaying, to behave with honesty and integrity. The *New Success* was drawing a new kind of road map to success; it was charting new ways of being masculine.[20]

By March of 1920 the magazine began to boast of its success, claiming that it was now printing 185,000 copies.[21] In 1921 the magazine updated its format, adding color printing and running many more articles and some fiction, and changed its name to *Success*. Though its circulation was not large compared to many other monthlies, *Success* was unusually successful at attracting

19. On Marden and New Thought, see Huber, *American Idea of Success*, 145–64.

20. Marden, "Make a New Year Compact with Yourself," *New Success,* January 1918, 17; Marden, "Little Lessons from a Great Life," *New Success,* February 1918, 33–34; "Personality as a Success Force," *New Success,* May 1919, 53; Marden, "Look Successful If You Would Be Successful," *New Success,* March 1918, 37; "The Influence of Appearances," *New Success,* January 1920, 25.

21. *New Success,* March 1920, cover; Mott claims that the magazine reached a maximum circulation of 150,000 in 1925. See Mott, *"Success,"* 291.

advertisers, who appeared in the magazine in droves nearly from the outset of its publication. Though the magazine was not specifically directed toward men—in fact, Marden and his contributors made special efforts to include women and even African Americans in their invocations to pursue success— advertisers in the first few years tended to offer products most suitable to a male audience. Advertisers flocked to *Success* because it was one of the few magazines whose ethos was thoroughly compatible with the message being promoted by advertisers. For both advertiser and editor spoke the language of happiness through consumption, the language of the perfectible man.

The very first issue of the *New Success* carried a surprising number of ads: the Pelton Publishing Company and the American Institute of Business Psychology offered advice on raising one's earnings; the Society for Self Improvement offered stories of inspiration; Thomas Crowell publishing offered "Books That Will Help You Succeed"; and Alois Swoboda asked, "Why Live an Inferior Life?" Later advertisers included bodybuilders Lionel Strongfort, Earle E. Liederman, and Charles Atlas; an array of techniques and practices for succeeding in business and love; and a variety of improvement products including chest expanders, muscle builders, memory expansion exercises, and so on. By 1922 and 1923, when the economy began to pick up, there appeared many guides to investing in the stock market or getting money quickly. The number of small ads looking for salesmen increased dramatically at about the same time. And finally, there was an abundance of ads for the products that men needed to wear as the garb of success—He-Man razors, the right clothes, a good shoe polish. In all, the ads offered men every possible opportunity to use goods and services to improve their chances of achieving the success that the readership of this magazine implied they sought. The sheer number of advertisements that embraced the rough agenda I have sketched here is daunting.

Nowhere was the congruence between advertising and editorial policy more pronounced than in Marden's comments about appearance. In one of his periodic "Talks on the Psychology of Clothes," Marden offered his opinion that "It doesn't pay to wear your clothing too long, if there is any possibility of getting fresh new clothes." While clothing advertisers no doubt appreciated this kind of support, Marden did not stop with such practical advice, for he believed that "Smart clothes make [every man] feel smart. He is a new person, a new being." "*The consciousness of being properly dressed* not only liberates our powers of self-expression, but is also a tonic to success, a stimulus to achievement, and increases our ability very appreciably. . . . Dress up and you will brace up. When we change our clothes we change our minds."[22]

22. Marden, "Talks on the Psychology of Clothes," *Success,* February 1924, 82–83.

The number and variety of ads and articles promoting appearance and personality speaks with the voice of a new social group, a go-go assemblage of businessmen, salesmen, and stockbrokers whose dynamism and energy helped drive the nation's economy in the 1920s. In *Prosperity: Fact or Myth* (1929), Stuart Chase described the businessman as "the dictator of our destinies. . . . He has ousted the statesman, the priest, the philosopher, as the creater [*sic*] of standards of ethics and behavior, and has become the final authority of the conduct of American society."[23] And the salesman, as the point man for the new economics of distribution and marketing, was heralded as the quintessential businessman. Such men had clearly found in *Success* a magazine that expressed their optimism about their prospects. Yet this heady optimism, this perfectible vision of man, did not emerge unbidden out of a dynamic 1920s economy, but rather out of a sometimes uneasy attempt to reconcile past truths with new possibilities. There is an agony in the transformation that sometimes gets lost in the magazine's rosy, forward-looking gaze, but it appears in the contradictions of reconciling the old language with the new, with speaking about character while wearing new clothes.

One of the magazine's recurring features was the "I Am—" column. Written by Marden, the column began with the words *I Am* and proceeded with a series of amplifications leading to the final word, which was always one of the cardinal traits of men who were successful, traits like thrift, industry, peace, optimism, and so on. A typical such column read: "I AM—The very essence of character. The first essential of happiness and success. . . . I make [man] the master of circumstances, the ruler of conditions that otherwise would fill him with despair. Without me, a man is like a mariner without a compass—at the mercy of every wind that blows; the slave of every passion and impulse. . . . I am anchored in the eternal calm of principle. I AM SELF-CONTROL."[24] Such columns indicated that success was predicated upon the consistent application of certain eternal and transcendent rules of behavior, a fairly old-fashioned version of the key to success, and one not unlike that promoted by the likes of Lorimer or Siddall. Yet while Marden promoted such principles, he also advised men to pay close attention to their appearance and he filled his magazine with ads suggesting that the key to success lay in one's ability to take up and discard when necessary a variety of behaviors, appearances, and attitudes. What were men to think when presented with one story that suggested that the key to success lay in obeying immutable laws while another story—and every ad—suggested that the key to

23. Stuart Chase, *Prosperity: Fact or Myth,* 40, quoted in Huber, *American Idea of Success,* 186.

24. Marden, "I Am—," *Success,* October 1921, 16.

success lay in molding one's personality to the requirements of the situation? What were they to think when a paean to self-control shared the same space with an ad for "Personality Supreme"?

Occasionally one gets the sense that contributors to the magazine were aware of the incompatibility of these two very different sets of values. In "Look Who's Here: The Superfake Stock Salesman," William G. Shephard warns readers to look out for the salesman who, though "scientifically trained in popular psychology, energetic, plausible and often personally honest, . . . leaves behind him a trail of shattered bank accounts and broken hearts."[25] The salesman Shephard warns of is the very salesman who has read the articles and bought the personality manuals offered in *Success* magazine, but he may be personally disreputable or the pawn of a company who has duped him into offering a bogus product. The problem is, the target of his attention has no way of judging whether the man is reputable or not. Is this article warning people against the very kind of salesman this magazine has aided in creating? And if people cannot trust the salesman, how can they trust the magazine that helped create the salesman? This question gets to the very crux of the dilemma of old values surviving in a new medium. How do you trust a medium (the magazine) whose very purpose is to sell both itself and the products advertised within? Perhaps all Marden's talk about character and integrity is mere window dressing, the right garb that will enable him to sell his wares. Such questions are similar to those that puzzled Americans nearly a century earlier, when the rapid expansion of the economy placed people in towns where they could no longer rely on a web of acquaintances to verify the character of those with whom they would do business.[26] In the nineteenth century, Americans resolved their concerns about authenticity by erecting social notions of identity that grew into the prescriptions of Victorian masculinity, but now those prescriptions were coming undone all over again in the face of the modern embrace of personality, appearance, and imagery. This inability to determine the authenticity of the people one met and the magazines one read was (and is) one of the more terrifying elements of the cultural embrace of modernity.

Success did not tarry too long over the ideological inconsistencies it raised by simultaneously offering Victorian and modern masculine ideals. The magazine did take steps to shield itself from the worst excesses of its paradox, namely by eliminating from its pages those ads that were deceitful. "Under the present management of this department," publisher Walter Hoff Seely wrote in 1923,

25. William G. Shephard, "Look Who's Here: The Superfake Stock Salesman," *Success*, April 1923, 11.

26. See Karen Halttunen, *Confidence Men and Painted Women: A Study of Middle-Class Culture in America, 1830–1870*.

"a strict investigation is made of advertising matter, and with the assistance of the Associated Advertising Clubs of the World, of which *Success* has become a member, higher standards will be enforced."[27] It was a common step taken by American magazines to console worried readers, but it was unclear how well such self-policing worked. In the meantime, the magazine had a product to sell and it continued to pursue this basic agenda with diligence.

Success was never one of America's great magazines. Magazine historian Frank L. Mott summarizes the magazine's career well when he comments that "It was a handsome and interesting magazine, though its persistent optimism was eventually a little galling."[28] Its singular dedication to the doctrines of Orison Swett Marden limited the number of people it might reach. In the end, *American Magazine* editor John Siddall would prove a better promoter of Marden's doctrine of success than Marden himself, for Siddall succeeded at mixing the success stories with other interesting material to produce a magazine with variety. Marden had one tune and he hummed it every issue. When Marden died in 1924 the magazine went into a predictable decline, scrambling to come up with material to fill the magazine, trying to lure women readers with articles on housekeeping and child rearing, and pleading with advertisers that their magazine had "circulation power." In its death throes this magazine was like all others, desperate and a little pathetic. After a name change, it ceased publication in April 1928.

Success-hungry salesmen were not the only ones who were offered new ways of understanding their masculinity. Beginning in the early 1920s, sports magazines also began to reorient their presentations of masculinity to encourage men to embrace perfectibility, consumerism, and personality. *Sporting Life* magazine traced its history back to the late nineteenth century, and it existed for many years as a newssheet for sports fans. Overwhelmingly devoted to baseball coverage—box scores occupied the central portion of the publication—the large-format weekly also offered some coverage of other sports, including shooting and cycling. In the 1890s the paper was filled with patent medicine advertising, including one pitch with the headline "Vigor of Men Easily, Quickly, Permanently Restored." Notwithstanding this pitch, the thrust of the magazine was not to provide men with the means to transform themselves, but rather to provide them with information. By the 1910s the magazine had purged the questionable ads, and its editor, Francis C. Richter, boasted of "the scrupulous cleanliness of the paper—a cleanliness embracing every department. . . . No

27. Walter Hoff Seely, "The Publisher—Talks Business," *Success,* November 1923, 8.
28. Mott, "*Success,*" 291.

unclean or doubtful advertisement is ever to be found in "Sporting Life's" columns; never a line in the reading columns to bring offense to men, blushes to women, or evil suggestions to youth."[29] In all, the magazine made every effort to provide just the facts, for that was all its editors imagined readers wanted.

In 1917 *Sporting Life* took an unexplained five-year break from publication. When it reappeared in March of 1922, the publication was under new ownership and editorship and it had adopted a substantially more modern format and editorial policy. These changes were just the beginning of the transformation that the magazine would undergo under editor Edgar F. Wolfe, who went by the name "Jim Nasium." Jim Nasium clearly saw the magazine as providing not just news but entertainment, for he filled it with comic illustrations, humorous stories, and personality profiles. In its first issue under new management, *Sporting Life* declared that it would no longer concern itself with the business side of baseball but would concentrate on the games and on the feats of the players.[30] The tenor of the magazine under Jim Nasium was soon confirmed when the magazine went to a monthly publication schedule. Announcing this change, Jim Nasium explained:

> A vast majority of readers are interested in stories of PEOPLE rather than in stories of events. They would rather hear something about the MAN who wins a race than to read about the RACE itself; the INDIVIDUAL hero of a World Series is discussed long after the final score is forgotten; persons who are NOT interested in baseball ARE interested in discussing Babe Ruth and Ty Cobb. . . . It is the HUMAN INTEREST appeals that gets and hold readers. It is the same thing which creates hero worship, the principle commercializing factor of any game.[31]

So much for the box scores. For the next four years, the staff of *Sporting Life* struggled to figure out what it meant to put together such a magazine. Though the sports focus always meant that the magazine was edited primarily for men, the editor soon took steps to make the magazine's relationship to American men somewhat more didactic. Announcing that the magazine would cover a

29. *Sporting Life,* March 8, 1913, 4. I suspect but cannot confirm that this cleanliness boast was also a dig at a competing sports publication, the *National Police Gazette,* which was known for its racy pictures and stories.

30. "THE BUSINESS OFFICE IS NOT OURS TO INVADE," wrote the editors in their declaration of policy. "We are not interested so much in what a player GETS as we are in what he GIVES in return; we are more interested in what a player is WORTH than in what he COSTS. We confess less interest in what a club owner PAYS than in what he PRODUCES. Furthermore, SPORTING LIFE is NOT the organ of any one man, any one faction, any one league, or any one policy but its own—'FOR THE GOOD OF THE GAME'" ("The Policy," *Sporting Life,* March 18, 1922, 6).

31. *Sporting Life,* August 1922, inside front cover.

wider range of sports, Jim Nasium declared in September of 1922 that "the aim of *Sporting Life* is to make its columns of such wider interest to MEN readers that it will be recognized as THE NATIONAL MAN'S MAGAZINE," offering stories with "MAN APPEAL."[32] But what was "man appeal"? Despite Jim Nasium's earlier pronouncements about hero worship, the magazine did not rush to a committed celebration of professional sports personalities; that was not what the magazine's embrace of commercialism meant. Indeed, its depictions of sporting men were far more Victorian than these early editorial pronouncements would lead one to believe.

Famous football coach Amos Alonzo Stagg provided the justification for the *Sporting Life's* representation of men in an essay called "Athletics and the Press," which the magazine reprinted from the *Christian Science Monitor.* Stagg, a firm believer in the character-building qualities of sports, calls for greater promotion of amateur athletics, claiming that "you cannot possibly get the fullest results in the developing of character from a sport that is tainted with commercial interest." Amateur ideals—loyalty, unselfishness, self-sacrifice, cooperation, team play, and so on—could all be promoted to the benefit of the morals of the nation. *Sporting Life* heeded Stagg's call with articles such as the one that profiled Yale football coach Tad Jones. In "Making Men Rather Than Football Stars," the anonymous author claims that "College coaches, for the most part, are learning that there is something finer and bigger, something more lasting and valuable, that they can impart and instill in the mind of the college athlete, rather than a mere desire for victory. The college coach today is conditioning and pointing his men, not for victory in the big game of the year, but for success in the greater game—the Game of Life."[33]

Effie Maurine Page's September 1923 editorial also sought to establish the respectability of the sporting life. In "Can a Sporting Man Be a Christian Gentleman?" Page claims that most people associate the sporting man with loving play, luxury, gambling, and "the age-old game of women." The "Christian Gentleman," on the other hand, is "a man quiet and religious, strong of mind and will, gentle and loving, but foremost—a man of God." But if we think about the true qualities of the sportsman, she continues, we will realize that he can also be a Christian gentleman. "Look underneath the surface and study the

32. Inside cover announcement, *Sporting Life,* September 1922, 2.
33. Amos Alonzo Stagg, "Athletics and the Press," *Sporting Life,* October 1923, 24–25; "Making Men Rather Than Football Stars," *Sporting Life,* November 1923, 4. Other such articles include Bill Dooly, "Football Stars Who Have Scored in the Game of Life," *Sporting Life,* December 1922, 6–7, 33; and John K. Tener, "The Influence of True Sportsmanship," *Sporting Life,* November 1923, 24–25.

man and you'll find that many, many of them are [Christian gentlemen]." The argument is so simple as to be almost specious, but it illustrates the desire of the editors to promote sports as something acceptable to respectable middle-class people, even to the outdated vision of the Christian gentleman. By July of 1924 the magazine even changed its title to *Sportlife* to lay claim to respectability. This "more dignified title," claimed the announcement, "is more expressive of the dignified nature and high class of [the magazine's] editorial contents," more reflective of a magazine that is "clean, wholesome, instructive and has a vital reason for existence." That reason for existence, the editorial explained, was the promotion of "the religion of FAIR PLAY," the "gospel of better MEN, not greater ATHLETES."[34]

Since *Sporting Life/Sportlife* wanted to make sports safe for a respectable middle class, it soon took to depicting the man-making qualities of sports in which middle-aged men could actually participate. The magazine thus took special care to promote the benefits of bowling and billiards. In stories like "Billiards His Stepping Stone to Success" and "The Bowling Parson," the sport and the healthful environment that surrounds the sport were credited with producing high-caliber citizens. The endorsement of such sports did not stop with mere profiles of happy bowlers, however. A text box next to the "Bowling Parson" article declared that "Keeping physically fit is a man's duty, first to his country, and to himself," and recommended bowling as "the one game or sport where you can play and exercise any old time and regardless of the weather." Another editorial in the same issue pitched exercise as the key to lifelong health, and then concluded with the injunction to "TRY BOWLING FOR WHAT AILS YOU." Lest the reader be unconvinced by such subtle advice, Arthur Brisbane condemned baseball fans for being passive—"The athlete competes and grows stronger— / The weakling looks on and grows weaker"—and then noted that "The character building qualities of bowling are little appreciated. Followers of this game consciously or unconsciously are developing such character building qualities as self-control, patience, honesty, courtesy, unselfishness. No other game or sport offers the same inducement, where all who are interested derive direct benefit."[35]

34. Effie Maurine Page, "Can a Sporting Man Be a Christian Gentleman?" *Sporting Life,* September 1923, 24–25; "Important Announcement," *Sporting Life,* July 1924, 1. The word *sporting,* the announcement explained, had come to have a "certain stigma" with which they no longer wished to be associated.
35. "Billiards His Stepping Stone to Success," *Sporting Life,* October 1922, 4; "The Bowling Parson," *Sporting Life,* November 1922, 6–7; "Exercise and Health," *Sporting Life,* November 1922, 24; Arthur Brisbane, "100 Per Cent American—They Watch and Stretch," *Sporting Life,* December 1922, 24.

Every editorial pronouncement was aimed at assuring readers of the respectability and the virtue of sports; the tone with which such assurances were made was one of authenticity, trustworthiness, candor. Yet this agenda was not nearly as pure as it pretended to be. For every article that lauded the character-building qualities of billiards, there was an advertisement for Brunswick billiards tables. An attentive reader must have noted that for every editorial column devoted to the manly art of shooting, there were ads for guns and shotgun shells. A call for advertisers boasted that "Your advertising in *Sporting Life* will produce *real* results," and by the mid-1920s, it began to seem that the editors of the magazine were not beyond shaping their editorial agenda precisely in such a way as to guarantee that readers would be thoroughly open to advertisers' inducements to buy.

No charge is harder for the historian to prove than the charge that a magazine acts in collusion with an advertiser. No editor left a record admitting that he shaped his magazine's editorial policy to best present certain products, and no advertiser confessed to planting editorial material suitable to its interests. Indeed, the pressure to provide a friendly editorial environment need not have been so direct or so sinister. It may have been that an editor like Jim Nasium was flexible enough in his notions of editorial policy that increasing his coverage of billiards and bowling seemed perfectly acceptable if it meant that his magazine would be displayed in bowling alleys or billiards rooms. Offering more coverage of the sports that his advertisements promoted probably did not seem like selling out, but rather like good business. And so the magazine's editorial content came to reflect quite closely the interests of its advertisers. A special issue on bowling was filled with ads for bowling products; an expanded shooting department was chock full of ads for Elmer Richards and L. L. Bean outdoor clothes, hunting coats, binoculars, and a variety of other accessories for hunters.[36] Where the editors developed new content, the advertisers followed—or was it the other way around? Did advertisers request just a little more coverage of hunting or a special issue on their sport? Did they provide the magazine with good pictures and an interview with the latest shooting champion, who just happened to endorse their product? The collusion was everywhere and nowhere, but it was hard to ignore.

The most telling example of the coordination of editorial policy and advertising comes from the magazine's treatment of billiards. As the editorial matter steadily promoted the appeal of a game that was once considered somewhat disreputable, the advertisements happily joined in seconding this vision of the sport. In 1922 the Brunswick-Balke-Collender Company had run

36. See *Sporting Life*, November 1922 and October 1924.

advertisements in the magazine that promoted the company's reputation for quality and its seventy-five years in business; they were rather typical appeals to rationality and quality. By 1924, the Brunswick brand billiards table ads took a very different line. "Billiards, a gentleman's game," read the headline for one such ad, beside a picture of an aristocratic-looking gentleman playing billiards with his son. The text of the advertisement read: "There are thousands of high-class billiard rooms in this country where fathers and sons meet regularly for an hour's healthy recreation. . . . [B]illiards is a character builder—a game that makes better citizens. It develops self-control, patience and perseverance. It requires keen concentration, inspires quick thinking, improves the judgment and makes one accurate, even-tempered and self-reliant."[37] It was difficult to differentiate the ad copy from the editorials, for the two spoke with the same voice.

While editor and advertiser may have spoken with the same voice, it was a voice that was deeply duplicitous or, at best, deeply conflicted. Both parties adopted the language of Victorian masculinity, with all its talk of building character and developing prosocial habits, yet they did so to the end of getting men to purchase the products that would allow them to develop those traits. But if any man with fifty cents could play billiards, then how meaningful was this notion of character anyway? Was not character degraded, indeed perverted, if one could attain it simply by purchasing the right form of recreation? It was an issue that was raised again and again over the course of the next decade as magazine after magazine that promoted some version of Victorian masculinity came to terms with the commercialism of the American magazine market. One thing at least was clear: as more ads used appeals to Victorian ideals, those ideals were stripped of their meaning. And as they ceased to have meaning, new ideals more suited to encouraging consumption came to take their place.[38]

The drama of this transformation from Victorian to modern masculinity stopped playing out in *Sportlife* just as it got really interesting. In August of 1924 new kinds of advertisements began to appear in the magazine: ads for bodybuilding equipment, song and dance records, Wurlitzer organs, and the National Salesmen's Training Association. Within a few months Earle Lieder-man pitched his books on "Muscular Development," as good a sign as any that

37. Advertisement, *Sporting Life,* November 1922, back cover; *Sporting Life*, April 1924, back cover.

38. Although it is beyond the scope of my study to question the intentions of those who created the advertisements, Roland Marchand suggests that those in the advertising trade thought of themselves as playing a game of "benign deception" that legitimated their evacuation of meaningful cultural ideals for the sake of commerce. See Marchand, *Advertising the American Dream,* 48–51.

the magazine was willing to embrace the "perfectibility" ethos. And well it might have, for the magazine had a new owner, one Bernarr Macfadden, physical culturist and magazine builder extraordinaire. Macfadden had dedicated his life to promoting physical and mental health, and his publishing efforts were experiencing a resurgence thanks to the success of *True Story* magazine. This success had helped him revive *Physical Culture* magazine, and Macfadden soon slanted the editorial stance of *Sportlife* toward his bodybuilding health-cure agenda.[39] But there was no use having two magazines promoting the same agenda, so by 1926 Macfadden eased *Sportlife* into oblivion.

Like John Griffith, J. D. Fetzer also started a sports magazine in 1921. Its initial impulse and audience seemed to mirror that of the *Athletic Journal.* Fetzer's *Football World,* "A Magazine with a Mission to Serve the College Man," was "devoted to Inter-collegiate Athletics and sports of Amateur standing only," heralded the first masthead. But Fetzer's approach to sports proved to be quite different from *Athletic Journal* editor Griffith's, and quite a bit more popular. Fetzer justified the magazine by arguing that "Among men, no heroes of the day have more popularity than the sportsman. . . . If the sport mania is one of the reactions after the war, it is the healthiest of all."[40] By the third issue, the magazine claimed a circulation of two hundred thousand (though there is little likelihood that it was this high). The magazine soon changed its name to *Athletic World* and began to cover a wide variety of sports, including women's sports, especially swimming.

The *Athletic World* quickly developed an identity quite different from the *Athletic Journal* or *Sporting Life/Sportlife.* Where the latter publications stressed the character-building qualities of athletics, the former celebrated the dynamism and entertainment of the games and the personalities of the athletes. Where the *Journal*'s tone was stern and moralistic, the *World*'s was light and entertaining. The two magazines had initially shared the same advertisers—makers of sports equipment and apparel that appealed to consumers on name and quality, not image. The *Journal* never left this core of advertisers, while the *World* soon picked up an array of advertisers who promised to make men strong, popular, and wealthy, and to educate them sexually. The *World*'s editorial offerings reflected a growing emphasis on personality and self-absorption as

39. Had *Physical Culture* not been so well-covered elsewhere I would certainly have covered it in this survey. On *Physical Culture* and masculinity, see White, *First Sexual Revolution.* On Macfadden, see Mary Macfadden and Emile Gavreau, *Dumbbells and Carrot-Strips: The Story of Bernarr Macfadden;* Harold Brainerd Hersey, *Pulpwood Editor;* and Harvey Green, *Fit for America: Health, Fitness, Sport, and American Society.*
40. *Football World,* October 1921, 4.

it offered articles on gaining strength, diet, and nerves. Its photographs also accentuated the physical body and most often featured women and bare-chested men in swimming suits. From the same starting point, these two magazines took radically different approaches to constructing the masculine athletic ideal.

In short, where the *Athletic Journal* celebrated self-control and looking inward, the *Athletic World* celebrated dynamism and the extension of the self outward. In editorial material and ads, this magazine viewed men in terms of their expansive power, their ability to develop strength and vitality. "Strength lies dormant in us all," wrote George O. Pritchard. "It is up to ourselves to bring it to life and develop it."[41] If editorials provided the motivation to develop one's body, the many ads that filled this magazine during its muscle stage (1923–1925) promised men that becoming strong was quick and easy. "If you were dying to-night," asked Earle E. Liederman's ad, "and I offered you something that would give you ten years more to live, would you take it? Well fellows, I've got it." That "thing" being offered was physical training, and Liederman and other "physical culturists" made a cult of the perfectible body. Liederman boasted that "When I'm thru with you, you're a real man"; Charles Atlas claimed that "muscles that are powerful . . . will make you the *admired* instead of the *pittied*" [sic]; Professor Henry W. Titus promised that his ten-cent book would make a man "MASTER of all that you desire to achieve"; Lionel Strongfort, creator of Strongfortism, advised men to avoid the devastating sentence of "Sexual Death" and try his system that has "reinstated thousands of despairing souls in the manpower of the nation."[42]

Like *Sporting Life/Sportlife,* this magazine showed a remarkable congruity between what was said and what was sold. The *Athletic World* sold a seamless package of perfectible masculinity, from advice on what to eat to dance lessons that promised overnight popularity, from an African bark extract that promised "Vim, Vigor and Vitality" to a book promising "Sexual Knowledge."[43] The dynamic and powerful masculinity the magazine promoted was purchasable and available to anyone; it did not rely on character but on following the easy steps outlined in some ten-cent guide. As kitschy as such ads and ideas often

41. Pritchard, "Gaining Strength at Home," *Athletic World,* October 1923, 41, 53; see also William T. Todd, "Strength—What Is It? The Dynamic Power of Man," *Athletic World,* September 1923, 24–25; Fred W. Tilney, "What Is the Strong Man's Diet?" *Athletic World,* August 1924, 10, 45.

42. *Athletic World,* October 1923, 53; August 1924, 45; January 1924, 53; June 1924, 47. These ads and many more like them appeared regularly in this magazine. Italics from source.

43. *Athletic World,* February 1924, 65; October 1923, 53; May 1924, 61. Kevin White traces similar images in the pages of *Physical Culture* magazine ("The Masculine Image in an Age of Cultural Revolution, 1910–1930," in *First Sexual Revolution,* 16–35).

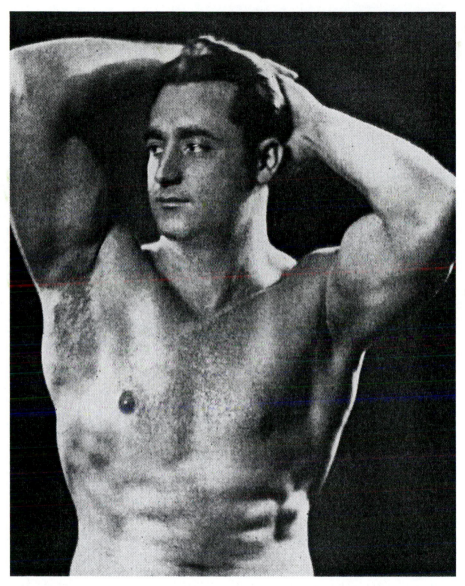

One of the many photos of Charles Atlas that filled the early sporting magazines like *Athletic World,* this image was used to promote Atlas's claim that any man—even a 98-pound weakling—could develop a powerful physique. The logic of Atlas's appeal—that a man could transform himself—soon suffused much of the advertising and editorial matter directed toward men (*Athletic World,* August 1924, 11).

were, they marked a clear distinction between old and new masculinity.[44] What differentiated the *Athletic World* from its competitors was the fact that what it said and what it sold were not mutually contradictory. Both the editorial content and the advertising in the *Athletic World* intimated that modern masculinity was a game of appearances and bluffs.

Vanity Fair was a magazine like no other in the American magazine marketplace, and it portrayed masculinity in ways unlike any contemporary publication. Confident where magazines like *Success* and the *American Magazine* were insecure, sophisticated where others were anti-intellectual, *Vanity Fair* spoke to men who laughed at high-blown expressions of idealism, wore the latest fashions, and were unconcerned with money. The men who read *Vanity Fair* had arrived, or so one gathered by reading its pages. And they did not like to talk much about what it meant to be men—*Vanity Fair* did not offer its readers formulas for success or for developing their personality. What *Vanity Fair* makes clear in the late 1910s and 1920s is that wealthy, educated men did not indulge themselves in reflections about developing their character *or* their personality—you either had it or you did not—and actively mocked that class that did. What the magazine also makes clear is that in the true consumer publication, advertising and editorial content could work hand in hand to promote the magazine's agenda.

Publisher Condé Nast began what was then called *Dress & Vanity Fair* in 1913 for selfish reasons: he wanted to protect his four-year-old magazine *Vogue* from the competition offered by *Dress*, so he bought the latter magazine and combined it with *Vanity Fair*, a magazine that had flourished in the 1890s as "a sort of refined *Police Gazette*," according to *New Yorker* contributor Geoffrey Hellmann. As might be expected from the result of the combination of such a melee of interests, *Dress & Vanity Fair* was scattered and indistinct. A friend of Nast's named Frank Crowninshield did not hesitate to tell him so, and he explained how he would edit such a magazine if given the chance. Nast, noting Crowninshield's experience as an editor with *Bookman* and *Century* as well as his connections to New York high society,

44. They also marked a distinction between producer and consumer, athlete and fan. *Athletic World* soon dropped its muscular emphasis in favor of a "field and stream" approach to men's sporting activities. The move seems to have been promoted by reader interest, for a 1925 article on fishing got a huge reader response and moved the editor to add more such articles. Eventually these articles came to dominate the magazine, which changed its name to *Outing* in December 1924 and slowly dropped all the bodybuilding ads. Perhaps the magazine's readership was always older than the editors had realized and thus less interested in building muscles; perhaps *Physical Culture* magazine had cornered the market on the bodybuilding niche.

invited Crowninshield to edit the magazine. "Stipulating that *Dress* must be dropped from its name and female fashions from its contents," writes Hellmann, Crowninshield set about to make *Vanity Fair* a magazine of distinction and taste.[45]

From its opening issues, *Vanity Fair* oozed wealth, sophistication, and breeding. "We shall not lack authority in those things which go to make the smart world smart," promised the opening editorial, and it was a promise the magazine kept. Devoted to staying abreast of drama, opera, music, fine art, and books, the magazine offered insightful reviews and articles of opinion, and, over time, came to feature some of the best writers of the day, including Dorothy Parker, Robert Benchley, Edmund Wilson Jr., Clive Bell, Aldous Huxley, Jean Cocteau, and Gilbert Seldes. By the time Crowninshield came aboard in March of 1914, the magazine toned down its fascination with European culture and focused more attention on the New York intellectual and cultural milieu. For the better part of the magazine's career, the main focus of its attentions would be the drama, art, and literature that appealed to wealthy and cultured New Yorkers. Defending the charge that the magazine was for wealthy dilettantes, Crowninshield explained that it was edited for readers with a "sophistication which is the natural and happy result of wide travel, some little knowledge of the world and a pleasing familiarity with the five arts and the four languages."[46]

Vanity Fair was edited from the first to appeal to both males and females, though the first few issues had little to appeal to men other than a column called "For the Well Dressed Man." As the magazine pulled away from the fascination with female fashions that it inherited from *Dress*, it announced: "If any Man has honored us by wandering thus far through these lines of purely feminine interest, let him take heart, for right here we announce that *Vanity Fair* is by no means to be a woman's magazine."[47] *Vanity Fair* soon added coverage of sports like tennis, golf, and motoring, and published articles on developments in motorcars, boats, and airplanes; the "Well Dressed Man" column ran throughout the magazine's history. While it contained editorial matter of interest to men, *Vanity Fair* was decidedly not about masculinity in the same way that magazines like the *American Magazine* or *Success* were about masculinity. *Vanity Fair* would never run an article suggesting ways that men could improve themselves or increase their chances for success in business; their profiles were always of people in the arts, and the subjects were not held

45. Geoffrey Hellmann, "Last of the Species—II," *New Yorker,* September 26, 1942, 24.
46. Editorial, *Dress & Vanity Fair,* September 1913, 15; editorial, *Vanity Fair,* May 1914, 19.
47. "In Vanity Fair," *Vanity Fair,* January 1914, 13.

out for emulation by readers in need of instruction. Though *Vanity Fair* was not about masculinity, it did nonetheless express some distinct views about the nature of the American male.

Vanity Fair cast a satirical eye on the concern with self-making that was so prevalent in the middle-class magazines. A number of articles penned in the late teens and early twenties caricatured the sense of striving and malleability that so characterized the articles that appeared in the likes of *Success* or the *American Magazine*. "Careers For Young Men," written by *Vanity Fair's* anonymous "success editor," parodies the career advice of other magazines by suggesting that "any young man with a college education who has ambition, ideals and stick-to-it-iveness can undoubtedly succeed in . . ." bootlegging, business, or literature. Stephen Leacock's "How I Succeeded in My Business" cited his dedicated application of advice on improving one's diet and personality as the keys to his success, though he admitted he did not have the foggiest idea what his company did. And Patrick Kearney's "The Great American University" satirized the claims made by "get smart quick" mail-order education schemes from Dr. Eliot's "Five Foot Shelf of Books" to Pelmanism to Alois P. Swoboda's *The Subtle Principle of Success*. "Their total purpose," writes Kearney, "seems to be to inculcate superstitions which were laughed at in Aristotle's day, and which have been the common belief and practice of all savage tribes since the beginning of mankind."[48] By ridiculing the assiduous efforts of middle-class men to improve themselves, *Vanity Fair* makes it quite clear that one cannot express a proper masculinity by such unseemly striving.

Vanity Fair singled out for special scorn the version of masculinity articulated in the pages of the *American Magazine*. In a feature called "Our Esteemed Contemporaries," *Vanity Fair* contributor Brighton Perry mocked the editorial mannerisms of the *American*. Perry's lampoon of Siddall's "Sid Says" punctured the optimism of the self-made man and his truisms:

Sid Says: Don't try to fail—it can't be done

> There are some folks who think that they are "sure-fire" failures until they
> have "tried it out." You may be "on the rocks" but don't forget that "every cloud
> has a silver lining," and when anyone tells you that "it is all up with you," just
> take your last "nickle" and go to a "barber-shop" and "get a shave." You will be
> surprised to find how smooth it makes your "face" feel.

48. "Careers for Young Men," *Vanity Fair,* July 1921, 35; Stephen Leacock, "How I Succeeded in My Business," *Vanity Fair,* September 1921, 46; Patrick Kearney, "The Great American University," *Vanity Fair,* April 1923, 45, 110. See also Frederic C. Nelson, "Can You Resist Salesmanship?" *Vanity Fair,* March 1920, 116, 118, 120.

And, after that, everything will be "easy sailing,"—that is, provided you are made of "the right stuff." Follow what Sid says each month and you will come out "all right."

And the *American Magazine* articles that promoted men's rise to success were also artfully lampooned, as in this brief look at how a man who had been failing as a salesman finally made it big:

> I began to sell my personality. Every man that came into my store I took aside and showed him different moods. First, I would tell him a funny story, to prove to him that I was more than a mere business automaton. Then I would relate a pathetic incident I had seen on the street a week or two ago. This disclosed my heart. Then I did a fragment of a bare-foot dance and sketched a caricature of Lloyd George, to let him see that I was a man of the world. After this, I was ready to sell him what he came in for, and he would go away carrying a very definite impression of my personal characteristics—and some of my goods, in a bundle.
>
> A week of selling rubber-goods in this manner, and I was on the vaudeville stage, earning $250 a week. How much do *you* earn?

Perry so perfectly captured the tone of the *American Magazine*'s absorption in self-creation that he collapsed the whole idea down upon itself. After all, how was self-creation any different than vaudeville?[49]

The one column that might well have been expected to sell men on the act of self-creation was the fashion column, "For the Well Dressed Man." Yet this column managed to take a tone that assumed that the reader had already arrived at a standard of good taste and merely needed to be informed about what was being worn this season. The kind of aristocratic assumption that informed the column was revealed in the unnamed columnist's remark about the outfit worn by a friend: "The *tout ensemble* showed the hand of a well trained servant and a master who is careful and knows."[50] The column would have never assumed to advise the reader why they should wear certain clothes, for this reader did not need to be convinced of the necessity of being well dressed.

In an age where so many of the advertisements in middle-class magazines strained to convince readers why they needed to buy such and such a product, the advertisements in *Vanity Fair* spoke with an entirely different tone. The first ad for a man's product in this magazine was a half-page spot for Arrow collars that ran in January of 1915. Depicting a clean-cut young man playing billiards, the ad sold the shirt on its features and value, its "smart tucked bosom . . . at a very low price." Other ads for men's clothing quickly followed, and they followed Arrow's rhetorical cue by promoting the quality and durability of their

49. Brighton Perry, "Our Esteemed Contemporaries: The *American Magazine*—Tabloid Edition," *Vanity Fair,* April 1919, 51. Idiosyncratic spelling from source.
50. "The Well Dressed Man," *Dress & Vanity Fair,* October 1913, 61.

products. Dobbs hats were "the aristocrats of finer hats"; Brooks Brothers suits offered the finest in custom tailoring. Through the 1920s, ads for men's clothing and accessories constituted a major portion of the magazine's advertising pages.

Ads for personal care products for men were never prevalent in *Vanity Fair*, but even they obeyed the standards of decorum established by the clothing advertisers. A 1917 ad for "Odorono" suggested that "In the worlds of crowds and pleasures, no woman can have perfect, exquisite daintiness—no man can be truly well groomed—no one can have the highest degree of personal cleanliness without Odorono." The illustration accompanying the ad was of an attractive couple dancing at a ball. Compare this to an ad that played off a man's fears that smelling bad would lose him business or a woman and this ad looks remarkably subtle. Even Listerine, which began to advertise in *Vanity Fair* in the late 1920s, offered more restrained appeals to the fear that the rank evidence of bodily functions would lead to social doom.[51] In the end, while other advertisers boasted that their products would give men the qualities they needed to get ahead, *Vanity Fair*'s advertisers remained remarkably respectful of the consumer's ability to make up his mind without excessive persuasion.

Unwinding the tangled strands of snobbery—or, as Crowninshield would have it, taste—in *Vanity Fair* to find its way of understanding masculinity is no easy task. *Vanity Fair* did not experience the same degree of self-consciousness about masculinity betrayed by middle-class (or middlebrow) publications. Perhaps because of the certainty of their income, their breeding, or their social prestige, male *Vanity Fair* readers were not subjected to the kinds of lures toward self-improvement and personality-building that advertisers used to allure those less certain of their status. Thus the basis for their masculinity—their ability to provide for themselves and related others—was never an issue in *Vanity Fair* in the way it was for those striving classes who might have needed the motivation offered by the *American Magazine*. What was at issue, however, was the notion of taste, and advertisements in this magazine were carefully crafted to appeal to readers who wanted very much to distinguish and differentiate themselves based upon their discrimination. Or perhaps *Vanity Fair*'s readers had been consuming long enough and confidently enough that they were able to elevate consumption to an art, rather than to an activity central to the constitution of identity. To put it another way, for the upper class consumption was but another of the arts that they might pursue.

Let me develop this point further, for it cuts to the core of this magazine's vision of masculinity. The rhetoric of consumerism encouraged individuals to

51. Odorono advertisement, *Vanity Fair*, May 1917, 112; the first Listerine ad appeared on the inside front cover of *Vanity Fair* in January of 1927.

In *Vanity Fair* men were deemed so sure of themselves that they were offered neither Victorian nor modern masculine images to emulate, but were instead encouraged to go their own way. Where other magazines presented boxer Jack Dempsey as a tough, *Vanity Fair* revealed his "pensive mood" (*Vanity Fair*, February 1923, 68). (© Ira Hill/*Vanity Fair*, Condé Nast Publications, Inc. "Jack Dempsey," February 1923.)

think of themselves not as objective cores of values but as highly subjective and malleable potentialities, capable of achieving multiple expressions through the goods they purchased and the way they presented themselves. Because of their wealth, elites had been able to express themselves via consumption for a much longer time, and thus had become acclimated to the world of goods that rising incomes, expanded production, and the boom in advertising were just now promising to the middle class. Robert C. Benchley expressed just such a view in the magazine's trademark style in his review of Thorstein Veblen's *The Theory of the Leisure Class.* Mocking Veblen for coming so late to the idea that consumption drives the culture of the upper class, Benchley writes:

> It is the private opinion of the reviewer that Dr. Veblen wrote this originally for Vanity Fair, to be used as the advertisement for the magazine which is usually run on the page immediately preceding the frontispiece. Or, perhaps Dr. Veblen has been writing the Vanity Fair advertisements all along, who knows? Listen:
> "The growth of punctilious discrimination as to the qualitative excellence in eating, drinking, etc., presently affects not only the manner of life, but also the training and intellectual activity of the gentleman of leisure. He is no longer simply the aggressive male—the man of strength, resource and intrepidity. *In order to avoid stultification he must also cultivate his tastes, for it now becomes incumbent upon him to discriminate with some nicety between the noble and ignoble in consumable goods. He becomes a connoisseur in creditable viands of various degrees of merit, in manly beverages and trinkets, in seemly apparel and architecture, in weapons, games, dances, and the narcotics.* This cultivation of the aesthetic faculty requires time and application, and the demands made upon the gentleman in this direction therefore tend to change his life of leisure into a more or less arduous application to the business of learning how to live a life of ostensible leisure in a becoming way."
> "*A copy of Vanity Fair each month will do all this, and more, for you,*" is the logical ending to that paragraph.[52]

Indeed, this is exactly what *Vanity Fair* attempted to do. For not only was it the declared intention of the magazine to use its editorial pages to offer readers an introduction to the best that was acted, written, or painted, but it was equally their intention to use the advertising pages as a true complement to the editorial matter. In *Vanity Fair,* the ads spoke with the same authority as the articles. A very early editorial makes this intention clear. Discounting the idea that advertisements merely provide the financial might needed to publish a magazine, the editorial states that such advertisements "furnish an independent and entirely different element of interest—an element that no

52. Robert C. Benchley, "The Dullest Book of the Month," *Vanity Fair,* April 1919, 39. Italics from source.

editorial department can either duplicate or replace." Each advertisement in the magazine:

> . . . is a special message definitely planned to interest the small and homogeneous circle of which you, gentle reader, form a part; and as carefully as any page of letterpress, each page of advertising is attuned exactly to those standards of individuality, refinement and distinction we conceive the most marked characteristics in common of those who do us the honor regularly to read this publication. . . . Frankly, we ask you to make this advertising a regular part of your reading—not on our account, not on the advertisers' account, but because these pages are worthy of it in their own right.[53]

The signal accomplishment of *Vanity Fair*, then, was to place the narrative force of advertising on equal terms with that of the editorial content. That they did so without apology or self-consciousness indicates a degree of comfort with the culture of consumption unheard of in American magazines up to this time.

In January of 1917, James Montgomery Flagg dashed off a spoof on magazine serials called "The Art of Editing a Serial Story." Pretending to be the editor of a magazine that runs such serials, Flagg suggests rewriting a paragraph that begins: "Leroy Maitland stepped out of his car. He was immaculately dressed in his top hat, his morning coat, his buckskin gloves and his exquisite boots. With his Patrician nose he rubbed the gardenia in his buttonhole" to read thus: "Leroy Maitland stepped out of his Scripps-Booth car. He was immaculately dressed in his Brooks Brothers' morning coat, his Dunlap hat, his Martin and Martin buckskin gloves, and his exquisite, Douglas' $3.50 shoes. With his Dr. Woodbury-improved nose, he rubbed the Thorley gardenia in his buttonhole."[54] Given the magazine's obvious policy of embracing advertising, Flagg's mockery was either misplaced—a slip that it is hard to imagine Crowninshield allowing— or aimed at the obviousness, the crassness, of such attempts to merge the appeals of advertising and content.

Vanity Fair was never so obvious nor so crass. It never used its stories to pump particular brands of products, but what it did quite capably was orient its reading matter with its advertising matter so as to get the most out of each. The "For the Well Dressed Man" column, for example, was always accompanied by advertising for men's clothing and accessories; an article on automobiles was paired with ads for Ajax and Lee tires; the book review column, written by Edmund Wilson Jr., was bracketed by ads for new books; and Merryle Stanley Rukeyser's finance column stood amidst ads for investments, insurance,

---

53. Editorial, *Dress & Vanity Fair*, November 1913, 19.
54. James Montgomery Flagg, "The Art of Editing a Serial Story," *Vanity Fair*, January 1917, 63.

and other financial services.[55] The articles provided one kind of information, the advertisements another. And the advertisements were so smartly done, so tasteful, just like the articles, that the discriminating and educated reader would never be offended by either. This was the vision promoted by *Vanity Fair* and, along with its smart, satirical tone, it was its major contribution to the changing nature of the American magazine. Many magazines would emulate this seamless joining of editorial content and advertising, a joining that placed *Vanity Fair* at the forefront of magazines carrying "general and class advertising."[56]

For all its success at attracting advertisers and the attention of the well-off and sophisticated, *Vanity Fair* never attracted a large number of subscribers. Its circulation "never rose above ninety thousand," wrote Hellmann, and "its advertising fell off sharply after 1929 and it began to lose money."[57] Adding serious articles by leading thinkers in politics and economics did not help, nor did it make editor Crowninshield very happy. As much as he had enjoyed the magazine's success, publisher Condé Nast was a businessman, and by 1936 he had had enough of losing money. In February of that year he slipped this announcement into the magazine: "I have decided on the amalgamation of *Vanity Fair* with *Vogue*—its sister periodical—for the reason that the lessening advertising patronage now accorded to periodicals like *Vanity Fair*—magazines so largely devoted to the spread of the arts . . . has made the publication of it, as a single publishing unit, unremunerative. It is for that reason that the magazine now closes its independent career."[58]

Taken together, *Vanity Fair, Success, Sporting Life/Sportlife,* and the *Athletic World* represent the emergence of a cluster of new ideas in the American magazine marketplace. Each of the magazines brought to the discussion of masculinity in America a new set of assumptions; each formulated a new set of ideals and guidelines for how American men might conceive of themselves. And they did so, not coincidentally, within the milieu of the commercialized magazine, a magazine that was driven by advertising as much as by any editorial agenda. These magazines offered new possibilities for the ways men might conceive of themselves, orienting manhood toward such ideals as flexibility, personality, other-directedness, and other "modern" traits. By the mid-1920s the force of such trends had reached the larger magazines and begun to trans-

55. For examples of the juxtaposition of like editorial and advertising material, see *Vanity Fair,* May 1915 and January 1923.

56. This last claim comes from an editorial boasting of the dramatic increase in the number of pages of advertising that the magazine carried. See editorial, *Vanity Fair,* October 1915, 37.

57. Geoffrey Hellmann, "Last of the Species—II," 27.

58. Condé Nast, "Important Announcement . . . ," *Vanity Fair,* February 1936, 11.

form them. The cultural imperatives of youth, consumerism, and personality echoed through the *American Magazine* and *Collier's* in odd ways, challenging editors to modify their editorial policies (if not their beliefs) and turning them in directions they may not have wished to go.

Modern Masculinity Enters the Mass Market

Even under John Siddall's stalwart editorship, modern ways of constructing masculinity began to gain a foothold in the *American Magazine* in the early 1920s. Modern masculinity moved into the domain of the self-made man first in advertisements that evoked images of men who achieved success via consumption, like buying Listerine to eradicate halitosis *(bad breath)*, acquiring the pleasing personality that assured the sale, or adding pep or vigor to life by eating the right breakfast cereal. These easy means to attaining success stood in stark contrast to the self-sacrifice demanded by Victorian masculine idealism. Superficial attributes began to appear as keys to success in fiction as well, though they never were heralded outright as such.[59] Eventually, after Siddall's death in 1923, the path to business success—always the true marker of masculine success in a capitalist society—began to be portrayed as resulting from a man's personality, his attention to the details of his appearance, his salesmanship. Masculinity came to be constructed in terms of how men presented themselves, not who they were. From roughly 1920 onward, the *American Magazine* engaged in an anguished struggle to reconcile Victorian masculinity with modern advertising and modern culture.

If ever there was a medium antithetical to Victorian masculine ideals, it was modern advertising. Advertisers wanted men to buy goods and sold to them based upon who they thought men were and what they thought men wanted. Once advertisers had promoted their products with a description of the product and a price, but as advertising became professionalized, skilled admen crafted elaborate advertising campaigns that prompted consumers to purchase based upon the image that the product could give the consumer. Such a change did not occur overnight; indeed a majority of advertisements still attempted to sell the product via a direct appeal to its quality, value, or price. But the pages of any magazine that carried paid advertisements reveal the increasing appeal of image in the modern era.[60]

59. In Roy P. Churchill's "The Hidden Powers of 'E. T.,'" *American Magazine* (January 1919), aging clerk Ellery Tilford finds business success after purchasing a good pair of shoes and socks and walking back and forth to work (10–14, 68).

60. Roland Marchand's *Advertising the American Dream* remains the standard against which interpretive studies of advertising should be judged, and I borrow from it the periodization of advertising's modernity and all that that entailed. See also Ewen, *Captains of Consciousness;* and Lears, *Fables of Abundance.*

"AND JONES, DON'T FORGET—THIS JOB CALLS FOR PLEASING PERSONALITY"

Grouches—bad temper—are often signs of a run-down physical condition

PERSONALITY has a lot to do with holding down a job. If you're edgy . . . depressed mentally . . . and carry a chip on your shoulder, you can't expect to make a good impression.

Often, people are called difficult to get along with—when the truth is they are overtired, physically run-down.

The cause is usually an "underfed" condition of the blood. Your

Genial and friendly in *all* your relationships—that's your normal state when you're glowing with health. But when your energy gets below par, it's difficult to do your work and keep pleasant.

blood feeds your body. When it is "underfed," not enough nourishment is carried to your nerves and muscles. Your energy suffers. You become low-spirited and out of sorts.

How a simple food stabilizes the nerves

Fleischmann's fresh Yeast increases the activity of the digestive organs—and helps to put more food into the blood stream. In this way more nourishment is carried to the muscle and nerve tissues. Your whole system responds with new energy.

Eat 3 cakes of Fleischmann's Yeast regularly each day—before meals. Eat it plain, or on crackers—or dissolved in a little water or fruit juice. Start today!

It's your blood that "FEEDS" your body

ONE of the important functions of your blood stream is to carry nourishment from your food to the muscle and nerve tissues of your entire body.

When you feel "overtired" at the least little extra effort, it is usually a sign that your blood is not supplied with enough food for your tissues.

What you need is something to provide the full nourishment from your food, so that there is more food for your blood to take up and carry to your tissues.

"I WORRIED when I realized I was no longer as alert as I should be. I was tired before the day began—could hardly drag myself out of bed. I was irritable. Then I took Fleischmann's Yeast, in two or three days the inertia disappeared. You ought to see me in the morning now. After a good sleep I can tear off hours of work without a stop."

Rhodes A. Patterson, Ruston, La.

corrects Run-down condition
by feeding and purifying the blood

Modern masculinity first emerged in advertisements that evoked images of men who achieved success via consumption, like buying Listerine to eradicate halitosis, eating yeast to acquire the pleasing personality that will assure the sale, or adding pep or vigor to life by eating the right breakfast cereal (*American Magazine,* March 1936, 75).

Some of the most remarkable advertisements to appear in the *American Magazine* in the years just after World War I promoted the skills that men needed to succeed in business. In 1919, the Independent Corporation dramatized one of the essential uncertainties of modern corporate life—how to conduct business relationships with unfamiliar people—in ad copy that read, "How to Size People Up from Their Looks." "What I have learned about judging people . . . has already added 25% to my sales," a person trained in Dr. Blackford's Course on Reading Character at Sight reveals. "It is all as clear as a book when you know the simple alphabet of signs that spell out a man's character and his mental 'slants'— an alphabet that is surprisingly easy to learn. . . . And yet learning it was a matter of only a few spare half-hours, while smoking my after-dinner cigar."[61] The ad promised that Dr. Blackford's course would teach you how to read character, but if one could learn to read character then one could also potentially learn to project the attributes of character. Advertisers were ready to show men how.

Several organizations suggested to men reading the *American Magazine* that the key to success lay in developing a more powerful, dynamic, or forceful personality. Their lead lines read "Why Live an Inferior Life?" "How the Biggest Thing in Life Almost Passed Me By," and "How a Failure at Sixty Won Sudden Success," and their text-heavy copy told of men who had made successes of themselves by projecting their will outward. Success, advised the Pelton Publishing Company, marketers of the book *Power of Will,* "was simply a question of dominating will power—determination that brooks no interference, commands respect, and easily leaps all obstacles." One could obtain such a will by buying their book and enacting their program, "For the will is just as susceptible to exercise and training as any muscle of the body." The Mentor Association pitchman, confiding in the reader in a conversational, man-to-man style, says he "had somewhat prided myself on being a self-made man" until he met men whose "broader view of life as well as their ease and fluency in talking marked them as men who were bound to succeed. They had *personality.*" Joining the Mentor Association, he learned personality in his spare time—and so could the readers. Most extravagant of all were the claims made for Alois P. Swoboda's system of Conscious Evolution. Following his system would make men "dynamic, vital, brave, authoritative, forceful, lively, dominant, courageous, self-reliant, daring, progressive, masterful, aroused, powerful and creative." "Do it today! This is your opportunity! Now is your turn! This is your day! This is your hour! Write Now."[62]

61. *American Magazine,* January 1919, 85.

62. Pelton Publishing Company ad, *American Magazine,* January 1919, 101; Mentor Association ad, *American Magazine,* January 1919, 9, 90; Alois P. Swoboda ad, *American Magazine,* March 1919, 84–85.

Ads for personal care products tended to reinforce the notion that by spending just a little men could reshape the way they presented themselves. Durham-Duplex promoted their "He-Man's Razor with the He-Man Blades"; Mifflin Alkohol aftershave depicted a bare-chested, clear-eyed man above copy that read "Moving blood—stamina—the decks of his mind cleared for action— it's going to be a mighty good day in business for him"; a Boncilla facial gave a man "confidence in himself" and earned him the sale.[63] Such advertising tactics, repeated throughout the period in ads directed at men, represented the primary rhetorical vehicle which image-based advertisers used to sell goods to men. It would be naive to argue that men saw these ads and decided that appearance mattered more than substance, that personality mattered more than character. No one ad, no dozen ads, could have such power. But as advertising came to hold a growing number of pages in American magazines and as advertisements developed into an important medium for displaying idealized cultural archetypes, men could not help but be aware of the notion that they might fashion and refashion themselves by purchasing the goods they saw advertised.

Something very curious began to happen to the *American Magazine*'s editorial content in the years following the death of its beloved editor John Siddall in 1923. Both nonfiction and fiction moved away from the celebration of Victorian masculine ideals and into a tenuous embrace of many of the tenets of modern masculinity. The *American Magazine* began to construct masculinity in terms initiated (at least within the magazine) by advertisements, thus suggesting that the ideal man was flexible, eager to conform his identity to the requirements of his increasingly corporate workplace, and interested in the benefits of a pleasing personality. Thus the *American* reconstructed masculine ideals around the flexibility and subjectivity of the male identity.

Under Siddall's editorship, the *American* had revealed a deep distrust of "personality," which Siddall and several of his contributors depicted as a facade that men erected to present themselves to others. Personality was acceptable if it was a clear window on the essential self, but personality followed from and did not take the place of good old Victorian masculine ideals.[64] "Men Who Over-Advertise Themselves," wrote one contributor, were not likely to succeed in the business world, and he marshaled several business stories to prove his point. He concluded: "It may sound too absurd to say that the most

63. *American Magazine*, October 1923, 161, 169.

64. In the unsigned article "What Is Personality?" (*American Magazine*, January 1920, 32–33, 131–33), the author concludes that one's true personality will always be revealed, that real personality must emanate from within. Such was true of the heroic Teddy Roosevelt and Abe Lincoln. False personality was likened to false advertising.

effective form of self-advertising which a man can do is to forget himself. Yet in that seeming absurdity is hidden a very profound truth." These authors were especially concerned with the extent to which young men pursued self-image over competence in a business task.[65]

Following Siddall's death in September of 1923, the magazine began to take a different approach to salesmanship and personality under the editorship of Merle Crowell. Profiles of prominent businessmen continued but tended to emphasize men who had achieved success by working within corporations rather than by building a corporation from scratch. Ads began to feature younger men, mirroring an overall trend toward youth in advertising. And personality, far from being a false god, was something that the *American's* readers were being told how to acquire. In an article titled "Personality—Its 20 Factors and How You Can Develop Them," University of Pittsburgh professor Werrett Wallace Charters related how men could cultivate certain traits that would make them successful in business and in social life. Though Charters's list of "20 Factors" included the old standbys, it also promoted forcefulness, friendliness, adaptability, cheerfulness, neatness, and health habits. Charters advised that men try to see themselves as others saw them and recreate themselves to make up for the qualities that they lacked. "The remedy" for social faults, he declared, "is to become less self-centered." French Strothers carried personality promotion even further in his 1928 piece titled "Cut Loose, and Give Your Personality a Chance," in which he advised readers to "Yield to your impulse to do things that you really want to do," but also to "develop the habit of thinking about the other fellow instead of thinking about yourself."[66] Men were to express their inner selves but in such a way as to respond to the needs and desires of an external audience; they were to combine self-expression with other-direction. What a difference from the advice given to men just a few years earlier.[67]

65. "Men Who Over-Advertise Themselves," *American Magazine,* May 1919, 47, 110–19; see also "He's Slipping," *American Magazine,* October 1920, 15, 86–100. My hunch is that these unsigned articles are written by Siddall himself—they have his tone.

66. Siddall is eulogized in a profile worthy of those done of corporate captains, and the editors vowed to follow in his footsteps ("John M. Siddall," *American Magazine,* October 1923, 7); Werrett Wallace Charters, "Personality—Its 20 Factors and How You Can Develop Them," *American Magazine,* April 1924, 9–10, 74–78; French Strothers, "Cut Loose, and Give Your Personality a Chance," *American Magazine,* February 1928, 42, 171.

67. Medical doctors seemed to concur in this evolving notion of the malleability of the self and joined the magazine's efforts to show men how to create the self they wanted. See William S. Sadler, M.D., "Pep," *American Magazine,* October 1924, 29, 178–84, which advises that "clean living, loyal affection and devotion to those who have the highest claim on you . . . [are] a marvelous help in conserving the power of your personality engine"; and Edward H.

For all the changes I have indicated, it is important to remember that through the 1920s the *American Magazine* remained a magazine dedicated to the success of American men and American business. The majority of its editorials, articles, and stories argued for the maintenance of old-fashioned morality and against the rages of youthful exuberance. Thus influential Baptist minister Harry Emerson Fosdick's claim in 1929 that "Our loosening of moral grip . . . is a national disaster. . . . We Americans need to relearn the serious meanings of self-denial and self-discipline," is more indicative of the overall thrust of the magazine than are assertions that men should cut loose and express themselves.[68] Yet it is precisely because of this Victorian backdrop that the emerging expression of modern masculinity appears so striking. It is as if the editors and writers of the magazine were testing how much of modern masculinity could be allowed to filter in without killing off the old styles altogether.

Collier's also went through a transformation in the way it presented masculine images in the 1920s. The transformation really began in 1924 when the magazine found a new editor, William L. Chenery, who was willing to play a stronger role in shaping the editorial identity of the magazine. Before Chenery, *Collier's* had been a blandly progressive, rural, Republican mix of fiction and nonfiction; under Chenery, the magazine eschewed stodgy nonfiction articles, added energetic and fast-paced fiction, and dramatically updated its layout and illustrations. As Chenery explained to John E. Drewry, "In mood, we particularly like the note of gayety. Characters in bold relief, with good strong silhouettes, against a background of stimulating color, suit us best. We prefer optimistic themes and happy endings, but this doesn't mean that we are afraid of veracity— for we are persuaded that there is no essential incompatibility between truth

---

Smith, "Your Emotions Will Get You If You Don't Watch Out," *American Magazine*, August 1925, 32–33, 72–74.

68. Harry Emerson Fosdick, "America's Biggest Problem," *American Magazine*, May 1929, 86. For support for my statements about the overall conservatism of the magazine, see these editorials: Robert Quillen, "Men Must Speed Up to Hold Their Time-Honored Rank," *American Magazine*, January 1927, 25; Quillen, "There Is Less Chance of Mutiny If Dad Is Captain of the Ship," *American Magazine*, August 1926, 55; and Merle Crowell, *American Magazine*, July 1928, 3; see these articles: Albert Payson Terhune, "They Are Hell Bent!" *American Magazine*, June 1928, 11–13, 108–12; and Harry Emerson Fosdick, "What Is Happening to the American Family?" *American Magazine*, October 1928, 20–21, 96–102; and see these stories: Priscilla Hovey, "The Father Who Didn't Understand," *American Magazine*, April 1925, 57–59, 109–10; and Robert Buchmann, "Boys Will Be Boisterous: The Story of Two Sentimental Sailors and a Pair of Sophisticated Flappers," *American Magazine*, February 1927, 52–55, 179–82.

and romance."[69] The magazine became, in a word, jazzier, and thus expressed far better than before a spirit of youthful optimism and energy. Circulation boomed in response, from 850,000 in 1924 to over 1,500,000 in 1927.[70]

The changes soon became evident: short stories like "The Fortunate Woman" were far racier than anything the magazine had previously published; nonfiction pieces like "The Book of Crime Wave Etiquette" and "What Good Are Lawyers?" took a satirical (rather than a sober) look at contemporary issues; and "The Old Familiar Faces," a sports survey written by Grantland Rice, was unusually studded with close-up pictures of the young athletes.[71] The illustrations that accompanied the articles showed the influence of modern magazine design, with cleaner, more dynamic lines. Perhaps most startling, the editors seemed to have reviewed the results of their Prohibition poll and decided they were on the wrong side of the issue; under Chenery, Prohibition became the butt of jokes and satirical asides. In all, the magazine seemed far more intent on entertaining than on instructing.

The sudden embrace of this upbeat editorial policy also meant the abrupt disappearance of Victorian masculine imagery: profiles of dour achievers no longer had a place in Chenery's magazine. According to Scribner's contributor Hickman Powell, Collier's "dispenses a dependable quota of murderous fictional villains and of young women in shorts and halters, with long, slim athletic legs, vibrantly in love with young men who have long slim legs, hair on their chests, and a wallop in each fist." Love stories like "Flamingoes," by Struthers Burt, captured the change. A light love story set in a tropical location, "Flamingoes" was driven by a boy-gets-girl narrative told without recourse to an extended description of the man's character and accompanied by illustrations that highlighted the near nudity of the female subjects. Victorian man was removed from the magazine's nonfiction as well. In "Izzy and Moe Stop the Show," John K. Winkler relates the story of two "famous hooch hounds" who "had a collection of more than a hundred true-to-life disguises—with a convincing line of patter to go with each one"; thus the very heroes of the conservative Prohibition movement are cast as clever masters of disguise. A photo spread called "Enter the Hardboiled Era" compared contemporary film stars with those of an earlier generation. The current stars were described as "beefy,"

69. John E. Drewry, "Collier's, The National Weekly," The Writer, February 1936; quoted in Drewry, Contemporary American Magazines, 18.

70. Hickman Powell, "Collier's," Scribner's, May 1939, 19–23, 36.

71. Juliet Wilbor Tompkins, "The Fortunate Woman," Collier's, January 2, 1926, 9–10, 43; H. I. Phillips, "The Book of Crime Wave Etiquette," Collier's, January 2, 1926, 11–12, 36; Judge Ewing Cockrell, "What Good Are Lawyers?" Collier's, January 2, 1926, 20, 36; Grantland Rice, "The Old Familiar Faces," Collier's, January 2, 1926, 21.

"ferocious," "steely," while yesterday's idols were merely "dee-vine" or "dainty." Their pictures seconded the language, showing old stars as melancholic, even effeminate, while the new stars were stern, aggressive, "hard-boiled."[72] What was most unique about this pictorial was not the preference for new stars over old, but the holding up of film stars as models for masculine emulation. It was as if modern masculine imagery had rushed in to fill the void left by the disappearance of the Victorian man.

The changing character of the magazine soon attracted advertisers eager to reach the *Collier's* audience. The magazine carried many of the same advertisements found in the *American Magazine*, though it never received as many of the self-improvement ads as the more success-oriented *American*.[73] Arrow collars began to advertise in 1929, and in the same issue Gene Tunney pitched a product called Nujol and promised that "Health Can Be Earned." A series of ads called "Why Famous Men of the Day Use Barbasol" featured celebrity pitches for Barbasol shaving lotion and skin freshener, and the ad copy claimed that "Women like their men young looking, bright and keenly fresh looking. Men like to be this way too." Ads for socks and deodorant tapped into the same rhetoric, trying to convince men that ever more elements of their appearance were crucial to their success in business and their success at attracting women. "He'd be in the market for a solitaire today if his socks had been as smooth as his wooing. But she said: 'No'—quietly, but firmly. She detested slovenly habits—and sloppy socks were her pet peeve. (Don't think that women are 'funny that way.' It's the little things in life that count for the most after all.) A modern Romeo needn't be a Sheik, but he dare not be . . . a Freak!" read the ad for Paris garters. Clearly, the language of modern masculinity had come to *Collier's* magazine.[74]

The embrace of modern masculine tropes in both editorial content and in advertising was accompanied by an emphasis on youthfulness and action. Stories that had focused on the development of a character were replaced with stories that accentuated action. The pivotal moments of stories, once merely alluded to, were now dramatized in pictures: where once a love story would have had a picture of man and woman looking at each other across a crowded room,

72. Powell, *"Collier's,"* 19; Struthers Burt, "Flamingoes," *Collier's,* February 6, 1926, 18–19, 43–45; John K. Winkler, "Izzy and Moe Stop the Show," *Collier's,* February 6, 1926, 15; "Enter the Hardboiled Hero," *Collier's,* June 4, 1927, 14–15.

73. That it carried many of the same ads is not surprising, since the Crowell Publishing Company, which published the *American Magazine,* bought *Collier's* in 1919.

74. Such advertising strategies began to appear shortly after Chenery's arrival and were quite prevalent by 1929. For specific ads in *Collier's,* see Arrow collars, February 2, 1929, 29; Barbasol, April 6, 1929, 47; Paris garters, June 7, 1930, 3.

Like the gentleman depicted on this 1925 cover, *Collier's* seemed slightly puzzled by the emphasis on male style and personality that began to influence magazines in the 1920s (*Collier's*, September 12, 1925).

now they were inches apart, just about to kiss—or just quitting; where once you saw policeman arriving at a crime that was already over, now you saw the bad guy pointing the gun in the victim's ribs. Moreover, whereas women were always featured prominently in illustrations, their level of dress now became increasingly skimpy; by 1933 *Collier's* presented a woman in a see-through full-length gown, her body positioned so that nothing is revealed. But the covers captured the change best. A typical cover of the pre-Chenery *Collier's* appeared in 1925 and featured a nice old codger smiling ruefully at the cover of a modern magazine; the more modern *Collier's* appeared in August 1930 and featured a strapping college-age man in a bathing suit.[75]

Modern Masculinity and the Depression

The economic depression precipitated by the stock market crash of October 1929 is widely considered to be one of the pivotal events of the twentieth century, changing everything that it touched. Increasingly dependent on advertising dollars, which were themselves a barometer of economic prosperity, magazines felt the impact of the Great Depression as soon as advertisers felt it necessary to cut back on their expenditures. The cutback in advertising dollars affected every magazine and destroyed some, but it did not alter the underlying economic dynamic that allowed for the mass magazine. Magazines did not look for new ways to underwrite their efforts; most just cut back on pages and weathered the storm. The depression also shaped the way magazines expressed their vision of American masculinity, forcing them to reconcile their notions of manhood with the limited prospects for success brought by the depression. The *American Magazine*, which had tied masculinity so closely to economic success and Victorian values, floundered in its attempts to speak optimistically about men's prospects for getting ahead but could not embrace modern masculinity fully. The *Athletic Journal* went on championing Victorian masculinity, and eventually found in the coming of war some way of reclaiming the legitimacy of its ideals. But *Collier's*, which had embraced modern masculine values most readily, found that those values were not incompatible with the newly difficult circumstances facing men and emerged as the magazine most capable of weathering the depression.

Within the span of a year, two events changed the nature of the *American Magazine*. The first event was the "stock market upheaval" of 1929, which

75. The kiss is in Bernard DeVoto, "The Girl Who Saved Herself," *Collier's,* August 26, 1933, 17, 32–34; the crime scene in Ernest Haycox, "Wild Enough," *Collier's,* September 16, 1933, 14–15, 51–53; the skimpy dress in Damon Runyon, "What, No Butler?" *Collier's,* August 5, 1933, 7–9, 30; old man cover, *Collier's,* September 12, 1925; young man cover, *Collier's,* August 2, 1930.

contributor M. K. Wisehart listed as just the sixth biggest news story of 1929, behind such celebrated occasions as the concordat between the Vatican and the Italian government and the formulation of the Young reparation plan.[76] For months to follow, the *American* barely deigned to notice the crash. The second event occurred in April of 1930, when the magazine got a new editor, Sumner Blossom. Blossom quickly updated the magazine: new artists used cleaner, less-cluttered illustrations and tended to draw women in shorter dresses and more revealing bathing suits; stories were set in the city rather than the country and were racier and more frivolous; the titles of both stories and articles were louder and catchier.[77] The magazine, in short, became more like *Collier's.* It is difficult to tell which of these two events changed the *American Magazine* more, the Great Depression or the new editor. But within six years the *American* would change its identity completely.

The most striking change in the articles printed in the *American* as the depression progressed was the abandonment of the optimism that had accompanied Victorian masculinity, the attitude that American men could achieve whatever they desired. Merryle Stanley Rukeyser said it well in his January 1930 article: "In the rail-splitting pioneer days, leadership went inevitably to forceful men—men with a powerful will and a sense of mastery. . . . But since America has come of age in a business sense, the older qualities are not enough." These days, Rukeyser quoted Paul H. Nystrom, "Fashion is one of the greatest forces in present-day life," and the man who understands how to make people want something they do not have is the one who will succeed. In May of 1930, Emil Ludwig advanced the unique proposition that "Greatness is always masculine. It is always productive, never receptive. Always gives, never receives." But this, he claimed, is not an age for greatness, for democratization and the rough equality produced in this country create the conditions in which greatness is unlikely. In the language of our day, Ludwig was saying that a culture driven by consumption is not productive of the greatness associated with older styles of masculinity. Editor Blossom stated the implications best in a memo he sent to his staff. "Horatio Alger doesn't work here any more," it read.[78]

76. M. K. Wisehart, "Extra! Who's Who and What's What in the News," *American Magazine,* January 1930, 92.

77. In the April issue alone there are stories titled "About the Length of Skirts" and "Goddess in the Car," and articles titled "Men Wanted" and "Living for the Fun of It."

78. Merryle Stanley Rukeyser, "The Kind of Men Who Get Along Today," *American Magazine,* January 1930, 66, 133; Emil Ludwig, "What Makes a Man Stand Out from the Crowd," *American Magazine,* May 1930, 15, 163–66. Such views again counter the notion that the Great Depression was the pivotal event in changing American masculinity; these

If Horatio Alger stories were not going to work for the *American* any more, what would? There were several answers to this question. First, a number of articles suggested that men scale back their expectations. Bruce Barton, former profiler of corporate captains, put his talents to work relating the success stories of one man who goes door to door offering to wash people's dogs, another who raises chickens out in his backyard, and still another who rents rowboats to vacationing rich folks. Edgar C. Wheeler's piece, whose subtitle reads "Fortune rides with many a man who has mounted his hobby to chase the wolf from the door," held similar lessons. Throughout the articles both writers emphasized ingenuity and flexibility over dogged determination or pride. The authors tried to relate the skills needed to survive the depression back to values like integrity and control, but their efforts seemed strained.[79]

Victorian masculinity as it was framed by the *American* had once presented a uniform ideal of male success, which the magazine had made tangible by depicting dashing and well-dressed college men, salesmen, and corporate executives sharing a set of core values as they pursued their upward trajectory. In the 1930s distinctively different images began to appear. Articles suggested the valor of physical labor and often depicted working-class men, as in Edmund M. Littell's 1930 feature on steelworkers titled "Men Wanted." And a new subgenre of fiction began to appear that told stories of working-class men, usually drawn with bare chests and jutting chins, whose courage saved the life of some weaker man in a more powerful position.[80] The point of view of such fiction also shifted to accommodate the diminished expectations the magazine had for American men. In the past, stories had been told primarily from the position of one who had succeeded; now they were told from the position of one who looked upon success, perhaps even one who had been blocked from success. Another departure from the older stance toward men was the growing emphasis on youth and personality. Youth had been seen as misguided and a little dangerous in the very early 1920s, especially under Siddall's leadership; by the 1930s young people were lauded for their willingness to accept challenges

---

writers assume that men had changed *prior* to their realizing the full import of the crash. Blossom's memo is quoted in Peterson, *Magazines,* 143.

79. Bruce Barton, "Out of a Job, What Would You Do?" *American Magazine,* December 1931, 49–50, 104–7; Edgar C. Wheeler, "What Can You Do to Make Money?" *American Magazine,* July 1932, 44–45, 70–72. See also John T. Flynn, "What Chance Have You in a Small Business?" *American Magazine,* November 1932, 11–13, 86–88.

80. Edmund M. Littell, "Men Wanted," *American Magazine,* April 1930, 46–51, 115–22; Frank Knox Hockman, "White-Hot," *American Magazine,* October 1931, 22–25, 90–96; Stanley Paul, "A Bit of Brass," *American Magazine,* November 1933, 46–49, 122–24.

and for their gumption.[81] Paul Gallico explained the popularity of sports heroes like Jack Dempsey, Babe Ruth, Dizzy Dean, and Walter Hagen in terms of their charisma and personality; notably missing from his list of those who "got the crowd" was Lou Gehrig, the iron man whose record stood as a modern-day testament to the virtues of bygone masculinity. Gehrig, implied Gallico, was boring.[82]

Two articles published a year and a half apart indicate the extent to which the *American* had abandoned its earlier conception of masculinity. In February of 1934, the *American* published a short piece called "A Young Man Speaks His Mind," in which "J. W." suggests that all the values his parents and his schools have taught him are useless in the modern world. In the most direct challenge to Victorian masculine values ever published in the magazine, J. W. writes, "So one good reason, please, Mr. Editor, why an ambitious young man should be honest. It's got to be a real, practical reason, too. And don't talk to me about great men having been honest. I don't want to be great. I want to be comfortable." The death of the Victorian masculine archetype was dealt a further blow in July of 1935, when Jack Dempsey authored a piece called "He-Men Wear Aprons," in which the boxing great provides his favorite cooking stories and recipes alongside pictures of himself in an apron.[83]

With its editor and its contributors no longer able to sustain the idealism of the Victorian self-made man, the *American Magazine* slowly transformed itself into a women's magazine. Articles written by and for women proliferated, and they mirrored the kind of domestic advice given in popular women's magazines.[84] The fiction became far more romantic, its illustrations featuring swooning damsels and brawny men.[85] And the advertising was increasingly pitched toward women. By 1936, the *American Magazine* had ceased to be a magazine for men at all. It seemed that if they could no longer present Victorian values as the key

81. Hubert Kelley, "Youth Goes into Action," *American Magazine,* February 1935, 12–13, 110–12.

82. Paul Gallico, "Why They Get the Crowd," *American Magazine,* April 1935, 51, 146–48.

83. "A Young Man Speaks His Mind," *American Magazine,* February 1934, 44–45; Jack Dempsey, "He-Men Wear Aprons," *American Magazine,* July 1935, 16–17, 100–104.

84. A good example is Agnes Sligh Turnbull's "She's Doing Her Own Work," *American Magazine,* August 1933, 30–31, 84–86, which validates the woman who cannot hire household servants and does her housework herself. A recipe is provided, and the editor claims to like it. See also "How to Get Along with the Neighbors," *American Magazine,* January 1936, 69, 82–83; and "I Hate Housework," *American Magazine,* January 1936, 63, 142–43.

85. Ruth Burr Sanborn, "His Endurance Test: A Week-End Party . . . a Wild Night Ride . . . and at the End, Romance, Superb and Unforgettable," *American Magazine,* June 1930, 22–25, 142–48; Margaret E. Sangster, "The Way of a Man," *American Magazine,* March 1936, 28–31, 90–93.

By the 1930s, the *American Magazine* presented even the toughest men—in this case boxing great Jack Dempsey—in garb that suggested that men reconsider traditional roles (*American Magazine*, July 1935, 16).

to success for American men, then they would abandon the championing of masculine values altogether.

Athletic Journal editor John Griffith, another fervent champion of Victorian masculine values, reacted to the depression in a suitably Victorian way: he dug in his heels and fought with all his might against what he saw as the diminishment of America and American men. As the depression worsened and Roosevelt implemented the New Deal, Griffith's defense of the masculine athletic code became increasingly embattled. The Great Depression was a test of men, he argued. Strong men would stand up to the challenge; weak ones would succumb to the "cults of the under men, the cult of incompetence." Griffith's stance offers one way of complicating our easy understanding of the relationship between economic decline and masculinity, which holds that men were "emasculated" by the depression and looked to a protective state for succor.[86] But Griffith urges that men not dwell on their decline in economic status but view it as a challenge to overcome. In increasingly ideological editorials, Griffith aligned himself against the New Deal and what he saw as its various foreign equivalents: totalitarianism, fascism, communism, and socialism. Yet by 1940 Griffith had found in the impending war some hope that the masculine ideals he defended might still have a place in America. Beginning that year, Griffith began to promote athletics as preparation for war, showing athletic men as warriors, and he was pleased to see resistance to his Spartan code diminishing. "Today, with a world war in the offing, we hear very little criticism of the manly sports which place an emphasis on courage, strength, and a fighting spirit," he exulted. The nation's need for a fighting force thus might redeem it from twenty years of dissipation.[87] Little could he know that the war would further women's entrance into the economy, reassert the guiding power of the state, and spark a boom

86. Quote from Griffith, "Strength or Weakness," *Athletic Journal,* January 1935, 20; for appropriate male reactions to the depression and "state capitalism," see "Christmas 1932," *Athletic Journal,* December 1932, 21; "Looking Ahead," *Athletic Journal,* June 1937, 22; and "An American Type," *Athletic Journal,* June 1939, 20. Peter Filene holds that the widespread unemployment associated with the Great Depression challenged the strict correlation between a man's job and his masculine identity: "If a man could not say 'I am an accountant' or a lawyer or a pharmacist, it became harder to say 'I am a man' " (*Him/Her/Self,* 176). Peter Stearns, who argues that the relationship between work and masculinity identity had been loosening for some time, contends, "The Depression was a severe blow to man-as-breadwinner" (*Be a Man!* 127).

87. Griffith, "Twenty Years," *Athletic Journal,* March 1941, 28. See also "Athletics and the National Defense," *Athletic Journal,* December 1940, 12; "Are the People of the United States Too Soft?" *Athletic Journal,* January 1941, 16; "Athletics and the National Defense," *Athletic Journal,* April 1941, 14; and "The Value of School and College Athletics in the Present Crisis," *Athletic Journal,* May 1941, 18–19, June 1941, 18–19.

in mass culture and consumerism unlike anything the country had ever seen. Griffith's warriors might serve the country in time of war, but the ideals those warriors represented—character, courage, integrity—were part of a unitary self that was no longer fully embraced by popular magazines.

Griffith's stand on the importance of strenuous masculinity was in many ways an anachronism. No other editor or publication stuck so steadfastly to such a view of essential maleness. Yet Griffith's position is also important, for it emphasizes the endurance of certain elements of masculinity in the face of widespread change. Griffith carried the banner for the martial spirit, for male aggression as an end in itself, for what he called "athletic asceticism." That ascetic martial spirit had been dramatically de-emphasized in a culture based upon mass entertainment, consumerism, and corporate capitalism. In times of peace, the character traits developed by such training served no useful purpose except on the field of play. But war could and did call forth the remnants of the martial masculine ideology that were useful. Until the potential need for organized violence is either eliminated or abstracted (via technology, for example, in the Gulf War), it seems that our culture will find ways to maintain the athletic ascetic mode of masculinity, either by segregating it into an appropriate domain—for example, the military subculture of the armed forces, military academies, and quasi-military boy's organizations—or ritualizing it in organized sports.

Collier's had a far easier time adjusting its portrayal of masculinity to the exigencies of the Great Depression. Since *Collier's* had never been a big promoter of self-improvement or an incessant commentator on what it took to make a man, like the *American*, it was not forced to confront the paradox of promoting success in an economy of decline. Its way of expressing an opinion on masculinity was to offer stories that accentuated the importance of personality and physical vitality, including illustrations that highlighted appearance, and advertising the benefits of improvement through consumption. But the magazine had to come to grips with the fact that men who were just coming to see themselves as consumers might react to economic hard times by retreating to a sense of identity removed from the consumer marketplace. Could they continue to offer men the same kinds of images, or would the pressures of the depression force *Collier's* to change its tone and its personality?

For the better part of 1932, it seemed that *Collier's* would go the way of the *American Magazine*, reorienting the contents of the magazine to appeal to women, trustworthy consumers that they were. Even more of the stories were centered around love, and increasingly they were written from the viewpoint of the woman in the story, an implicit narrative pitch to a feminine audience. In stories like "Men Don't Understand" and "The Primrose Path" (whose come-on line read: "They told her St. Louis was a bad, wicked town. So she hopped on the ten-two and went there"), both the story and the accompanying illustrations were projected via the female character. The nonfiction took a similar tack, as in the article "From Hand to Hand," which commented on the proliferation of manicure salons in America.[88] But the advertising did not follow suit, and the sense of a panicked pursuit of women readers soon disappeared.[89]

The story of this crucial editorial indecision and of the coinciding decision at the *American Magazine* to adjust the contents of their magazine to appeal to a feminine audience is one of the mysteries that I have been unable to solve. *Collier's* and the *American Magazine* were owned by the same company and it is hard to imagine that management would not have sought for these magazines to appeal to different audiences so as not to steal readers from one another. But when the *American* downplayed its success-story agenda and updated its stories and typographic style, it began to look much like *Collier's*. How would the magazines differentiate themselves?

I believe that the magazines' respective success at drawing advertising dollars had something to do with the decisions that led to the *American* reorienting itself to a feminine audience while *Collier's* continued its more masculine appeal to a general audience. The *American Magazine* had long relied on self-improvement ads to fill a large block of their advertising pages, but these advertisers dropped off precipitously during the depression. Their choice was to turn to a more reliable source of advertising dollars, the women's market. *Collier's*, on the other hand, tried a different approach. According to Hickman Powell, *Collier's* executive Tom Beck said to advertising manager Theodore Lee Brantly: "Come on, we're going out and sell advertising. They don't know it now, but they're still going to need it." The two embarked on a shoe-string-budgeted canvass of advertisers that convinced many clients to continue to place ads despite the financial decline. Thus *Collier's* was not forced to radically change its advertising strategy because it aggressively pursued the same types of advertisers it had always carried. According to Powell, the number of other magazines carrying "lipstick and lingerie" ads made it easier for *Collier's* to get the "industrial accounts," because the two "don't mix."[90] By 1937 and 1938, such a philosophy allowed *Collier's* to carry even more advertisements than the venerable *Saturday Evening Post*.

88. Dana Burnet, "Men Don't Understand," *Collier's*, August 6, 1932, 9, 48–52; Stephen Morehouse Avery, "The Primrose Path," *Collier's*, August 6, 1932, 14–16, 47; John B. Kennedy, "From Hand to Hand," *Collier's*, October 1, 1932, 13, 30.

89. See Powell, "*Collier's*," 36.

90. Ibid.

Collier's soon returned to a more balanced array of stories, featuring such manly fare as a "superb sea drama" called "The Hero" by Albert Richard Wetjen and some good detective stories, including "They Can Only Hang You Once" by hard-boiled crime writer Dashiell Hammett and "Too Many Miles" by William MacHarg. If anything, the men portrayed in *Collier's* during the depression got tougher. In "Fighting Man," for instance, Quentin Reynolds tells the story of a boxer whose girlfriend, Lota, tells him he must choose between her and his sport. As the fight begins, Terry, the boxer, decides to throw the fight, but he wants to throw it "like a man"—he will let himself get knocked out. After getting saved by the bell following his opponent's big punch, Terry realizes that he would not be a man if he let a punch like that take him out. Throwing away the happy prospects of a life with Lota, Terry regains command and knocks out his opponent. The story ends with Lota apologizing for ever tempting him away from his manhood and promising to be a good, submissive wife.[91] It seems that once Chenery got over his fear that male readers would disappear in droves, he returned to giving them the same kind of stories they had seemed to enjoy in the late 1920s. Thus *Collier's* editorial content weathered the storm of the depression largely unchanged from the pattern that it had developed under Chenery in the late 1920s.

Though Chenery seemed not to display much anxiety over the challenges the depression posed to American manhood, the advertisers who continued to pitch their products to men certainly did. Advertisements had long pointed out to men conditions such as dandruff or bad breath that their products could help eradicate, but during the 1930s the tenor of the ads for such products often became shrill or desperate. Listerine ads had always tapped into the fear that people noticed dandruff, but the ad that appeared on June 4, 1932, took this paranoia to a new level. At the center of the ad is a large picture of a man looking with concern at the dandruff he brushes off his shoulder; floating in the air all around him are accusatory pointing fingers, and the ad copy above reads "It disgusts—it repels—it's inexcusable!" in increasingly larger type, followed by the imperative: "get rid of that dandruff." Another Listerine ad that appeared slightly later had the bold headline "Men Women Despise" and related the news that "There are a half-dozen of them in every large office. If your luck's bad you often draw one as a partner at the bridge table." This time the offender is bad breath, but the message is the same. A 1937 ad for Ipana toothpaste depicts the unmanning of a fellow who has failed to educate himself as a consumer, failed

91. Albert Richard Wetjen, "The Hero," *Collier's,* November 19, 1932, 12–13, 48–49; Dashiell Hammett, "They Can Only Hang You Once," *Collier's,* November 19, 1932, 22–24; William MacHarg, "Too Many Miles," *Collier's,* April 8, 1932, 11, 55; Quentin Reynolds, "Fighting Man," *Collier's,* December 7, 1935, 12–13, 29–30.

to learn about toothpaste. "Child-like in his Dental Knowledge—thousands of grown-ups *never* take care of their gums" the headline above a picture of a man wearing a baby bonnet reads. Ads this shrill in their appeal seemed determined to frighten men into buying the product, or to chasten them for not consuming wisely enough to avoid such pitfalls; perhaps advertisers thought this was what was necessary to get money out of men's pockets during economic hard times.[92]

In all, the approach used by Grape Nuts seemed a more astute analysis of what might appeal to men eager for improvement in their condition. The ad is a full-page comic strip titled "Red Gets His Chance," and it features a youth named Red who walks through a woods worrying about being out of a job and unable to send his mother any money. Soon a wealthy aristocrat and his daughter pass him on horseback and the daughter's horse gets out of control. Red runs after the pair, taking a shortcut through the woods and appearing just in time to save the girl. "Young man, that was marvelous," says the father. "I can use your spirit and energy in my business! Come home with us and talk it over. Tell me, where in the world do you get all that energy?" The youth replies, "Well, Sir,—I was brought up on Grape-Nuts." Not only does the young man get the job, but the daughter's comment—"Red always was my favorite color"—hints that he'll get the girl as well.[93] The premise of this ad was no more plausible than the scare ads, but it coincided more easily with the cheery tone of the editorial pages.

In the end it seemed to make more sense for both editors and advertisers to take an optimistic approach to crafting their messages. People turned to magazines like *Collier's* for entertainment, not for scary reminders of the difficulty of their situation. In taking this optimistic and forward-looking stance, magazines like *Collier's* continued to promote the modern masculine ideals that they had come to embrace during the 1920s. Modern masculinity continued to thrive in many magazines despite the undeniable chastening effects of the depression. After all, modern masculinity did not center around a man's commitment to his job or to his reliability as patriarchal head of the family, elements of manhood that the depression had called into question. Modern masculinity allowed men to understand themselves through their personality, their physical vitality, and their ability to enjoy their leisure time, and men could continue to see themselves as successful in these terms despite the difficulties they may have been facing in other areas of their life.

92. Listerine, *Collier's*, June 4, 1932, 21, and April 6, 1935, 3; Ipana, *Collier's*, April 10, 1937, 10.
93. Grape Nuts, *Collier's*, October 1, 1932, 31.

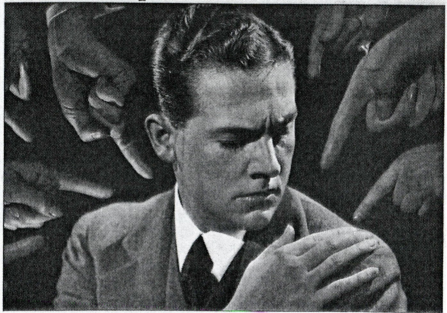

it disgusts—it repels—it's inexcusable!

get rid of that dandruff

Ads such as this suggested that men needed an array of products to fit in to the corporate workplace—and that they were in danger if they didn't use such products (*Collier's,* June 4, 1932, 21). (© Warner-Lambert Company.)

Collier's seemed to understand this dynamic, for it continued to put a positive spin on manhood during the depression. In a Chenery editorial called "Man to Man," the editor praises President Franklin Delano Roosevelt as a modern man whose skills at dealing with people, whose "capacity for friendship and human understanding," are what make him an effective president. The magazine did not heap praise on hard work, for plenty of hard-working people were now unemployed, but it offered a generous profile of actor Robert Taylor, who reached his position of stardom entirely on his good looks. Taylor rose to the top every time the right person noticed how handsome he was, and he "is the first to tell you that he had very little to do with [his success]."[94] Such articles suggested that plenty of real men were getting by on a good personality and good looks. These were hardly serious analyses of the prospects for manhood in a time of crisis, but they were what *Collier's* had to offer.

The masculinity portrayed in American magazines underwent significant and undeniable changes in the two decades following World War I. By the mid-1930s, Victorian masculine ideals—self-control, hard work, character—were no longer championed as keys to success in mass-market publications. Instead, most magazines promoted an outer-directed, flexible notion of manhood. How did such a transformation come to pass? One of the most compelling forces driving this change was modern advertising. Modern advertisers learned to craft sophisticated appeals to men that openly promoted male absorption in appearance, personality, and an ongoing process of self-creation. But it is hard to imagine that advertising would have succeeded at transforming the normative ideals of masculinity had it not worked in conjunction with the editorial content of the magazines.

While magazines like the *American Magazine* and *Collier's* offered visions of Victorian masculinity alongside advertisements that promoted modern values, other magazines showed no such inconsistency. Many of the magazines that appeared in this period sought to align themselves with new trends in modern culture. Their editors offered images of modern masculinity that were aligned with shifts in the economic marketplace and sympathetic to emerging popular fascinations with celebrity, youthfulness, sports, and fashion. These editors were not self-consciously creating images of masculinity to suit the needs of consumer culture, but rather were often unconsciously intimating a new understanding of masculinity that was already committed to the images and ideals that made modern masculinity so suitable to consumer culture. In short, while I argue that many of the editors of modern magazines—Frank Crowninshield of *Vanity Fair*, Orison Swett Marden of *Success*, Jim Nasium of *Sporting Life*, and J. D. Fetzer of the *Athletic World*—offered up images of modern masculinity that were consistent with those offered by advertisements, they seemed to do so out of a sincere belief in the efficacy of those ideals (both as ideals and as effective strategies for attracting a wide readership) rather than as a craven caving in to the wiles of corporate interests. As new editors came to take control of the *American Magazine* and *Collier's*, they too reshaped their magazines to accommodate an increased emphasis on modern masculinity. Only John D. Griffith expressed

94. William Chenery, "Man to Man," *Collier's*, February 3, 1934; Kyle Crichton, "Heart Thumper," *Collier's*, October 3, 1936, 55.

the kind of anxiety with the coming of modern masculinity that those who have decried the transforming effects of consumer culture predicted. For the great majority of those who expressed themselves in American magazines, modern masculinity suited their needs just fine.

Modern masculinity was at once the creation of advertisers eager to create consumers and editors and writers eager to offer understandings of masculinity that were consonant with larger cultural changes and exciting enough to attract readers in a competitive magazine market. In the years to come, visions of modern masculinity would become even more widespread as they were taken up as the reason for being by such magazines as *Esquire, True,* and *Argosy.* These magazines developed the central images of modern masculinity in such a way as to make them workable for an ever wider variety of white men, from urban sophisticates to rural workers. Even *Ebony,* which in 1945 became the first mass-market magazine for African Americans, managed to find in modern masculinity some ways to integrate black men into the embrace of American consumer culture.

4

From the Ground Up

Reclaiming the Basis for Masculinity in African American Magazines, 1910–1949

By 1910, one thing was clear to anyone trying to publish a magazine for African Americans: commercial success was still a long way off. Too few blacks could afford to subscribe to a general-interest magazine, or they were not interested in spending their limited funds on a magazine that was not nearly as slick and expensively designed as white counterparts; too few advertisers were willing to subsidize its publication; and editors found it impossible to present the happy overview of life that seemed to be required of a medium of entertainment. After all, who wanted to relax after a hard day's work by reading about discrimination, the minor stars of a distant black theater scene, or the meager successes of a black undertaker's assistant? While white magazines of the day presented a lush and optimistic vision of a world of goods and success, black magazines offered an emaciated imitation of the same. And so the black general-interest magazine failed and was replaced by the race journal, a resource that offered very different visions of the prospects for African American men.

For W. E. B. Du Bois, the failure of one kind of magazine begat the success of another kind, and this transfer of his editing fortunes represented a kind of victory over Booker T. Washington in their battle to act as the leading spokesman for the concerns of their race. When the general interest publications the *Colored American* and *Alexander's* went under, they took with them the stories of black economic success that could occur only within the circumscribed realm of Washington's program for racial advancement. With the *Crisis* now the major magazine reporting on the black condition, readers could not help but see that Negroes in America were hemmed in, trampled on, mistreated, and maligned— nor could they escape Du Bois's claim that the way out of their predicament was to stand up and agitate for their rights *like men*. To be sure, the *Crisis* was not the only magazine reporting on the black condition in this era. Among the number of black publications that sprang up in these decades, especially just following World War I, the *Crusader* and the *Messenger* stand out as examples of successful African American periodicals. But these magazines were as different from the *Crisis* as a magazine like the *Masses* was from the *Saturday Evening Post*. Committed to a truly radical political agenda—the *Crusader* to communism, the *Messenger* to socialism—these magazines just do not belong in a study of magazines that were devoted at least in part to promoting success within a capitalist economic system.[1]

In the *Crisis,* Du Bois succeeded in articulating a vision for gaining full access to economic and political equality; that vision included within it a vision of black masculinity. While Du Bois did not hesitate to recognize black success, he refused to accept limited economic gains coupled with the appropriate adherence to Victorian values as the proper end of the black man's ambition. For Washington and the publications that embraced his ideology, playing the game of economic ascension, mouthing the truths of hard work, sincerity, and trustworthiness, and slowly gaining some measure of economic success were the appropriate paths toward claiming some form of legitimate cultural space for black Americans. For Du Bois and his magazine, such achievements were inadequate if they were not accompanied by a public and legal recognition of the rights of Negroes as men (and women). Du Bois insisted that until black men were accepted as men—as equal participants in American society with the same rights and opportunities—any achievements would be less than complete, for they would exist in a black world apart. Thus his magazine advocated a masculinity that had to be reconstructed from the ground up and on the same terms as the white man's masculinity—it must be based on the full protection of the law, on full citizenship, and on the assumption of the essential dignity of the individual, and not on the mere achievements that "good" Negroes could carve out in the limited space made available to them in Jim Crow America.

What is so ironic about the career of the *Crisis* is that it was begun with the supposition that a black magazine could not make it, and it ended up as the first black magazine to make it; it recognized from the outset that it would have a hard time gaining either advertisers or subscribers, and then went out and won over both.[2] By 1916 the magazine had gathered enough subscribers to pay

1. On the *Crusader,* see Robert A. Hill, introduction to *The Crusader*; on the *Messenger,* see Theodore Kornweibel Jr., *No Crystal Stair: Black Life and the* Messenger, *1917–1928.*

2. Two good accounts of the early years of the *Crisis* are Charles Flint Kellogg, *NAACP: A History of the National Association for the Advancement of Colored People,* vol. 1, *1909–1920;* and David Levering Lewis, *W. E. B. Du Bois: Biography of a Race, 1868–1919,* 408–34.

the salary of its editor, who had until that point been "paid for" by the NAACP. And it achieved all of these successes while promoting an openly radical vision of black masculinity. Of course it never obtained the support of white national advertisers.

The *Crisis* would be the reigning black magazine for the next thirty or so years, its dominance never seriously challenged by the other race-issue magazine, *Opportunity,* published by the National Urban League, or by the sprinkling of other general-interest publications that appeared and quickly disappeared in these years. Together with *Opportunity* and Robert Vann's *Competitor,* the *Crisis* established advocacy for manhood rights as the baseline from which most other magazine representations of the black experience sprang. But this advocacy for manhood rights bumped into the color line all through these years, and the collision sent representations of black masculinity scattering off in a number of directions. On the one hand, black men were encouraged to reject the individualism implicit in the capitalist visions of manly achievement and to embrace instead economic cooperation, if not outright socialism. On the other hand, the early rise of black culture "stars"—athletes (especially runners and boxers), musicians, and literary artists—took black representations in a direction that was rapidly becoming mainstream in white culture. The promotion of black celebrities offered a back door into mainstream acceptance that Washington had never imagined. Such representations of black masculinity continued to develop independently of the pressures that consumer culture placed on white masculinity.

Du Bois and the *Crisis*

From the very first issue, *Crisis* editor Du Bois made clear his intention to dedicate the magazine to a serious purpose. "The object of this publication," he announced, "is to set forth those facts and arguments which show the danger of race prejudice, particularly as manifested to-day toward colored people. It takes its name from the fact that the editors believe that this is a critical time in the history of the advancement of men."[3] No "general magazine," the *Crisis* was dedicated to a problem that involved brutality, murder, and the continuing belief by members of one race that members of another race were inferior. "The policy of THE CRISIS will be simple and well defined," continued Du Bois:

> It will first and foremost be a newspaper: it will record important happenings and movements in the world which bear on the great problem of inter-racial relations, and especially those which affect the Negro-American. . . .

3. Du Bois, "The *Crisis*," *Crisis,* November 1910, 10.

> [I]ts editorial page will stand for the rights of men, irrespective of color or race, for the highest ideals of American democracy, and for reasonable but earnest and persistent attempts to gain these rights and realize these ideals. The magazine will be the organ of no clique or party and will avoid personal rancor of all sorts. In the absence of proof to the contrary it will assume honesty of purpose on the part of all men, North and South, white and black.

Those who knew Du Bois and his earlier magazines must have wondered whether he could avoid personal rancor, which had been the bread and butter of the *Horizon,* but they would not have been surprised that Du Bois wished to bring black men into full possession of the fundamental rights and assumptions of equality that white men enjoyed.

But what exactly was this basis for manhood Du Bois always referred to but never explicitly defined? The concrete element of the manhood that Du Bois demanded was rooted in the rights that adhere to citizens in America's democratic society: the right to vote, the right to own property, the right to move freely. In short, all the specific rights that were systematically denied to American blacks, especially in the South. Such rights were the very air that white men breathed, the ground they walked on—white men so took these rights for granted that they probably did not consider them as the very basis for their definition of masculinity. When white men subscribed to the creeds of hard work, virtue, and honesty, or later to visions of sexiness, personality, or charisma, they did so from the secure basis of a set of manhood rights. Black men, however, were forced to constitute definitions of masculinity in the absence of these fundamental supports for white masculinity. This dilemma—having to advocate manfully for the very rights that would make black men men—put Du Bois in the position of defining manhood or manliness as something that came prior to such rights and, later, of placing himself in an adversarial position to the very system within which those rights had been defined. Here was his problem: How do you claim to be a man when you lack the rights upon which the hegemonic bloc bases its notion of masculinity?

There were several answers, revealed over the years of Du Bois's editorship of this essential American magazine. The first and most powerful of Du Bois's answers was to take the definition of masculinity to a higher ground, a domain of principle from which black men could critique the actions of those who did not meet his rigorous definition. Such a tactic was well-suited to Du Bois's lofty intellect and penchant for scorching critique. From such a position he could attempt to shame the powers that be into allowing black men rights, revealing the contradictions and hypocrisies that lay within their refusal of those rights, both legally and morally. This strategy, which defined the *Crisis's* editorial policy for roughly the first ten years, was born out of a rejection of the Washingtonian solution to the problem, a solution that called for blacks to make slow gains in areas where they were already accepted, gradually bringing to public attention the inherent acceptability of the black race. Du Bois was unwilling to go slowly, and he stoked the fires of the manly vision to urge black men to advocate for their rights now.

Another answer to this dilemma evolved out of Du Bois's reaction to the failure of his first solution and his perception of the possibilities for black advancement in white America. As Du Bois realized that white America was not going to simply open its doors to the first forceful intellectual argument for racial equality, he began to offer visions of manhood that existed outside the realm of white masculinity, manhood that was based not on the competitive individualism of white capitalism but rather on a more cooperative vision of economic advance. These models, never fully realized in the pages of the *Crisis*, indicated nothing less than an alternative vision of manhood.

The vision of masculinity offered by the *Crisis* developed out of a rejection of the policies of Booker T. Washington and the place of black men intimated by Washington's philosophy. Du Bois had been sharpening his rhetorical claws on Washington's tough hide for years, but it was in his role of editor of the *Crisis* that Du Bois finally articulated his opposition to Washington in such a way as to make his own leadership seem a credible, principled, and worthwhile option for the race. Gone were the bitter jibes, the smirking references to Washington's failures—in the *Crisis*, Du Bois took the high road. In an editorial called "The Simple Way," Du Bois let the reader see the logic of his rejection of Washington. Listing the tenets of "a solution to the Negro problem so ridiculously simple that those who did not receive it as gospel were hooted if not stoned"—among them "The Negro must work out his own salvation," "The Negro must not complain," "Negroes must let politics alone," and "Money talks—let the Negro get a $5,000 brick house and his individual problem is solved"—Du Bois charges:

> The mass of Negroes has been so ground down and oppressed that they do not know what complaint is. If they did, segregation, the "Jim Crow" car and disfranchisement would disappear to-morrow. We have shivered in the storm like dumb driven cattle and forgotten our rights before we learned them. We have "let politics alone" so effectually that we practically have no voice in our own government, and we have accumulated brick houses so fast that from Boston to Galveston white nerves are being strained to drive us out of them.
>
> We are therefore listening to those eminent and distinguished solvers of the Negro problem, white and black, who, with hat in hand, have in the last twenty years been lulling this nation to sleep and also feathering their own nests; we are listening for further advice and direction along the simple way.[4]

4. Du Bois, "The Simple Way," *Crisis*, November 1913, 337–38.

Cartoonist John Henry Adams nicely illustrated the outcome of "the simple way" in a two-page diptych that featured, in the first panel, a prosperous looking young black man working in his office above the caption "1900: The colored man that saves his money and buys a brick house will be universally respected by his white neighbors." On the second panel, the same black man pockets his bank book as he leaves the teller window, receiving the glances of white patrons; the caption reads "1910: New and dangerous species of Negro criminal lately discovered in Baltimore. He will be segregated in order to avoid lynching." Such a comic illustrated the belief that simply having money would never be enough in a society where deeply felt racial hatred took precedence over rationality. Thus the truths of black advancement in 1900—Booker T. Washington's truths—are not those of 1910, intimates the cartoon.[5]

At the root of Du Bois's complaint was his sense that blacks who followed Washington's policies had traded in their dignity, their manhood, for a few dollars. Sarcastically labeling Washingtonians optimists, he claims that they have given up hope for their race and are willing to take what scraps they can get. Gaining influence by adopting "a cheerful, sunny attitude," the optimist "pockets his substantial check, remarking 'Optimism pays!' " The "pessimist," on the other hand, believes in the abstract principles of justice and right. "He, therefore, insists on the Truth, that the truth may make us free. He finds himself greeted by frowns and shrugs."[6]

Du Bois even took the opportunity of Washington's death to call his readers' attention to the inadequacies of the departed leader's vision. Admitting that Washington was "the greatest Negro leader since Frederick Douglass, and the most distinguished man, white or black, who has come out of the South since the Civil War," Du Bois nevertheless laments that Washington's understanding of the solution to the Negro problem was based on caste and charges that "we must lay on the soul of this man, a heavy responsibility for the consummation of Negro disfranchisement, the decline of the Negro college and public school and the firmer establishment of color caste in this land." Though he does not repudiate Washington's efforts, Du Bois urges the Negro race in America to "close ranks and march steadily on, determined as never before to work and save and endure, but never to swerve from their great goal: the right to vote, the right to know, and the right to stand as men among men throughout the world."[7]

It was not that Du Bois rejected Washington's call for black men to make an economic success of themselves, to improve their condition through steady

5. John Henry Adams, *Crisis,* February 1911, 18–19.
6. Du Bois, "The Optimist and the Pessimist," *Crisis,* March 1912, 200.
7. Untitled obituary, *Crisis,* December 1915, 82.

work, saving, and thrift. In fact Du Bois celebrated those very qualities in the pages of his magazine, enshrining them in the "Men of the Month" column that ran in every issue, and publishing a number of articles that described the efforts of black men to make a financial success of themselves.[8] The difference between the two was that Du Bois did not make a cult of the Victorian virtues of individual competitive capitalism in the way that Washington and his publications did. Rather, he drew attention to the "character" of black achievers. Du Bois was after a definition of manhood that came prior to economic success and that did not depend on financial gain for its very existence.

The definition of manhood that Du Bois began to spell out in the *Crisis* in the 1910s was in part a product of his own experience, as he related to readers in "The Shadow of Years," an autobiographical essay he wrote for the "Editor's Jubilee" edition of his magazine in February of 1918. Recalling a youth when he thought he could accomplish anything—and did just that— he next traces his "Days of Disillusion," in which he came to realize "how much of what I had called Will and Ability was sheer luck." Supposing that a variety of circumstances had been different—that he was born to a mother who did not care to educate him, attended a school whose principal had "no faith in 'darkeys,'" or encountered a scholarship board with "distinct ideas as to where the education of Negroes should stop"—he imagines that his life could have been very different. "Was I the masterful captain, or the pawn of laughing sprites?" he asks rhetorically.[9] The answer was that he was a black man in America, irrevocably buffeted by the winds of racism and prejudice that threatened his ability to decide his own fate. People could talk all they wanted to about how hard work, perseverance, and integrity would open all doors, but the plain fact was that for the Negro these "truths" were lies.

Realizing the limits placed on him and his people by their race, he rejected Washingtonian visions of self-determining manhood and began his fight to claim for black Americans those rights that had been denied them. When he was in his forties, he wrote, "I found myself suddenly the leader of a great wing of my people, fighting against another and greater wing." His cardinal goal was to convince Negroes not to accept the lower status to which Washington's accommodationist policies threatened to relegate them. "We

8. This column began including women in September of 1911, when Mary F. Gunner became the first woman to be featured in the "Men of the Month." There was never any mention of the inclusion of women in this column, nor did they rename it "Person of the Month," as they no doubt would today.

9. Du Bois, "The Shadow of Years," *Crisis*, February 1918, 169.

simply had doggedly to insist, explain, fight and fight again until, at last, slowly, grudgingly we saw the world turn slightly to listen."[10]

Du Bois meant it when he declared that blacks must fight for their rights. Fighting, struggling, claiming what was due to them even when it meant trouble—these traits were to the Du Boisian Negro what self-control and hard work were to the Victorian white middle class, the basis upon which they would build their identity. Du Bois spelled out what this meant on any number of occasions. In the editorial "Social Equality," for example, he takes up the issue upon which Washington made his peace with white southerners and reverses it. Discussing a black man who accepted inferior seating on a train, Du Bois argues:

> Social equality is simply the right to be treated as a gentleman when one is among gentlemen and acts like a gentleman. No person who does not demand such treatment is fit for the society of gentlemen. Of course, what the speaker [who said he did not want social equality] meant to say was that he had no desire to force his company on people unnecessarily if they objected to him, but such a right does not imply "equality" but "superiority," and this speaker knows or ought to know that every time a black man says publicly that he is willing to be treated as a social pariah, he is forging the chains of his social slavery. Let intelligent black men stop this sort of talk. If they are afraid to demand their rights as men, they can, at least, preserve dignified silence.[11]

This is Du Bois at his best, clearly staking out a moral high ground that can sustain black men while they seek access to real social equality.

Du Bois's New Year's resolution for 1912 was an even more explicit statement of this philosophy. "I am resolved in this New Year to play the man—to stand straight, look the world squarely in the eye, and walk to my work with no shuffle or slouch," writes the editor. "I am resolved to be satisfied with no treatment which ignores my manhood and my right to be counted as one among men. . . . I am resolved to defend and assert the absolute equality of the Negro race with any and all other human races and its divine right to equal and just treatment."[12] A man who could do these things, Du Bois implied, could resist the impulse to give in to the indignities inflicted on black men, could stand for what he believed on principle.

In a 1912 portrait of J. Max Barber, former editor of the *Voice of the Negro,* Du Bois exalts these very traits. When Barber became the editor of this publication at a young age, writes Du Bois, there "came the severest temptation a young

10. Ibid., 170, 171.
11. Du Bois, "Social Equality," *Crisis,* September 1911, 197.
12. Du Bois, "I Am Resolved," *Crisis,* January 1912, 113.

man can meet. A little dishonesty to his own ideals, a little truckling diplomacy, and success and a fine income awaited him. This he refused to give. Perhaps there was some arrogance of youth in the decision to hew to the line of his thought and ideal, but it was fine arrogance, and when defeat came and the *Voice* stopped publication, he simply set his teeth and started life again. Only menial employment was open to him, but he took it, faced poverty, and began to study dentistry." Barber made it *and* he maintained his true manhood, rather than the false manhood implied by "success and a fine income." The attentive reader of the time knew well that the tempter to whom Du Bois refers and whom Barber resisted was Washington himself, giving his resistance even greater moral import for Du Bois.[13]

The little fiction published in the magazine prior to the 1920s offered similar moral lessons. "The Man Who Won—(A Story)" by Harry H. Pace has the setting of a Charles Chesnutt novel, the narrative hooks of any good magazine romance, and references to a bevy of the problems facing blacks in America. Pace tells of a light-skinned New York Negro named Russell Stanley who returns to the South to help out his successful (and darker-skinned) farming family, the Wyatts. Despite Stanley's near whiteness, the black family and all the laborers love him and he settles happily in his new life, despite the anxiety caused by the presence of a bigoted white politician, Edgefield, who would like to see blacks returned to slavery. After he saves the life of Edgefield's beautiful daughter when her horse runs away, she invites him back to the house, but when he reveals that he is part of the black Wyatt clan, she snaps "[My father] hates Niggers and so do I" and hurries away.[14]

The next installment begins by telling the story of Edgefield, who has been elected to Congress for several terms despite being a loudmouthed racist in a majority black district. But this year the Republicans have nominated Russell Stanley, and it turns out that Stanley and the Wyatt clan have a special reason for winning, for Edgefield is the white father that Stanley never knew, which makes his daughter Stanley's sister. As it appears that Stanley may win the election, Edgefield's henchmen burn down the Wyatts' ginhouse, and Stanley wonders what to do. Then the girl, his sister, comes to him and pleads with him not to shame her and her father by defeating them. He is touched but unconvinced, and as he prepares to ride off:

> She caught his bridle menacingly and hissed at him: "Don't you dare refuse me! Nigger—I need only scream, here, now, and your life wouldn't be worth that!" and she snapped her fingers in his face.

13. "Men of the Month," *Crisis,* November 1912, 16.
14. Harry H. Pace, "The Man Who Won—(A Story)," *Crisis,* April 1913, 295.

The blood flamed in his brain, and his anger burst all bounds. With his flat hand he struck her full across the face!
"Scream!" he cried. "Scream, sister, scream with all your might!"

She screams and "A minute later the sharp crack of a rifle broke the spell of his words. She saw the shadow of his dead body as it lurched and fell, and the echoing hoofs of a riderless horse smote on her horror-stricken ears." Though he dies, Stanley reveals his true manhood by refusing to stand down in the face of the restrictions that would deny his rights. He would rather die defending what is right than give in to the indignities that the white man, with his hidden miscegenation and fear of black political power, would subject him to. The story is a perfect explication of Du Boisian manhood in action.[15]

From 1910 to 1920 the *Crisis* enjoyed uninterrupted growth. On the occasion of the magazine's second anniversary, Du Bois recalled trembling as he pondered whether to order the printing of 500 copies or 1000. By November 1912 they were regularly publishing 22,000 copies. And circulation rose from there, to 32,000 in December of 1913, 44,000 in December of 1917, and finally 100,000 in 1919. By 1916 the magazine generated enough income—$57,000— to allow the NAACP to stop subsidizing Du Bois's salary and pay all its own expenses.[16] The magazine's success was not directly related to its institutional affiliation with the NAACP, for at a time when NAACP membership stood at 448, the *Crisis's* circulation topped 22,500.[17]

What accounted for this unprecedented success? Why, when no black magazine had ever sold more than 12,500 issues, did the *Crisis* sell so well? Several circumstances can be called to account for the magazine's success. First, the *Crisis* had the general magazine field to itself following the collapse of the *Colored American* and *Alexander's*. (Competitors the *Crusader* and the *Messenger* were too radical to be considered general magazines and circulated primarily in the city of their publication.) Second, the magazine was well-edited and nicely printed by Robert N. Wood, a New York printer. Du Bois had learned from his own mistakes and from those of his peers, and he offered a combination of positive news of Negro achievement, unflinching criticism of the problems facing blacks in America, and—something that Du Bois claimed

15. Pace, "The Man Who Won," *Crisis,* May 1913, 36.
16. Circulation figures are drawn from various issues and from Du Bois, "Editing the *Crisis*," *Crisis,* March 1951, 147–53, 213. Du Bois's "independence" as editor of *Crisis* had always been an issue of hot dispute within the leadership of the NAACP, and his assertion that he was out from under the wing of the parent organization drew the ire of leadership as well. For further discussion of these disputes see Kellogg, *NAACP;* and Lewis, *W. E. B. Du Bois.*
17. "Publisher's Chat with Readers," *Crisis,* April 1912.

was quite important—"pictures of colored people."[18] Third, the black exodus from the South was beginning to concentrate black populations into northern urban areas, especially Chicago and Harlem, where they were better reached by the still-developing circulation arms of the magazine; the magazine's highest circulation was in the states of Pennsylvania, Illinois, Ohio, and New York.[19] Fourth, if magazines act as a kind of mirror in which readers are able to see themselves, the *Crisis* provided a flattering portrait of the race. While other race magazines had overstated examples of black achievement, the *Crisis* presented black accomplishments as a natural result of black talent. The profiles of successful people rarely resorted to the race qualifiers that undermined the very achievements they sought to exalt, and they featured people pursuing a variety of occupations, from athletes to businessmen, dramatists to professors. The editorials were written clearly and plainly, and did not resort to under-handed attack or slanderous innuendo. And the advertisements revealed to black readers a world of possibility that might have gone unrealized without such a publication.

The *Crisis* and Consumption

Magazines create an environment, indeed a set of environments, within which readers are invited to situate themselves. One of the environments the *Crisis* staff worked diligently to develop was the arena of consumption. From the very first issue it carried more advertising than any black publication, and advertising manager Albon L. Holsey developed a series of pitches designed to get more firms to advertise. "People Who Read THE CRISIS Find it intensely interesting because it is different from the ordinary," read Holsey's back-cover pitch of June 1911. "When a magazine is so interesting that the reader says 'I was sorry because there was no more to read' it is very valuable as an advertising medium, because, when 'there is no more to read,' the advertisements are invariably read with the same zest and enthusiasm as the reading matter. Advertisements read in this frame of mind always leave an after-thought and are more likely to 'make the sale.' Let us tell you WHY the CRISIS is different as an advertising medium. Let us tell you HOW we co-operate with our advertisers."[20] Such claims, furthered in September 1911 by a similar pitch called "Magazine Efficiency—The Real Test," claimed that the *Crisis* was a particularly efficient means of delivering ads, but had nothing to say about the Negroes' long-standing incapacity to consume. By 1917 Holsey began to orchestrate a more pointed approach to

18. Du Bois wrote that other black papers published only pictures of celebrities who paid to get themselves in print or criminals; Du Bois, "Editing the *Crisis*," 148.
19. *Crisis*, April 1915, 97.
20. *Crisis*, June 1911, 87.

gaining advertisers. His back-cover pitches stated that there were twelve million Negroes in the United States spending "a thousand million dollars every year," and claimed that the *Crisis* "reaches *more* Negroes with *intelligence and money than any periodical in the world.* If you have *anything* to sell which these people *want* advertise it in THE CRISIS."[21] This appeal operated on a very different principle, for it announced not only that readers paid attention but that they had money to spend.

Black advertisers bought the pitch and bought space in the magazine, at the cost of forty-five dollars for a back cover, forty dollars for an inside cover page, front or back, and thirty-two dollars per page for other pages in December of 1913, double the rates of just two years earlier.[22] Black colleges always advertised heavily in the magazine, knowing that they were reaching the most educated readers (or those readers who most likely wished to be educated). They were followed closely by booksellers offering works by Washington, Kelly Miller, Du Bois, and others. But there was always an array of ads for goods and services as well. Music instruction and performances, wigs and hair beautifiers, dentists and lawyers, resorts and hotels, and clothing by mail order—all of these were advertised in the *Crisis*. And if the ads were not as nicely laid out or lush as their counterparts in white publications, they did offer black readers a sense of what was available to them in a marketplace newly cognizant of African Americans as consumers. Unlike the ads that black readers encountered in white publications, these ads featured black models, they promoted stores that were located in black communities, and they sought black consumers. For those who had recently left the confines of rural southern life, where they might have depended upon a single general store for all their goods, the landscape of consumer culture—a landscape they were being invited to imagine themselves as part of—must have looked nearly limitless.

It is not stretching the point to say that both advertisers and magazine staff were trying to create an environment in which black consumers would feel welcome. Upon raising advertising rates in March of 1912, the publishers promised: "To those whose support and encouragement we owe the existence of THE CRISIS we promise that our most sincere efforts will be made to bring together the best representatives of the world's commercial highway, with a tempting variety of luxuries and necessities, making our advertising department a real department store where each member of the family may shop 'by the fireside.'" This effort was consolidated into what they called the Dunbar Company by November of the same year. The Dunbar Company would

21. *Crisis,* December 1917, 104.
22. *Crisis,* December 1913, 97; April 1911, 35.

Advertising

There are **twelve million** Negroes in the United States.

They spend a **thousand million dollars** every year.

THE CRISIS reaches **more** Negroes with **intelligence and money** than **any periodical** in the **world.**

If you have **anything** to sell which these people **want** advertise it in THE CRISIS.

Remember that if our **rates** seem **high** it is because our **service** is **exceptional.**   If you want **testimonials** to this, *write us.*

Circulation — 47,500

As early as 1917 the *Crisis* began to promote itself as the best way to reach the potentially huge audience of black consumers—but advertisers failed to flock to the magazine, perhaps because of its call for full black civil rights (*Crisis*, December 1917, back cover).

offer books, pamphlets, postcards, music by Negro composers, jewelry, toilet articles, wearing apparel, and so on, at a low price. "We believe that such price and quality will appeal to those in 'Jim Crow' localities, where direct shopping is robbed of its pleasures by discourteous salespeople and shopkeepers." And they promised a Christmas catalog.[23] Thus the *Crisis* was configured as a black consumer heaven, offering high quality goods and insulating consumers from the insults of a prejudiced marketplace.

But this consumer heaven had its limits, limits that must have been clear to readers and reinforced their awareness of their segregation. The Ocean House resort in Sea Isle City, New Jersey, advertised its ocean views—but it was the only such hotel advertised. Ads for the Paragon Tailoring Company,

23. "Publishers' Page," *Crisis,* March 1912, 178; "Publishers' Page," *Crisis,* November 1912, 41.

American Woolen Mills Company, and the Chicago Tailors Association seemed to offer the latest cut in suits, but they were not inviting black men to come to a retail store and try those suits on, but rather trying to attract salesmen to go to buyer's homes to take fittings for suits to order. And throughout the 1910s no white advertiser of national brand products deigned to place an ad. "The 'Big' advertisers remained aloof"; wrote Du Bois years later, "some looked us over, but nearly all fell back on the rule not to patronize 'propaganda' periodicals. Besides they did not believe the Negro market worth entering."[24]

That the commercial success of the *Crisis* had its limits is not surprising, given the limits placed on any black achievement in that era. What is important is that the *Crisis* was selling more—more copies, more ads—than any black magazine had before. And Du Bois was certainly not displeased with the progress of his latest publishing venture. In anniversary editorials and in other comments, Du Bois expressed clear satisfaction with the trajectory of the *Crisis*. Perhaps such satisfaction led him to believe that with continued work in this vein he and his race would be able to achieve the rights he had championed.

Whatever sense of satisfaction Du Bois may have derived from the success of his magazine, the events surrounding his qualified early support and later criticism of African American involvement in World War I demonstrated to Du Bois that black men still faced an uphill battle to claim equal status in America. As America began to prepare itself for possible entrance into World War I, African Americans faced a difficult choice: did they support American involvement, thus proving the loyalty and patriotism of their race, or did they protest the inevitable segregation that black troops would face in order to stand fast to the principle of their quest for equal rights? Surely no one felt this dilemma more strongly than Du Bois, whose very career had depended on making hard choices between accommodation and resistance.

Early on in the war, in March of 1917, Du Bois framed his decision to back segregated training for black troops as yet another tough choice in what he called "The Perpetual Dilemma." Negroes are always faced with terrible choice in America, he explained, "between insult and injury; no schools or separate schools; no travel or 'Jim Crow' travel; homes with disdainful neighbors or homes in slums." Now they are faced between limited duty in a white man's war or segregated forces that are at least led by black officers. Du Bois reluctantly advocated forming all-black regiments headed by black officers, because he knew that when conscription comes the choice will not be between volunteering or not volunteering, "The choice will be between conscription and rebellion."[25]

24. Du Bois, "Editing the *Crisis*," 150.
25. Du Bois, "The Perpetual Dilemma," *Crisis*, March 1917, 270–71.

Fighting in segregated regiments was not the only alternative for blacks during wartime, however, as Du Bois's June 1917 editorial, "We Should Worry," reveals:

> If they do not want us to fight, we will work. We will walk into the industrial shoes of a few million whites who go to the front. We will get higher wages and we cannot be stopped from migrating by all the deviltry of the slave South; particularly with the white lynchers and mob leaders away at war.
> Will we be ousted when the white soldiers come back?
> THEY WON'T COME BACK!
> So there you are, gentlemen, and take your choice,—
> We'll fight or work.
> We'll fight and work.
> If we fight we'll learn the fighting game and cease to be so 'aisily lynched.'
> If we don't fight we'll learn the more lucrative trades and cease to be so easily robbed and exploited.
> Take your choice, gentlemen.
> "We should worry."[26]

Du Bois clearly saw opportunities for African Americans during wartime, though he was not yet sure how to attain them.

By 1918, however, NAACP leader and personal friend Joel Spingarn came to Du Bois with what seemed like an ideal opportunity. Under Spingarn's plan, Du Bois would become an army captain in the War Department's Military Intelligence Branch and they would work together to promote the idea that African Americans made good soldiers and loyal patriots. In order to secure the captaincy, however, Du Bois had to prove that he was not in fact a radical leader calling for dissent on the part of his people. That proof came in the form of a July 1918 editorial called "Close Ranks," in which Du Bois explained to his readers that it was time to "forget our special grievances and close our ranks shoulder to shoulder with our white fellow citizens and the allied nations that are fighting for democracy." It was an editorial, claims historian Mark Ellis, that Du Bois would recall "with a mixture of shame and bitterness for the next forty years."[27]

Du Bois's decision to advocate the suspension of civil rights protest during World War I has been the source of much debate among historians and biographers, who have generally pictured Du Bois's decision either as a rea-

26. Du Bois, "We Should Worry," *Crisis,* June 1917, 62.
27. Du Bois, "Close Ranks," *Crisis,* July 1918, 111; Mark Ellis, "'Closing Ranks' and 'Seeking Honors': W. E. B. Du Bois in World War I," 96. Ellis's article attempts to explain Du Bois's editorial as "a conscious deviation in the trajectory of his wartime writings [that] was specifically included in the July 1918 issue of the *Crisis* to help get him into military intelligence" (124).

soned and pragmatic retreat to an accommodationism that was neither out of character nor unique among members of the black community, or as an aberration in his behavior and policies caused by personal pride and overreaching ambition.[28] Given the tone of Du Bois's other editorials on the subject—both those that came before and after "Close Ranks"—it seems best to view this editorial as a mistaken attempt to reach ends that were in accord with Du Bois's general (and not accommodationist) principles. Historian Mark Ellis and biographer David Levering Lewis both stress that Du Bois penned this particular editorial as a kind of quid pro quo to guarantee his participation in a federally led program to encourage and value black participation in the war.[29] Du Bois clearly expected black men to gain from their involvement in the war effort, and he wanted to exert an influence on those gains by gaining a position within the Military Intelligence Branch. Thus he was willing to use accommodationist means—the editorial—to reach his more radical end—an enhanced place for African Americans in American culture.

Though Du Bois's support of the Wilsonian war effort may have seemed an unlikely accommodation for this great radical, it was in fact well suited to his overall vision of improving the prospects for black Americans. Du Bois wanted full recognition of the rights of citizenship for Negroes, and he believed that the draft—a draft of citizens—recognized that status; he wanted higher wages and better employment, and the boom in wartime industries provided both. Further, black men could not help but gain by acquitting themselves with valor on the field of battle, especially as they fought against a Germany whose colonial record was "the most barbarous of any civilized people." On a more abstract

28. William Jordan argues in "'The Damnable Dilemma': African-American Accommodation and Protest during World War I" that Du Bois's "decision to adopt an accommodationist position during the war made sense to him in the face of this excruciating dilemma. And it should make sense to us in light of the historical context and Du Bois's past ideological flexibility" (1565). In his response to this argument, Mark Ellis argues that the editorial "represented a major shift in his advice to black Americans and a negation of his own behavior hitherto" ("W. E. B. Du Bois and the Formation of Black Opinion in World War I: A Commentary on 'The Damnable Dilemma,'" 1588.) Du Bois biographer David Levering Lewis largely concurs with Ellis's interpretation, describing Du Bois's decision to write the editorial as "a radical departure from activities that had defined him for others, and an exercise in personal conceit" (W. E. B. Du Bois, 554). These statements represent the tip of an iceberg of scholarly commentary on this issue.

29. Ellis, "W. E. B. Du Bois," 1590; Lewis writes that "Du Bois struck a deal, through Spingarn, with the War Department to use the enormous influence of his magazine toward rallying African-Americans behind the war in return for the heady opportunities he and Spingarn persuaded themselves their military commissions would yield" (W. E. B. Du Bois, 555).

level, Du Bois also knew that black participation in a "war for democracy" ought to prick the consciences of those who would deny democracy at home.[30]

But what of these hopes? Within a few months of the armistice, Du Bois began to take a distinctly different tone toward black participation in the war. As he became aware of the malicious and false reports concerning the failure of black officers and the rape of white women by Negro soldiers, and as he learned of the general poor treatment meted out to African American fighting men, Du Bois soon returned to his more customary indignant rhetoric. Welcoming soldiers back to the land of lynching, disfranchisement, ignorance, theft, and insult, Du Bois declared that "we are cowards and jackasses if now that the war is over, we do not marshal every ounce of our brain and brawn to fight a sterner, longer, more unbending battle against the forces of hell in our own land. We return. We return from fighting. We return fighting. Make way for Democracy! We saved it in France, and by the Great Jehovah, we will save it in the United States of America, or know the reason why."[31] But for all the high hopes that Du Bois had for the war's ability to improve conditions for black Americans, little actually improved and much worsened.

In fact, during the "Red Summer" of 1919, white Americans seemed intent on proving to blacks that they had gained nothing from their participation in the war. "The tribal and institutional power of those 'forces of hell in our own land,' editorially challenged by Du Bois, were starkly manifested in the lynching of seventy-eight African-Americans during 1918 and in the boasts of white newspapers in the South about the bloody fate in store for any black man daring to come back from the war expecting to be treated like a white man," writes Du Bois biographer David Levering Lewis. As attacks, murders, and race riots swept black communities across the country, the Chicago *Whip* noted that the rioters "really fear that the Negro is breaking his shell and beginning to bask in the sunlight of real manhood."[32] Though Du Bois may have wished that this were the truth, he knew that the path to "real manhood" for African Americans remained a long and difficult one.

Du Bois's first ten years as editor of the *Crisis* had been tumultuous. He had begun this project with a clear sense of his mission and, though he knew that gaining full citizenship rights for African Americans would be a long and

30. See especially Du Bois, "Our Special Grievances" and "The Reward," *Crisis,* September 1918, 217–18; on Germany, see "World War and the Color Line," *Crisis,* November 1914, 29.

31. Du Bois, "Returning Soldiers," *Crisis,* May 1919, 14. Lewis has called this Du Bois's second most famous editorial (*W. E. B. Du Bois,* 578).

32. Lewis, *W. E. B. Du Bois,* 579; *Whip* quoted from Lewis, 579, quoted from Robert T. Kerlin, *The Voice of the Negro, 1919,* 67.

difficult task, he had reason to believe in the success of his efforts. At least, the success of his magazine led him to believe that he was accomplishing something, for he had offered his openly radical views in the marketplace and they had met with unprecedented success. But the failure of his efforts to position blacks as citizens and men through their war effort posed a tremendous challenge to the Du Boisian vision of manhood. This failure reinforced what must have remained of the fear that merely declaring a principled manhood might not be enough. In the wake of the challenges to Du Bois's vision posed by the war and its aftermath, and in the light of a variety of changes taking place in both the African American populace and in popular culture, the *Crisis* in the coming years began to discuss the prospects for black Americans in ways that intimated alternative visions of black masculinity.

The *Competitor*

After 1920, the *Crisis* was no longer alone in promoting different views of black masculinity. For eighteen months, Robert Vann's *Competitor* offered a view of the black experience that was less partisan than any magazine since the early *Alexander's*. Vann, the publisher of the popular black newspaper the *Pittsburgh Courier*, invested great amounts of time and money into producing his large, lavish magazine, but the high costs of publishing, the relatively high price asked for the magazine (20 cents), and the continued failure of advertisers to underwrite the publication of a black general-interest magazine eventually drove Vann from the market.[33] In its brief life, however, the *Competitor* indicated some of the variety of interests that now existed in a black community that was becoming increasingly diverse.

Vann began his magazine hoping to avoid the divisiveness that he believed had characterized other magazines. "The Competitor," he wrote in the opening editorial, "comes before the reading world in answer to a pressing need for a journal national in scope, constructive in policy and replete with matter calculated to inspire the race to its best efforts in everything American." Vann supported black demands for full citizenship rights, but he was not willing to put calls for such rights above the pursuit of other aspects of "Americanization," which seems to have been a euphemism for business success. Such an editorial agenda combined elements of both Du Boisian and Washingtonian ideologies; Vann would be Washington without his hat in hand, Du Bois in a business suit, without the outrage. But Vann did not style himself as a race leader, but a spokesman for blacks who just wanted to join in the great flow of American

---

33. Andrew Buni takes brief note of the *Competitor* in his biography of Vann, *Robert L. Vann of the* Pittsburgh Courier: *Politics and Black Journalism,* 117–19.

life. "The Negro," he declared, "wants to be swallowed up in the great scheme of Americanization."[34]

Judging from the content of the first issue, the Negro was indeed swallowed up in the great scheme of Americanization. The first editorials echoed standard Republican Party rhetoric, notably in opposition to Wilson's League of Nations; an article deplored the recent race riots in Washington, D.C.; Mary Terrell wrote the lead piece for the "Women's Department"; and the sports section covered the Lincoln-Howard football game. Two stories were particularly notable. Ira F. Lewis told the Horatio Alger-like tale of C. H. James, who lifted himself from pack peddler to successful business owner; the successful James says, "I would advise every young man who believes he can make it to go in business. Matters not how small, go in business, for it is *business! business! business!* that we need." Rose Atwood offered a melodramatic story about a poor man who renounces money and glamour in favor of proving his honesty and valor and devoting himself to the woman he loves.[35] What makes these stories so remarkable is the absence of any distinct reference to race. These stories, with their formulaic faithfulness to convention, could have appeared in any number of white publications of the period in nearly identical form. Part of Americanization, it seemed, was swallowing Negroes up in the stock narratives of love and success.

Succeeding issues of the magazine went even further in urging blacks to join in the optimistic Chamber of Commerce boosterism and updated fealty to Victorian virtues that characterized the white mainstream of the time. In "Why Work," Dr. Jesse E. Moorland advises that "In this land most men are at liberty to change their status of living quite quickly, if they are willing to work and practice thrift and control. . . . Work begets character. . . . Great honor awaits the faithful worker." In the space available beneath this story the editor chose to print the poem "If," by Rudyard Kipling, with verses that perfectly accompanied the article.

> If you can fill the unforgiving minute
> With sixty seconds' worth of distance run
> Yours is the Earth and everything that's in it
> And—which is more—you'll be a Man, my son!

The editorial optimism that seemed to offer black men entrance into the heart of the American economy—not to mention the white manliness of Kipling's

34. Robert L. Vann, "Why This Magazine," *Competitor,* January 1920, 2.
35. Ira F. Lewis, "How C. H. James Rose from a Pack Peddler to Head of a Quarter-Million-Dollar Business," *Competitor,* January 1920, 18–19, 84; Rose Atwood, "A Man's Duty," *Competitor,* January 1920, 56–61, 81–82.

poem—was echoed in the first ads that appeared in the magazine, one of which featured two returning black soldiers who had opened a drugstore that they promoted with the line, "We did our bit; can you do less?" Another, for the Homestead Development Association, offered lots "improved and developed, with fruit trees planted on them in a beautiful cherry grove."[36] Taken together, these stories could have come straight out of the *American Magazine* or the *Saturday Evening Post*, and they offered the same happy message of prosperity and peace in a nation of Americans working hard to better their lives.

Similar stories followed in the coming issues of the *Competitor;* such stories follow the conventions of their genre so closely that quoting individual pieces would hardly be informative. Nor is it worthwhile to give undue notice to a magazine that lasted so short a time. But the *Competitor* is notable as a kind of precursor to *Ebony,* for it established some conventions that *Ebony* would follow. Offering a message of happy prosperity and downplaying the importance of race as a determinant of success or happiness would be keys to the later magazine's success. So why did they not work in the early twenties? Financial considerations must be at the forefront of any explanation of the *Competitor*'s failure. Vann was a good businessman if nothing else, and though he thought it important to spend the money to produce a good-looking, nicely laid-out magazine, he also knew that such a venture had to pay its own bills. Two things kept the *Competitor* from that goal: it failed to gain sufficient advertising, and not enough people subscribed. The advertising drought affected all black magazines. But the lack of subscribers is a factor less readily understood. Vann's biographer Andrew Buni and black magazine scholar Walter Daniel attribute the failure to gain subscribers to the high price of the magazine at a time when Negro weekly newspapers sold for as little as a nickel a copy.[37] Buni also suggests that the magazine was too "literate and cultured" for black readers, though the content of the magazine hardly bears out that hypothesis. But we also should consider that perhaps an audience for such a publication did not exist yet—that the number of black Americans who were living the reality described in the *Competitor* or who honestly believed that the magazine's vision of success was attainable were simply too few for it to gain an audience. Was this vision of success still too foreign to the Negro experience of life in America to sell? And if so, what would have to change to make an eclectic and optimistic magazine palatable to a black audience?

36. Jesse E. Moorland, "Why Work," *Competitor,* February 1920, 43–45; Rudyard Kipling, "If," *Competitor,* February 1920, 45; ads appear on pages 81 and 82.
37. Buni, *Robert Vann,* 118; Daniel, *Black Journals,* 138.

Opportunity: A Journal of Negro Life

By 1923 another magazine had entered the Negro market, and it proved to be a more formidable competitor, in longevity if not in circulation. Entitled *Opportunity: A Journal of Negro Life* and edited by Charles S. Johnson, the magazine began by proposing to offer "scientific" explorations of the problems of Negro life. The title and the timing of its beginning—at the end of the postwar depression, in a time the editors called an "age of opportunity"—indicated that it would take an "optimistic" approach similar to that of the *Competitor*, but what distinguished the magazine was the serious and often scholarly approach it took to the problems of the day. As the official organ of the National Urban League, the magazine offered reports of the investigations pursued by the N.U.L., news of the league's activities, as well as a survey of Negro news and culture.[38]

Though the first issues of the magazine were heavy on sociological analysis, offering articles on such topics as Negro housing, the placement of retarded orphans, and churches and social work, within a year the magazine began to demonstrate a real broadening of content. As it entered its third year of publication, the magazine typically offered two or three longer nonfiction articles; several short stories; some poems; a "Survey of the Month" section with short pieces on the arts, housing, health, sports, and other topics; book reviews; and some pictures. Johnson's decision to initiate a literary contest in 1925 soon led *Opportunity* to become what Daniel called "a foster parent for the literary movement of the day," the Harlem Renaissance. Publishing the first works by such noted writers as Countée Cullen, Langston Hughes, Claude McKay, Angelina W. Grimke, Zora Neal Hurston, and others, *Opportunity* became one of the leading literary magazines of the period.[39]

Throughout the 1920s and into the 1930s, both the *Crisis* and *Opportunity* discussed the African American experience in terms that differed from the earlier emphasis in the *Crisis* and the emphasis in other early race periodicals.

38. The single best discussion of the magazine is in Nancy J. Weiss, *The National Urban League, 1910–1940*, esp. 220–33. Weiss is actually quite critical of the magazine's approach to the race issues of the day, especially its whitewashing of the issues facing black workers and its easy embrace of "traditional bourgeois values: education, hard work, thrift, sobriety, self-effacement, concern for others, and above all, self-help" (226).

39. Daniel, *"Opportunity: A Journal of Negro Life,"* in *Black Journals*, 305. Although Countée Cullen, the literary editor of the magazine from 1926 to 1929, deserves much of the credit, the initial outpouring of fiction came to the magazine as the result of a call meant to "stimulate creative expression among Negroes" (*Opportunity*, August 1924, 228). Richard Robbins, author of a good biography of Johnson, devotes far more of his attention to Johnson's literary efforts than he does to other elements of Johnson's activities as editor of *Opportunity* from 1923 to 1928; see his *Sidelines Activist: Charles S. Johnson and the Struggle for Civil Rights*, 40–57.

During its heyday, *Opportunity* presented the best in black literature and the arts—and offered images of powerful black manhood (*Opportunity*, July 1940, cover). (Courtesy of Lee A. Daniels.)

Du Bois, whose early efforts to establish the legitimacy of Negro claims to full citizenship had led him to emphasize the "manliness" of his positions, largely abandoned that sort of rhetoric following World War I, and *Opportunity* never engaged the questions that had largely defined the earlier debates about black masculinity. Early in the century, writers and editors pondered the implications of 1) striving to succeed in a business world in which opportunities for Negroes were so limited or of 2) advocating immediate justice and equality based on the principles found in the Constitution and the Declaration of Independence. These questions had posed the issues facing black men as a choice between a manhood based on production or one based on citizenship. These choices were not mutually exclusive, of course, but as they were posed in the debate between accommodationists and radicals they took on a moral weight that made them seem that they were. With the demise of the magazines that supported the Washingtonian vision of masculinity, the emphasis on economic success as the primary determinant of manhood largely disappeared from the magazine market. In its place was the widespread assumption that blacks first must demand full justice and citizenship.[40]

I do not mean to suggest that there was a "winner" in the Washington–Du Bois debate, because neither view vanquished the other. The differences between Washington and Du Bois were never posed in "either/or" terms. Du Bois's vision gained emphasis—thanks to his role as editor of the *Crisis*, to Washington's death, and to the demise of the major accommodationist magazines—but blacks remained focused on making an economic success of themselves and their communities. To the extent that the older visions of black masculinity remained a part of black mass culture, they did so in certain features that appeared in *Opportunity*. A large part of the National Urban League's mission was to press for the employment of black workers in northern industry, and several articles took pains to demonstrate how well-suited black men were to such jobs; as such the magazine was performing a crucial role in helping those participating in the black migration northward find work to which they were not accustomed. An editorial in the first issue claimed Negro workers are treated as "appendages rather than members, 'robots' rather than men." At a time when white workers were being encouraged to develop a commitment to an organization, the editorial continued, black workers were thought of as

---

40. "The Sense of Belonging," *Opportunity*, January 1923, 5. For a representative sampling of *Opportunity*'s approach to such issues, see J. O. Houze, "Negro Labor and the Industries," January 1923, 20; W. P. Young, "The First Hundred Negro Workers: The Frank Story of the Experience of a Negro Welfare Worker," January 1924, 15–19; W. P. Lawall, "The Worthington Pump and Machine Works," February 1926, 58; "Negroes As Workers: A Page of Comments," March 1926, 90.

expendable. But *Opportunity* sought to convince employers that Negro workers were reliable and committed, and it did so by celebrating those workers who had fit in to an industrial environment. One such article stressed the "sunny disposition" of black workers, their strength, and their hard-working nature.[41] Ignoring the ongoing discrimination against such workers and the difficulties they faced in organizing, these articles tended to portray black workers as committed to the long haul of slow advance. Moreover, *Opportunity* took the field as the representative of a viewpoint whose very existence was to balance the political, rights-based focus of the *Crisis* with a practical, job-oriented focus.

But to say that the early debate over the definition of black masculinity subsided is not to say that the outlets for black mass culture no longer concerned themselves with issues of manhood. While masculinity was no longer foregrounded in the discourse of black magazines, it remained a subcurrent in discussions over what constituted black success, in determining who would be black heroes and role models, and indeed in the very struggle for the financial existence of black magazines. Both the *Crisis* and *Opportunity* continued to debate how blacks would gain entrance into the economic life of the nation. Both magazines continued to tell stories of black success, and both began to look to athletes and entertainers as models for the kind of success that Negroes might achieve in America. Finally, both magazines struggled to draw advertisers to the Negro market, an effort that had profound implications for both the history of black magazines and for the representation of black men within those magazines.

Negotiating Their Way to Modernity: The *Crisis* and *Opportunity*, 1923–1949

One of Du Bois's most piercing critiques of Washington's philosophy of race improvement was that blacks were dupes to follow the "work hard and play fair" path to economic success when the cards were so decidedly stacked against them. Washington, it was said, clung to these bromides of competitive capitalism long after they had become untenable, long after it became impossible for large numbers of men, let alone black men, to be self-made men starting their own business from scratch and rising to success through the strength of their character. Washington's vastly influential autobiography, *Up from Slavery*, offered this as the model for success, and Washington continued to insist on it, when in reality there was little room remaining for such small-capital ventures

41. E. Franklin Frazier, "Some Aspects of Negro Business," *Opportunity*, October 1924, 293–97; "The Sense of 'Belonging,'" *Opportunity*, January 1923, 5; "sunny disposition" comment from J. O. Houze, "Negro Labor and the Industries," *Opportunity*, January 1923, 20.

and far more of the available jobs were in increasingly unionized factories and shops controlled by large corporations. Washington's vision was twice deceiving, first because it failed to reflect the economic reality and second because it inadequately recognized the limits posed by white racism.

The emphasis on manhood rights was thought by radicals to offer a way of opening both of these doors, for when blacks had political power they might open access to the available jobs and tear down the legal structures of white racism. But gaining those manhood rights was a slow process, and in the meantime people had to put food on the table. To this end, both the *Crisis* and *Opportunity* began to advocate an economic strategy that had profound implications for black masculinity. "The first duty of a modern citizen is to earn a living," wrote Du Bois in an editorial entitled "Co-Operation," "but earning a living today is a complicated thing and it would be a great mistake for Negroes to try the old, individualistic *laissez-faire* method." Instead, the *Crisis* proposed a new method called "co-operation," which is devoted "to the principle that things should be done and commodities produced for use rather than for exchange," reads the quote from a pamphlet written by Dr. J. P. Warbasse. The pamphlet goes on to explain:

> Food, clothing, housing, fuel, insurance, transportation, and entertainment are all provided by co-operative societies for their members. To attain these things has meant, first, the organization of people as consumers, and then production for these organized consumers. . . . There have been many conflicts with the forces of capitalism, but co-operation has won.
>
> The consumer has the money; if he has not he cannot consume; or he consumes with somebody's else [*sic*] money. He and his purse are the aim and object of business. . . . It is for him that the honey of trade is spread, music plays, lights sparkle, and all the prostitution of business is made as alluring as genius can contrive. . . .
>
> Whenever the people organize as consumers, then they begin to enjoy the economic advantages of their organization; not at some remote day, but from the moment they organize; not when all are organized, but when even a few are gathered together.

Du Bois closed these long quotes from Warbasse with this endorsement: the *Crisis* "firmly believes that this is our economic way out, our industrial emancipation."[42]

This was not outright socialism that Du Bois was advocating, but rather an attempt to take advantage of two emerging changes in the black population— the growth of black incomes and the concentration of blacks in communities

42. Du Bois, "Co-Operation," *Crisis,* November 1917, 9; also see J. P. Warbasse, "The Theory of Co-Operation," *Crisis,* March 1918, 221–24.

in the North where they might safely organize—to further black economic goals. Pursuing economic progress in this way prompted a further movement away from the Victorian masculine ideals advocated by Washington, and a movement toward the very masculine ideals that were taking shape concurrently in white magazines, albeit in somewhat different form. For to join a consumer co-op distanced men from the individualistic self-made man ethos while also encouraging them to think of themselves as consumers, a way of thinking that also challenged the Victorian masculine ethic.

Cooperation of the type described by Du Bois and Warbasse carried an implicit challenge to producers. The challenge was meant to encourage producers to make their consumer goods more readily available to African Americans, and to recognize that some of their profits already came from African American households. But E. Franklin Frazier—noted scholar and author of *Black Bourgeoisie*—drew readers' attention to another element of cooperatives when he contributed an essay titled "Some Aspects of Negro Business" to *Opportunity* in October 1924.[43] For Frazier, cooperatives offered blacks first, an opportunity to pool their limited resources to gain the necessary capital to start a business, and second, access to consumables at a low price for those who take out a membership or hold shares. This latter arrangement, far from drawing Negroes into the market of white consumption, placed the black consumer outside the reach of the middleman who, while taking a share of the cost of the goods, also sells to the consumer an image of himself that goes along with the purchase of the product. This is an important point, for when a black consumer purchases his goods from a warehouse owned by his cooperative rather than from a retail establishment, he remains outside the blandishments of retail selling and advertising that attach image to item in the open market. If consumerism is a web of social and cultural entanglements peculiar to capitalist societies, then cooperatives provided a way to remain outside that web. This was far closer to the socialist practices that white producers feared than the more benign version of cooperatives proposed in the *Crisis*.

Cooperatives, then, posed two kinds of challenges to American capitalism. The first challenge represented a positive stimulus—it suggested that blacks organize to prove to producers the efficacy of their wooing the growing Negro market; it wished to entice white producers to make their goods more readily available. The second challenge offered a negative stimulus—it declared that if capitalists were not going to look after the interests of the Negro market, then the Negro market would organize to short-circuit the system and its stimulation (advertising); it threatened the loss of existing profits derived from

43. Frazier, "Some Aspects," 293–97.

the Negro market. In either case, however, the proposal of cooperatives had the goal of encouraging white producers to break down racial barriers within the consumer economy. I have excluded the possibility that the editors of these magazines were seriously urging their readerships to consider the creation of an alternative black economy, perhaps a socialist economy, outside the circuits of white consumer capitalism. While this may have been the agenda of more radical black publications like the *Messenger*, it was clearly not the agenda of the *Crisis* or *Opportunity*. The management of both of these magazines clearly wanted to have greater access to the larger economy and wished to convince producers of the benefits of appealing to the Negro market.

Of even greater importance than the challenge to white producers, perhaps, was the rhetorical challenge, even the ideological challenge, that the idea of cooperation presented to black men. While Washington and even Du Bois had earlier urged them to think of themselves as "manfully independent," though for different ends, the language of cooperation urged them to think of themselves as dependent on their power as a mass of people pursuing their shared interests. To cooperate was to go along, to meld oneself into the demands of the group, much as white workers were doing as they incorporated themselves into the large bureaucracies that were employing more and more white workers. To behave as a member of a cooperative was to give up strict notions of independence and orient oneself toward a different horizon.

But to behave as a consumer was something even more distant from the vision of African American masculinity than cooperation. Note the language Warbasse used to entice people into accepting the idea of consumer cooperatives: "He [the consumer] and his purse are the aim and object of business. . . . It is for him that the honey of trade is spread, music plays, lights sparkle, and all the prostitution of business is made as alluring as genius can contrive. . . ." Who would not want to have honey spread, music play, and lights sparkle on his behalf? If the lures of consumer society had not yet been aimed at African Americans, it was because they had not forced them to be, implied Warbasse. By organizing to present themselves as a market worthy of enticement, blacks could be courted in the American marketplace.[44]

Thinking of themselves as consumers acting cooperatively to bring themselves to the attention of advertisers and producers and thus to gain a fair break in the consumer marketplace was not antithetical to believing in the primacy of men's claims to full equality. It might even be compatible, if it eventually led to

44. In "Theory of Co-Operation," Warbasse waxes so rhapsodic about the possibilities for consumer cooperatives that he says that "when one grasps its significance and its possibilities he becomes filled with a holy zeal for its promotion" (224).

black men's full recognition as citizens. But it held very different lessons about how men should conceive of their identities. Up until this time, black men had almost never been exposed to articles or ads in black publications that asked them to think of themselves in terms of their image, their appearance, their personality. The cooperative movement began to offer black men an alternative set of images with which they might identify.[45]

While the consumer cooperative movement provided the first alternative frame of reference for conceiving of black masculinity, the growing number of advertisements aimed at black men and the increasing visibility and attention paid to black athletes served to reinforce this change. Though no black magazine was ever flooded with advertisements, a number of advertisers—especially black colleges, black hair care producers, and local businesses—stayed with the *Crisis* and *Opportunity* over the years. In addition to the black colleges and personal care products, *Opportunity* carried ads for the Asbury Park resort—"where the elite, the wealth, and the beauty of the race meet"—Nepperhan Home Building Corporation, and a variety of hotels, books, and retailers offering to serve the needs of a racial elite, one that seemed to reside mainly in New York. Carter, the editor, once boasted that "OPPORTUNITY . . . is read by that class of Negroes who are able to buy automobiles. More than that its reading clientele make up the leadership in the Negro race." As the *Crisis* reached a circulation of 104,000 in 1919, these advertisers reached the largest black audience ever to read a single magazine. According to editor Elmer Anderson Carter, who had succeeded Charles Johnson, *Opportunity* attracted a similar and perhaps even slightly higher class of advertisers, though its circulation was much smaller, reaching a high of approximately 11,000 in 1927 and 1928 (and some 40 percent of those readers were white, according to Ann Douglas).[46] What characterizes the majority of the advertisements placed in these magazines is their singular lack of "modernity." While white ads pitched products based on style, appearance, and allure and tried to convince the consumer that they would be better off for purchasing the product, through the 1920s black ads continued to employ archaic techniques, selling strictly on issues of quality, durability, and—not least—"race interest." But all this would soon change, just as it had earlier changed in the white magazine market, though never to the same degree until the late 1940s.

45. This is not to say that they had not been exposed to such images in white magazines, but rather that they had not seen black men figured as consumers, for black men were almost always pictured as laborers or servants in white advertising.

46. Carter quoted in Weiss, *National Urban League*, 221–22 nn. 16, 22; however Carter may have esteemed his readership, no automobile advertisers chose to place advertisements. Ann Douglas, *Terrible Honesty: Mongrel Manhattan in the 1920s*, 85.

As white magazines readers were introduced to a consumer-based masculinity, they were taught to value image over reputation, personality over character, style over substance. The same process occurred in black magazines, though it was extended over many more years and was indelibly tinged by race. Black magazine editors, for example, had always felt that it was important to have pictures of successful Negroes in their magazines, in order to show the readers what those who succeeded looked like. In the early years of black magazines, these images had most often been of successful businessmen, like Washington's Sweet Potato Farmer (or, in a ghoulish inversion of success, of blacks who had been successfully lynched by white mobs). During and after the war, the *Crisis* and later the *Competitor* and *Opportunity* had prominently featured pictures of black soldiers, especially those who had served with valor. Even the early treatments of black football in the *Competitor* stressed not the excitement and action of the game but the sportsmanship of the players. When the *Crisis* published its first sports piece in March of 1929, the purpose of the article seemed to be to document that good colored players existed, not to discuss their athletic abilities.[47] In all, the purpose of such photos seemed to be to document the fact of black success, to assert that black success existed in a culture that often denied it was so.

Such images began to change only in the 1930s, and they changed for two reasons: the celebration of black sports and culture stars and the introduction of image-based ads, often working in tandem. The very first attempt to sell a retail product directly to men appeared in the *Crisis* in July of 1930, and it was placed by the leading entrepreneur of personal care products for Negroes, the Madame C. J. Walker Manufacturing Company. In large print the ad beckoned "To Men," and the copy instructed that "business men, professional men, tradesmen, students, in fact men in all walks of life have learned to pay strict attention to their hair in seeking the genteel ensemble. . . . Wonder Pomade is a real wonder-working 'he-man's' preparation." (This was not the first product designed for men to be advertised in the magazine, but given that earlier ads for men's clothing were not in fact ads for the clothing but ads attempting to attract traveling salesmen to sell the clothing, the ad is quite notable.) Similar ads soon followed, and they expanded on the premise of the first. In October of 1931, Johnny Hudgins, star of the play *Blackbirds,* advised that "Well-Groomed Hair is demanded by stage and society" as spokesman for Virtus Brilliantine pomade; a month later Frank Wilson, star of "Singin' the Blues," offered men a similar

---

47. Paul W. L. Jones, "Football in Negro Colleges in 1928," *Crisis,* March 1929.

Jesse Owens was the first sports hero to be promoted on the cover of an African American magazine (*Crisis,* September 1936).

motivation for buying Coffo hair dressing. By February of 1938, boxer Joe Louis was telling readers that "Murray's Hair Pomade is just right for me!"[48]

Ads such as these invited consumers to participate with known celebrities in a world of glamour, and black magazines took steps to make that world of glamour known to their audiences. These magazines celebrated the emergence of black mass culture, boosting the literary movement we now know as the Harlem Renaissance, and in the late 1920s and early 1930s providing a forum for a discussion of black theater, films, and sports.[49] Sports drew special attention from both *Opportunity* and the *Crisis,* with both magazines providing extensive coverage of Negro Olympic efforts from as early as 1932. *Opportunity* editor Carter promoted the successes of four blacks who made the 1932 team as good examples of what blacks could accomplish, and both the *Crisis* and *Opportunity* devoted a great deal of attention to Jesse Owens and the other black Olympians in 1936. James D. Parks, whose style most closely approximated the active and jocular style of white sports writers of the day, provided a dramatic narration of the Olympic trials, calling Jesse Owens a "superstar" and Ralph Metcalfe "the peerless Marquette Meteor" with the "driving finish."[50] By the mid-1930s the black magazines joined the many black newspapers in celebrating the career of boxer Joe Louis.

What are we to make of the introduction of such images into issue-oriented black magazines? On the one hand, not terribly much can be made of such images, for the articles celebrating black personalities appeared very infrequently. White magazines of the 1920s fell all over themselves in covering the career of Jack Dempsey; every major white magazine of the period attempted to repackage Dempsey to fit the vision of their magazine. But black magazines reported on these celebrities infrequently and, by comparison, matter-of-factly. The articles on such subjects concerned themselves predominantly with documenting the existence and growth of the phenomena they discussed— black films, black athletes—rather than providing detail on the nature of the

48. "To Men," *Crisis,* July 1930, inside back cover; Virtus Brilliantine pomade ad, *Crisis,* October 1931, inside back cover; Coffo hair dressing ad, *Crisis,* November 1931, 399; ads such as these were ubiquitous in white magazines of the era, but the ads I have selected were virtually the only ones to appear in black magazines.

49. The *Competitor,* a far more "general" magazine than the *Crisis* and *Opportunity,* offered two articles on black theater in its first issue, and they later pumped the prospects of a black boxer named Sol Butler and declared Harry Wills a better boxer than champion Jack Dempsey. See Romeo L. Dougherty, "Progress of the Drama," 53–55; and Salem Tutt Whitney, "The Colored Thespian," 56–57, *Competitor,* January 1920; "Will and Dempsey," *Competitor,* March 1920, 73.

50. James D. Parks, "Negro Athletes in the 1936 Olympiad," *Opportunity,* May 1936, 144–46.

By the 1930s, black celebrities began to appear in advertisements that mimicked those in white magazines. Such ads brought these magazines one step closer to the consumer dynamic that funded the white mass-market magazines (*Crisis,* February 1936, back cover).

experience. Perhaps such an approach was the most suitable, given the nature of the magazines' missions. Nevertheless, their presence alongside articles on lynching or housing made for an odd contrast. Were the magazines concerned with improving the deplorable conditions that faced most American Negroes, or were they concerned with glamorizing the entertainments that kept those troubles from getting people down?[51]

While the fascination with celebrity in black magazines of this period never reached the level of that in white magazines, it remains a significant departure from the history of black magazine publishing. Such ads and articles hinted at the existence of a black culture that had simply not existed ten years earlier, a culture that was urban, valued sophistication and appearance, and had recognizable stars. And they spoke of an image of masculinity that was without precedent in black America, at least as that culture was represented in its magazines. By invoking images of success that arose out of physical vitality, talent, "genius," or personality—as opposed to hard work, frugality, honesty, humility, and the like—these ads and articles offered the first real evidence of a masculinity that was not first and foremost based on race.

In the only real attempt to make sense of athletic celebrity, Edwin Bancroft Henderson provides a telling theory of how the success of black athletes may be leading to racial advancement. His reasoning suggests a rather striking counterpoint to the professed mission of both the *Crisis* and *Opportunity*. Despite the persistence of bigotry, Henderson was convinced that Negro success in athletics may be improving matters. "The mass of humanity still is motivated by feelings and emotions," he explained in a 1936 article in *Opportunity*, and among these emotions those that value fighting and struggle are primary: "[W]e still respond readily to the call of the chase, the fight, the race or the hunt and live over something of our early ancestral experiences when we thrill or despair with the runner, boxer or other athlete. The world still loves a fighter, whether he be the winner or loser." As evidence, he cites a number of black athletes—Joe Louis, Jesse Owens, Ralph Metcalfe—who "are emulated by thousands of growing youth of all races, and above all they gain for themselves and the Negro the respect of millions whose superiority feelings have sprung solely from identity with the white race."[52] Such an argument is not so different than that advanced by Washington or Du Bois, who contended that acquiring economic success or

51. Neither the *Crisis* nor *Opportunity* resolved this seeming paradox by avoiding it: following Du Bois's departure, the *Crisis* became the house organ of the NAACP and abandoned the goal of entertaining readers, and *Opportunity* vacated the field when it ceased publication in 1949.

52. Edwin Bancroft Henderson, "The Negro Athlete and Race Prejudice," *Opportunity*, March 1936, 77–79.

political equality were key. But athletic success and the other kinds of success for which Negroes were gaining public attention relied on different attributes than the kinds of success championed by the race leaders. Henderson's argument works only within a society that is giving more credence to the physical and outward expressions of human achievement—to a society that is willing to value winning over striving. Whereas Victorian culture sought to wall off the physical, to concentrate its rewards on the expression of the qualities like self-control and character, modern culture chose to exalt the physical, the exterior, over the interior. And in some limited ways, black Americans were beginning to partake of that cultural dynamic through their magazines.

Despite the growing importance of the consumer-driven economy, and the increasingly evident influence of that consumer economy in the white magazine market, black consumers and black magazines remained largely outside the circuit. They remained outside for a variety of reasons: white racism kept blacks from participating in many retail experiences, black incomes remained so low compared to white incomes that African Americans often did not have the resources to enter the consumer marketplace, and advertising firms, still predominantly white, had never sought to make separate appeals to the Negro market.[53] So while white magazines served as a vehicle for transmitting to whites the road maps for how to negotiate a successful passage into a culture of consumption, black magazines still largely agitated for basic issues like political equality, equal justice, fair housing and employment, and a host of other race concerns. In "A Survey of the Negro Press," Eugene Gordon wrote that "the Negro press is religiously, almost fanatically, race conscious, and, hence, is doing more than any other agency to develop and sustain this consciousness in its readers." Recent scholarship that discusses the historical consciousness of whiteness has made us aware that white magazines were equally obsessed with race, though they never drew attention to race as such.[54] The point—mine and

---

53. Marchand notes that advertisers automatically excluded between 30 and 65 percent of the American populace from consideration because of their low income, and the majority of African Americans fell into this bracket (*Advertising the American Dream*, 64). Dwight Ernest Brooks examines the discourse of advertisers in trade journals in his "Consumer Markets and Consumer Magazines: Black America and the Culture of Consumption, 1920–1960," while lamenting the fact that the origins of the black consumer market remained understudied.

54. Eugene Gordon, "A Survey of the Negro Press," *Opportunity*, January 1927. Historians of whiteness are now being subject to the same objections that historians of masculinity once faced, and in some cases still do: that history has always been about whiteness. Two works by David R. Roediger begin to make the case for a history of whiteness: *Towards the Abolition of Whiteness: Essays on Race, Politics, and Working Class History*, and *The Wages of Whiteness: Race and the Making of the American Working Class*.

Gordon's—is that race magazines were so concerned with race as such that they failed to participate in the concerns of the majority culture.

Race Magazines and Advertising

It was not for lack of trying that black magazines remained outside the net of advertising dollars that supported white magazines. Indeed, they wanted in most desperately, as their frequent calls for advertising support indicated. But producing a commercially successful magazine in America required a careful weighing of the desire of the editor and publisher to produce a distinct editorial product, the desire of the audience to be entertained and informed about issues they found important, and the desire of advertisers to reach the people they envisioned as their consumers, all within a constantly shifting cultural milieu. While black magazines like the *Crisis* and *Opportunity* had come to satisfactory resolutions of the first two issues, solving the dilemma of gaining advertising support puzzled them throughout the 1920s and 1930s.

As I have already noted, dunning the black community for advertising support was a major occupation for black magazine editors throughout the first forty years of the twentieth century. But the efforts to gain the support of white advertisers became more organized in the 1920s and 1930s. Among the first people in black publishing known to have explored the possibilities of attracting white advertisers was Claude A. Barnett, founder of the Associated Negro Press, a news service that provided news and feature articles to black newspapers and magazines throughout the United States. (The A.N.P. was the equivalent of today's U.P.I.) Because the A.N.P. always flirted with financial failure, Barnett sought in the 1920s to strengthen his business by linking his press service to an advertising exchange. This advertising exchange—the Associated Publishers' Representative and, later, the National Feature Service—worked by giving black periodicals national news stories in exchange for advertising space in their pages. The advertising space was then sold to advertisers. It was an ingenious way to eke a profit out of an entire industry—Negro publishing—that offered few profits. But Barnett quickly ran into the same troubles that magazine editors and managers had already encountered: namely, that few black businesses had the money to invest in heavy advertising.[55]

55. Linda J. Evans, "Claude A. Barnett and the Associated Negro Press," 52–54. As associate curator of the Chicago Historical Society's Manuscripts Collection, Evans has helped to organize the Barnett Papers, which contain 320 boxes of information on the Negro press from 1918 to 1967. Although Barnett was more closely linked to black newspapers, his efforts at attracting advertisers closely paralleled and sometimes joined with those of magazine publishers and are thus worth examining within the context of my argument. Thanks to Susan Curtis for pointing me in the direction of this valuable archive, one of the

The biggest problem, according to Barnett, was to convince white advertisers that the Negro market was substantial enough to merit the cost of advertising to it. In a letter to Robert R. Moton of the Tuskegee Institute, Barnett lamented that black periodicals:

> get practically none of the millions of dollars poured out into white publications. . . . Whether the advertisers see in the strengthening of Negro newspapers a stimulus to Negro growth and prosperity and do not want to encourage it, I do not know, but almost universally, they have built up a defense which sounds as though they had arrived at an [sic] uniform conclusion. . . . . They have built up a defense mechanism against using Negro newspapers which is marvelous and indicates concerted thinking and agreement. We must find a way to marshal our buying power so as to force them to realize our value.[56]

What was needed, Barnett wrote to the editor of the *East Tennessee News,* was "a definite effort . . . to impress advertising men with the importance of the Negro market and the value of Negro newspapers." He wrote to J. B. Bass of the *California Eagle* newspaper that he had attracted the interest of Louis Meyers & Son, Kellogg Company, and American Tobacco Company, but they wanted proof that their money would be well invested. "We must do for our advertisers all that the white dailies will do in our districts for their advertisers," Barnett informed Bass.[57] Soon Barnett made more definite plans to bring his plan to fruition.

Using his influence to place a black adviser to small business in Secretary Herbert Hoover's Department of Commerce, and working closely with Albon Holsey of the National Negro Business League (formerly advertising manager of the *Crisis*), Barnett sought to document the emergence of a black market that advertisers ought to be eager to exploit. "They saw the 1930 federal census as a chance to document the considerable economic gains made by black citizens over the previous decades and thus to gather official evidence that a substantial Negro market existed in the United States," writes Barnett papers curator Linda J. Evans. "[Barnett] hoped that better statistics would persuade major national advertisers that they could reach a worthwhile audience of potential consumers by placing their ads in the black press."[58]

---

very few sources of information about efforts by African Americans to penetrate the white marketplace.

56. Claude A. Barnett to Robert R. Moton, September 22, 1930, Claude A. Barnett Papers, Manuscripts Collection, Chicago Historical Society (hereinafter referred to as Barnett Papers), Box 131, Folder 6.

57. Claude A. Barnett to *East Tennessee News,* n.d., and Barnett to J. B. Bass, n.d., Barnett Papers, Box 131, Folder 6.

58. Evans, "Claude A. Barnett," 53.

But Barnett's plans, formulated in the 1920s, foundered in the harsh economic climate of the early 1930s. With the failure of a major client and a lawsuit brought against him by the competing W. B. Ziff Company of Chicago, not to mention a declining advertising market that sharply diminished the number of ads in even the largest circulation white magazines, Barnett exited the advertising business in 1934.[59] But Barnett was not the only member of the black press to imagine the possibilities of promoting the growing Negro market to white producers and advertisers. The managers of *Opportunity* also hoped to lure advertisers with this potential gold mine of consumer dollars.

It is rather appropriate that the magazine dedicated to providing a scientific approach to understanding Negro problems should have come up with the first scientific approach to increasing the number of white ads in a black magazine. For a scientific appeal is clearly what editor Carter or his advertising manager had in mind when they placed a call for advertisers in the December 1931 issue of *Opportunity*. This appeal, laid out to look like a news story, is worth quoting at length. "A U.S. Government Official Speaks: 12,000,000 Negroes Represent a Vital Consumer Market," began the ad, which goes on to claim that "in many southern cities the Negro represents from 5 to 45 per cent of the total consumer buying power, while *Negro purchases in New York City alone are estimated to exceed $150,000,000 yearly*" (italics from source). Also headlined is an editorial from the *Chicago Daily News* that mentions the twelve million figure and says:

> But the market furnished by the American Negro lies at our door and is largely neglected. It would be more profitable, and certainly more business-like, for producers to inquire whether that market does not present a great opportunity. . . . Now intelligent Negro leadership is challenging white America to give its Race a chance to prove that . . . millions were not invested unwisely.

Beneath these dual appeals is appended "Advertisers Please Note," followed by the claim that: "*Opportunity* . . . is a splendid medium through which to reach much of this tremendous consuming power. . . . Advertisements in *Opportunity* are read by the class of colored and white people who can afford to pay for the things they need or want. WRITE TODAY for a sample copy of *Opportunity* and a rate card."[60]

It sometimes seems that the early history of black magazines is a history of "despites"—despite the best efforts of determined and skilled editors and

59. Ziff had also made plans to convince advertisers of the importance of the Negro market, as their pamphlet called "The Negro Market" indicates; Barnett Papers, Box 131, Folder 5.
60. *Opportunity*, December 1931, 397.

publishers, despite some very high quality writing on issues of great social importance, despite the institutional support of the strongest Negro organizations—the Negro magazine failed to thrive. Add another despite to this list: despite tremendous efforts to document the viability of advertising to the Negro market, decidedly few white advertisers chose to advertise in black publications. Barnett imagined a kind of conspiracy of white advertisers to deprive black publications of their financial support, but in the 1930s he probably needed no conspiracy theory to explain the problem. With African Americans suffering the Great Depression even harder than white Americans, the very market that had just become viable instantly lost that viability, or at least the appearance of viability. In a decade when advertisers were taking no risks and exploring no new markets, there would be no influx of white advertising into black magazines. Though it seemed that they might have entered into the nexus of relations that had made white magazines so prosperous, black magazines remained outside and would remain so until the 1940s and early 1950s, when a renewed push to make white producers aware of the Negro market and a new approach to black magazine publishing finally came together to create a commercially successful black magazine.

Black magazines suffered greatly during the 1930s, though both the *Crisis* and *Opportunity* survived the decade. Du Bois looked back on the decline of his magazine in a retrospective essay written in 1951:

> Our income in 1920, was $77,000, that was our high water mark. Then began a slump which brought the circulation down to 35,000 copies in 1924. . . . The causes of this were clear and strike every periodical: the reading public is not used to paying for the cost of the periodicals which they read. . . . Advertisers pay for most of the costs and advertisers buy space in periodicals which circulate widely among well-to-do persons able to buy the wares offered. The CRISIS was known to circulate among Negro workers of low income. Moreover it antagonized many white powerful interests.[61]

When the depression hit the Negro economy—which Du Bois claims occurred as early as 1926—circulation and advertising fell even further, and the *Crisis* was forced once again to accept subsidization from the NAACP. Chafing at losing complete control over the editorial output of "his" magazine, and embroiled in clashes with NAACP officials over its policies toward segregation, Du Bois admitted by 1934 that the magazine would never again support itself and resigned his editorship. Roy Wilkins, assistant executive secretary to NAACP head Walter F. White, took over the reins of what would now be strictly a house organ. Du Bois later commented that "all large organizations need such

61. Du Bois, "Editing the *Crisis*," *Crisis*, March 1951, 149–50.

a publication. But it is never self-supporting nor widely read. So far as it tries to be literary or artistic, it misses its main function and is too narrow to achieve any other."[62] Though the magazine went on after Du Bois, it no longer represented an attempt to make a commercial success.

Perhaps because *Opportunity* was always the acknowledged house organ of the National Urban League, it was never forced to weather the depression under its own power. Funded for the first three years by the Carnegie Corporation and supported thereafter by the N.U.L., the magazine always had it easier than the *Crisis*. Though it only reached a circulation of 11,000 subscribers and was continually plagued by a scarcity of high-paying ads, *Opportunity* made it through the depression and well into the 1940s, by which time it declared its purpose—to represent the concerns of black Americans—well covered by other publications. Daniel suggests that *Opportunity* enjoyed the support of industrialists concerned with the issues facing Negroes in large cities, and that it secured needed support from the League when it was required.[63]

Retreating from the cultural emphasis that had characterized the magazine in the 1920s and even in the 1930s, *Opportunity* refocused its attention on political and racial issues in the early 1940s, but the strain of publishing a magazine with few subscribers outside the N.U.L. and few advertisers forced the magazine to begin publishing quarterly beginning in 1943. Carter left the editorial work in the hands of "acting editor" Madeline L. Aldridge beginning in January of 1943, and Aldridge served in this capacity until the summer of 1947, when Dutton Ferguson took over just in time to celebrate the magazine's twenty-fifth anniversary. Though the magazine was updated in format to mimic modern mass-circulation magazines, offering a "cover girl" and continuing Aldridge's efforts to appeal to female readers, the magazine shrunk steadily. In the winter issue of 1949, the Executive Board of the National Urban League announced the termination of the magazine with this explanation: "Production costs have risen more rapidly than either the Magazine's income or the ability of the Urban League to cover the financial deficit in the Journal's operations. Today, national publications, both popular and scientific, welcome well-written articles by Negro authors as by those of any other race. We find that several highly successful Negro publications keep the American public abreast of the facts of Negro living and race relations."[64] By 1949, they were right, for *Ebony* had finally succeeded in going where no black magazine had gone before, into the heart of the commercial marketplace.

62. Ibid., 151.
63. "An Open Letter," *Opportunity,* winter 1949, front cover; Daniel, *"Opportunity,"* 305–6.
64. "An Open Letter," *Opportunity,* winter 1949, front cover.

5
A Pleasing Personality Wins the Day

The Cultural Hegemony of Modern Masculinity

For years, the intimations of new styles of masculinity had been emerging in the American magazine market. In advertising for Earl Liederman's bodybuilding programs; in articles describing how a vibrant personality can boost a corporate career; in stories glorifying men whose winning smile and taste in clothes made them the envy of all the other guys; and in editorials urging men to dedicate themselves to self-improvement, a cluster of images and values had emerged to challenge the dominance of Victorian cultural norms for masculinity. At times these new notions of masculinity were the product of an editor's vision, at times they served the needs of an advertiser who needed to sell a product, and at times they reflected the momentum of a faddish social fixation on youth or sports. The emergence of new notions of masculinity reflected the rise of corporatism and consumerism, the post–World War I disenchantment with nineteenth-century values, the faddishness of mass culture—in short, these new notions of masculinity emerged out of and reflected a changing cultural milieu, in all its chaotic variety. And yet, prior to 1933, these new images and values had not been joined together in such a way as to represent a coherent cultural idea. Though all the attributes and qualities of modern masculinity had been hinted at before, there was no single coherent embodiment of modern masculinity until the 1933 birth of *Esquire* magazine.

From its first issue, *Esquire* encouraged men to identify themselves with leisure, good reading, stylish clothes, fashionable accessories—all the accoutrements that a consumer economy could make available to men. The magazine offered an attitude to match, encouraging men to think of themselves as tough nonconformists, iconoclasts, sophisticates unspoiled by their knowledge. And the magazine threw into the mix a fascination with sexuality never before seen in a respectable publication. It was, like *Vanity Fair* twenty years before, a new kind of magazine, and it expressed a new kind of masculinity. To the surprise

"But I can't see you tomorrow, darling, I'm getting married—how about the day after?"

The *Esquire* man was young, handsome, and a bit of a rogue (*Esquire,* May 1936, 38). (By permission of *Esquire* magazine. © Hearst Communications, Inc. Also, *Esquire* is a trademark of Hearst Magazines Property, Inc. All rights reserved.)

of many, the magazine worked, surging in circulation during the nation's worst economic depression and despite a cost—fifty cents—that was nearly unheard of in the American magazine market.

Where *Esquire* led, others followed. By the mid-1940s, two magazines— *True* and *Argosy*—offered themselves as the *Esquire* for everyman. Rejecting *Esquire*'s urban sophistication and fascination with style, *True* and *Argosy* made themselves into the men's magazines for the hunting, beer, and poker set. Forget highbrow stories and the latest cut in suits, the editors of these magazines declared, men are interested in reading a true adventure story, learning about good fishing areas, and buying a good hunting jacket, a new rifle, or a cool-smoking pipe. In the process of recreating *Esquire*'s formula for a different demographic, these magazines succeeded in bringing a whole new class of men into the cultural logic of consumerism and modern masculinity.

Together, *Esquire*, *True*, and *Argosy* framed the terms of modern masculinity for white men no matter their social class. But what about African American men? Were they too to be invited within the embrace of modern masculinity? Black men, as we have seen, had faced a long and difficult struggle in coming to terms with the images and ideals of Victorian masculinity. Victorian masculinity had posited a notion of manhood based on economic success and ascension, but American racism had made it extremely difficult for black men to succeed economically. Because black men were barred from the networks of economic interaction that defined the greater American marketplace, they were also excluded from direct consideration by the creators of mass-market magazines. Mass-market American magazines had only served as venues for the expression of masculine values that were pertinent to the consumerist dynamic that allowed those magazines to exist. As long as black men were economically marginal, and as long as American manufacturers declined to make an effort to appeal to black consumers, it seemed that no mass-market magazine would appeal to black men.

For nearly as long as there were mass-market magazines, black magazine editors and publishers had been trying to figure out how to navigate their way to commercial success and how to formulate a vision of masculinity suited to African Americans' peculiar place within American culture. The economic insignificance of black advertisers and the disregard of white advertisers had forced black editors and publishers to develop magazines quite unlike their white counterparts. These magazine's visions of black masculinity were equally unlike their white counterparts. While white magazines sorted out the increasing irrelevance of Victorian masculinity and the rise of modern masculinity, black magazines struggled to formulate arguments for the very terms through which they could lay claim to legitimate expressions of manhood in American culture.

Yet not long after *Esquire, True,* and *Argosy* had succeeded at championing modern masculinity for white readers, a new magazine for black readers succeeded at revolutionizing the nature of black magazine publishing. *Ebony,* created in 1945 by publisher John Johnson, modeled itself after the hugely popular *Life* magazine and proposed to show the "happy side" of Negro life in America. With lavish photo spreads and optimistic articles about Negro accomplishment, *Ebony's* content was unprecedented in its ability to portray African Americans participating in the full range of pleasures available to the American middle class. Johnson took the idea that black Americans lived lives very much like white Americans—that they lived in homes they owned, bought and drove new cars, and were interested in leisure and recreation—and made that vision central to his magazine. With one stroke Johnson rewrote the book on publishing a black magazine, and no sooner had he done it than he found advertisers—white advertisers—who were happy to reach the market that Johnson made available to them. In reinventing the black magazine, Johnson steered depictions of black masculinity away from the rights-based agenda that had characterized the race magazines and toward the agenda of consumerist modern masculinity. In short, Johnson brought black men into the realm of modern masculinity.

The story of this chapter is the domination and spread of modern masculinity. The terms of modern masculinity, which had floated about the American magazine market for nearly twenty years, were taken up by *Esquire* and combined into a package that was immediately popular with American men. Following *Esquire's* lead, magazines like *True* and *Argosy* revised modern masculinity just enough to make it appealing to its readership, and to a readership that grew with the magazines. Finally, *Ebony* succeeded at translating the terms of modern masculinity into a language that was available to African American men. By turns, these magazines worked out what it meant to embrace modern masculinity fully, and the encounters these magazines had with issues of sexuality, attitudes toward women, class, and race have informed the nature of manhood to this day. The masculinity presented in these magazines was confident and buoyant, deriving its meaning from issues that would have struck a Victorian man as ephemeral, meaningless. But for the modern men imagined and presented in these magazines, concerns with personality, leisure, consumption, and self-realization were what gave life meaning.

Esquire: " An Unholy Combination of Erudition and Sex"

The magazine that came to epitomize modern masculinity in the 1930s was founded in the midst of the nation's worst depression by a trio of salesman who had never edited a real magazine. Such beginnings would have doomed nearly every other American magazine, but *Esquire* was, from its very beginnings, a different kind of magazine. *Esquire* managed to pull together the most unlikely combination of elements from the broader magazine market: from *Vanity Fair* it borrowed its sense of urban sophistication, its adoration of things expensive, and its heavy, glossy pages; from *Captain Billy's Whiz Bang* it took its gutter humor about sexuality; from *Vogue* it took its aim of selling its audience on a consumer lifestyle, though it changed the sex of that audience. But *Esquire* became something more than any of its predecessors. It became, in the words of one critic, an "unholy combination of erudition and sex," and, in the words of one of its copyeditors, a three-ring circus featuring fashion, off-beat masculine writing, and sex; more than anything, it became one of the most notably successful magazines of the 1930s.[1]

The desire to sell goods to men was not new to publishers David Smart and William Hobart Weintraub and editor Arnold Gingrich. Indeed, they had been working together in this effort for several years before they created *Esquire,* creating trade magazines like *Gentlemen's Quarterly, Club and Campus, The Etonian,* and *Gifts for a Gentleman.* These magazines displayed pictures and descriptions of the latest offerings in menswear and were provided to retailers as an aid in selling to their customers. Gingrich recalled that "*Gentlemen's Quarterly* was forcing men's stores into the unaccustomed role of actively stimulating their customers' hitherto unsuspected wants, as opposed to catering passively to their routine needs." In 1931, the trio advanced the genre by supplementing the promotions for men's clothing with editorial matter; they called their new magazine *Apparel Arts* and modeled it after Henry Luce's *Fortune.* As the depression knocked the wind out of retail sales at men's stores, many retailers offered the magazine to consumers as a catalog from which they could order. Instead of carrying lots of clothes, retailers could carry the magazine. But that strategy would not make the publishers any money. So Gingrich, Smart, and Weintraub started bandying about ideas for a new magazine that combined fashion features, advertising for menswear, and more editorial matter. "The more they talked, the more expensive the proposed new magazine became. Its cover price rose from a dime to half a dollar."[2] Its name, chosen after much deliberation, would be *Esquire.*

---

1. Henry F. Pringle, "Sex, Esq.," *Scribner's,* March 1938, 33; interview with Martin Mayer, November 30, 1989, cited in Hugh Merrill, *Esky: The Early Years at* Esquire, 32 n. 8. The rivals for *Esquire's* claim to fame in the 1930s are *Fortune,* the magazine that celebrated American capitalism that started in 1930, and *Life,* the picture magazine that started in 1936.

2. Arnold Gingrich, *Nothing but People,* 28; Merrill, *Esky,* 29–30. For a complete discussion of the early publishing efforts of the trio, see Merrill, *Esky,* 13–30.

Everything was wrong with the idea: the magazine cost too much, especially during the Great Depression; men were not that interested in fashion and could not be expected to buy a fashion magazine; and they could hardly afford to pay for the top-quality editorial matter they hoped to publish. But somehow, the creators of *Esquire* made it work. The financial problems proved to be the least worrisome. Most of the printing of the first issue was presold to clothing retailers and carried ample advertising, so there was never a question of it earning a profit. And Gingrich begged or borrowed enough editorial material to publish an initial issue that listed as contributors Ernest Hemingway, John Dos Passos, Erskine Caldwell, Dashiell Hammett, James T. Farrell, actor Douglas Fairbanks Jr., golfer Bobby Jones, and boxer Gene Tunney. But getting men to buy a fashion magazine was the biggest challenge, and *Esquire* met that challenge with an editorial package that was nothing short of astonishing.

Gingrich seemed to sense that if he were going to pitch consumer goods to a male audience, he would have to make the magazine aggressively masculine from the outset. In his opening editorial, Gingrich explained that they formed *Esquire* because "the general magazines, in the mad scramble to increase the woman readership that seems to be so highly prized by national advertisers, have bent over backward in catering to the special interests and tastes of the feminine audience." "ESQUIRE aims to become the common denominator of masculine interests—to be all things to all men," continued Gingrich. "The one test that has been applied to every feature that is in this first issue has been simply and solely: 'Is it interesting to men?' How often were we wrong? Come on, let's have it—we're leading with the chin."[3] This chin-thrusting defined the editorial tone of the magazine under Gingrich's editorship: it was Gingrich's way of translating barroom banter between tough guys into editorial policy. Gingrich wanted the magazine to speak directly to its readers, and its readers to speak directly to it, so he addressed men as a friend might, with bluster and directness. Gingrich dared readers to accept the publication of a story by Langston Hughes, "a brilliant young Negro author," claiming that "there ought to be one magazine in America in which a man can read stories like this." And he told men to muffle their complaints when the magazine began to run some ads directed at women, arguing that "the magazine isn't edited for women and won't be."[4] The magazine seemed to listen as well, for it frequently responded

3. "Editor's Box," *Esquire,* autumn 1933, 4. Gingrich's untitled comments customarily appeared on the contents page, but also in an untitled box elsewhere in the magazine, thus the appellation "Editor's Box." *Esquire* was a quarterly for one issue only, becoming a monthly with its second issue in January of 1934.
4. "Editor's Box," *Esquire,* January 1934, 15; "Editor's Box," *Esquire* November 1935, 5. The query about Hughes produced a huge number of responses both for and against

to requests from readers for changes in the magazine and published a very large selection of reader mail, much of it quite critical.[5] Thus from its very opening *Esquire* attempted to cast masculinity in terms of its toughness, confidence, and lack of fear of challenge.

Gingrich also led with his chin when he presented Ernest Hemingway as the lead author in every issue he could. Gingrich had long admired Hemingway and collected his works, and after he met Hemingway early in 1933 he sought out the writer to contribute something—anything—to his new magazine. Gingrich wrote to Hemingway that his new magazine "will try to be to the American male what *Vogue* is to the female. . . . It aims to have ample hair on its chest, to say nothing of adequate cojones. It won't, on the other hand, have that self-conscious bad-little-boy-behind-the-barn air that was emanated by [earlier] magazines-for-men. . . . Just short of splitting a bowel, I'll try anything to sell you the idea of being in that first issue."[6] It was an audacious request from a man who had never edited a consumer magazine before, but Gingrich had high hopes for his venture. He wanted to pitch a consumer lifestyle to the Hemingway man, and what better spokesman to hire than Hemingway himself?

Hemingway agreed, albeit after conning Gingrich into paying him double the going rate and throwing in some free clothes to boot. *Esquire* rarely got Hemingway's best work, though it did publish the short story "The Snows of Kilimanjaro."[7] Hemingway sent in journalistic stuff on fishing and hunting and boating, and occasional political commentary. But it did not matter, really, for the point was not that the magazine published the best Hemingway but that it published Hemingway at all. Hemingway's contributions were a kind of endorsement, a guarantee that this magazine was not for "sissies." Hemingway ended his association with *Esquire* late in 1936, writing to Gingrich that "by staying out of the magazine now I am probably fucking up my commercial career as badly as I fucked up my critical status (the hell with it) by staying in it. But I haven't any choice. . . ."[8] It was the kind of closure that Gingrich, with his tough-guy attitude, must have appreciated.

---

publication, reported Gingrich the next month, and in April of 1934 he printed the story, "A Good Job Done."

5. One letter writer called *Esquire* the "magazine for lechers," complaining bitterly about the nudity in cartoons and smutty stories (November 1935, 8). Gingrich responded indirectly in June of 1936, saying "Morality does not, as most of these letter-writers seem to believe, consist of attempting to remake the world in your perhaps slightly sour image" (5).

6. Arnold Gingrich to Ernest Hemingway, February 24, 1933, Box 4, Folder 2, Gingrich Papers.

7. Ernest Hemingway, "The Snows of Kilimanjaro," *Esquire,* August 1936, 27, 194–201.

8. Ernest Hemingway to Arnold Gingrich, August 25, 1936, Box 4, Folder 3, Gingrich Papers.

Hemingway was the most overtly "tough" of the many famous writers *Esquire* managed to feature in its pages; according to Hugh Merrill, "there was no hairier literary chest than Ernest Hemingway's." Hemingway was, in many ways, the quintessential modern male: hostile to Victorian masculine archetypes, he had reinvented himself as a swashbuckling world adventurer and his art as a gauntlet thrown down before writers of sentimental fiction. This was the man who had written in *A Farewell to Arms,* "I was always embarrassed by the words sacred, glorious, and sacrifice and the expression in vain."[9] Not all the writers fit into Hemingway's tough-guy image, but none of them wrote the kind of light, clean fiction that could be found in the *American* or the *Saturday Evening Post.* F. Scott Fitzgerald, John Dos Passos, Langston Hughes, Dashiell Hammett, James T. Farrell, and others provided a stream of material that led the magazine to boast that it published more Nobel and Pulitzer Prize winners than any other magazine. Some of the writing was of high quality, and it pushed men to engage the narrative styles of the best modernist authors, whose work explored the world through the guise of the individualized sensibility and not an overarching moral code.[10] *Esquire* somehow made it manly to read serious fiction.

The editorial tone and the fiction published in *Esquire* helped to allay Gingrich's fears that men would be put off by "the lavender [homosexual] whiff coming from the mere presence of fashion pages."[11] But no single element of the magazine was more calculated to counter whatever sense of effeminacy remained attached to fashion than the magazine's absorption in heterosexual sexuality, especially via the illustration and the cartoon. While *Esquire's* fiction appealed to men's more intellectual side, its cartoons and its "figures," forums for the display of female breasts and sexual innuendo, were as bawdy as those

9. Merrill, *Esky,* 32; Ernest Hemingway, *A Farewell to Arms* (New York: Charles Scribner's Sons, 1929, 1957), 177. The Hemingway that I present is the Hemingway of Gingrich's imagination, rather than the particular Hemingway of one of his many biographers and hundreds, perhaps thousands, of interested scholars. That is, he is the Hemingway that Gingrich offered to readers in his editorial comments, a man as known for his adventures as his writing. For a discussion of Gingrich's portrayal of Hemingway, see Merrill, *Esky,* 32–35.

10. Not all of the writing in *Esquire* was good, however. In order to fill the first several issues, Gingrich purchased the "excess inventory that had been accumulated to distressing proportions by Ray Long for *Cosmopolitan* magazine," recalled Gingrich in a draft of his unfinished autobiography (Box 1, "biographical material" folder, Gingrich Papers). Once they exhausted *Cosmopolitan's* reject pile, *Esquire* often accepted manuscripts that leading authors had had rejected elsewhere. *Esquire* was often more concerned with the name of the author than with what he wrote. See also Merrill, *Esky,* 35–37.

11. Gingrich, *Nothing but People,* 81.

found in the naughtiest of the pulps.[12] The women who appeared in *Esquire* were young, long-legged, and full-breasted, and they seemed to exist to give men pleasure, to acquiesce to men's ever-present sexual urges. By presenting images of such women as the natural object of male desire, *Esquire* made it perfectly clear that its readers were "real men."

Kenon Breazeale, author of an excellent analysis of the use of female images in *Esquire,* argues that *Esquire*'s use of eroticized female images is "one of modern popular culture's most influential attempts to embody represented femininity as a signifier for specifically heterosexual masculinity." The magazine's regular illustrated features certainly had this effect. E. Simms Campbell's "Sultan" cartoons featured a heavyset, vaguely Arabic-looking man who surrounded himself with a harem of white women—blondes, brunettes, and redheads. In one cartoon, the Sultan is warned not to touch the merchandise at an auction of half-naked women. In another, a trader delivers the Sultan several half-naked women but the Sultan complains, "There's some mistake. What I ordered was two elephants and a camel." For the Sultan, women were a product to be selected, purchased, and used at will. George Petty's finely drawn female figures, his Petty Girls, were studies in the idealized female form; Breazeale called them "exemplars of the fetishizing possibilities inherent in airbrush: bodies encased in a flawlessly taut sheath of skin that resembles inflated rubber."[13] One purpose of Petty's single-page sketches was to show off as much of the female body as possible; the see-through lingerie or body-hugging clothes were mere nods to propriety, for the Petty Girl may as well have been nude.[14] Yet the milieu in which the Petty Girl appeared fulfilled another purpose. The props—a phone, a riding crop, a pistol—and the caption reminded men that such girls did not come easy. When the Petty Girl spoke to a man it was to tease; when she spoke to her girlfriend it was to commiserate about the difficulties of dating rich millionaires. At the same time that the girl's attire and pose seduced, her props and her words held men off. The intent of such framing was to remind men that women were to be pursued and won; the images stimulated both sexual desire and pursuit.

12. Though I claim no extensive knowledge of low-brow men's publications, the material found in *Esquire* is quite comparable to that found in *Captain Billy's Whiz-Bang,* a satirical magazine that included "French postcards" and "artistic studies" of nude women, which I examined for the years between 1921 and 1933.

13. Kenon Breazeale, "In Spite of Women: *Esquire Magazine* and the Construction of the Male Consumer," 10; E. Simms Campbell, *Esquire,* April 1936; January 1936 (numerous other cartoons of Campbell's would have served equally well as examples); Breazeale, "In Spite of Women," 12.

14. And sometimes she was—see especially *Esquire,* August 1938, 35.

"Please do *not* handle the merchandise!"

E. Simms Campbell's "Sultan" cartoons reminded *Esquire* readers that everything was for sale (*Esquire,* January 1936, 31). (By permission of *Esquire* magazine. © Hearst Communications, Inc. Also, *Esquire* is a trademark of Hearst Magazines Property, Inc. All rights reserved.)

Though illustrator E. Simms Campbell published his sexy drawings in the best white magazines, including *Esquire*, it was in the black magazine *Opportunity* that he was celebrated as a role model (*Opportunity*, March 1932, 83). (Courtesy of Lee A. Daniels.)

Esquire's treatment of women had its darker side as well. Breazeale argues that in order to cast men as consumers, *Esquire's* editors had to make "a thoroughgoing attempt to detach the imputation of femininity from that arena of domestic consumption *Esquire* planned to open for its male readers." In a number of articles concerning food and liquor, clothing, and household decorating, *Esquire's* contributors took pains to point out how poorly women managed the tasks of discrimination and consumption. One writer claimed that his wife had turned their dining room into "a valentine store after an explosion"; another complained that women cannot cook because "pro primo, they are less generous, pro secondo, they have less imagination, and pro tertio, they just do not enjoy good food"; another accused women of "cluttering up the home with antiques of the most unlivable type"; and yet another boasted that people like men's parties better because "you get better drinks." All in all, such articles recuperated "a female-identified role for men" by "arguing against traditional sex-linked roles."[15] Or, in simpler terms, they rescued consumerism for a male audience.

Of course all this chin-leading, girl-ogling, tough-guy stuff was designed to prepare men to accept the steady stream of advertisements that would be directed their way. *Esquire* began with an advantage that few other magazines enjoyed—it already had a bevy of clothing advertisers that the publishers had brought along from their past ventures. And *Esquire* soon added many new accounts. By its second issue, the magazine carried ads for shaving creams, razors, accessories, liquor and, of course, clothing. Most of these ads followed the formulas long used to sell products to men, promoting the products for their quality, their value, and their good taste. According to Merrill, "*Correct* seem[ed] to be the watchword in these advertisements [for clothing]. And for the newly urbanized man who fear[ed] his small-town roots will show, being correct means fitting in to his new world."[16] Such ads for Arrow shirts, Stetson shoes, Hart Schaffner & Marx, and others were the same ads that appeared in magazines like *Collier's*, the *Post*, and the *American Magazine*. They cast the man as a consumer and appealed to him by flattering his rationality and by tweaking—ever so slightly—his desire to conform.

Advertisers soon learned to cast their advertising in the context of the heightened masculine atmosphere created by *Esquire*, and in so doing they

15. Breazeale, "In Spite of Women," 6; Donald Hough, "Dinner Bits Man," *Esquire*, October 1936, 46; Dick Pine, "Women Can't Cook," *Esquire*, September 1939, 51; E. McKay Jackson, "The Bachelor at Home," *Esquire*, November 1935, 109; William B. Powell, "Cocktail Party, Masculine," *Esquire*, September 1936, 118; all quoted in Breazeale, "In Spite of Women," 6–7; Breazeale, "In Spite of Women," 9.

16. Merrill, *Esky*, 52.

completed the project of casting men as consumers that advertisers had been perfecting for years. The first element of *Esquire*'s masculine agenda to appear in advertising was the appeal to men's sexual longing, and it was used by Rolls Razor in the magazine's second issue, published in January 1934. Addressing the male reader, a buxom woman with a very low cut dress says, "Hello Smoothy, That tip of yours was absolutely swell. . . . [T]his Christmas they're not going to kid me about fool, female presents."[17] This small ad combines a powerful appeal to sexuality and consumption. Lured by the erotic image of a woman addressing him alone, the man is flattered several times over: he is called "Smoothy," he is told that his "tip" was "absolutely swell," and he is lauded for giving good advice about what to purchase. The Rolls Razor ad compliments the man for already being smart enough to purchase their product; the sale had already been made, and it has won the reader what he desires. This was one of the most directly sexual appeals to the male consumer ever to appear in the magazine, and it set the tone for ads to come.

Several advertisers used the very female images provided by *Esquire* to pitch their goods. In October of 1935, Hart Schaffner & Marx clothiers signed E. Simms Campbell and his Sultan and harem of women to advertise their clothes. In this first ad, the Sultan and his harem have just arrived in America, and the women eye an American magazine (*Esquire?*) advertisement. "Oh boy America! and Hart Schaffner & Marx clothes!" reads the caption. The Sultan looks warily on—he better get himself some Hart Schaffner & Marx clothes if he wants to keep his harem happy. Similarly, Old Gold cigarettes hired the Petty Girl to mouth their copy. "Hitched to a Humdrummy? Light an Old Gold," recommends the shapely pitchwoman. "When the slipper-snoozer to whom you're shackled is pepless as a senile snail . . . don't let it make you a bitter woman." Assuming that the ad is for men, despite the fact that it addresses a woman, we can see that the appeal is to the man who wishes to have more sexual spunk—and what man would not wish such a thing if he read *Esquire*, which continually reminds men that conquest and sexual performance is what counts with women?[18]

Lest readers not get the hint that appropriate consumption could ease fears of sexual inadequacy, Hart Schaffner & Marx spelled it out quite clearly in a January 1937 advertisement. This advertisement was aimed at the wealthy but slightly older man who is experiencing competition from young sharpies. The half-page color illustration depicts a group of six tuxedoed young men bidding

17. Rolls Razor ad, *Esquire*, January 1934, 150.
18. Hart Schaffner & Marx ad, *Esquire*, October 1935, 19; Old Gold ad, *Esquire*, October 1935, 19, 135. Petty's independent cartoons almost never contain male figures, but his ads do. In this ad, the aging man appears more interested in his newspaper than in the girl.

farewell to a Mrs. Van Sickle, above this caption: "Goodby, Mrs. Van Sickle—and remember us to Mr. Van Sickle." The copy below reads:

> You just know Mr. Van Sickle doesn't own a Hart Schaffner & Marx tailcoat. If he did this situation could never have developed.
> As a matter of fact, all that would be necessary for Mr. Van Sickle to completely dominate the picture would be for him to appear in a new Robert Surry Tailcoat!
> How about yourself—are you prepared against an invasion like this? Think of how decidedly awkward it might be to find yourself in such a position. The solution is simple, sensible and sure—step into the Hart Schaffner & Marx store in your town.[19]

In this formulation, appropriate consumption trumps youth and protects men from sexual competition. There is no flattery implied in this ad, merely a preying on the aging man's fear that his wife may be courted by younger men.

Esquire's own self-promotional copy articulated a similar logic. In one appeal to readers, *Esquire* posed the situation of a man who was eager to attract the attention of a woman but "couldn't get into Her Grace's graces." "Then one day my best friend told me! It was because I was a mug. Hadn't been anywhere. Hadn't seen anything. Didn't know anything. Did I say he was a friend? YES— because then he told me how to know everything a young man-about-town should know." The friend told him about *Esquire,* and the man quickly used *Esquire* to guide him in all matters of taste. "I can truthfully say that had it not been for *Esquire* I would still be the simple hill-billy that my wife, the ex-duchess, first knew. You, too, can be a brilliant wit and beau this easy way."[20] The "buy me and you'll get the girl" appeal seemed to lay at the very heart of *Esquire's* approach to its readers. A full-page Petty Girl illustration from 1938 placed this whole sexual appeal dynamic in an interesting context. The girl is completely nude, with folded legs and arms shielding the parts of her body that would have attracted the censors. She says to her friend on the phone: "I'm not posing for that account any longer. It seems that I took the consumer's mind entirely off the product." Saying this, she is in fact posing for the *Esquire* account, and keeping its consumers' minds right on one product, *Esquire* magazine, which uses sex to sell a variety of other products. This illustration is a good example of what the magazine has been doing all along—feinting one way while leading the other, drawing men into consumerism while acting like it is all bunk, laughing at men who look at women while providing men with women to look at. This dynamic allowed *Esquire* to merge its version of masculinity and consumerism into a seamless whole.

19. Hart Schaffner & Marx ad, *Esquire,* January 1937, 34.
20. *Esquire,* October 1934, 162A.

An anonymously written article published in 1939 summed up the picture of the American man that *Esquire* had been creating. "The gigolo," the article claimed, "is the forerunner of a new type of American man, subtle and intelligent, who, instead of opposing the fair sex, of laying himself on the slaughter block in usual American male fashion, is learning to deal with the American woman in a practical, efficient manner, on terms which she seems to understand and admire." For too long, American men have assumed that women want a man who works hard to achieve success in the world. But the modern man realizes that:

> Fame, high ideals, world acclaim, or greatness, in a man are minor qualities as far as a woman's real personal appraisal of him is concerned. The American man, who concentrates so ardently on such goals, is wasting his time if he hopes thus to make himself worthy of feminine affection. . . . It is not the big achievements or winning of high honors, but the little things a man does, that count with women; the way he wears his dinner suit, the manner in which he orders supper in a fashionable café, his generosity with unexpected gifts, the tilt at which he sets his hat, his adeptness with the latest dance steps, his playing of a superior game of contract bridge. . . . Not by his slaving ceaselessly at an office, ruining his health and personal appearance by long hours of toil, nor by self-sacrifice of his own interests and pleasures, does a woman gauge a man's love for her. Rather, it is by his close attention to trifling courtesies and chivalries in the insignificant things of life.[21]

With this article—which expresses well the sum of *Esquire's* appeal—*Esquire* denies the significance of the vestiges of Victorian masculinity and insists that the things that are important to the modern man are appearance, manners, taste, and personality. This article vacates the moral structure of Victorian masculinity and replaces it with a conception of manhood that relies strictly on the show of pleasing social traits that *Esquire* and its advertisers have been tutoring men in.

Esquire peddled its vision of the masculine experience into unparalleled success in the 1930s. Circulation climbed from 180,000 in May of 1934, to 400,000 by March of 1936, to 600,000 by May of 1937, and to its peak of 728,000 copies in January of 1938. Advertising dollars kept pace with this steady circulation growth. *Esquire's* appeal to advertisers was explained partially by the demographics of its audience—surveys revealed that *Esquire* readers were better off than the average American and avid consumers—and partially by the very congenial environment that it offered advertisers. An *Esquire* promotional booklet told advertisers that the average reader "is a sailor with his money— he sails for every new thing that comes into his ken and, more often than not, for no good reason. He's rather inclined to be vain and self-indulgent. . . .

21. "In Defense of the American Gigolo," *Esquire,* January 1939, 35, 127.

There's an even chance that you would hesitate to accept him for some things. Quite possibly you would hesitate to take him into the bosom of your family, or even to propose him for membership in your club. But you couldn't possibly hesitate to accept his business because the Grade-A spender is the prime prospect." *Esquire* was a good place to place an ad because the right people saw the ads within a context that actively celebrated the consumption of goods. It was this steady record of booming circulation and profitable advertising that led *Scribner's* contributor Henry F. Pringle to call *Esquire* "the current phenomenon of the publishing business."[22] But it was the magazine's rewriting of the terms of American masculinity that paved the way for other magazines to follow in *Esquire's* footsteps.

Esquire maintained its distinctive attitude until about 1940, when, for a variety of reasons, the magazine began to change its orientation. The changes came first as a response to declining circulation in late 1938 and early 1939. Publisher David Smart "tried to boost the sagging circulation by doubling the size of the racy Petty Girl drawing to a two-page foldout in December 1939," writes Merrill. It was the beginning of the magazine's increased emphasis on what Gingrich derided as "big bosomed pin-ups," and the beginning of Gingrich's disillusionment with David Smart.[23] The pinups not only remained an important part of *Esquire*, but they increased with the coming of World War II. *Esquire* began a feature on "The Types of American Beauty" and hired a new illustrator to draw visions of the ideal woman. The illustrator, a Peruvian named Alberto Vargas, created the Varga Girl, and her fame grew to eclipse that of the Petty Girl. It was the Varga Girl who most commonly graced the nose sections of U.S. warplanes; the Varga Girl whose pinup traveled across enemy lines with U.S. soldiers. She soon became the subject of calendars, playing cards, drinking glasses, and a variety of other products. The Varga Girl soon replaced Esky, the pop-eyed playboy who graced the cover of *Esquire* through the 1930s, as the magazine's dominant image.[24]

Circulation rose on the popularity of the Varga Girl and her scantily clad sisters, both drawn and photographed. Much of that circulation gain was attributed to the immense popularity of the magazine with U.S. soldiers. "In effect," writes Merrill, "the United States government was *Esquire's* biggest customer, accounting for 200,000 copies of its magazines . . . and 49 percent of

22. My circulation figures come from Gingrich's editorial page musings (*Esquire*, May 1934, 11; March 1936, 5; May 1937, 5) and Merrill's *Esky*, 51, 54; promotional booklet quoted in Merrill, *Esky*, 58; Pringle, "Sex, Esq.," 33.

23. Gingrich is quoted in a memo from Jerry Jontry to All Salesmen, January 21, 1958, Box 11 (*Esquire Magazine* Office Files Advertising [3]), Gingrich Papers.

24. Merrill, *Esky*, 89–96.

calendar sales." The magazine reacted to its popularity with soldiers by casting itself as a morale-boosting patriotic organ. "Esquire's role in wartime is perfectly clear. This magazine's primary job is to purvey diversion, not as an escape but as a tonic." But it was not the kind of diversion the magazine had once offered. More and more of the magazine was war related: the stories were about brave soldiers who got the girl; there were full-page color illustrations of warplanes; and nonfiction pieces educated readers about wartime production, the enemies' armed forces, and other such topics. Advertising took on a military cast, as Hart Schaffner & Marx compared the clean cut of its suits to that of the uniforms of U.S. soldiers and Kentucky Tavern bonded whiskey admitted that "There's only one better buy in bonds—War Bonds!" And cartoons picked up the military theme, depicting women discussing their affairs with military men or posing in front of tanks. One cartoon indicated that the magazine was conscious of its changed attitude. Two admen sat around a table laying out copy. One said to the other: "How will we keep public confidence after the war when we switch to—'Throw It Away—Buy a New One!'?"[25]

Gingrich, bored with the magazine's changed focus and perhaps worn out by the magazine's run-in with the postmaster general, left the magazine shortly after the war's end, and David Smart took over the duties of editor before handing them over to Frederic Birmingham. Without Gingrich, the magazine steadily declined in popularity through the 1940s. Gingrich remembered that the magazine "chased circulation . . . by following for several years a blood and thunder policy, with heavy stress on mysteries and westerns, garishly made up and sensationally presented. *Esquire* was given a 'man in the street' approach. It worked, and circulation climbed steadily, and the rate per page per thousand steadily went down, while the original character of *Esquire*, as a class magazine and a fashion force, went equally steadily into a gradual and partial eclipse."[26] When Gingrich returned to the magazine in 1952, he helped return it to a position of respect, but it was no longer the preeminent men's magazine. *Esquire* had done its best work in the 1930s, paving the way for magazines like *True* and *Argosy* to usher working-class men—and for *Ebony* to usher African American men—into the modern masculine fold.

In the seven years of its greatest influence, *Esquire* had come a long way in redefining American masculinity. On the one hand, *Esquire* took up some strands of thinking about masculinity that had first appeared in other magazines.

25. Merrill, *Esky*, 93; editorial, *Esquire*, February 1942, 3; Hart Schaffner & Marx ad, *Esquire*, May 1943, 9; Kentucky Tavern ad, *Esquire*, January 1944, 153; cartoon, *Esquire*, May 1943, 16.
26. Arnold Gingrich to Jerry Jontry, August 15, 1955, Box 11, Gingrich Papers. On the magazine's troubles with the post office, see Merrill, *Esky*, 103–23.

The notions that men were to pursue an identity based on personality and appearance, or that they might consume their way to a more fulfilling life were not new, nor was the representation of men as blunt-speaking tough guys. But *Esquire* was utterly original in its ability to tie together toughness, personality, consumption, and sexuality into a complete package of expectations about the nature of masculinity. Those expectations differ in nearly every way from those articulated by the many magazines that had valorized the Victorian self-made man. The *Esquire* man, the modern man, was not interested in abstract ideals to guide his life. He was relatively young, like the male figures in the advertisements with whom men were invited to identify. He was concerned with wearing appropriate fashions, and *Esquire* provided him with plenty of information on the latest cut in suits and sporting attire. He was forthright about his sexuality, if somewhat baffled by the hold that women seemed to have over him. The *Esquire* man was above all else a consumer, looking for the latest and best in fiction, fashion, and flesh. Ads, articles, and stories combined to evoke a masculinity that is other-directed and yet intent on projecting an image of individuality, as if one could simultaneously defy categorization and pursue fashion. The *Esquire* man was driven by the pleasure he may acquire in his leisure time rather than by abstract notions of success that must be deferred while he scales the ladder of self-made masculinity.

True: Esquire for the Beer-and-Poker Set

Through the late 1930s and early 1940s, *True* magazine seemed like an unlikely venue to translate the meaning of modern masculinity to a working-class readership. One of a number of the "true" magazines that had gained great popularity with working readers beginning with the introduction of Bernarr Macfadden's *True Story* in 1919, the magazine was filled with "guaranteed true" stories of adventure, danger, and romance. A typical issue from 1940 featured a lurid cover depicting a pair of Nazis grappling with a woman whose blouse is nearly unbuttoned; "I was tortured in a Nazi prison camp for women" read the headline. Inside, readers could find stories about a woman accused of being a mad murderess, men who endured an attack by German gunships, or "Ace Government Undercover Man" Thomas W. Murray, who "Was a Coast Guard Spy."[27] The titles of *True* stories most often began "I Was" or "I Saw"; the numerous photos accentuate the most lurid or risqué details of the story, exposing a woman's breast or a gaping wound. Advertisers must not have been confident that this magazine reached an audience of avid consumers, for there

27. "I Was Tortured in a Nazi Prison Camp for Women" and "Ace Government Man Was a Coast Guard Spy," *True*, June 1940, front cover.

were few ads for expensive items or from big-name national advertisers. Instead the magazine was littered with small ads promoting such things as quick cures for asthma and rheumatism. With a formulaic editorial product and no agenda for capturing the attention of consumers, *True* remained one of a number of cheap pulps.

According to a study funded by the McCall Corporation in 1939, the "true story" magazines were immensely popular with families of limited economic means. Breaking down magazine distribution by standard of living, the study found that the two most popular "true" magazines, *True Story* and *True Confessions,* were overwhelmingly popular in the homes of those who were either "getting by" or "poor." Eighty-five percent of the readership of these magazines came from these lower-standard-of-living groups, compared to 44 percent for the *American Magazine,* for example, or 53 percent for the *Saturday Evening Post.*[28] Given the limited means of this readership, and given the fact that *True* was hardly the most popular of the "true" magazines, its editors sought to reshape the magazine to appeal to a larger audience that would be more appealing to advertisers. Beginning in June of 1944, *True* began to reformulate its editorial content to a distinctly male audience. The change was announced by the simple addition of a subtitle on the cover: *True* was now *True: The Man's Magazine.* Making *True* a man's magazine did not require too many changes. The magazine had always featured male adventure stories and all it had to do to let those stories dominate was to get rid of the stories for and about women. The ongoing war provided ample fodder for stories of masculine heroism— stories about a man who shot down five planes in a day, a man who single-handedly battled thirty German warplanes—and the editors added stories about sports and a new feature called "Man to Man," in which "noted adventurer and raconteur" Tex O'Rourke would settle arguments that occurred between men.

From the beginning of this revised policy, one could see the impact of *Esquire*'s example. *True* introduced a new class of men to the idea that clothes and accessories—for hunting, cooking, drinking, smoking—were important, and it helped to define a distinctly masculine space in which men could rest comfortably in their role as consumers. While *True* borrowed from *Esquire* the dynamic for promoting a consumerist masculinity, the precise attitudes and expectations it presented about manhood were colored by the editor's expectations about the very different tastes and desires of *True*'s readership. A *Magazine Industry* survey of the men's magazines noted the real differences between the magazines' readerships: the average *Esquire* reader was thirty-eight years old,

28. Frank R. Coutant, "Who Reads Magazines?" in *A Qualitative Study of Magazines: Who Reads Them and Why,* 7.

owned a home, had gone to college, drank Scotch, and had an income of $8,429 a year; the average reader of *True* was between thirty-two and thirty-four, was likely a skilled laborer or white-collar worker, enjoyed hunting and fishing, drank beer, and earned between $4,000 and $5,000 a year.[29] Where *Esquire* assumed its readers would seek leisure in urban environments—nightclubs, concerts, even literary events—*True* gauged that its readers would spend their time hunting, fishing, and playing poker with their buddies. *Esquire's* readership was already inclined to think in terms of style and image, but *True's* was not. Thus *True* faced an uphill battle in convincing its readers to orient their sense of self toward goods and leisure, and this sense of battle tinged its editorial policy with defensiveness and misogyny.

Just as *Esquire* constructed a reader who was youthful, urban, interested in sexuality and good reading, *True* began to construct its typical reader. The foundation of *True's* representation of masculinity was, not surprisingly, an abiding sense of pragmatism and common sense. In February 1945, editor Horace Brown rejected an article on improving the human race and told his readers why: "It's one of our pet beliefs that men prefer facts over fiction, and our whole magazine is built on that belief—all true yarns."[30] Many of *True's* features played up to this side of men. The "Man to Man" column, for example, was a forum in which men could get the facts straight. In this column, O'Rourke and later Robert E. Pinkerton helped men sort out such questions as "When did the first Mercury automobile come out?" and "How tall was Babe Ruth?" The implication was that if a man knew the facts he needed nothing else, that life was not a matter of image or self-promotion but of ascertaining reality.

This same sense of determined realism seeped into a series of features on, of all things, art. Recognizing that his readership might be somewhat skeptical about having art in their magazine, Brown explained that "Your new *True* is planned as a he-man's magazine, written for *masculine* men—the kind of men who hunt and fish and now and then try their damndest [*sic*] to figure out what women are all about, anyway. . . . About Art we don't know much, either. . . . Art always sort of scared us. It got worse every time somebody tried to explain it. And when we tried to read so-called simplified explanations, it became positively confusing." But art, too, could be reconciled with the pragmatic approach. To this end, *True* hired John Morse, a staff member at the Metropolitan Museum of Art and editor of the *Magazine of Art*, to select a series of "all-male masterpieces—everyone of them the kind you would like to hang up alongside your guns" to present to *True* readers. Morse soon offered up

29. Carle Hodge, "For Men Only," *Magazine Industry,* winter 1950, 10.
30. Horace B. Brown, "The Editor Speaking," *True,* February 1945, 6.

a print by Winslow Homer called *The Portage.* Lauding the painting's realism, he claimed "This is one test of a good picture—people who look at it should be able to say, 'This is the real stuff. This is how things are.'" Another Homer painting, *Huntsman and Dogs,* was once faulted for its over-realism, explained Morse. But this is exactly what makes the picture: "Homer was a hard-headed Yankee who saw things as they are, and he was a big enough man not to be too much distressed by what he saw."[31]

Other features of the magazine indicated that the *True* man was rugged, an outdoorsman, interested in hunting and fishing and drinking with the boys. During the war, the figure of the soldier was often used to encapsulate *True* masculinity. In August of 1944, for example, Lowell Thomas wrote an article in praise of "The Infantryman." "The infantry today is an *elite corps.* The foot soldier, the man who is closest to the enemy, wins the war. He is a swash-buckling, dare devil, to-hell-with-hardships, let-me-at-'em, singing, cursing, fighting hero. And he will grumble like hell to hear himself called such a thing." Such a persona seems crafted precisely to fit the image of the *True* reader, a man of no pretension, of quick wit but no bombast who heroically does what is asked of him. The same attitude is captured in a story by Albert Richard Wetjen titled "When Guts Were Tough." One of Wetjen's anecdotes tells of a man whose lower leg is crushed. The captain and steward decide his leg will have to come off, so they pour whiskey down the injured man's throat and clear a spot to perform the operation. The mate puts some old canvas down, so as not to get his hatch covers any more stained than they already are: "After all, a mate has to take care of the ship. You can always get another man but an indent for a new hatch tarp might be denied." The description of cutting off the guy's leg with an old hacksaw dipped in brandy is pretty rough stuff, ending, "The old man had drunk close to a bottle of brandy but was still ghastly sober, and it seemed like he had blood from his wrists to his elbows. I don't know how he'd stood it, except I do know that when you have to do a thing you somehow get it done, especially when you're skipper or in charge." The *True* reader, such stories suggested, knew that life mattered little and that a real man sucked it up when times got tough. A series of magazine covers painted by Rico Tomaso put a face on the man that *True* glorified; strong jawed and steely eyed, the soldiers painted by Tomaso were the Marlboro Man before the Marlboro Man was invented.[32]

31. Brown, "The Editor Speaking," *True,* January 1945, 100; John D. Morse, "The Portage," *True,* February 1945, 53; Morse, "Huntsman and Dogs," *True,* July 1945, 57.

32. Lowell Thomas, "The Infantryman," *True,* August 1944, 23; Albert Richard Wetjen, "When Guts Were Tough," *True,* September 1946, 45, 46; for a representative Rico Tomaso cover, see August 1944.

While writers and illustrators presented the nicer side of the *True* man, a reader's letter summed up the raunchier side of this same figure. Complaining about liquor ads featuring men leaning on the rail of a yacht or saddling up a thoroughbred, this reader asks: "Must one belong to an exclusive club and own a bundle of tuxedos before one gets a load on? Why not entice just one likker merchant into showing about four ordinary Joes sitting around a well-used bottle with a neat load on, telling dirty jokes and happily discussing the sex life of a *True* critic?" The editor obliges with a cartoon picturing just that, with the caption: "When Jolly Guys Meet Old Panther Is Always Drunk."[33] At least you could not accuse the editor or readers of taking themselves too seriously.

There was one major problem with this way of casting masculinity, however. This *True* man hardly seemed like a good consumer: his professed "devil may care" attitude made him unlikely to purchase personal care products, he probably worked in a job where what he wore mattered little, and his pragmatic approach to life meant that he was not susceptible to goads to self-improvement. If the editors of *True* would draw in the advertisers they needed to make the magazine a financial success, they would need to figure out how to reconcile the attitudes of the men they claimed to appeal to with the ethos of modern consumerism. They began that process of reconciliation soon after they became a "man's magazine."

True's staff was clearly interested in figuring out how to make their magazine an appropriate venue for advertisers to reach men who had not previously been assumed to be avid consumers. A questionnaire included in the magazine for several issues beginning in August of 1944 tried to get men to reveal their consuming interests. Offering a free copy of the magazine to those who filled out the survey, *True* gathered information they could use to sell their readership to advertisers: information about leisure activities; use of aftershave, hair tonic, or talcum powder; the amount of money spent on apparel, accessories, alcohol, and amusements; and whether men carried life insurance or owned a home or a car. Though the editor never reported on the results of the survey, the number and size of ads increased steadily over the next year. In March of 1945 a new column called "*True* Goes Shopping" began featuring a range of gadgets for men (cuff links, watches, a revolving tie rack, and the like), and the column was bracketed by stacks of small ads for similar goods. By June of 1945, ads for "Buck Skein Joe" gabardine jackets, Swank wallets, suspenders "For the Modern Man," books with such titles as *How to Relax and Be Happy*, and every variety of alcohol had replaced the earlier ads for modern-day patent medicines.

33. "When Jolly Guys Meet Old Panther Is Always Drunk," *True,* July 1950, 4.

True did more than just hunt up advertisers and hope that their readers would prove susceptible to the siren song of consumption. In fact, the magazine actively persuaded men to conceive of themselves as consumers. In February of 1945 *True* published its first article on fashion. "They Get Wilder Every Hour," by Sidney Garfield, began by ridiculing the wildness of modern neckties and the dandies who wore them, but shifted gears in the middle of the article to suggest that wearing bold ties was an expression of American liberty. Posing the freedom to choose a tie against the fascism American troops were fighting abroad, Garfield boasted that "the dungeon-dark, sepulchral colors of men's clothes have been replaced by vivid, flashing hues that loudly proclaim the new world and the free world for men. This is good stuff, brethren. This is the stuff of freedom. . . . And I commend them to you men who yearn for emancipation from *anything!*"[34] Garfield subtly took the reader from a position they were comfortable with—a tough opposition to fascism—and led them to equate antifascism with an appreciation for fashion as a form of self-expression. It was a rhetorical move quite similar to what the editor negotiated with respect to art. Subtly, carefully, such articles led men to an appreciation of the world of goods.

In 1946 *True* initiated a column that would be its most forthright attempt to induce working men into the world of consumerism. Called "Mr. Hobby," the foldout column combined color illustrations of "Mr. Hobby" at work and at leisure and commented on what he would do and wear for each occasion. "We at *True* hope that you other bozos will take the hint," reads the note introducing the column. "We aren't crusading—we think a gent is entitled to spend as much on his hobby as he wants—but we'd like to remind you that the clothes you wear every day are damned important to you and to the people around you. You should get the best you can afford. Therefore, read about Bill Hobby, businessman, . . . after you learn about his fisherman's outfit below." The text mentions Bill Hobby's fishing attire, and then goes on to describe his business attire as well, explaining "Basically, good taste is good common sense. Bill Hobby shows that. Nothing he wears is loud or outlandish. Everything combines to make him appear well-dressed among his friends and business contacts, and yet allows him individuality."[35] The column was nested among an array of ads for men's clothing, and it was patently designed to encourage men to think of themselves as consumers of clothing.

Mr. Hobby quickly became a regular feature of the magazine. Succeeding columns depicted Mr. Hobby as a hunter, a fisherman, a golfer, a "do-it-yourself" handyman, and an array of other typically masculine pursuits. These

---

34. Sidney Garfield, "They Get Wilder Every Hour," *True*, February 1945, 71.
35. "The Double Life of Mr. Hobby," *True*, May 1946, 101–4.

activities were consistent with the fishing and hunting emphasis that had always characterized the magazine, but the advice that accompanied the pictures and the consistent depiction of Mr. Hobby as a white-collar businessman seemed out of sync with other of *True*'s representations of manhood. In December of 1945, for example, Harvey Fergusson's "A Hunter Is a Kind of Man" lauds hunting as a way for men to get back in touch with their primal, savage roots. Comparing modern hunters to their "savage" ancestors who "always let the women do the work" and to "pioneer hunters" who "always moved on when matrimony and farming threatened to catch up with them," Fergusson heralds hunting as a "return to blood and earth." "A hunter," he concludes, "truly sheds the burden of his civilized consciousness and lives for a day or a week upon another level of being." Mr. Hobby is also depicted as getting away from it all, but his absorption in manly hobbies carries with it a different lesson. Mr. Hobby's hobby often was cast as an excuse for him to get all dressed up: "Bill . . . has a hobby, for the pursuit of which he enjoys shucking the familiar garments of civilized living and rigging himself out in something special." Getting dressed up was good fun for Mr. Hobby whether he was working or playing, the copy intimated. "As long as you're doing the swanky thing," the copy told the reader, "you might as well dress the part and get all possible enjoyment out of it."[36]

The dissonance between these opposing attitudes was sometimes jarring, as *True* readers soon revealed. *True* regularly published letters from readers, and these letters allow us to look into the way men reacted to the magazine's changing content. One thing was clear: readers disliked all the advertising and attention paid to fashion. "I haven't missed a copy of *True* in five years," wrote one reader, "but it's beginning to look like a Montgomery Wards catalog." "Keep on changing *True* and it will end up looking more like a ladies' housekeeping journal or a Sears Roebuck catalog," wrote A. M. Jacobson of St. Louis, Missouri, "Stick to your 1943 style; or have you gone sissy like everything else?" Another reader particularly hated the Mr. Hobby features: "Do you really think that the average old boy gives a damn about what some pipsqueak flunky with $500 a month might wear when he fishes for those little trout, or the cute little pajamas and those perfectly lovely house slippers that cover his pinkies! What the hell, we fish in G.I. clodhoppers and sleep in our shorts most of the time! That Mr. Hobby of yours is unadulterated manure."[37] Fewer readers wrote in to say what they liked, although there were always a few letters from readers "oohing and

36. Harvey Fergusson, "A Hunter Is a Kind of Man," *True*, December 1945, 55, 102; "The Double Life of Mr. Hobby," *True*, July 1946, 82, 85.

37. "*Truely* Yours," *True*, July 1945, 5; January 1946, 4; December 1947, 4. Other critical letters appeared in the "*Truely* Yours" column in September 1946, 3; September 1947, 8; and December 1947, 4.

"We at *True* hope that you other bozos will take the hint," wrote the editors when they introduced working-class men to the pleasures of modern masculinity with their "Mr. Hobby" series, which promoted the best clothes for all a man's activities (*True*, May 1946, 101–2).

aahing" over the latest pinup girl. But it was clear that the decision to bring in more ads and pay more attention to fashion was far from popular.

The problem was the same one that had faced *Esquire:* how to reconcile men's sense of who they are with advertisers' sense of what they want men to be (or rather, what they want men to buy). In many ways, *Esquire* had a far easier time reconciling these notions, for urban, college-educated men had long been schooled in the appropriateness of consumption and self-creation. Because working-class men had not always been avid readers of commercial American magazines and because advertisers had only recently begun to think of the American working class as a market worth exploiting, such men were relatively unschooled in the language and habits of consumption. It was up to *True* to offer them a crash course in modern masculinity. And they had to offer that course while still appealing to men who thought of themselves as tough, no-nonsense, hard-drinking guys.

Urging men to enter into the realm of consumption and image threatened to break down the barriers between men and women, for it had long been a truism that only women were concerned with fashion and with making themselves look good. One of the ways that the magazine tried to code their upholding of male privilege, their refusal to turn men into women, was through the regular use of sexual imagery. Like *Esquire, True* offered men a regular stream of pictures, illustrations, and jokes aimed at establishing their sexual interest in women. *True* offered men foldout Petty Girl illustrations, cartoons filled with sexual innuendo (A woman enters the door of her apartment and says to her female roommate, "Well, No—I didn't exactly have to sing for my supper"), galleries of pinups like Rita Hayworth, Betty Grable, and Jane Russell, and true articles on burlesque or South Seas islands that contained frontal nudity.[38] *True* never framed women as items of consumption in the knowing and playful manner of *Esquire.* Instead, *True's* presentation of sexuality was a not-so-subtle reminder to men that no matter what they wore or read they were united in their attitude toward women.

One advertisement seemed to capture *True's* efforts to balance the contradictions between "hunting man" and "consuming man" on the sexualized figure of the woman. For a number of years Gillette had advertised its razors in spots covering the bottom third of a page; the ads featured a short bit of verse about the product and an unrelated illustration of a man and a woman together. The men are always broad shouldered, young, and athletic; the women always lightly dressed and buxom. But the ad that ran in December of 1945 (the same issue in

---

38. Untitled cartoon, *True,* June 1945, 77; pinup gallery, *True,* December 1945; "A Street Named Bourbon," *True,* December 1948.

which Fergusson boasted of hunting as man's return to his savage origins) was far more explicit in its sexual themes than any other ad in the campaign. In this ad, the man and woman are in a boat and the man holds up a long narrow fish to show the girl, who leans back with her arms up in the air, her legs spread apart and her breasts uplifted. The effect is to accentuate the girl's open legs and to place the fish as phallic symbol directly between them. In this ad, man the hunter has brought home the trophy and with it he acquires the right to sexually dominate the woman—it is the *True* formula condensed into one small image, an image used to sell men a product to improve their appearance. Through the woman, savagery and consumption are thus reconciled.[39]

One of the latent fears hinted at in the letters cited above is the fear that the growth in advertising and the focus on fashion was turning *True* into a women's magazine. Men who were leery of the feminine influence in their magazine had some cause for complaint. Sid Garfield, who often advised men on what to purchase, instructed men how to buy gifts for women in January of 1946; an ad for FTD suggested that men use the service to buy flowers; a "Mr. Hobby" feature in July of 1946 mentioned the make of an accompanying woman's swimsuit.[40] A perceptive woman reader even wrote in to applaud the magazine for introducing men to the use of deodorant and mouthwash. But these relatively minor and benign feminine influences could hardly explain the vituperation that was directed at women from the pages of the magazine.

Though numerous men over the years had written in to complain about the number of advertisements that were appearing in the magazine, tying the appearance of advertisements to the feminizing of the magazine, Ben Gurney of Detroit, Michigan, evoked a different level of distrust toward women with his September 1946 letter. "Women have been the downfall of men ever since Eve started playing with that snake," wrote Gurney. "[T]hey cannot bear to let a man have something alone, and now they are trying to take over *True*. There should be a law forbidding its sale to anything wearing a skirt, or overstuffed slacks. . . ." Editor Bill Williams picked up on Gurney's fear in his editorial. Noting that their research department had found that women often read *True*, Williams huffed: "This shocks us, no end. We have been trying to put out a magazine for men. Personally, we don't want women in here. What's going on, anyway? Are there women readers of this book? If so, why? Why don't they get out?"[41] Gurney's letter and Williams's (tongue-in-cheek?) support of it initiated a string

---

39. Gillette ad, *True*, December 1945, 155.

40. Sidney (Jerk) Garfield, "Men Are Jerks!" *True*, January 1946, 70–71, 91; FTD ad, *True*, January 1947, 23; "The Double Life of Mr. Hobby," *True*, July 1946, 85.

41. Ben Gurney, letter in "*Truely* Yours," *True*, September 1946, 3; Bill Williams, "The Editor Speaking," *True*, September 1946, 10.

of complaints against women in the magazine and eventuated in a remarkable antiwoman campaign, for this latent distrust of feminizing influences turned, in the hands of editor Bill Williams, into a campaign to defend American manhood by enshrining man as the real consumer in America. It was a daring rhetorical move that allowed Williams to reconcile retrograde notions of masculinity with elevated levels of masculine consumption, all to the benefit of his magazine.

Williams's opening editorial, subtitled "Never Underestimate the Power of a Man," tied together hostility to the feminizing influence of women, a reassertion of man's primacy, and an appeal to advertisers to subsidize *True*.

> We've been getting madder and madder. A slow burn. For years the myth has been growing in America that woman is the boss in the home. It's a racket. Like most rackets, it has a purely commercial origin. It has been built up by the women's magazines. The spearhead of the attack has been *The Ladies' Home Journal* . . . [which] for years has been circulating a series of devilishly clever little cartoons under the heading, "Never Underestimate the Power of a Woman." [These magazines and their advertising salesman have] convinced the advertising agencies, for instance, that women "buy 80 per cent of the purchases made at retail stores." From this premise, they have drawn the conclusion that the wives run American homes like dictators . . . [and] that the wives run their husband like dictators. Their purpose is obvious: They want advertisers to spend the bulk of their advertising money in the women's magazines.
>
> But we're sore as hell at their methods. And we're especially sore at the secondary effect which their methods have brought about. They, damn them, have just about convinced American men that all men are Caspar Milquetoasts. [But] In our home . . . we tell her [what to buy]. She goes out and buys it.
>
> We're not trying to sell any of you advertising. To hell with that. We got an advertising department. What we are trying to do is to stamp out the idea that American men are henpecked men.
>
> Up until now, the women's magazines have had all the play. The reason is simple. Up until our little book came along, there never has been a mass circulation men's magazine! (Circulation guarantee of 1,000,000). . . . We're not going to rant and roar, nor start any revolt. We're just going to ask you men to re-appraise yourselves; we want you to recognize the myth as a complete myth. Don't fall for this propaganda campaign!

To counter this vicious propaganda campaign, announced the editor, *True* will start running an "Never Underestimate the Power of a Man" cartoon in every issue.

> And we're going to continue giving you strong men's fare for reading material every month. And any time we meet a cartoonist who has turned out a henpecked husband gag, we're going to punch him in the nose.
>
> After all, who signed the Declaration of Independence? Were there any women there?

Out of this improbable mélange of arguments Williams had found a way to act tough defending real manhood while also arguing for the importance of his pages for advertising.[42]

For years afterward, *True* simultaneously promoted masculine dominance and masculine consumption as the foundation of American masculinity. The caption beneath the first "Never Underestimate the Power of a Man" cartoon argued: "It's always been a man's world; it's still a man's world—in spite of the sly propaganda of the women's magazines to the contrary. As editors of The Man's Magazine, we of *True* intend to do our bit toward keeping it a man's world. Don't let them kid you, gentlemen. Woman's biggest job today remains what it always has been: To latch onto a man to feed her." Williams explained that such a position was only a natural defense of man's proper role: "We, as the only man's magazine of outstanding circulation, apparently stand alone in reminding American man of his proper place, his rights, his prerogatives—and his responsibilities." Williams even claimed at one point that women "actually adore a man who cave-mans them a little bit."[43] As vituperative and bold as such pronouncements seem—especially to modern ears—they were not the real point of *True*'s campaign. Williams's defense of man's natural privilege always took a backseat to the promotion of ever greater levels of male consumption. And when Williams died, the retrograde campaign for male dominance faded into insignificance while the pro-consumption campaign continued.

The suspicious reader might well have suspected that all the chest beating about a man's proper role was the Trojan horse that concealed the consumerist message, for the amount of space and editorial attention given to the promotion of masculine consumption always outpaced that given to masculine privilege. Editorial pronouncements, the "Never Underestimate . . ." cartoon series, the increased space given to consumption-promoting articles, and the increasing number of advertisements all spoke of the magazine's effort to make itself *the* source for promoting consumption to a certain class of men. The initial concern of the editors was to convince men and advertisers that men were making consumption decisions. *True* commissioned a full-length article on the phenomenon in April of 1949. The illustration that accompanied Hardy Burt's "Who's Passing the Buck?" explained the intent of the article: it pictured a bevy of marketers pushing their products—clothes, food, appliances, and automobiles—at a lady buyer. But the lady was merely a puppet, for standing behind her pulling the strings was the American man. The "true" story that Burt

42. Bill Williams, "The Editor Speaking," *True*, March 1948, 8–9.
43. "Never Underestimate the Power of a Man," *True*, April 1948, 8; Bill Williams, "The Editor Speaking," *True*, June 1948, 10–11; Williams, "The Editor Speaking," *True*, May 1948, 8.

relates was of his quest to determine who ever really believed that women made purchasing decisions. That assertion, he concludes, is purely imaginary: "It is my contention that the average woman—bless her little heart!—acts as purchasing agent for her husband. She buys merchandise either on direct instructions, or in consultation with him, or to please him."[44] The man is master of consumption after all.

But editor Williams was the best spokesman for this viewpoint. Railing against women's magazines, Williams contended that "We're pretty sure that the women go out and make most of the family purchases—*but only after their husbands have told them what to purchase.*" His research indicated, in fact, that "eighty per cent of the family brand changes in purchases may be attributed to suggestions made by the husband." In June of 1948 Williams complained that the propaganda of the women's magazines had "infected all other mediums of communication," and responded directly to a claim by the *Ladies' Home Journal* that men's magazines "can't and won't remedy" the alleged sloppiness of men: "This is a neat little double lie. All the surveys we have seen on the readership of men's magazines, our own included, show that their features concerning men's clothing rate close to the top in reader interest. Men not only are not 'naturally sloppy' as the LHJ would have you believe, but they are intensely interested in their own clothes."[45] Such arguments flew in the face of earlier editorial matter and letters from readers, and hardly jibed with some of the magazine's presentations of rough and tough men, but they indicated that Williams was willing to follow this crusade into new territory. He was going to convince men that consuming was what they were really interested in after all.

Although *True*'s "Never Underestimate the Power of a Man" cartoon was introduced as a counter to the cartoons in women's magazines that mocked men's foibles, the cartoons had a somewhat different effect than was initially intended. One cartoon pointed out that when a man comes into an office all the women decide to take care of themselves; another indicated that once a man starts wearing horse riding gear, women will follow. In yet another, a woman in charge of Christmas buying comes home with a tiny tree and a few small gifts, while the man returns with a huge tree and abundant presents for everyone. Another cartoon even suggested that men were better cooks than women. The gist of the cartoons was thus to demonstrate that men are better at promoting consumption, not that they were tough or masterful.[46]

44. Hardy Burt, "Who's Passing the Buck?" *True,* April 1949, 81–82.
45. Bill Williams, "The Editor Speaking," *True,* May 1948, 8, and June 1948, 13.
46. "Never Underestimate the Power of a Man," *True,* February 1949, 9; "You Can't Overestimate the Power of a Man," *True,* March 1949, 7; "Never Underestimate the Power

Of course there could be no better proof of the magazine's increased emphasis on masculine consumption than an increase in articles promoting consumption and advertisements. Both soon appeared. In May of 1948 the magazine added two new columns, "What's New in Casual Wear?" and "What's New in Men's Apparel?" running near the familiar Mr. Hobby column. Advertising for men's clothing picked up apace. Ken Purdy soon introduced a column on automobiles, and a few months later the first ad for an automobile graced *True*'s pages.[47] In October of 1949 Mr. Hobby was replaced by a new column promoting men's clothing. Called "Your Clothes Do the Talking," the column went further than any article in *True* in promoting the relationship between clothes and success. Describing the dress of a real-life salesman named Gordon Johnstone, the copy read:

> Being a realistic young man, Gordon doesn't mind admitting that his clothes help do the trick. . . . "Sure," says Gordon, "clothes do for a man what good packaging and design do for a product. The smart, streamlined appearance of our new Dictaphone Time Master plays a big part in its popularity, just as my appearance plays a big part in successful selling." Gordon Johnstone is only one of thousands of successful men these days who realize that clothes are a professional investment. Naturally, therefore, he selects his clothes with care, wears them properly, and is alert to the dividends paid by intelligent, tasteful dressing.[48]

Such a pitch could have come straight from the ads in a middle-class men's magazine.

There was more, for *True* soon offered a column called "*True* Tested Trends," "a sound, down-to-earth guide to help you choose quality products," and offered to sell men "*True*'s Guide to Good Appearance," a booklet "packed with straight, helpful advice for every man," with "man-styled answers to the problems of dressing for success." The blatant and unabashed attempts by editors and article writers to promote male consumerism were accompanied by a rush of new ads in late 1949 and through the early 1950s. In addition to the gun and fishing-rod advertisements that had always appeared in *True*,

---

of a Man," *True,* December 1948, 8; "You Can't Overestimate the Power of a Man," *True,* April 1949, 8.

47. The sudden appearance of an automobile ad in this magazine has to be understood within the larger context of the American magazine market. Ads for cars had long been among the mainstays of the middle-class magazine, for car marketers assumed that these were the people who were buying the cars. The appearance of the ad in *True* indicates that marketers were becoming newly aware of the viability of the working-class market. Nobody places an ad in a magazine if they do not think the readers of that magazine can afford to buy their product.

48. "Your Clothes Do the Talking," *True,* October 1949, 54–55.

there were now ads for radios, car batteries, dog food, gum, Murine eyedrops, Alka-Seltzer, and so on. If the goal of the campaign was to bring in advertisers, it certainly worked, for the commercial side of the magazine had been utterly transformed since the campaign began. The tough-guy reader who just wanted to read a true yarn while knocking back a whiskey must have wondered what had happened. But the editors never published his letter if he wrote one.

The *True* magazine that greeted the new decade of the 1950s had changed dramatically in its six years as "The Man's Magazine." The magazine still tried to appeal to men through the relation of true stories, but the way it addressed the concerns and attitudes of these men—the way it constructed its readership—had changed dramatically. The magazine's editors had inherited and initially claimed an audience that stood outside the consumerist dynamic of modern masculinity and slowly introduced those men to the formula for masculinity that would make their magazine a financial success. Ingratiating themselves to the tough-guy ethic and appealing to men's taste for sexual imagery and straight talk, these editors allied themselves with working readers and then announced that the battle that those readers needed to fight was the battle to claim consumption for men. By 1950 *True* had so succeeded in framing issues of masculinity in terms of consumption that it no longer seemed contradictory to peddle true war stories and hunting advice alongside the latest men's suits and personal care products to a readership estimated at 1.5 million. In the end, it was not that the *True* man had been feminized, as he had initially feared, it was just that he had been consumerized, modernized.

Argosy: *True* Minus the Misogyny

Argosy magazine also took the plunge into the men's magazine market in the 1940s, and its construction of American masculinity offers an interesting counterpoint to the vision offered by *True* and *Esquire.* Like *True, Argosy* had roots in the pulp trade and appealed to and expected an audience with limited financial means. Founded in 1882 by Frank A. Munsey as a juvenile magazine, the magazine had switched to an all-fiction format and found phenomenal success around the turn of the century. By 1905 *Argosy* reached half a million readers. Though it kept the all-story format in the years to come, the magazine fell on hard times following Munsey's death in 1925 and had declined to a circulation of forty thousand by 1940. In 1942 *Argosy*, along with several other old Munsey publications, were sold to Popular Publications, a major publisher of pulps. Henry Steeger took on the task of editing the magazine, and he announced that the editorial staff would experiment until they had made *Argosy* the best possible magazine.[49]

The early tinkering with editorial content initiated by Steeger did little to change the magazine's all-fiction format: through 1943 and into 1944 the magazine offered stories about sports, adventure, and romance. Beginning in mid-1944, however, *Argosy* began to experiment with more masculine contents, picking an All-American basketball team and featuring more stories on themes like hunting, war, and murder. Beginning in June of 1946, *Argosy* began to experiment with subtitles on the cover that would indicate the masculine focus of the content; "The Complete Man's Magazine" finally won out over "New and Better Stories for Men," "Fiction and Fact for Men," and "For Men." It seemed to capture the difference between *Argosy* and *True*, which published only "true" stories. When one reader wrote to suggest that *Argosy* go to an all-true story format, the editor responded: "We and most of our 1,250,000 customers like fiction. Other men's magazines, from time to time, try the all-true pattern and it just never works out."[50]

Though *Argosy* thumbed its nose at *True's* format, the magazines had a great deal in common. Indeed, *Argosy* seemed to follow closely in the footsteps left by *True*. Its "Men's Mart" department featured a variety of gadgets for men, just like *True;* its column called "Getting the Most for Your Wardrobe Dollar" followed *True* in pitching clothes to working-class men. And *Argosy* had cheesecake illustrations and photos of women. But despite these similarities in the genre of their contents, the intent of these contents was quite different. The most significant difference was that *Argosy* made no attempt to appeal to the he-man, tough-guy, misogynistic sensibility that *True* worked so hard to exploit. *Argosy* had articles on hunting, but the articles were intended to point out the best places to hunt, not to claim for hunting the ability to transport men to their primitive biological homeland. *Argosy* had pictures of women, but these pictures were not accompanied by leering asides. Indeed, a 1951 feature called "A Short Guide to the Understanding of Cheesecake" presented pictures of starlets with a tongue-in-cheek article that refused to take too seriously men's desire to look at pretty women. Another such article was accompanied by the explanation that "It is our policy never to use pictures in the pin-up category unless there are good and sufficient reasons for using them," reasons like making men aware

49. Mott, "The *Argosy*," in *History of American Magazines,* 4:417–23; editorial, *Argosy,* November 1944.

50. "Cooking with Dynamite," *Argosy,* August 1951, 10.

of important actresses.[51] In all, *Argosy* appealed to a man with a more refined sensibility and a greater moral sense, but also a man who was far less interested in consumption.

Though *Argosy* was most likely aimed at a working-class audience, as evidenced by its low-end advertisements and articles on topics such as "Businesses You Can Start on Little or Nothing," the magazine did not assume that such men were cretins. The magazine's fiction, though set in working-class locales, offered a fairly enlightened view of manhood. "Carnival Pitch," by Philip Clark, finds its hero and heroine working as game operators for a traveling carnival. Their discussion is strictly hard-boiled: "Bourke said, 'Season's late this year.' Midge put a plaster doll carefully on the shelf. 'They average out,' she said. 'Have a good winter?' 'Good enough,' Bourke said. 'Anyway, I lived through it.'" It turns out Bourke has a soft spot for a kid whose mom is hospitalized, and he follows the kid and his dad when they go to the hospital. Bourke feels sheepish when Midge finds him at the hospital: "'How does it feel?' she said. 'How does what feel?' 'Being human,' Midge said. 'Rejoining the human race.' 'It feels all right,' Bourke said. He took a long breath. 'What the hell! It feels fine.'"[52] Bourke's expression of humanity wins Midge's heart and imparts a moral lesson to *Argosy*'s readers. It was a lesson *True* would have scorned.

"Me and the Muscle Maid" by Jerome Brondfield draws even more attention to the magazine's view of masculinity. In this story, Joe Davis meets a pretty girl named Hester and quickly takes a shine to her; but his attraction diminishes when Joe finds out that she is quite an athlete, a former judo teacher in the armed services. Though he likes her, he cannot imagine spending his life with a girl who was stronger and tougher than he is. He imagines her doing the heavy lifting around the house and opening jars for him: "How long could a red-blooded man put up with a situation like that? How cozy to know that any time he got out of line this shy little judo expert could reach out and flip him halfway across the love nest!" Despite his attraction Joe resolves to give her up, and he plans to tell her so on a farewell ride through Central Park when their horse runs away with the carriage. Joe imagines being shamed by headlines that read "Beauty Bests Beast When Escort Fails to Halt Runaway," and before he knows it he has jumped atop the horse's back and brought it screaming to a halt. "'Oh, Joe,' Hester whispered. 'That was the bravest thing I ever saw. I was so scared I couldn't even move.'" Joe reflects on his experience: "Sure, she'd been petrified. It was natural. Hester had a man's strength, but Hester, after

51. "*Argosy*'s All-Male Jury Picks: The Top New Movie Girls," *Argosy*, September 1951, 42–43.

52. Philip Clark, "Carnival Pitch," *Argosy,* February 1949, 34–35, 94–95.

all, was a woman. She didn't have that old masculine initiative. You know—
executive ability. . . . Hester's lovely muscles didn't worry me now; they were
no substitute for a masculine mind—my masculine mind. She needed me,
and that's just what *I* needed."[53] Following the incident, their romance gains
new strength and it appears that they will live happily ever after. Thus *Argosy*
presents a man resolving one of the fears of inadequacy that appeared to plague
men in this era. The masculinity depicted here is confident, though not cocky;
it values women rather than wishes to put them down. Again, the contrast with
True is striking, for while *True* railed against women, posing them as infringing
on men's domain, *Argosy* confronts and resolves the feminine threat into a
vision of gender compatibility.

Argosy addressed other of men's concerns as well in several articles about
sexuality. In "The Truth about Sex Hormones," Joseph Bernstein tried to allay
the fears of men who may have found their virility declining. He told the
story of one J. W., who lost interest in sex, suffered lapses in memory, and
found the company of his closest friends distasteful: "Terrible danger seemed
lurking in wait for him." When hormone therapy returned J. W. to normality,
Bernstein exulted that the male hormone "may grant you your birthright of
manhood." Amram Scheinfeld's "Are You Sexually Mature?" asked men: "Do
you think only of yourself and your own desires when you're with a woman?"
"Are you habitually a heavy drinker?" "Do you feel you're being a he-man
when you constantly swear or use coarse language?" and "Do you spend your
evenings whenever possible with other men?" If you answer yes to these types of
questions, then you are sexually immature, says Scheinfeld. (One has to imagine
that the typical *True* reader would have answered "yes.")

> Let's say you're a married man of the rugged type, who never lets his wife
> forget "who's boss," doesn't go in for "romantic nonsense," and misses no chance
> to get out for a wild time with the boys.
>
> Or let's say you're a bachelor (young or old), who's a regular wolf, sees women
> as prey in a continuous chase, likes 'em when he wants 'em and has no use for
> them otherwise.
>
> In either case it may come as a surprise to be told that you are *sexually
> immature.*

The article explains that this immaturity is something that must be conquered,
for it is really a sign of weakness and a failure to develop into an adult. He
concludes, "In any event, as more and more men and women move toward
full sexual and emotional maturity, and train their children in that direction,
we can expect to see a steady diminution in the basic factors which now

53. Jerome Brondfield, "Me and the Muscle Maid," *Argosy*, March 1949, 28–29, 78–81.

are wrecking many marriages, ruining home life, producing failures of many kinds and bringing personal tragedy to vast numbers of people." In all, his prescriptions for sexual maturity seemed like a direct critique of *True*'s he-man masculinity.[54]

Argosy's presentation of masculinity was always a pale imitation of *True*'s, but it was also a critique of *True*'s misogyny and brutishness. It was *True* shorn of the locker-room bravado. One would have thought that such an approach would have been more palatable to advertisers, for *True*'s blatant editorial pronouncements sometimes seemed calculated to offend. But *Argosy* never proved able to attract the number and variety of advertisers that *True* began to attract in the very early 1950s. Despite a circulation of some 1.25 million in 1951, *Argosy* continued to carry mostly small ads for unglamorous men's products. Perhaps the reason *Argosy* proved unable to draw more advertising was its failure to aggressively woo men *as consumers*. Its articles on men's clothes were always pragmatic, discussing quality and durability, and neither articles nor editorials tried to argue that men could consume their way to a satisfying male identity. The reduced number of ads would seem to indicate that it was not marketers' decisions to appeal to a working-class audience alone that turned the tide in bringing ads to such publications—those publications had to be willing to embrace a way of talking about masculinity and consumption before they could really draw ads.

Ebony: "The Happier Side of Negro Life"

While white men's magazines like *Esquire* and *True* (and to a lesser extent *Argosy*) drew much of their popularity from their claims to originality and freshness, they were not without precedent. Working within the well-tested domain of the mass-market, advertising-driven magazine, they had any number of examples to follow in terms of distribution, marketing, and advertising. Even *Esquire*'s male-oriented contents—its most original contribution—were an amalgamation of lessons learned from men's clothing trade magazines, highbrow "little" magazines, and mass-circulation giants. *Esquire* took up the pieces of consumerist masculinity that lay about and combined them into a coherent whole, and *True* and *Argosy* mimicked *Esquire* for a less affluent and more outdoorsy audience. But *Ebony*, which would come to frame black men in much the same terms that *Esquire* and *True* framed white men, was rooted in the least fertile soil imaginable, for no black magazine had managed to solve the problems that *Ebony* solved.

54. Joseph Bernstein, "The Truth about Sex Hormones," *Argosy*, March 1949, 55–56, 77; Amram Scheinfeld, "Are You Sexually Mature?" *Argosy*, May 1949, 50–52.

Since the turn of the century, black editors and publishers had struggled to devise a magazine that would be both profitable and true to the black experience. Yet profits and racial reality did not seem to mix, as many an editor who had struggled to attract advertisers to his magazine realized. One after another, magazines that tried to reflect and comment on black culture failed because they could attract neither adequate advertising support nor ample circulation. Neither rage at racial injustice nor forbearance with slow but noticeable progress provided the motive force to build a commercially successful general magazine. The few magazines that lasted were official organs of large organizations like the NAACP or the National Urban League; while these magazines attempted to approximate the breadth of white general magazines, they were unavoidably tied to the needs and the ideology of their parent organization. In the end, they just did not compare to the white mass-market magazines.

Yet a number of conditions existed after 1940 that would prove advantageous to the creation of a black commercial magazine. As I discussed in the previous chapter, black magazines had been utilizing social surveys to indicate that black Americans had money to spend, but by the mid-1940s advertisers were beginning to acknowledge that they ought to "fix their sights on the underdeveloped markets of the U.S." According to Dwight Brooks, "The legitimation of the Black consumer market was aided, if not sustained, by . . . considerable scholarly attention [that] had been given to Black income and consumption patterns, Black marketing strategies, Black media, and other social and economic aspects of Black life that most scholars found relevant to Black participation in the national market." Such factors combined with a continuing northward migration of blacks, improved salaries in war-related industries, and enhanced race relations resulting from wartime cooperation to indicate the existence of an important market left largely untapped. By 1945 a magazine named *Ebony* finally proved capable of linking black consumers to the larger commercial marketplace in a mass-market magazine. In the process of offering a vision of the black experience that embraced consumer culture, *Ebony* brought black men within the fold of modern masculinity. *Ebony* was, according to Brooks, "the major vehicle to bring Black consumers to manufacturers and advertisers. As a cultural artifact, it was the major forum for the circulation of consumer ideology."[55]

John H. Johnson was twenty-eight when he founded *Ebony*, and it was not even his first magazine. Three years earlier, in 1942, he had founded *Negro Digest*. This small-format magazine collected nonfiction by and about

55. "Negro Market: An Appraisal," *Tide*, March 7, 1947, 15, cited in Brooks, "Consumer Markets," 133; Brooks, "Consumer Markets," 153.

Negro Americans from a variety of sources and brought it together in one place. It was the *Reader's Digest* of race, and it took a very moderate line on race issues, championing no single cause and striving not to offend. Johnson's unprecedented financial success with the *Negro Digest* led him to consider a more commercial magazine aimed at entertaining and informing a general audience. That magazine, which modeled itself on the hugely successful *Life* magazine, first appeared in November of 1945 and quickly sold every issue that it printed. Johnson's opening editorial set the tone for the magazine's development:

> We're Off! Like a thoroughbred stallion, we've been straining at the starting gate for months now waiting for the gun from the almighty, omnipotent, superduper War Production Board. As you can gather, we're rather jolly folks, we *Ebony* editors. We like to look at the zesty side of life. Sure, you can get all hot and bothered about the race question (and don't think we don't) but not enough is said about all the swell things we Negroes can do and will accomplish. *Ebony* will try to mirror the happier side of Negro life—the positive, everyday achievements from Harlem to Hollywood. But when we talk about race as the No. 1 problem of America, we'll talk turkey.[56]

Johnson's words, as well as his tone and his rhetorical style, announced that this would be a new kind of Negro magazine, and the contents bore him out. The cover photo depicted a happy interracial group of school children, and the accompanying article detailed the Reverend Ritchie Low's efforts to ease racial hatred by bringing kids of different races together to play; a long profile on black entertainer Eddie Anderson, who makes "more than $150,000 a year being stooge for Jack Benny"; smaller features on commercially successful black musicians and writers; photo spreads featuring cheesecake shots of singer Hazel Scott and Sheila Guys; and cartoons depicting sexy, curvaceous black women. This combination could have come out of any number of white magazines of the day, for such magazines readily portrayed happy examples of success and beauty; but the fact that these articles were about African Americans was breathtakingly original.

---

56. "Backstage," *Ebony*, November 1945, 2. All of *Ebony*'s unsigned editorials are written in the voice of John Johnson, but there is reason to believe that Johnson wrote few if any of the editorial comments. Ben Burns, who was always listed as executive editor to Johnson's editor and publisher designation, claimed in his 1996 autobiography that he was in fact the author of every editorial, though he acknowledged that the opinions were Johnson's (Burns, *Nitty Gritty: A White Editor in Black Journalism*, 83–153). Johnson, however, insists throughout his autobiography that the magazine was his creation and that Burns was an employee who sometimes defied his employer's direction; Johnson, with Lerone Bennett Jr., *Succeeding against the Odds*, 235–36.

Take the "profile of a successful person" genre, for example. The very early black magazines had made such articles a regular part of their editorial product, but in such magazines the success a black men achieved was either "in spite of" the barriers presented by race or explained entirely in terms of the possessor's allegiance to the cult of hard work and integrity. Moreover, early success stories were always indelibly tainted by the ceiling that race placed on achievement. The bleakness that informed such early success stories encouraged later black magazines like the *Crisis* and *Opportunity* largely to drop the genre, which did not fit in to their emphasis on black men's access to citizenship and workplace rights. Prior to *Ebony*, black magazines largely avoided the profile of success because such articles revealed the limits that black men faced in American culture, turning a profile of success into a portrait of failure.

White magazines, on the other hand, had perfected a success-profile formula that showed how a man's dynamic talents led him to the enjoyment of fame and earthly goods; they focused not on the qualities that made a man but on the accouterments that a made man enjoyed. It was this latter formula that *Ebony* used so well, from the very first profile to appear in its pages. The Eddie Anderson profile, titled "Rochester: Radio Star Finds Long Green Buys Lots of Comfort and Ease," hurried through Anderson's rise to success and lingered on his lifestyle of consumption. Anderson's home contains a "nice-sized movie theater," an "upstairs library with well-thumbed volumes showing the books are not there for display only," and a maid; Anderson's hobbies include toy railroads, gun collecting, and woodworking in his fully equipped shop.[57] In presenting such stories, *Ebony* took the narrative of white success and replaced the hero of that story with a black man. It was a daring and original move, and one that *Ebony* soon made a part of its trademark style.

In coming issues, *Ebony* devoted many of its pages to profiles of heroes of consumption, to use Leo Lowenthal's term. A profile of Duke Ellington delved into his personal life and daily habits; a feature on Adam Clayton Powell focused on Powell's role as typical husband; a profile of black model Maurice Hunter highlights his "perfect physique"; cartoonist E. Simms Campbell is notable for the parties he gives in his home. By March of 1949, such profiles are even detailing the amount of money singer Billy Eckstine spends on his hats, shirts, and shoes.[58] All these figures are discussed in terms of how they live lives of success, rather than in terms of how they acquired the success that has allowed

57. "Rochester: Radio Star Finds Long Green Buys Lots of Comfort and Ease," *Ebony*, November 1945, 13–18.

58. The term "heroes of consumption" is one I borrow from Leo Lowenthal, who used it as part of his argument concerning a cultural progression from "heroes of production" to "heroes of consumption." I use the term without borrowing Lowenthal's sense that these

them to live that way. They are profiles of how these men spend their money, not how they make it.

Profiles of success that focused on consumption were not the only features that *Ebony* had in common with white mass-market magazines. The magazine often featured pretty (black) women on its covers and frequently ran photo spreads on attractive actresses, dancers, and singers—just like *Liberty* or *Life* or *Look* or any number of other white magazines. *Ebony* often printed cartoons by Jay Jackson or E. Simms Campbell that poked fun at sex, money, or social customs—the ads could well have appeared in *Esquire* or *True* or any of the white magazines. And it frequently ran nonfiction articles on entertainment, sports, and social trends—similar to material that appeared in the *American Magazine* or *Collier's*. In all, *Ebony* looked much like any other successful American magazine, with the exception that all of its material was about African Americans. For nearly fifty years of American magazine publishing, a magazine that focused on the lives of African Americans seemed doomed to failure. But *Ebony* thrived by shifting the way it talked about race in America. Where magazines like the *Crisis* and *Opportunity* used their sense of injustice at racism as a guiding light in searching out editorial material, Johnson used his optimism to search out evidence of black accomplishment. And, in the somewhat improved racial conditions of postwar America, he found enough to be optimistic about to fill a magazine.

If John Johnson understood one thing about publishing a magazine for and about black Americans, it was that racism is bad for business. If there was one theme that united the magazine's contents, this was it. Johnson foregrounded the notion that racism is bad for business in his editorial comments, in the personality profiles he published, and, most clearly, in the nonfiction articles. Businesses had always succeeded in America when they focused on what they would accomplish, not on the impediments in their way, and Johnson wanted to teach this lesson to black Americans. "*Ebony's* purpose in life," wrote Johnson in February 1946, "is to mirror the deeds of black men, to help blend America's blacks and whites into interracial understanding through mutual admiration of all that is good in both." In the New Year's pronouncements for 1947, Johnson opined that "The outlook for the morrow . . . is basically hopeful if

---

"heroes of consumption" were necessarily pawns of a corporate class exerting social control over the masses. See Lowenthal, *Literature, Popular Culture, and Society.*

"Two Decades with the Duke," *Ebony,* January 1946, 11; "The Powells: Happily Married, Famous N.Y. Couple Anxiously Awaits Heir," *Ebony,* May 1946, 35; "The Man in the Ads: Maurice Hunter Pops Up on Billboards All over U.S.," *Ebony,* January 1947, 35–37; "Country Gentleman," *Ebony,* August 1947, 9–15; "The Private Life of Billy Eckstine," *Ebony,* March 1949, 54–59.

only because more and more white Americans are becoming convinced that the Negro deserves a better opportunity to earn a living and take his place as a citizen of the community."[59] And in an editorial titled "The Carrot or the Club," Johnson argued that:

> A happy omen of days to come is the increasing awareness by Negroes that there is much more in America today than "the problem." In reaching out to flex their intellectual power in the white world, an ambitious, alert pioneering band of creative Negroes is demonstrating their capacity for becoming well-rounded, unbiased, progressive-minded men of the highest calibre. Indicative of what is happening in this sphere are the thrilling success stories of up-and-coming Negroes in the arts, business, education, religion and science—men who are doing brilliant work that has nothing to do with "the problem."[60]

Johnson thus urged his readers to look beyond "the problem" and on to the brighter horizon that was theirs if they focused on success.

Accommodationist magazines had once urged Negroes to pursue the success ideal in terms that were distinctly Victorian, stressing hard work, character, integrity, and other qualities. Yet they were constantly forced to acknowledge the severe impediments to black success posed by a racist white society. The obstacles racism placed in the way of black success became a common element of all the success stories told in black magazines, thus foregrounding "the problem" even in discussions of success. In *Ebony*, however, all talk of the preparatory work necessary for success disappeared, and with it went the inevitable narrative of the obstacle of racism. By presenting the baubles of success, the goods and the lifestyle of the successful person, without reminding readers that the odds against African Americans reaching such success were great, *Ebony* certainly focused on the "happy side of Negro life," while significantly downplaying racism.[61]

Downplaying racism as a factor in impeding black success was a common element in many of the magazine's features. A short profile of Clifford Blount, who lost both his arms when he was sixteen years old and still managed to build a successful business, suggested that if an armless man can succeed, then anyone can (and they draw no attention to his race). A feature of New York's Café Zanzibar noted that "Zanziboss Howard gambled a quarter-million dollars and with clever publicity and the public's love of Negro entertainment proved that racism is not only bad manners but also bad business." Another story on a hattery run jointly by a black and a white man opened with a nearly

59. John Johnson, "Backstage," *Ebony*, February 1946, 2; Johnson, "What's ahead for the Negro in 1947?" *Ebony*, January 1947, 40.

60. "The Carrot or the Club," *Ebony*, August 1947, 46.

61. Johnson discusses the magazine's optimism at length in *Succeeding against the Odds*, 155–59.

identical line: "Racism is bad business in more ways than one." And in that initial profile of Rochester, the anonymous writer noted that Eddie Anderson "mixes well with the fellow in the street but steers clear of arguments about racial prejudice. He 'refuses to propagandize' as he puts it. He thinks 'a performer is a performer first and last. He has no business making propaganda. People want to be entertained, not educated.' "[62] This last comment expressed well the magazine's philosophy—*Ebony* wanted to entertain, not educate.

While *Ebony*'s presentation of the good life was consistent with similar visions promoted in white magazines, *Ebony* faced expectations and criticism that no one would have directed at white magazines and that had everything to do with race. Because it was a black magazine, readers and critics expected, even demanded, that *Ebony* take a position on race issues. If it wanted to please black readers, *Ebony* had to take notice of the problem of racism in America. And yet if it wanted to make a commercial success, *Ebony* had to broach the problems of racism without alienating advertisers wanting a safe forum in which to sell their goods or readers who were looking for an optimistic message. It was difficult terrain to negotiate, for every black magazine that had come before *Ebony* had failed commercially when it embraced a radical racial agenda. Remembering that racism was bad for business, *Ebony* embraced the idea that things were looking up for blacks in America and wooed advertisers who were willing to integrate black consumers into the postwar consumer matrix. This strategy dominated the magazine, allowing room for *Ebony* to fend off its critics with honest editorials that acknowledged the existing impediments to full equality.

Prior to *Ebony*, no black magazine had taken so optimistic a view of the racial situation in the United States. But *Ebony* was determined to see the good side of life for blacks in this country. In sports, wrote contributor Hy Turkin, there was a new color line: "It's the color line of PERFORMANCE. Yes, in several sports there are 'lines' which have never been surpassed by anyone but Negroes." In radio, wrote another contributor, "Uncle Tom is doing a fadeout." And even in movies, black musicians were rapidly proving that they were the best men for the job. Johnson hired "one of America's crack photographers" to photograph black women in order to show that they were as beautiful as the white women whose images appeared on "the billboards, magazines, and pinup posters of America."[63] Such sentiments were the norm for the better part of the content

---

62. "Zanzibusiness," *Ebony*, April 1946, 23; "Harlem Hatters," *Ebony*, February 1946, 3; "Rochester," *Ebony*, November 1945, 18.

63. Hy Turkin, "Brown Supermen," *Ebony*, January 1946, 6; "Radio and Race," *Ebony*, January 1946, 41; Dixon Gayer, "Meet Mr. Moore," *Ebony*, December 1945, 41; Johnson, "Backstage," *Ebony*, May 1946, 4.

of *Ebony*, for the magazine was determined to find the good in every aspect of Negro life.

Johnson made sure that readers understood his optimistic message in a number of his editorials. Answering a reader's request for a clear statement of his editorial policy, Johnson wrote in the "Backstage" column that:

> Essentially our policy is based on the principle that what's best for the Negro is what's best for all Americans and vice versa. . . . We believe in crusading and militance in their places but can't see it as a 24-hour chip-on-the-shoulder job that never allows time for enjoying an occasional night club session, a good meal or most important, doing a job to take pride in. . . . *Ebony* wants to reflect the Negro's everyday life on Main Street from coast to coast, to present him to both white and Negro readers as an ordinary mortal human being—not a freak or a stereotype, not a debate or a resolution.[64]

On the magazine's two-year anniversary, Johnson's gushing was even more optimistic:

> Is it so terrible to be a Negro in the United States? Certainly not! . . . American Negroes live a more prosperous, more enjoyable, more creative life than at least 90 per cent of the world's population. . . . Yes, the Negro is deprived of his vote and sometimes of his life in many Southern states but where else in the world can a person yell as loud and long about it except in America? . . . No, being a Negro American is not so much of a handicap as a privilege. For here in the richest, most advanced country in the world, the Negro has made his most significant advancements in history and has a brilliant outlook for the future. Much remains to be done to give the Negro his just due in the American way of life. But it cannot be done by bitterness, by cynicism, by singing the blues.[65]

Judging from the sampling of reader mail that *Ebony* printed in its "Letters" column, many readers appreciated the sunny outlook. "I was extremely glad to see that you did not play the old worn-out harp of discrimination," wrote one reader. "I wish that Negro editors in general would realize that their public no longer wants to hear about something which they know exists, and which each individual is doing his best to fight in his own way." When *Ebony* did probe into some of the problems facing Negroes in America, one reader complained that this magazine was not the place for such material: "Your magazine is nice but for God's sake, lay off this mess about Negroes living in a ghetto and the horrible conditions that the Negro lives under. . . . You cannot help a person that is too

---

64. Johnson, "Backstage," *Ebony*, August 1947, 8.

65. "Time to Count Our Blessings," *Ebony*, November 1947, 44. For other similarly optimistic editorials see: "When Bouquets Are Brickbats," *Ebony*, June 1948, 46; "Do Negroes Really Want Equality?" *Ebony*, June 1949, 56; "The Carrot or the Club," *Ebony*, August 1947, 46.

lazy to help himself. They are nothing but poor black trash and we cannot help them any more than the white people can help poor white trash." Reader Thomas Green indicated just how much some readers identified with *Ebony*'s take on race issues when he wrote to urge the editors not to publish letters that revealed disagreement and acrimony in the black community: "*Ebony* readers are growing daily and you showed little discretion in printing letters by Carolyn Morrison . . . and Gladys Brown. . . . Remember, everybody will be reading about us."[66] Clearly, at least this reader had embraced Johnson's sense that this magazine was an ambassador for the black race to white America.

To its credit, *Ebony* did not present *only* the sunny side of Negro life. From the very first issue and in every issue thereafter, *Ebony* ran articles and editorials that took note of the special difficulties facing African Americans. The *Ebony* photo-editorial (a full-page dramatic photo paired with a full-page editorial) was the most common forum for the magazine's hard look at race problems. It was in this column that Johnson and his editors once acknowledged that the Negro "is an outcast among his own countrymen—feared and despised, unknown and uncared for," and in this column that they called for more jobs for black workers and lambasted Walt Disney's presentation of Negroes in the film *Song of the South.*[67] Several articles on the prospects facing returning black soldiers argued that these men had faced better treatment abroad than they did at home.[68] These and other such articles provide ample evidence that *Ebony* did address issues of racism, but their role within the magazine and the tone with which these articles were offered signaled to readers that this magazine was no rabble-rouser about race. *Ebony* was about entertaining, not about exploring "the problem," so it was only natural that the articles on racial trouble would not be promoted on the cover or highlighted in the "Backstage" column. These articles were in the magazine because they were a necessary complement to the magazine's generally optimistic approach to race relations, a way of acknowledging that the magazine was realistic enough to see the other side of the coin. But the racism articles never called for action, never urged black Americans to engage in protest, never stoked the fire of resentment. As often as not, a discussion of bad racial conditions was concluded

66. "Letters," *Ebony,* March 1946, 51; "Letters," *Ebony,* May 1946, 50; "Letters," *Ebony,* June 1947, 5.
67. "Labor's Love Gained," *Ebony,* March 1946, 44; "Sixty Million Jobs or Else . . . This Again?" *Ebony,* November 1945, 50; "Needed: A Negro Legion of Decency," *Ebony,* February 1947, 36.
68. "Heroes Find Peacetime Battles Rougher Than War," *Ebony,* January 1947, 9–10; Allan Morrison, "What Price Heroism?" *Ebony,* January 1947, 11; "Two GI's Go Back to Paris," *Ebony,* March 1947, 16–18.

with the thought that things were improving and racism was receding into the background.

There is no reason to believe that *Ebony's* optimistic editorial policy was anything but a sincere ideological and editorial position, but it is worth considering that it was also the only editorial policy possible for a publication that wanted to break into the commercial magazine market. For years black magazines had been trying to attract advertisers, but to no avail. Black advertisers had not enough money to subsidize a national publication, and white advertisers either did not know that there was a Negro market worth entering, did not care to enter that market, or did not wish to associate their products with rabble-rousing, radical race opinions. Rising black incomes, market research that demonstrated the viability of the African American consumer market, and an increased desire on the part of capitalists to exploit heretofore unexploited markets all combined to encourage white advertisers to extend their advertising efforts into the African American market.[69] *Ebony* wanted to be the magazine to communicate the advertiser's message to that market.

John Johnson made clear his own intentions in creating the magazine in his autobiography. Citing a comment that he had invented a new Negro journalism, Johnson demurred, claiming that "I wasn't trying to make history—I was trying to make money." Johnson had clearly borrowed rather than invented his style of journalism, but he was happy to lay claim to another invention: the invention of the black consumer market. According to Johnson, creating a black magazine was easy; the real problem was getting advertising, and it was a problem he solved, single-handedly, through his superior salesmanship. "I can sell anybody anything," Johnson boasted, and he gleefully described how he enticed advertisers into his publication.[70]

For the first six months of its publication, *Ebony* carried no advertising. But in April of 1946 Johnson indicated that advertising was on its way:

> [W]e might as well break the news that beginning with next month's May issue, *Ebony* will run advertising—and in four colors. You may be sure that we intend to be particular about the character of the "company" we introduce to the privacy of your home or office or study or wherever you enjoy your copy of *Ebony*. The editors of *Ebony* are determined that the standards of the advertising in its pages will be up to the merits of its editorial material. You have our promise that our

---

69. For a good discussion of the transformation of the black consumer market from its undeveloped pre–World War II state to it postwar emergence, see Brooks, "Consumer Markets," 42–156. I am indebted to Professor Brooks for providing me with a copy of this excellent piece of scholarship, and for discussing with me the problems in studying the early black consumer market.

70. Johnson, *Succeeding against the Odds,* 156, 226.

advertisers shall come a-calling with only the best. Perhaps the choosing will be slim at first. We haven't any idea at present. But we will be selective in rejecting advertisements which are of a doubtful nature. In so doing, we wish to encourage your support of the products advertised in *Ebony,* since income from advertising means your enjoyment of each issue will increase as our editorial department has more funds to bring you the best in photo stores [*sic*] on Negro life.[71]

This was quite a welcome to extend to advertising, but it was fitting for a magazine that had every intention of doing what no Negro magazine had done before. As announced, the ads began appearing in May of 1946, with full-page ads for Murray's pomade and HairGlo and Supreme Liberty Life Insurance Company occupying the first pages. The rearmost pages contained an abundance of small ads for cheap watches, Nadinola bleaching cream, Chesterfield cigarettes, and other such products. These initial ads hardly indicated that *Ebony* was breaking new ground, for hair and cosmetic products had long been advertised in black magazines, to the dismay of those who thought such products (especially bleaching creams) were evidence of racial self-hatred. And John Johnson was the major stockholder in Supreme Liberty Life, meaning that this ad carried on the tradition of black publishers being their own best advertising clients. But the kind and number of advertisements would soon improve, lifting *Ebony* out of the gutters of the advertising world.

Though some "sleazy" ads continued to appear in *Ebony,* a number of higher grade advertisers soon began placing ads. The Book of the Month Club began running a spot in September of 1946, Chesterfield began promoting its cigarettes with boxer Joe Louis, and Old Gold hired Jackie Robinson to pitch their smokes. In August of 1947, the Holland Furnace Company bought the back cover to promote is furnaces, thus expressing its belief that African Americans owned homes and had the money to buy large appliances. It was a singular vote of confidence in the rising power of the black consumer. Other national advertisers followed the Holland Furnace Company into the magazine, including Beech-Nut gum, Colgate dental cream, Schenley whiskey, Armour bacon, and RKO Radio Pictures, and, in 1949, Zenith televisions. It was a slow process, but *Ebony* soon drew a wide variety of major advertisers, more by far than any black magazine had ever carried. Johnson would later claim that, through his efforts to attract advertisers, he had "invented . . . the Black consumer market."[72]

Ebony's booming circulation made it easy to attract advertisers. By October 1946 Johnson used the "Backstage" column to announce that *Ebony* had the largest circulation of any Negro publication in the world and the Audit Bureau of

71. "Backstage," *Ebony,* April 1946, 2.
72. Johnson, *Succeeding against the Odds,* 229.

Circulation's first report on *Ebony* in July 1947 listed the magazine's circulation at 309,715. The steady growth in circulation and in advertising allowed the magazine to expand from fifty-two to sixty-eight pages in February of 1948. "Making possible the expansion of *Ebony* have been the thousands of loyal readers who have shown their devotion not only by buying the magazine but also by buying the products advertised in its pages." The expansion was helped along by the power of *Ebony* to reach the audiences advertisers desired. "Best of all," Johnson boasted, "ad agencies tell us that *Ebony* 'pulls,' as advertising men say. Readers are patronizing our advertisers and as a result this month *Ebony* has more advertising than in any month since we opened our columns to ads."[73]

Of course, advertisers did not recognize the viability of *Ebony* as an advertising medium out of their own prescient analysis of the magazine field. In fact, *Ebony* and publisher John Johnson went out of their way to demonstrate to white advertisers that such a market existed and that it required a special kind of handling. According to Brooks, "Johnson initiated a comprehensive merchandising program for his magazines' advertisers," a program that featured on-site marketing assistance, surveys, and literature instructing businesses about the "dos and don'ts" of dealing with black consumers. Johnson "helped solidify the perceived need to market to Black consumers by providing, among other things, strategies and techniques for successful marketing, market research and, perhaps most important, a responsible and successful Black medium to reach these consumers."[74] In essence, by thoroughly linking manufacturers to consumers through appropriate advertising, *Ebony* had finally proved that the dynamic that drove white magazines could apply to black magazines as well.

Ebony's readers soon expressed a proprietary interest in the magazine's advertising, just as they had done with the editorial content. Margaret E. Kuhn, publication director for the USO division of the YMCA wrote in to complain about some crass novelties that had been advertised in the magazine. "The tone of this advertisement is such a marked contrast to the general level of the content of the magazine that this regrettably vulgar note seems in our opinion to undercut everything fine and constructive that is being established by *Ebony*." Another wrote to complain that "your stooping to permit such an advertisement for the sake of revenue is more of an insult to Negro America than any Disney film would ever be."[75] An eloquent reader asked, "How can you, *Ebony*, sacrifice your integrity and hypocritically continue to proudly devote

73. "Backstage," *Ebony*, February 1948, 10; "Backstage," *Ebony*, February 1947, 4.
74. Brooks, "Consumer Markets," 148, 146.
75. "Letters," *Ebony*, April 1947, 4–5.

pages to colored women, both dark and fair, who have attained commendable positions in life—and at the same time sell space to a product which forwards the opinion that success comes with a fair skin? Where is the policy, democratic thought, and common sense which should be so prominent and unerring in our Negro publication? Would you help us to segregate ourselves for an advertiser's fee? Is it worth it?" Another declared that "It is such a disgrace to our race for you to accept such advertisements as the Manor Company's sharp pointed shoes and pork-pie hats. . . . Such apparel makes us the laughing stock of the world. . . . I wouldn't wear such apparel to a dog fight."[76] Such comments indicated that readers saw the entire contents of *Ebony* as a reflection on their lives, and they wanted the world to know that Negro America had as much taste as the rest of the world.

One cannot blame *Ebony* for taking whatever ads came its way during those initial months of advertising; after all, black magazines had always been hard-pressed to attract much advertising at all. The fact that readers cared enough about the magazine to protest the quality of the advertisements, indeed the fact that readers suspected that the quality of middle-class black life would be judged based on the one magazine that had explicitly pitched itself to that class, forced *Ebony* to reconsider its policy toward advertising. The problems with taking "indecent" and "vulgar" ads typify "the problems not only of *Ebony* but of all Negro publications in getting decent copy," wrote Johnson in "Backstage." "Many advertisers believe they must 'talk down' to Negro readers and slant their copy accordingly. And because big advertisers of consumer items fail to recognize the immensity of the Negro market, which far exceeds Canada's total imports from the U.S., and are hesitant to buy space from colored newspapers and magazines, these publications must depend on Class B and C accounts."[77] But if *Ebony*'s readers can prove to advertisers that they purchase quality products, and if *Ebony* proves to the world that a Negro magazine can be a high-class forum for editorial content and Class A advertising, then together they can create a magazine of which they can be proud. This was the calculus by which *Ebony* meant to bring its readers fully into the culture of consumption.[78]

To enter in to the culture of consumption, the mainstream of American

76. "Letters," *Ebony*, May 1948, 8–9.
77. "Backstage," *Ebony*, May 1947, 8.
78. It was a calculus that ultimately resulted in the actual ejection of some twenty advertisers from the magazine in November of 1948, when Johnson claimed that he had written a letter to a number of offending advertisers—mostly peddlers of "sex books, skin lighteners, hair straighteners," etc.—asking them to either make their ads more subtle and attractive or get out. "Basically it is for [the advertisers'] benefit as well as our readers to raise the level of advertising copy and give their customers—and ours, incidentally—the benefit of a product that is sold within the bounds of dignity and with good taste and high standards" ("Backstage," *Ebony*, November 1948, 12).

middle-class culture, was to take part in a complex process of acculturation in which magazines played an important part. Magazines offered a particular kind of entertainment—fast-paced enough to be scintillating, yet not so scintillating as to be vulgar; high-class enough to appeal to an audience's best sense of itself, yet not so highbrow as to be exclusive. Magazines offered a set of readers a world with which they could identify; an important part of that world was a web of products and services offered for their consumption. Magazines offered advertisers controlled access to a group of consumers who might buy their products, and advertisers in turn paid for the creation of the editorial culture that would attract those consumers. Only now, only with *Ebony*, were Negro Americans introduced into the web of consumer culture defined by the American magazine. *Ebony* provided middle-class African Americans a forum to see their best selves, and its readers carefully monitored their reflection in the mirror that *Ebony* provided. According to Dwight Brooks, "*Ebony's* discourse, simply put, articulated consumption as a means to success and equated the ability to consume with political and social equality."[79] Advertisers saw that this group of readers was ready to and capable of spending money, and they embraced that audience in the only way they knew how—by inviting them to consume.

And soon, *Ebony* learned to nurture the consuming habits of its readers, schooling them in the habits of good consumers. The first fashion articles appeared in *Ebony* in April of 1946; aimed at women, they offered guidance in choosing the appropriate hats for spring. By September of 1948 *Ebony* also offered fashion advice for men. The many articles on popular nightspots promoted the club-going lifestyle, and many New York clubs came to place ads in the magazine. The profiles of popular Negro figures highlighted their consuming habits, as I have already noted. *Ebony's* editors had learned from their white counterparts that those magazines that promote a consuming lifestyle are more apt to get the ads, and they did. Just like the white magazines that had pioneered the formula, *Ebony* soon attracted ads that were making direct pitches to black consumer's desire to buy the latest fashion, learn the latest dance step, keep their hair looking good, and so on.

Ebony was helped in its quest to infiltrate the consumer magazine market by a group of professionals it named "The Brown Hucksters." "The 'brown huckster,'" read the article, "is a sales engineer whose job it is to establish contact between the 99 per cent of the country's manufacturers who are non-Negro and the 10 per cent of the consuming population that is Negro." These "brown hucksters" helped *Ebony* recognize that the biggest obstacle to increasing advertising in the Negro market is the lack of market data, for

79. Brooks, "Consumer Markets," 153–54.

ad buyers want hard data about the markets they are trying to penetrate. *Ebony* followed their lead and soon began to survey its readers with questionnaires. By September of 1950 the magazine was reporting the highlights of this survey, which revealed that 28 percent of *Ebony* readers earned more than four thousand dollars annually, 36.2 percent owned homes, 41 percent owned cars, and 22.3 percent owned TVs. Further results of the ongoing surveys, reported in March of 1951, revealed that "ads in *Ebony* were better read than in any other publication including every leading general weekly magazine and top women's magazines as well as the week-end newspaper supplements."[80] The survey thus provided *Ebony* with the evidence that its audience had the money to consume, and the added kick that its audience was still new enough to the blandishments of consumer advertising that it actually paid those advertisements a great deal of attention. In the end, the surveys, used heavily by the magazine to pitch itself to potential advertisers, sealed the case.

It was within the context of the rapid maturation of *Ebony* into a true consumer magazine that black men came to be included within the logic of modern masculinity. From its very first issue, with the profile of Eddie Anderson, *Ebony* eschewed the rhetoric by which earlier black magazines had framed black masculinity. Rejecting the self-made man rhetoric of the accommodationists or the rights-based radicalism of the *Crisis* and *Opportunity*, *Ebony* instead presented men who had made it on their personality and their looks. E. Simms Campbell, the cartoonist who made a big splash with *Esquire* after working for years for black magazines, was described as "Harlem's most dapper man-about-Harlem" whose "debonair presence was familiar in jazz-joints." The profile of singer Billy Eckstine attributes his tremendous popularity to his "manly voice plus romantic personality," and pays a great deal of attention to the specific kinds of clothes he wears (and their cost). Even the article "Negro America's Most Exciting Men," which argued that "the heyday of the glamour boy is gone," presented photographs of leading men like Paul Robeson, Duke Ellington, Lester B. Granger, Richard Wright, and E. Simms Campbell and commented how their brains and their achievements gave them sex appeal. The very act of placing these men within the context of such an article made them into "beefcake," the male equivalent to photo spreads on "Hollywood's Prettiest Women." Other articles in the "beefcake" vein included "Negroes Come Back to Pro Football," which featured shots of pro players getting a massage and taking a shower, and "Brown Giant," which had discreet nude photos of power-

80. "The Brown Hucksters," *Ebony*, May 1948, 28; "Backstage," *Ebony*, September 1950, 12; "Backstage," *Ebony*, March 1951, 12.

lifter John Davis.[81] These articles and the many others like them placed black men within the image and leisure-oriented sphere that had come to be the most common way for white magazines to frame masculinity. The magazine largely avoided tales of sacrifice and striving in order to present men as appealing, sexual, energetic pursuers of pleasure.

The growing number of ads aimed at male readers also operated within this now-familiar set of cultural norms. "Don't be 'Wire-Haired Willie,' the man nobody loves! Like Johnny Davis, let Snow White help you have smooth, richly gleaming hair," read the first men's personal-care product advertisement to appear in the magazine. "If you want the smart, well-groomed look that wins popularity and success, discover these two amazing, new preparations."[82] Similar ads followed: Hollyco marketed a Minute Gym to build powerful muscles and lasting stamina; Conversation Studies offered a book to "Make Your Conversation Pay Dividends"; a vitamin company claimed that "Hormones Promise Renewed Vigor to Men"; finally even Charles Atlas approached black men to ask, "Will You Let Me PROVE I Can Make *YOU* a New Man?" It did not take long for advertisers to pitch their whole array of personality-producing, bodybuilding, hair-improving, life-changing products at black men. Once advertisers acknowledged that black men had the money to spend, they proved eager to reach into their wallets and to try to change men's very perceptions of themselves. *Ebony* provided the perfect place for them to make their pitch.

Not only did *Ebony* provide a forum for the personality-type articles and advertisements that were the trademark of modern masculinity, it also imitated magazines like *Esquire* and *True* in wedding its content to its advertising. Not long after the magazine had begun running advertisements for men's clothing and accessories, it launched its first fashion article for men. Called "Stag Styles," the article tried to break down "men's reluctance to accept new styles" by promoting the comfort and attractiveness of the "bold California styles."[83] On the facing page was a full-page ad for Manor Fashions, a menswear retailer who had become one of *Ebony*'s regular clients. Such a linkage of content to ads was unprecedented in a black magazine, but then so was the formulation of black men as participants in the modern masculine absorption in leisure, personality,

81. "Country Gentleman," *Ebony,* August 1947, 10; "The Private Life of Billy Eckstine," *Ebony,* March 1949, 58; "Negro America's Most Exciting Men," *Ebony,* June 1949, 50–52; "Negroes Come Back to Pro Football," *Ebony,* October 1946, 12; "Brown Giant," *Ebony,* September 1947, 18.

82. Snow White Hair Beautifier and Creme Shampoo advertisement, *Ebony,* February 1947, 2.

83. "Stag Styles," *Ebony,* September 1948, 53–56.

and appearances. And menswear sellers could not have been hurt by an article like "What Women Notice about Men," which surveyed one hundred women to find what they liked about men. The comments of their celebrity survey participants were most revealing. Sarah Vaughan liked "men in sports clothes"; Pearl Bailey insisted on "a clean collar and a neat, well shaped-up hair line"; and Louise Beavers admitted that "the first thing I look at is a man's necktie and collar."[84]

Once black magazines had presented men with a choice between lashing themselves to a life of sacrifice and hard work in pursuit of limited business success or dedicating themselves to the cause of advocating for the manhood rights that had been promised to all men in the Constitution. But *Ebony* swept all such discussion aside in its presentation of an altogether different choice: black men, argued *Ebony*, could put aside their concerns with "the problem" and embrace the good life of leisure and consumption within an economy that now had room for them. In making the choice that *Ebony* held out, such men could become real Americans. In one editorial, Johnson brought together consumption and manhood in his distinctive formulation of how a Negro could claim his place in America. In "Why Negroes Buy Cadillacs," Johnson refuted claims that the popularity of Cadillacs among African Americans was a shameful example of how a race would invest in a car but not in itself. "The fact is that basically a Cadillac is an instrument of aggression, a solid and substantial symbol for many a Negro that he is as good as any white man. To be able to buy the most expensive car made in America is as graphic a demonstration of that equality as can be found. . . . To a Negro indulgence in luxury is a vindication of his belief in his ability to match the best of white men. It is the acme of dignity and stature in the white man's world."[85]

Johnson uses the example of the Cadillac to argue that consumption offers the Negro especially powerful and symbolic ways of signifying his rightful place in American culture. "Negroes have made it a part of their behavior pattern always to buy the best and most expensive items they can afford. They have always gone in for brand names with established reputations, survey after survey has discovered." Negroes consume to compensate for what remains unavailable to them in a racist society, but they do so in order to strive for equality. "To berate colored Cadillac owners for not spending their money instead on good race causes is to deny Negroes the right to reach for equality on every level of U.S. life. As long as there are rich and poor people in this country, there will be rich and poor Negroes. And that means there will be Negroes with Cadillacs.

84. "What Women Notice about Men," *Ebony*, November 1950, 46–47.
85. "Why Negroes Buy Cadillacs," *Ebony*, September 1949, 34.

It cannot but do every Negro's heart good to see one of their number driving the finest car, wearing the finest clothes, living in the finest home. It is a worthy symbol of his aspiration to be a genuinely first class American."[86] And providing a forum for the ads for such goods was clearly a worthy symbol of Johnson's aspiration to run a first-class American magazine.

The depiction of success as the means to live a good life, a life of consumption, meant that *Ebony* had more in common with white magazines than with other and earlier black magazines. *Ebony* was able to enter into the larger American magazine market because it celebrated consumption and economic progressivism and soft-pedaled the issue of race. Entering into the dynamic of relations that defined success in the consumer magazine market, *Ebony* also offered a transformed notion of black masculinity. Though *Ebony* did not explain away the problems that continued to face African Americans, it shifted its readers' attention from those problems to the good things that many African Americans were able to enjoy. This sleight of hand was itself a typical gesture of the modern magazine, which shifted the viewer's gaze from the process of achievement to the results of that achievement, which in America was always expressed as the life of goods and leisure purchased by economic success. Yet for *Ebony* to invite African Americans into the fold of modern masculinity was perhaps the greatest feat of all.

86. Ibid.

$Conclusion$

In this study I have tried to show that the images of masculinity that came to dominate American magazines were created by a multiplicity of forces: by corporate advertisers eager to construct avid consumers, by idealistic editors with a vision of how men should carry themselves in a changing social environment, by social forces such as racism and sexism, even by readers who shaped the content of magazines by applauding or contesting the images of masculinity they loved or hated. Emerging out of the collapse of proprietary capitalism in the latter half of the nineteenth century, and shaped by a myriad of forces over dozens of years, modern masculinity slowly penetrated the American magazine market until it became the norm. The images and ideals associated with modern masculinity were and are radically and irremediably different than those associated with Victorian masculinity, and their ascension felt and still feels like a loss to those who valued both the older style of masculinity and the cultural milieu within which it made sense. But to view the ascension of modern masculinity as a tragic loss seems to me tremendously counterproductive, for it blinds us to the alternative possibility that men exercised agency in constructing the masculine ideals that emerged from the melee of cultural interaction.

Up until the appearance of *Esquire,* the images and ideas that defined modern masculinity had appeared in magazines haphazardly, as a peripheral interest, a passing fancy. Though most American magazines relinquished their embrace of Victorian masculine norms by the late 1920s, there existed no coherent set of masculine ideals to which they remained attached. And then *Esquire* gathered together all the disparate ideas about masculinity and arranged them into one glossy, ad-filled magazine. *Esquire* editor Arnold Gingrich claimed that his was the first magazine for men, but this was not quite true. Most magazines had been edited at least in part for men and some—like the *Saturday Evening Post* and the *American Magazine*—took men as their primary audience. In truth, *Esquire* was the first magazine *about* men, for it took as its subject how men should act outside the workplace, how they should dress, what they should think about the opposite sex, and what they should read, eat, drink, and do in their spare time. Earlier "men's" magazines had been about *success* and they took pains to tell men how to succeed in the workplace, usually by advising men to adopt a set of prescribed values and habits in order to develop their character. Over time, as these magazines grew disillusioned with the cult of character, they began to talk about success in terms of personality and appearance. But it took *Esquire* to remove altogether the preoccupation with how to succeed and how to develop character. *Esquire* made personality, appearance, and "lifestyle" the bottom line by which a man was judged. *Esquire*'s creators—salesmen who wholeheartedly embraced the cult of personality that is central to modern masculinity—framed masculinity in ways that allowed men to negotiate their place in modern consumer culture.

Anyone who has learned a foreign language as an adult will perhaps recall the moment at which they began to inhabit the grammar, the internal logic, of their new tongue. There is a subtle shift in the way one thinks about the language, a sudden feeling of being at ease with a new way of expressing thoughts. Thoughts that once took shape in the original language and had to be adapted now originate in the new language. There was something of this process in the way that American magazines took up the grammar, the cultural logic, of what I have called modern masculinity. One by one, at different paces and at different times, the magazines I have studied tried and then embraced the images, ideals, stories, and tropes of a masculinity that best suited men for the consumer culture that by 1950 characterized the United States. The logic of Victorian masculinity that once shaped representations of American masculinity gradually (but never entirely) receded; in its place there developed a new masculine logic that stressed personality, self-realization, sexuality, youthfulness, and leisure. Magazines created new men for a new culture.

To the critics of the rise of consumer culture, the growing dominance of modern masculinity represented a loss of authenticity, a capitulation to the demands of bureaucratic corporate interests. The changes associated with the emergence of modern masculinity appear to such critics as a defeat, for they appear to deter men from achieving an authentic form of selfhood. Modern masculinity thus appears to consist of the leftovers, the sad remainders, of a viable masculinity that had once existed in a more stable cultural environment. Yet the magazines I have examined echo not with the laments of men robbed of possibilities, but rather with the vibrancy of editors, publishers, writers, and advertisers exploring and creating new possibilities for masculine expression, with the exuberance of people adapting to a new and evolving cultural environment. What I have described is not a process of capitulation or of begrudging acceptance of a fait accompli, but rather the more prosaic process of numbers of people with different functions and intentions contributing in various ways to the long-term re-creation of gender norms that seem more suitable to the changing social, cultural, and economic life of their day. In the early part of the century, in magazines like the *American*, the *Saturday Evening Post*, and *Collier's*, contributors struggled to reconcile what they had learned in their youth with what seemed to work at present, and the magazines sparked with the conflicts between old and new styles of masculinity. But by the 1930s and 1940s, the contributions of younger editors and writers to such magazines as *Esquire*, *True*, *Argosy*, and *Ebony* offered an unconflicted representation of modern masculine norms. In the end, the many contributors to American magazines had little cause to lament the emergence of a new social and economic order, for they participated fully in its pleasures, both personal and economic.

A perceptive reader may complain that just as critics of consumer culture have located bodies of evidence to justify their argument about the negative impact of consumer culture on notions of selfhood, I have located a body of evidence that justifies my argument that the rise of consumer culture invigorated emerging notions of masculine selfhood with largely positive consequences. Such conflicting evidence is not irreconcilable, for the emerging cultural hegemony of corporate capitalists created conditions in which some forms of cultural discourse were validated and others were not. I disagree with such critics of consumer culture as Jackson Lears, Christopher Lasch, and William Leach, however, when they suggest that the invalidation of some forms of selfhood by the emergence of consumer culture has had long-term detrimental consequences for modern identity, that the emergence of consumer culture placed individuals in an inauthentic relation to themselves and their culture. In fact, I believe that my study offers proof that new ways of articulating selfhood— in this case masculine selfhood—were avidly embraced by those producing magazines for the middle class, the working class, and—late in the game— for African Americans, and that these new styles of masculinity brought real benefits to American men (and some negative consequences as well, as I will discuss shortly).

I am not alone in proposing that we rethink the meaning of this crucial stage of cultural transformation. In his *Corporate Reconstruction of American Capitalism, 1890–1916*, Martin Sklar urges that we understand the transition of capitalism from its "proprietary-competitive" phase to its "corporate-administered" phase not as the result of the movement of "supra-human laws of economics" but rather as the product of a social and intellectual movement led by businessmen, politicians, and lawyers, with the consent of numbers of Americans. The ideology of corporate capitalism, which Sklar calls corporate liberalism, "was not, in its origins, a benefaction bestowed upon society by a sector of the capitalist class endowed with an enlightened disposition, nor by any other middle or upper class or stratum. It was instead the expression of a hierarchic but pluralistic web of class and political relations engaged in reconstructing American capitalism." James Livingston, in *Pragmatisn and the Political Economy of Cultural Revolution,* returns to early arguments among intellectuals, social critics, and economists to recover the potential they saw that the rise of consumer culture might offer real possibilities for individual identity, a notion embodied in Livingston's "social self." Livingston, writes Alan Trachtenberg in his foreword to the book, "revise[s] some fundamental premises about the 'new America,' especially about the possibilities for personal growth and social transformation that accompany a modernity more typically described by critics and historians as grimly repressive and limiting of freedom." And Matthew Schneirov, in his *Dream of a New Social Order,* argues that early magazines such as *Cosmopolitan, Munsey's,* and *McClure's* were not the mere agents by which corporate capitalists exerted social control but rather were a forum within which editors, publishers, and writers negotiated and articulated "a new culture for this new social order."[1] In different ways, each of these arguments asks that we revisit the dynamic that created modern consumer culture and consider the possibility that the process through which corporate capitalists came to attain cultural hegemony was more open and consensual than previous historians and cultural critics have led us to believe.

Revisiting the rise of consumer culture in these terms does not amount to an apology for or a defense of the dominance of corporations, the rise of the corporate ideology, or the undeniable ill effects of rampant consumerism in American life. Rather, this revised approach to understanding the period asks that we do not begin our interpretations of the period with the a priori assumption that corporate capitalist hegemony twisted and deformed authentic cultural life to fit its agenda, and thus seek out evidence of resistance that must eventually fail. In fact, what such an approach explicitly attempts to avoid is to either apologize for or lament the passing of the past. Livingston puts it in a slightly different way, arguing that for those who would apologize or lament, "the present always appears as radical departure from the past: the romantics feel they are exiled, and the positivists know they are liberated, from the more transcendent, transparent, or traditional past."[2] The approach that I have used to interpret cultural images of masculinity asks that we begin by assuming that the creation of culture is an open process, one in which a variety of people and

1. Martin J. Sklar, *The Corporate Reconstruction of American Capitalism, 1890–1916: The Market, the Lawn, and Politics,* 11, 35; Alan Trachtenberg, foreword to Livingston, *Pragmatism and the Political Economy,* xii; Schneirov, *Dream of a New Social Order,* 4.
2. Livingston, *Pragmatism and the Political Economy,* 215.

groups may make meaningful contributions, and not a closed process in which individuals either embrace the dominant cultural paradigm or fall victim to it.

In this study, such an approach has revealed that the shapers of early magazines were adjusting to more modern notions of masculinity from the very beginning, even before advertisers began to exert a greater influence; that those who actively championed modern masculinity in the late 1920s and onward saw in it possibilities for men to live richer, more meaningful lives than were made available by old styles of masculinity; and that there was real discussion and debate about the validity of modern masculinity throughout the period of my study. The evidence offered by the black magazines further complicates matters. Left outside the commercial dynamic that energized white magazines, black magazines sought to construct meaningful ideals for masculinity on very different terms than the white magazines. Yet when they had the opportunity, black magazines joined the consumer dynamic gladly, seeing in modern masculinity opportunities for participation in the larger cultural scene. In *Ebony*, black Americans were framed in the same ways men had been framed in white magazines for years, as successful businessmen, entertainers, intellectuals, consumers, and so on. The magazine celebrated the notion that black men could fully participate in consumer culture.

Could seeing themselves pictured as full participants in a consumer culture have motivated African Americans to take the more tangible steps of protesting and eventually ending widespread institutionalized racism? Was the depiction of African Americans as participants in consumer culture one of the factors that laid the cultural groundwork for the civil rights movement? This is not to suggest that merely because black magazine buyers were wooed by advertisers that they suddenly found themselves energized politically or embraced by white America; this is far from the case. But if we are to understand the complex process by which African Americans found the will to mount the protests associated with the civil rights movement, we ought to look at all areas of black social life to understand the conditions that might have created a cultural climate in which such a movement made sense. To put it another way, if we are going to allow that the military service and increased economic prospects that African Africans enjoyed during World War II were factors in precipitating the civil rights movement, then we ought also to consider the possibility that entering the culture of consumption played a role as well.

Having stated that the process of changing masculine norms was open and contested (and not closed and imposed), I want to be clear in stating that modern masculinity was not an unconflicted or monolithic cultural formation. There was much that was liberating in the development of modern masculinity:

it unchained masculinity from its strict ties to property ownership, and it thus allowed many more men access to the cultural markers for success; it expanded the standards for masculine success to include noneconomic criteria; it offered criteria for success that were not strictly tied to class or race; and all in all, it greatly expanded opportunities for individual expression.

Though the new gender roles arising out of the transformation to consumer capitalism were liberating, they were not liberating in quite the way members of the men's movements of the 1970s and 1980s construed them to be. Early men's studies scholars seemed eager to look back to the turn of the century as the turning point in a century-long transformation of masculinity. Positioned as they were in the midst of a period of rapid transformation of gender roles prompted by the women's movement, such scholars aimed to find a usable past in the changes that took place in the first half of the century. I would argue, however, that while the early changes that I have discussed may have helped set the stage for the changes of the 1970s and 1980s, they were not directly related. That is, the emergence of modern masculine roles in the first part of the century left largely intact the male-led nuclear family with its gender and family dynamics, the sexual prerogatives of the aggressive male, and the dread of homosexuality. Because the emergence of modern masculinity was— at least in American magazines—directed primarily by changing ideas of work and consumption, and not by gender and family dynamics, the areas in which males became "liberated" in the 1970s and 1980s were left relatively untouched by these early changes. The liberation that men underwent in this later period involved (and still involves) very different issues, including among other things the erasure of sexist stereotypes, the end of sexual harassment in the workplace, the full acceptance of women's labor, the acceptance of a greater role in child-rearing, and the acceptance (if not the embrace) of alternative sexualities. I would argue that we still need a study that traces the connections between men's early liberation from Victorian gender roles and their later liberation from sexist ideas and attitudes.

One of the most compelling of the critiques of modern masculinity—indeed, of modern selfhood—is that it was and is illusory, ungrounded, free-floating (recall Lears's invocation of a "sense of selfhood that had grown fragmented, diffuse, and somehow 'unreal' ").[3] Critics of modern selfhood charge that men cannot feel comfortable in their manhood because the standards for success or belonging are constantly shifting to suit the passing fads of consumer culture. This critique is compelling because most men have actually felt it: they have wondered how they measure up, whether they are good enough, whether they are or

3. Lears, "From Salvation to Self-Realization," 8, 4.

are not "manly." But just because men feel this does not mean that that feeling is historically unique. In fact, a more compelling case can be made that it is common to all people, a part of the human condition. What is probably more distinctly modern is the public debate over this private uncertainty. Modernity has made public our inner doubts—but there is little reason to think that our historical predecessors were any more sure of themselves than we are today. This critique is animated by a nostalgia for the past, for the days when masculine success was based in property ownership and there was little question about who had made it and who had not. Projecting present discomforts with masculine identity backward to a time when the foundations for modern masculinity were laid, such critiques locate a moment when we failed as a culture to sustain stable notions of selfhood and lay the blame for that loss at the foot of consumer culture.

When I began this study I shared the assumption that modern masculinity was characterized by this sense of ungroundedness, but the evidence available in American magazines convinced me that this was not the case. To be sure, men expressed confusion and uncertainty about how to navigate the gendered byways of a culture that was rapidly changing. Especially early in the century there was much that was unfamiliar in the cultural terrain that men had to learn to deal with. But a large majority of the articles and editorials I encountered showed men actively recreating the ways they understood masculinity, not lamenting the instability of gender roles. Magazines greeted the modern age with a real sense of its promise, and their representations of masculinity followed suit. These magazines suggested to me that the rise of consumer culture left masculinity not undermined but challenged, and that the contributors to the majority of magazines responded to that challenge with ingenuity and imagination.

The black men who contributed to early magazines would likely have found this question of groundedness laughable. Were black men in the first decades of the century grounded in their notions of masculinity? It is more accurate to say they were ground down. The struggle for black men was not to figure out how to understand masculine success in an unfamiliar consumer culture but how to attain the very foundations on which white masculinity rested—economic access and citizenship. Even *Ebony,* a magazine that shifted its focus from racial politics to entertainment and amusement, recognized the primary importance of black men and women gaining access to jobs and the vote. Thus the question of the illusory and fragmented nature of modern masculinity simply does not apply to African American men of this period.

As it developed in the magazines of the first half of the twentieth century, modern masculinity embraced the culture of personality while still valuing some of the ideals of the self-made man of character; it promoted leisure and recreation while still recognizing that most men still found validation in their work; it celebrated sexuality while upholding the sanctity of the family. Modern masculinity bound together a variety of cultural prescriptions and images, some of them potentially contradictory, to create a set of ideals that defined normality in America. These descriptions of modern masculinity should resonate with the contemporary reader, for they remain with us today. We are the children of a cultural transformation that began a hundred years ago, and we live within a consumer culture that has only become more entrenched and fully articulated in the years since the end of my study. The magazines that define masculinity today do so in terms that were initiated in the 1930s, 1940s, and 1950s. The masculine norms within which we live today are closely related to those that emerged in relation to the rise of consumer culture early in the century.

In terms of magazines, where *Esquire* led, others followed . . . and they still follow today. *True* and *Argosy* used the *Esquire* formula to recast images of working-class masculinity; *Ebony* borrowed from it (and from *Life*) to invite African American men into the folds of a consumer society. In the years that followed, other magazines used elements of the *Esquire* formula to find a place in the expanding American magazine market. *Playboy* stripped the last vestiges of clothing from the Petty and Varga Girl and presented real nude women as objects for male appreciation within an editorial package that looked much like the early *Esquire*. Magazines like *Penthouse* and *Oui* and later *Hustler* went several steps further and offered full frontal nudity to men within very different editorial formulas, ranging from the moderately high-brow "issues" stance of *Penthouse* to the downright gutter bawdiness of *Hustler*. If *Playboy* took *Esquire*'s lead and followed it one way, magazines like *Sports Illustrated* and *Road and Track* and *Car and Driver* followed it another way. Such magazines took one element of men's interest in sports and leisure and made a whole magazine out of it. The list of magazines that trace their history back to *Esquire* could go on and on: *Gentleman's Quarterly*, *Men's Health*, *Men's Journal*, *Details*, and *Vanity Fair* all work by casting men's interests in leisure and personality as the motive for their existence. And they are all funded by the mass of advertisers who are eager to reach an audience of consuming men.

As I have written this conclusion I have returned again and again to the local megabookstore to browse through the many magazines that are offered to men today. These magazines, nearly fifty of them, are grouped together in a section called "Men's Interest." The majority of the magazines still follow in *Esquire*'s footsteps, skewing either upscale or downscale in order to find their niche. The *Robb Report* pitches itself to the wealthy executive, with ads for high-end clothes and cars and editorial matter suited for the man who already has it all. At my store it came in a plastic wrapper, just like *Playboy* and *Penthouse* at the other end of the rack, but presumably wrapped for different reasons: to connote exclusivity, while the others are wrapped to keep the wrong eyes from viewing nude women. *Men's Journal* centers around active, outdoor lifestyles; *Men's Health* focuses on health issues. Many others aim down-market. Such magazines as *Maxim* and *Detour* and *Stuff* strip away the pretense of sophistication that *Esquire* clings to and dwell more fixedly on women's bodies and thrills and chills. *Maxim's* September 1999 cover boasted articles like "30 New Sex Tricks," "The 20 Beer Workout: Get Drunk! Look Great!" "Death Cruise," and "Wham! Bam! Brand New Pam!" (on recently breast-reduced Pamela Lee). And *Bizarre*, with its subtitle "More Balls, Less Bollocks," offers a British tabloid sensibility to American males. The venerable *Esquire* lingers on in the middle of the pack, appealing to about the same audience it imagined when it first started out— middle-class, twenty-five- to forty-five-year-old urban men. The magazine is still fixated on women and fashion and it still publishes some excellent short fiction, but it is no longer an innovator.

Though *Ebony* is still the dominant black general magazine, there are now a several magazines created specifically for black men, including *Blackmen* and a brand new magazine, *Code*. The former does not compare favorably with its white counterparts in photo quality and layout, though its content is quite similar. *Code*, however, is every bit the equal of *Esquire* in the quality of its photos and layout, and it carries a number of big-name advertisers. Its articles are intelligent and straightforward—they do not play games with readers, nor do they engage in the lowbrow humor and crassness that characterizes *Maxim's* fare. There are several magazines for gay men as well, including *Genre* and *BlueBoy*. The list could go on and on. There is, it would seem, a magazine for every man.

Despite all these magazines, despite all the discussion of masculinity that today can be found in the public sphere—on talk shows, in books, in stadium-filling men's rallies—there is much we still need to understand about the development of masculine gender roles in the twentieth century. We need to know much more about the ways that nonwhite, non-middle-class men conceived of their masculine identity. We need to explore the relationship between male and female gender roles, to understand how changes in one affect the other. We need studies that attempt to account for the different ways that men express their masculinity—as fathers, community members, workers, and spouses. What we need most is to remain open to the diversity and multiplicity of masculine roles. As I have argued, masculinity in particular and gender roles in general are tremendously complex cultural constructions that are constantly in flux. But these roles are amenable to change by individuals and groups seeking to make them more meaningful. If we understand that about the past, then we give ourselves the opportunity to effect meaningful change today.

Bibliography

Manuscript Collections

Barnett, Claude A. Papers. Manuscripts Collection, Chicago Historical Society.
Crowell-Collier Publishing Company Records. New York Public Library, New York.
Esquire, Inc., Records. Bentley Historical Library, University of Michigan.
Gingrich, Arnold. Papers. Michigan Historical Collections, Bentley Historical Library, University of Michigan, Ann Arbor.

Periodicals

Alexander's Magazine, 1905–1909.
American Magazine, 1914–1937.
Argosy, 1940–1950.
Athletic Journal, 1921–1941.
Athletic World/Outing, 1921–1925.
Collier's, 1919–1937.
Colored American, 1900–1909.
Competitor, 1920–1921.
Crisis, 1910–1940.
Ebony, 1945–1951.
Esquire, 1933–1950.
Horizon, 1907–1910.
McClure's, 1893–1913.
Munsey's, 1893–1906.
Negro Digest, 1942–1951.
Opportunity, 1923–1949.
Saturday Evening Post, 1899–1908.
Sporting Life/Sportlife, 1895–1926.
Success/The New Success, 1911–1928.
True: The Man's Magazine, 1940–1950.

Vanity Fair, 1914–1936.
Voice of the Negro/Voice, 1904–1907.

References

Allen, Frederick Lewis. "The American Magazines Grows Up." *Atlantic,* November 1947, 77–82.

———. *The Function of a Magazine in America.* University of Missouri Bulletin, vol. 46 no. 23, Journalism Series 101. Columbia: University of Missouri, August 10, 1945.

———. *Only Yesterday: An Informal History of the Nineteen-Twenties.* New York: Harper, 1931.

Allen, James Egert. *The Negro in New York.* New York: Exposition Press, 1964.

Anderson, James D. "Black Liberalism at the Crossroads: The Role of the *Crisis,* 1934–1953." *Crisis* 87, no. 9 (1980): 339–46.

Andreasen, Alan R. *The Disadvantaged Consumer.* New York: Free Press, 1975.

Archer, William. "The American Cheap Magazine." *Fortnightly Review,* May 2, 1910, 921–32.

Atwater, Tony. "Editorial Policy of *Ebony* before and after the Civil Rights Act of 1964." *Journalism Quarterly* 59, no. 1 (1982): 87–91.

Avery, Sheldon. *Up from Washington: William Pickens and the Negro Struggle for Equality, 1900–1954.* Newark: University of Delaware Press, 1989.

Baker, Ray Stannard. *American Chronicle.* New York: Scribner's, 1945.

Barnett, Margaret Ross. "Nostalgia as Nightmare: Blacks and American Popular Culture." *Crisis,* February 1980, 42–45.

Bauer, Raymond A., and Scott M. Cunningham. "The Negro Market." *Journal of Advertising Research* 10 (1970): 3–13.

Bederman, Gail. "Civilization, the Decline of Middle-Class Manliness, and Ida B. Wells's Antilynching Campaign (1892–94)." *Radical History Review* 52 (1992): 5–30.

———. *Manliness and Civilization: A Cultural History of Gender and Race in the United States, 1880–1917.* Chicago: University of Chicago Press, 1995.

Bigelow, Frederick S. *A Short History of the* Saturday Evening Post: *"An American Institution" in Three Centuries.* 1927. Reprint, with additional material, Philadelphia: Curtis Publishing Co., 1936.

Blackmore, David L. "Masculinity Anxiety and Contemporary Discourses of Sexuality in United States Fiction between the Wars." Ph.D. diss., University of California–Los Angeles, 1994. Abstract in *Dissertation Abstracts International* 55 (1995): 2387-A.

Blumin, Stuart. *The Emergence of the Middle Class: Social Experience in the American City, 1760–1900.* Cambridge: Cambridge University Press, 1989.

Bond, Horace M. "Negro Leadership since Washington." *South Atlantic Quarterly* 24, no. 2 (April 1925): 115–30.

Bontemps, Arna, ed. *Harlem Renaissance Remembered.* New York: Dodd, Mead and Company, 1972.

Boyenton, William. "The Negro Turns to Advertising." *Journalism Quarterly* 42 (spring 1965): 227.

Braithwaite, William. "Negro America's First Magazine." *Negro Digest,* December 1947, 21–25.

Breazeale, Kenon. "In Spite of Women: *Esquire* Magazine and the Construction of the Male Consumer." *Signs: Journal of Women in Culture and Society* 20, no. 11 (1994): 1–22.

Britt, George. *Forty Years, Forty Millions: The Career of Frank A. Munsey.* New York: Farrar and Rinehart, 1935.

Brodhead, Richard H. *Cultures of Letters: Scenes of Reading and Writing in Nineteenth-Century America.* Chicago: University of Chicago Press, 1993.

Brooks, Dwight Ernest. "Consumer Markets and Consumer Magazines: Black America and the Culture of Consumption, 1920–1960." Ph.D. diss., University of Iowa, 1991. Abstract in *Dissertation Abstracts International* 52 (1992): 2308-A.

———. "In Their Own Words: Advertisers' Construction of an African American Consumer Market, the World War II Era." *Howard Journal of Communications* 6, nos. 1–2 (October 1995): 32–52.

Brown, Richard D. *Modernization: The Transformation of American Life, 1600–1865.* New York: Hill and Wang, 1976.

Bullock, Penelope L. *The Afro-American Periodical Press, 1838–1909.* Baton Rouge: Louisiana State University Press, 1981.

Buni, Andrew. *Robert L. Vann of the* Pittsburgh Courier: *Politics and Black Journalism.* Pittsburgh: University of Pittsburgh Press, 1974.

Burke, Kenneth. *Attitudes toward History.* Rev. ed. Boston: Beacon, 1961.

Burns, Ben. *Nitty Gritty: A White Editor in Black Journalism.* Jackson: University Press of Mississippi, 1996.

Cancian, Francesca M., and Steven L. Gordon. "Changing Emotion Norms in Marriage: Love and Anger in U.S. Women's Magazines since 1900." *Gender and Society* 2, no. 3 (1988): 308–42.

Cann, Marvin L. "Robert Quillen: A Champion of Traditional Values." In *Proceedings of the South Carolina Historical Association,* 33–37. Columbia, S.C.: Carolina Historical Association, 1994.

Carnes, Mark C. *Secret Ritual and Manhood in Victorian America.* New Haven: Yale University Press, 1989.

Carnes, Mark C., and Clyde Griffen, eds. *Meanings for Manhood: Constructions of Masculinity in Victorian America.* Chicago: University of Chicago Press, 1990.

Carter, Purvis M. "The Negro in Periodical Literature, 1985–1989: Part I." *Journal of Negro History* 75, no. 1–2, (1990): 51–79.

Cawelti, John. *Apostles of the Self-Made Man.* Chicago: University of Chicago Press, 1965.

Chandler, Alfred D., Jr. *The Visible Hand: The Managerial Revolution in American Business.* Cambridge: Harvard University Press, 1977.

Chase, Stuart. *Prosperity: Fact or Myth.* New York: C. Boni, 1929.

Chenery, William Ludlow. "The Magazine and Public Opinion." *Vital Speeches of the Day,* August 15, 1936, 720.

———. *So It Seemed.* New York: Harcourt Brace and Company, 1952.

Clawson, Mary Ann. *Constructing Brotherhood: Class, Gender, and Fraternalism.* Princeton: Princeton University Press, 1989.

Coben, Stanley. *Rebellion against Victorianism: The Impetus for Cultural Change in 1920s America.* New York: Oxford University Press, 1991.

Cohn, Jan. "The Business Ethic for Boys: The *Saturday Evening Post* and the *Post* Boys." *Business History Review* 61, no. 2 (1987): 185–215.

———. *Creating America: George Horace Lorimer and the* Saturday Evening Post. Pittsburgh: University of Pittsburgh Press, 1989.

Connolly, Margaret. *The Life Story of Orison Swett Marden.* New York: Thomas Y. Crowell Company, 1925.

Cott, Nancy F. *The Bonds of Womanhood: "Woman's Sphere" in New England, 1780–1835.* New Haven: Yale University Press, 1977.

———. "On Men's History and Women's History." In *Meanings for Manhood,* ed. Mark C. Carnes and Clyde Griffen. Chicago: University of Chicago Press, 1990.

Coutant, Frank R. "Who Reads Magazines?" In *A Qualitative Study of Magazines: Who Reads Them and Why.* New York: McCall Corporation, 1939–1941.

Cowley, Malcolm. *After the Genteel Tradition: American Writers since 1910.* New York: Norton, 1936.

Dahlinger, Charles W. "The Rising Tide of Color." *Western Pennsylvania Historical Magazine* 4 (April 1921): 72–73.

Damon-Moore, Helen. *Magazines for the Millions: Gender and Commerce in the* Ladies' Home Journal *and the* Saturday Evening Post, *1880–1910.* Albany: State University of New York Press, 1994.

Daniel, Walter C. *Black Journals of the United States.* Westport, Conn.: Green-wood Press, 1982.

Dates, Janette L., and William Barlow, eds. *Split Image: African Americans in the Mass Media.* 2d ed. Washington, D.C.: Howard University Press, 1993.

Detweiler, Frederick. *The Negro Press in the United States.* Chicago: University of Chicago Press, 1922.

———. "The Negro Press Today." *American Journal of Sociology* 44, no. 3 (1938): 391–401.

Douglas, Ann. *Terrible Honesty: Mongrel Manhattan in the 1920s.* New York: Farrar, Straus, and Giroux, 1995.

Drewry, John E. *Contemporary American Magazines: A Selected Bibliography and Reprints of Articles Dealing with Various Periodicals.* 2d ed. Athens: University of Georgia Press, 1938.

———. *Some Magazines and Magazine Makers.* Boston: Stratford Company, 1924.

Dubbert, Joe L. *A Man's Place: Masculinity in Transition.* Englewood Cliffs, N.J.: Prentice-Hall, 1979.

Dumenil, Lynn. *The Modern Temper: American Culture and Society in the 1920s.* New York: Hill and Wang, 1995.

Eby, Clare Virginia. "Babbitt as Veblenian Critique of Manliness." *American Studies* 34, no. 2 (1993): 5–23.

Edwards, Paul Kenneth. *The Southern Urban Negro as a Consumer.* 1932. Reprint, College Park, Md.: McGrath Publishing Company, 1969.

Ehrenreich, Barbara. *The Hearts of Men: American Dreams and the Flight from Commitment.* Garden City, N.Y.: Anchor Press/Doubleday, 1983.

Ellis, Mark. " 'Closing Ranks' and 'Seeking Honors': W. E. B. Du Bois in World War I." *Journal of American History* 79, no. 1 (1992): 96–124.

———. "W. E. B. Du Bois and the Formation of Black Opinion in World War I: A Commentary on 'The Damnable Dilemma.' " *Journal of American History* 81, no. 4 (1995): 1584–90.

Evans, Linda J. "Claude A. Barnett and the Associated Negro Press." *Chicago History* 12, no. 1 (spring 1983): 44–56.

Ewen, Stuart. *Captains of Consciousness: Advertising and the Social Roots of the Consumer Culture.* New York: McGraw Hill, 1976.

Farrell, Warren T. *The Liberated Man: Beyond Masculinity.* New York: Random House, 1974.

Felker, Clay S. "Life Cycles in the Age of Magazines." *Antioch Review* 29 (spring 1969): 7–13.

Filene, Peter G. *Him/Her/Self: Sex Roles in Modern America.* Rev. ed. Baltimore: Johns Hopkins University Press, 1986.

————. "The Secrets of Men's History." In *The Making of Masculinities: The Men's Studies Movement,* ed. Harry Brod. Boston: Allen and Unwin, 1987.

Fox, Richard Wightman, and T. J. Jackson Lears, eds. *The Culture of Consumption: Critical Essays in American History, 1880–1980.* New York: Pantheon, 1983.

Fox, Stephen R. *The Guardian of Boston: William Monroe Trotter.* New York: Atheneum, 1970.

Franklin, John Hope, and Alfred A. Moss Jr. *From Slavery to Freedom: A History of African Americans.* 7th ed. New York: Knopf, 1994.

Franzen, Raymond. *Magazine Audiences in the Urban Negro Market.* New York: Our World Publishing Co., 1966.

Fraser, C. Gerald. "The *Crisis,* 1910–1980: A Record of the Darker Races." *Crisis* 87, no. 10 (1980): 468–72.

Frazier, E. Franklin. *Black Bourgeoisie.* Glencoe, Ill.: Free Press, 1957.

Friedrich, Otto. *Decline and Fall.* New York: Harper and Row, 1969.

Friend, Irwin, and J. B. Kravis. "New Light on the Consumer Market." *Harvard Business Review* 35, no. 1 (January–February 1957): 112–15.

Gaines, Kevin. *Uplifting the Race: Black Leadership, Politics, and Culture in the Twentieth Century.* Chapel Hill: University of North Carolina Press, 1996.

Gale, Zona. "Editors of the Younger Generation." *Critic* 44 (April 1904): 318–31.

Garvey, Ellen Gruber. *The Adman in the Parlor: Magazines and the Gendering of Consumer Culture, 1880s to 1910s.* New York: Oxford University Press, 1996.

Gecas, Viktor. "Motives and Aggressive Acts in Popular Fiction: Sex and Class Differences." *American Journal of Sociology* 77, no. 4 (1972): 680–96.

Gibson, D. Parke. *The $30 Billion Negro.* New York: Macmillan, 1969.

Gilmore, Glenda Elizabeth. *Gender and Jim Crow: Women and the Politics of White Supremacy in North Carolina, 1896–1920.* Charlotte: University of North Carolina Press, 1996.

Gingrich, Arnold. *Nothing but People.* New York: Crown, 1971.

Glazener, Nancy. *Reading for Realism: The History of a U.S. Literary Institution, 1850–1910.* Durham: Duke University Press, 1997.

Goffman, Erving. *Gender Advertisements.* New York: Harper and Row, 1979.

Goldberg, Herb. *The Hazards of Being Male: Surviving the Myth of Masculine Privilege.* New York: Nash, 1976.

Goodman, Walter. "*Ebony:* Biggest Negro Magazine." *Dissent* 15, no. 5 (1968): 403–9.

Gordon, Eugene. "The Negro Press." *American Mercury,* June 1926, 207–15.

———. "The Negro Press." *Annals of the American Academy of Political and Social Sciences* 140 (November 1928): 248–56.

Gorn, Elliot J. *The Manly Art: Bare-Knuckle Prize Fighting in Victorian America.* Ithaca: Cornell University Press, 1986.

Green, Dan S. "W. E. B. Du Bois: His Journalistic Career." *Negro History Bulletin* 40, no. 2 (March–April 1977): 672–77.

Green, Harvey. *Fit for America: Health, Fitness, Sport, and American Society.* Baltimore: Johns Hopkins University Press, 1986.

Griswold, Robert L. *Fatherhood in America: A History.* New York: Basic Books, 1993.

Halttunen, Karen. *Confidence Men and Painted Women: A Study of Middle-Class Culture in America, 1830–1870.* New Haven: Yale University Press, 1982.

Harlan, Louis R. "Booker T. Washington and the *Voice of the Negro,* 1904–1907." *Journal of Southern History* 44 (February 1979): 45–62.

———. "The Secret Life of Booker T. Washington." *Journal of Southern History* 38 (August 1971): 393–416.

Harlan, Louis R., and Raymond W. Smith, eds. *Booker T. Washington Papers.* Vol. 8, *1904–1906.* Urbana: University of Illinois Press, 1977.

Harris, Othello. "The Image of the African American in Psychological Journals, 1895–1923." *Black Scholar* 21, no. 4 (1991): 25–29.

Hays, Samuel P. *The Response to Industrialism, 1885–1914.* Chicago: University of Chicago Press, 1995.

Hersey, Harold Brainerd. *Pulpwood Editor.* New York: Frederick A. Stokes Company, 1937.

Higham, John. "The Reorientation of American Culture in the 1890s." In *The Origins of Modern Consciousness,* ed. John Weiss. Detroit: Wayne State University Press, 1965.

Hilkey, Judy Arlene. *Character Is Capital: Success Manuals and Manhood in Gilded Age America.* Chapel Hill: University of North Carolina Press, 1997.

Hill, George H., and Michael Nelson, eds. "John Harold Johnson: Publishing Magnate." *Bulletin of Bibliography* 42, no. 2 (1985): 89–94.

Hill, Robert A. Introduction to *The Crusader.* New York: Garland, 1987.

Hirsch, Paul M. "An Analysis of *Ebony:* The Magazine and Its Readers." *Journalism Quarterly* 45, no. 2 (1968): 261–70.

Hodge, Carle. "For Men Only." *Magazine Industry,* winter 1950, 9–15.

Huber, Richard M. *The American Idea of Success.* New York: McGraw-Hill, 1971.

Humphrey, Ronald, and Harold Schuman. "The Portrayal of Blacks in Magazine

Advertisements, 1950–1982." *Public Opinion Quarterly* 48, no. 3 (1984): 551–63.

Ikonné, Chidi. "Opportunity and Black Literature, 1923–1933." *Phylon* 40, no. 1 (1979): 86–93.

Jhally, Sut. *Codes of Advertising.* New York: St. Martin's Press, 1987.

Johnson, Abby Arthur, and Ronald M. Johnson. "Away from Accommodation: Radical Editors and Protest Journalism, 1900–1910." *Journal of Negro History* 62, no. 4 (October 1977): 325–38.

————. *Propaganda and Aesthetics: The Literary Politics of Afro-American Magazines in the Twentieth Century.* Amherst: University of Massachusetts Press, 1979.

Johnson, Charles S. "The Rise of the Negro Magazine." *Journal of Negro History* 13, no. 1 (January 1928): 7–21.

Johnson, John H., with Lerone Bennett Jr. *Succeeding against the Odds.* New York: Warner Books, 1989.

Jordan, William. "'The Damnable Dilemma': African-American Accommodation and Protest during World War I." *Journal of American History* 81, no. 4 (1995): 1562–83.

Joyce, George. *The Black Consumer: Dimensions of Behavior and Strategy.* New York: Random House, 1971.

Kellogg, Charles Flint. *NAACP: A History of the National Association for the Advancement of Colored People.* Vol. 1, *1909–1920.* Baltimore: Johns Hopkins Press, 1967

Kennedy, David M. *Over Here: The First World War and American Society.* New York: Oxford University Press, 1980.

Kerlin, Robert T. *The Voice of the Negro, 1919.* New York: E. P. Dutton, 1920. Reprint, New York: Arno Press, 1968.

Kern-Foxworth, Marilyn. *Aunt Jemima, Uncle Ben, and Rastus: Blacks in Advertising, Yesterday, Today, and Tomorrow.* Westport, Conn.: Greenwood, 1994.

Kerr, W. A., and H. H. Remmers. "Cultural Value of 100 Representative Magazines." *School and Society* 54 (November 1941): 476–80.

Kimball, Penn T. "The Non Editing of *Esquire.*" *Columbia Journalism Review* 3 (fall 1964): 32–34.

Kimmel, Michael. "Baseball and the Reconstitution of American Masculinity, 1880–1920." In *Sport, Men, and the Gender Order: Critical Feminist Perspectives,* ed. Michael A. Messner and Donald F. Sabo. Champaign, Ill.: Human Kinetics Books, 1990.

————. "The Contemporary 'Crisis' of Masculinity in Historical Perspective."

In *The Making of Masculinities: The New Men's Studies,* ed. Harry Brod. Boston: Allen and Unwin, 1987.

————. *Manhood in America: A Cultural History.* New York: Free Press, 1996.

Kinzer, Robert H., and Edward Sagarin. *The Negro in American Business.* New York: Greenberg, 1950.

Kolko, Gabriel. *The Triumph of Conservatism: A Reinterpretation of American History, 1900–1916.* New York: Free Press, 1963.

Kornweibel, Theodore, Jr. "Apathy and Dissent: Black America's Negative Responses to World War I." *South Atlantic Quarterly* 80 (summer 1981): 322–38.

————. *No Crystal Stair: Black Life and the* Messenger, *1917–1928.* Westport, Conn.: Greenwood, 1975.

Kriegel, Leonard. *The Myth of American Manhood.* New York: Dell, 1978.

Lasch, Christopher. *The Culture of Narcissism: American Life in an Age of Diminishing Expectations.* New York: Norton, 1979.

————. *Haven in a Heartless World: The Family Beseiged.* New York: Norton, 1977.

————. *The Minimal Self.* New York: Norton, 1984.

Leach, William. *Land of Desire: Merchants, Power, and the Rise of a New American Culture.* New York: Pantheon, 1993.

Lears, T. J. Jackson. *Fables of Abundance: A Cultural History of Advertising in America.* New York: Basic Books, 1994.

————. "From Salvation to Self-Realization: Advertising and the Therapeutic Roots of the Consumer Culture, 1900–1930." In *The Culture of Consumption: Critical Essays in American History, 1880–1980,* ed. Richard Wightman Fox and T. J. Jackson Lears. New York: Pantheon, 1983.

————. *No Place of Grace: Antimodernism and the Transformation of American Culture, 1880–1920.* New York: Pantheon, 1981.

Leuchtenburg, William E. *Perils of Prosperity, 1914–1932.* 2d ed. Chicago: University of Chicago Press, 1993.

Leverenz, David. *Manhood and the American Renaissance.* Ithaca: Cornell University Press, 1989.

Levinson, Daniel J. *The Seasons of a Man's Life.* New York: Knopf, 1978.

Lewis, David Levering. *W. E. B. Du Bois: Biography of a Race, 1868–1919.* New York: Henry Holt, 1993.

Livingston, James. "The Politics of Pragmatism." *Social Text* 14, no. 4 (winter 1996): 149–72.

————. *Pragmatism and the Political Economy of Cultural Revolution, 1850–1940.* Chapel Hill: University of North Carolina Press, 1994.

Lowenthal, Leo. *Literature, Popular Culture, and Society.* Englewood Cliffs, N.J.: Prentice-Hall, 1961.

Lyon, Peter. *Success Story: The Life and Times of S. S. McClure.* New York: Scribner's, 1963.

Lystra, Karen. *Searching the Heart: Women, Men, and Romantic Love in Nineteenth-Century America.* New York: Oxford University Press, 1989.

Macfadden, Mary, and Emile Gavreau. *Dumbbells and Carrot-Strips: The Story of Bernarr Macfadden.* New York: Holt, 1953.

Mangan, J. A. "Men, Masculinity, and Sexuality: Some Recent Literature." *Journal of the History of Sexuality* 3, no. 2 (1992): 303–13.

Mangan, J. A., and James Walvin, eds. *Manliness and Morality: Middle-Class Masculinity in Britain and America, 1800–1940.* New York: St. Martin's Press, 1987.

Marchand, Roland. *Advertising the American Dream: Making Way for Modernity, 1920–1940.* Berkeley and Los Angeles: University of California Press, 1985.

Marriner, Gerald L. "A Victorian in the Modern World: The 'Liberated' Male's Adjustment to the New Woman and the New Morality." *South Atlantic Quarterly* 76 (spring 1977): 190–203.

Marsh, Margaret. "Suburban Men and Masculine Domesticity, 1870–1915." *American Quarterly* 40 (June 1988): 165–86.

Maxcy, David Joseph. "Advertising, the Gender System: Changing Configurations of Femininity and Masculinity in Early Advertising in the United States." Ph.D. diss., University of Massachusetts, 1994. Abstract in *Dissertation Abstracts International* 55 (1994): 409-A.

May, Lary. *Screening Out the Past: The Birth of Mass Culture and the Motion Picture Industry.* New York: Oxford University Press, 1980.

McClure, S. S. *My Autobiography.* 1914. Reprint, New York: Frederick Ungar Publishing Co., 1963.

McDonald, Susan Waugh. "From Kipling to Kitsch: Two Popular Editors of the Gilded Age: Mass Culture, Magazines, and Correspondence Universities." *Journal of Popular Culture* 15, no. 2 (1981): 50–61.

McGovern, James R. "David Graham Phillips and the Virility Impulse of the Progressives." *New England Quarterly* 39 (September 1966): 333–48.

Meier, August. "Booker T. Washington and the Negro Press: With Special Reference to the *Colored American Magazine.*" *Journal of Negro History* (January 1953): 68–90.

———. *Negro Thought in America, 1880–1915: Racial Ideologies in the Age of Booker T. Washington.* Ann Arbor: University of Michigan Press, 1963.

Mellen, Joan. *Big Bad Wolves: Masculinity in the American Film.* New York: Pantheon, 1977.

Melosh, Barbara. *Engendering Culture: Manhood and Womanhood in New Deal Public Art and Theater.* Washington, D.C.: Smithsonian Institution Press, 1991.

Merrill, Hugh. *Esky: The Early Years at* Esquire. New Brunswick, N.J.: Rutgers University Press, 1995.

Miller, Cristanne. "Who Talks Like a Women's Magazine?: Language and Gender in Popular Women's and Men's Magazines." *Journal of American Culture* 10, no. 3 (1987): 1–9.

Miller, Jan. "Annotated Bibliography of the Washington–Du Bois Controversy." *Journal of Black Studies* 25, no. 2 (December 1994): 250–72.

Miller, Roger. "Selling Mrs. Consumer: Advertising and the Creation of Suburban Socio-Spatial Relations, 1910–1930." *Antipode* 23, no. 3 (1991): 263–306.

Moore, Jesse Thomas, Jr. *A Search for Equality: The National Urban League, 1910–1961.* University Park: Pennsylvania State University Press, 1981.

Morgan, W. L., and A. M. Leahy, "The Cultural Content of General Interest Magazines." *Journal of Eductional Psychology* 24 (1934): 530–36.

Mott, Frank Luther. *A History of American Magazines.* 5 vols. Cambridge: Harvard University Press, 1930–1968.

———. "The Magazine Revolution and Popular Ideas in the Nineties." *Proceedings of the American Antiquarian Society* 64 (April 21, 1954): 195–214.

Mullen, Robert W. *Blacks in America's Wars: The Shifts in Attitudes from the Revolutionary War to Vietnam.* New York: Monad Press, 1973.

Munsey, Frank A. "Getting On in Journalism." Address given at the Annual Meeting of the Press Association of Canada, Ottawa, March 10, 1898. N.p.

Nash, Roderick. *The Nervous Generation: American Thought, 1917–1930.* Chicago: Ivan R. Dee, 1990.

Nourie, Alan, and Barbara Nourie, eds. *American Mass-Market Magazines.* New York: Greenwood Press, 1990.

Oak, Vishnu. "What about the Negro Press?" *Saturday Review of Literature,* March 6, 1943, 4–5.

Ohmann, Richard. *Selling Culture: Magazines, Markets, and Class at the Turn of the Century.* London: Verso, 1996.

———. "Where Did Mass Culture Come From? The Case of Magazines." *Berkshire Review* 16, no. 106 (1981): 85–101.

Osofsky, Gilbert. *Harlem: The Making of a Ghetto.* New York: Harper and Row, 1966. Reprint, Chicago: Ivan R. Dee, 1996.

Ottley, Roi. *The Lonely Warrior: The Life and Times of Robert S. Abbott.* Chicago: Regnery, 1955.

Painter, Nell Irvin. *Standing at Armageddon: The United States, 1877–1919.* New York: Norton, 1989.

Partington, Paul G. *The* Moon Illustrated Weekly: *Black America's First Weekly Magazine.* Thornton, Colo.: C and M Press, 1985.

————. *"The Moon Illustrated Weekly:* The Precursor of the *Crisis." Journal of Negro History* 48, no. 3 (July 1963): 206–16.

Perry, Bruce. "Malcolm X and the Politics of Masculinity." *Psychohistory Review* 13, no. 2–3 (1985): 18–25.

Peterson, Theodore. *Magazines in the Twentieth Century.* Urbana: University of Illinois Press, 1964.

Pleck, Elizabeth H., and Joseph Pleck, eds. *The American Man.* Englewood Cliffs, N.J.: Prentice-Hall, 1980.

Pleck, Joseph H. *The Myth of Masculinity.* Cambridge: MIT Press, 1981.

Pleck, Joseph H., and Jack Sawyer, eds. *Men and Masculinity.* Englewood Cliffs, N.J.: Prentice-Hall, 1974.

Pope, Daniel. *The Making of Modern Advertising.* New York: Basic Books, 1983.

Powell, Hickman. *"Collier's." Scribner's,* May 1939, 20.

Pringle, Henry L. "Sex, Esq." *Scribner's,* March 1938, 33–39, 88.

Pugh, David G. *Sons of Liberty: The Masculine Mind in Nineteenth-Century America.* Westport, Conn.: Greenwood, 1983.

Regier, C. C. *The Era of the Muckrakers.* Chapel Hill: University of North Carolina Press, 1932.

Riesman, David, with Reuel Denney and Nathan Glazer. *The Lonely Crowd: A Study of the Changing American Character.* 3d rev. ed. New Haven: Yale University Press, 1969.

Riess, Steven A. "Sport and the Redefinition of American Middle-Class Masculinity." *International Journal of the History of Sport* 8, no. 1 (1991): 5–27.

Robbins, Richard. *Sidelines Activist: Charles S. Johnson and the Struggle for Civil Rights.* Jackson: University Press of Mississippi, 1996.

Roediger, David R. *Towards the Abolition of Whiteness: Essays on Race, Politics, and Working Class History.* New York: Verso, 1994.

————. *The Wages of Whiteness: Race and the Making of the American Working Class.* New York: Verso, 1994.

Rosenberg, Charles E. "Sexuality, Class, and Role in Nineteenth-Century America." *American Quarterly* 25 (May 1973): 131–53.

Rotundo, E. Anthony. *American Manhood: Transformations in Masculinity from the Revolution to the Modern Era.* New York: Basic Books, 1993.

Rubin, Joan Shelley. *The Making of Middle-Brow Culture.* Chapel Hill: University of North Carolina Press, 1992.

Ryan, Mary. *Cradle of the Middle Class: The Family in Oneida County, New York, 1790–1865.* Cambridge: Cambridge University Press, 1981.

Scanlon, Jennifer. *Inarticulate Longings: The* Ladies' Home Journal, *Gender, and the Promises of Consumer Culture.* New York: Routledge, 1995.

Schneirov, Matthew. *The Dream of a New Social Order: Popular Magazines in America, 1893–1914.* New York: Columbia University Press, 1994.

Scott, Joan Wallach. *Gender and the Politics of History.* New York: Columbia University Press, 1988.

Sedgwick, Ellery. *The* Atlantic Monthly, *1857–1909: Yankee Humanism at High Tide and Ebb.* Amherst: University of Massachusetts Press, 1994.

Sentman, Mary Alice, and Patrick S. Washburn. "How Excess Profits Tax Brought Ads to Black Newspapers in World War II." *Journalism Quarterly* 64, no. 4 (1987): 769–74, 867.

Shevelow, Kathryn. *Women and Print Culture: The Construction of Femininity in the Periodical.* London: Routledge, 1989.

Shockley, Ann Allen. "Pauline Elizabeth Hopkins: A Biographical Excursion into Obscurity." *Phylon* 33, no. 1 (spring 1972): 22–26.

Simmons, Christina. "Modern Sexuality and the Myth of Victorian Repression." In *Passion and Power: Sexuality in History,* ed. Kathy Peiss and Christina Simmons. Philadelphia: Temple University Press, 1989.

Sklar, Martin J. *The Corporate Reconstruction of American Capitalism, 1890–1916: The Market, the Law, and Politics.* Cambridge: Cambridge University Press, 1988.

Smith-Rosenberg, Carroll. *Disorderly Conduct: Visions of Gender in Victorian America.* New York: Bantam, 1991.

Staples, Robert. "Social Inequality and Black Sexual Pathology: The Essential Relationship." *Black Scholar* 21, no. 3 (1990–1991): 29–37.

Starch, Daniel. *Profile of the Black Consumer.* New York: n.p., 1973.

Starr, Michael E. "The Marlboro Man: Cigarette Smoking and Masculinity in America." *Journal of Popular Culture* 17, no. 4 (1984): 45–57.

Stearns, Peter N. *Be a Man! Males in Modern Society.* Rev. ed. New York: Holmes and Meier, 1990.

Steffens, Lincoln. *The Autobiography of Lincoln Steffens.* New York: Harcourt, Brace, 1931.

Steinem, Gloria. "Sex, Lies, and Advertising." *Ms.,* July/August 1990, 26.

Stinson, Robert. "McClure's Road to *McClure's:* How Revolutionary Were 1890s Magazines?" *Journalism Quarterly* 47, no. 2 (1970): 256–62.

———. "S. S. McClure's *My Autobiography:* The Progressive as Self-Made Man." *American Quarterly* 22, no. 2 (1970): 203–12.

Strasser, Susan. *Satisfaction Guaranteed: The Making of the Mass Market.* New York: Pantheon, 1989.

Stroman, Carolyn A. "The *Chicago Defender* and the Mass Migration of Blacks, 1916–1918." *Journal of Popular Culture* 15, no. 2 (1981): 62–67.

Sundstrom, William A. "The Color Line: Racial Norms and Discrimination in Urban Labor Markets, 1910–1950." *Journal of Economic History* 54, no. 2 (1994): 382–96.

Susman, Warren. " 'Personality' and the Making of Twentieth-Century Culture." In *Culture as History: The Transformation of American Society in the Twentieth Century.* New York: Pantheon, 1984.

Tarbell, Ida M. *All in the Day's Work.* New York: Macmillan, 1939.

Tassin, Algernon. *The Magazine in America.* New York: Dodd, Mead and Company, 1916.

Tebbel, John. *The American Magazine: A Compact History.* New York: Hawthorn Books, 1969.

———. *George Horace Lorimer and the* Saturday Evening Post. Garden City, N.Y.: Doubleday, 1948.

Tebbel, John, and Mary Ellen Zuckerman. *The Magazine in America, 1741–1990.* New York: Oxford University Press, 1991.

Testi, Arnaldo. "The Gender of Reform Politics: Theodore Roosevelt and the Culture of Masculinity." *Journal of American History* 81 (March 1995): 1509–33.

Thornbrough, Emma Lou. "More Light on Booker T. Washington and the *New York Age.*" *Journal of Negro History* 43, no. 1 (January 1958): 34–49.

———. *T. Thomas Fortune: Militant Journalist.* Chicago: University of Chicago Press, 1972.

Towne, Charles Hanson. *Adventures in Editing.* New York: Appleton, 1926.

Trachtenberg, Alan. *The Incorporation of America: Culture and Society in the Gilded Age.* New York: Hill and Wang, 1982.

Trotter, Joe William, Jr., ed. *The Great Migration in Historical Perspective: New Dimensions of Race, Class, and Gender.* Bloomington: Indiana University Press, 1991.

Weinstein, James. *The Corporate Ideal in the Liberal State, 1900–1918.* Boston: Beacon Press, 1968.

Weiss, Nancy J. *The National Urban League, 1910–1940.* New York: Oxford University Press, 1974.

Welter, Barbara. "The Cult of True Womanhood." *American Quarterly* 18 (summer 1966): 151–74.

White, Kevin. *The First Sexual Revolution: Male Heterosexuality in Modern America.* New York: New York University Press, 1992.

Wiebe, Robert H. *The Search for Order, 1877–1920*. New York: Hill and Wang, 1967.

Wiegman, Robyn. "The Anatomy of Lynching." *Journal of the History of Sexuality* 3, no. 3 (1993): 445–67.

Williams, Loretta J. *Black Freemasonry and Middle-Class Pillarization*. Columbia: University of Missouri Press, 1980.

Wilson, Christopher P. "The Rhetoric of Consumption: Mass-Market Magazines and the Demise of the Gentle Reader, 1880–1920." In *The Culture of Consumption: Critical Essays in American History, 1880–1980*, ed. Richard Wightman Fox and T. J. Jackson Lears. New York: Pantheon, 1983.

Wilson, Harold. "Circulation and Survival: *McClure's Magazine* and the Strange Death of Muckraking Journalism." *Western Illinois Regional Studies* 11, no. 1 (1988): 71–81.

———. McClure's Magazine *and the Muckrakers*. Princeton, N.J.: Princeton University Press, 1970.

Wolseley, Roland E. *The Black Press, U.S.A*. 2d ed. Ames: Iowa State University Press, 1990.

Wood, James Playsted. *Magazines in the United States: Their Social and Economic Influence*. 3d ed. New York: Ronald Press, 1971.

Woodress, James. "The Pre-eminent Magazine Genuis: S. S. McClure." In *Essays Mostly on Periodical Publishing in America*, ed. James Woodress. Durham: Duke University Press, 1973.

Wyllie, Irvin G. *The Self-Made Man in America: The Myth of Rags to Riches*. New Brunswick, N.J.: Rutgers University Press, 1954.

Wynn, Neil A. *From Progressivism to Prosperity: World War I and American Society*. New York: Holmes and Meier, 1986.

Zinkhan, George M., Keith K. Cox, and Jae W. Hong. "Changes in Stereotypes: Blacks and Whites in Magazine Advertisements." *Journalism Quarterly* 63, no. 3 (1986): 568–72.

Index

Printed in the United States
33820LVS00003B/1-14